Library of
Davidson College

UNCERTAIN DÉTENTE

Publications of the John F. Kennedy Institute,
Center for International Studies, Tilburg, The Netherlands

UNCERTAIN DÉTENTE

edited by
Frans A.M. Alting von Geusau

with contributions from:
L. Aćimović
F.A.M. Alting von Geusau
J. Bognár
R. Byrnes
E.O. Czempiel
M. Dobrosielski
A. Fontaine
V.-Y. Ghébali
W.E. Griffith
L. Mates
J. Pinder
I.L. Sheidina
P.J. Teunissen
Z.A.B. Zeman

SIJTHOFF & NOORDHOFF   1979
Alphen aan den Rijn, The Netherlands

ISBN 90 286 0818 4

Copyright © 1979 Sijthoff & Noordhoff International Publishers B.V., Alphen aan den Rijn, The Netherlands.

All rights reserved. No part of this publication may be reproduced, stored in a retrieval system, or transmitted, in any form or by any means, electronic, mechanical, photocopying, or otherwise, without the prior permission of the copyright owner.

Filmset in Great Britain by Eta Services (Typesetters) Ltd., Beccles, Suffolk
Printed in The Netherlands.

PREFACE

The evolution of East–West relations in an era of *détente* has been a primary and continuing focus of the John F. Kennedy Institute's research program ever since its creation in 1967. The program included intensive and extensive research-projects on many aspects of East–West relations; a series of international Colloquia; and the promotion of exchange of students, scholars and research with institutes especially in Poland, Hungary and Yugoslavia. Following the conclusion of the Final Act of the Conference on Security and Cooperation in Europe in 1975, primary attention was obviously focused on the interpretation and implementation of the Final Act, and its impact on the process of détente. Topics related to the Final Act were examined in several books and articles, as well as in regular bilateral consultations within the framework of our exchange programs.

Those who had participated in these programs and other scholars and officials from participating States, were brought together in the tenth anniversary Colloquium of the Institute on Uncertain Détente, held on April 20–23, 1977. Consultations preceding the Colloquium and a series of working papers produced a stimulating exchange of views and a useful overview of the problems of *détente*.

In this volume the Institute presents the result of its efforts.

Its distinguishing feature is that it is the outcome of intensive discussions between scholars and officials from several participating States belonging to NATO, the Warsaw Pact and the Non-aligned European countries.

The authors of Chapters 1–13 had prepared their papers in March/April 1977. Wherever necessary, they revised them after the Colloquium during June–September 1977. Chapter 14 reprints the text of Chapter 4 of the Second Semiannual Report of the President to the Commission on Security and Cooperation in Europe of the US Congress. The Epilogue has been completed after the termination of the Belgrade Review Conference.

The Institute is grateful to the authors for their contributions to this volume and to the US Government for permission to include the chapter on the Implementation of the Third Basket.

I am particularly grateful to Dr. J.W. Schneider s.j., Dr. L.L. Bartalits, Dr. George Embree, Drs. R. Kuster, Drs. J.A. van Lith and Dr. J. Pelkmans who constituted the research-team for this project.

The Institute is indebted to the Netherlands' Ministry of Science and Education, the North Atlantic Treaty Organization, the American Embassy and Tilburg University for their financial support towards the Colloquium and to A.W. Sijthoff International Publishing Company for publishing this volume.

I am most grateful to Miss M.C. Hinkenkemper, executive secretary and Miss Annelies Vugs, secretary, who—as always—have performed the most difficult tasks with a rare and unique dedication.

F.A.M. Alting von Geusau

TABLE OF CONTENTS

Preface	V
About the Authors	XIV
Abbreviations	XV
Prologue by *Frans A.M. Alting von Geusau*	XVII

Part one
DÉTENTE: PROBLEMS AND PRINCIPLES — 1

Introduction — 3

Chapter 1
East-West Détente in Europe — 5
by *William E. Griffith*
- Definitions — 5
- Causes — 6
- The German Settlement — 7
- CSCE — 8
- CSCE's Aftermath — 12
- MBFR — 13
- The Western Malaise about Détente — 16
- The Revolution in Weapons Systems — 19
- Regional Destabilizing Factors — 22
- Kissinger and Détente in Europe — 23
- The Carter Administration and Détente in Europe — 24

Chapter 2
Détente-Entente-Coopération — 26
by *André Fontaine*
- English Summary — 26
- L'Europe de l'Atlantique à l'Oural — 28

Le retrait de la France de l'OTAN	29
De Gaulle fait cavalier seul	30
L'invasion de la Tchécoslovaquie	31
Pompidou et le "condominium"	33
Le Kremlin et la campagne présidentielle en France	34
Le sommet d'Helsinki	36
La contestation à l'Est	37
Entre la gérontocratie et l'armée	38
Le choix de la direction soviétique	40

Chapter 3
The Future of Non-alignment in Europe 42
by *Leo Mates*
    Developments in the West after Helsinki 43
    Developments in the East after Helsinki 46
    The Effects of Developments in the East and the West on Nonalignment in Europe 48
    Prospects for a Non-aligned Europe in the World 52

Chapter 4
Les dix principes d'Helsinki: Interprétations et mise en oeuvre 57
by *Victor-Yves Ghébali*
    English Summary 57
    Les interprétations du Décalogue 58
        Le problème des frontières: immutabilité ou intangibilité? 59
        La "doctrine Brejnev" 62
        Les fondements de la troisième corbeille 64
        La démocratisation des relations paneuropéennes 65
        La "dimension mondiale" de la CSCE 67
    La mise en oeuvre du Décalogue 68

Part two
DÉTENTE AND DISARMAMENT 75

Introduction 77

Chapter 5
Arms Reduction in Europe and the Problem of Nuclear Weapons 79
by *Marian Dobrosielski*
    The Problem of Nuclear Weapons 81

Theatre Nuclear Weapons	82
No-first Use of Nuclear Weapons	87
Mutual Reduction of Armed Forces and Armaments	88
Further Problems	92

Chapter 6
The Vienna Negotiations on Mutual Reduction of Forces and Armaments and Associated Measures in Central Europe (MURFAAMCE) 93
by *Paul J.M. Teunissen*

Prelude to the Talks	94
Preliminary Talks	101
The Initial Proposals: the Warsaw Pact Draft-agreement	106
The Initial NATO Proposals	111
Further Course of Negotiations	113
Interim-assessment	121
Some Broader Considerations (1): Differing Perspectives on Security	123
Some Broader Considerations (2): The Continuing Strategic Arms Race	127
The Need for a New Approach	130

Chapter 7
The CSCE and Military Aspects of European Security 132
by *Ljubivoje Aćimović*

Different Approaches to the Problem	134
Basic Problems and Results of the Conference	136
Confidence building measures	136
Prior notification of major military manoeuvres	136
Prior notification of other military manoeuvres	139
Exchange of observers at military manoeuvres	139
Prior notification of major military movements	140
Other confident building measures	140
Measures intended to restrain military activities that might cause misunderstanding or tension	140
General considerations	141
Implementation of the Document on the Military Aspects of European Security	144
Future Tasks	145

Chapter 8
Military and Political Détente in American Foreign Policy   150
by *Ernst-Otto Czempiel*
    Détente in American Foreign Policy   153
    Domestic Forces and Détente Policies   157
    Evaluating Détente   162
    The Contradiction Remains   167

Part three
COOPERATION IN THE FIELD OF ECONOMICS   169

Introduction   171

Chapter 9
East–West Trade and the Process of Détente   172
by *József Bognár*
    The Development of Economic Relations and the Security System   173
    Trends in East–West Economic Relations   177
        Benefits to the socialist countries   179
        Benefits to developed capitalist countries   180
        Benefits to developing countries   181
        New forms of cooperation   182
        The need for CMEA–EEC discussions   185
    Changes in the Economic Policies of Socialist States   186
        Efforts to improve the system of economic management   187
    Coping with the Changes in the World Economy   189

Chapter 10
Economic Integration and East–West Trade: Conflict of Interest or Comedy of Errors?   192
by *John Pinder*
    The Slow March through Institutional Contacts towards Negotiations   192
    Political Obstacles   194
        Soviet and East European views of Community and Comecon   194
        Community attitudes towards Comecon   196

Differing Economic Interests	198
The European Community: substantial exports to the East, but what is reciprocity?	198
Substantial Soviet exports to the Community, but they encounter few trade barriers	201
The East Europeans' interest in negotiations	203
Forms of Negotiations	204
Can existing channels suffice?	204
What more would bilateral trade negotiations achieve?	206
The Future Development of Economic Relations	208
The content of East–West negotiations	209
The present prospects for negotiations	211

Part four
COOPERATION IN HUMANITARIAN AND OTHER FIELDS   213

Introduction	215

Chapter 11
Cultural Exchange and Ideological Struggle: A Soviet View   216
by *Inna L. Sheidina*

Cultural Exchanges: Problems and Points of View	217
Progress in Promoting Cultural Exchanges	220
Cultural Exchanges and the Ideological Struggle	223
Ideological Struggle and Psychological Warfare	226
Prospects	230

Chapter 12
Cultural Exchange and Competition Between Societies: An American View   231
by *Robert F. Byrnes*

Advantages of Exchange and Competition	232
American benefits	232
Soviet benefits	233
East European benefits	234
Perspectives Since Stalin's Death	234
Progress since the mid-fifties	235
Progress in recent years	237

The Paradoxical Reversals of Position on Helsinki	240
The Significance of Helsinki	244
The Dilemmas	245
The Soviet dilemma	245
The American dilemma	246
The Future	247
Some proposals	248

Chapter 13
The Final Act, its Implementation and 'Human Contacts' by Z.A.B. Zeman	250
The Flow of Information	250
Human Contacts	252
Emigration	255
Other Areas of Human Contacts	256
Conflicts and Limitations	257

Chapter 14
Implementation of Basket Three*	259
Introduction	259
Cooperation in Humanitarian and Other Fields	260
Human contacts	261
Family visits and reunification	262
Binational marriages	267
Travel for personal or professional reasons	268
Religious contacts and information	269
Tourism; meetings among young people; sports	270
Expansion of contacts	271
Information	271
Dissemination of information	272
Broadcasting	272
Cooperation in the field of information	274
Working conditions for journalists	274
Cooperation and Exchanges in the Fields of Culture and Education	276
General considerations	276
Cooperation and exchanges in the field of culture	277
Books and publishing	277
Films and broadcasting	279

* Text of Chapter 4 from Second Semiannual Report by the President to the Commission on Security and Cooperation in Europe.

Performing arts	280
Exhibits	281
Exchange visits among specialists	282
Multilateral activities	283
Cooperation and exchanges in the field of education	284
Extension of relations: access and exchanges	284
Other educational programmes and visits	284
Science	286
Language	287

Epilogue:
A Deepening sense of Uncertainty 288
by *Frans A.M. Alting von Geusau*
    The Belgrade Follow-up Conference 288
    Détente and Disarmament 291
    Cooperation in the Field of Economics 293
    Cooperation in Humanitarian and Other Fields 294
    The Growing Malaise 296

INDEX 299

ABOUT THE AUTHORS

Frans A.M. Alting von Geusau is Professor of the Law of International Organizations at Tilburg University and Director of the John F. Kennedy Institute.

L. Aćimović is Director of the International Relations Department of the Institute of International Politics and Economics, Belgrade.

J. Bognár is Professor and Director of the Institute for World Economics of the Hungarian Academy of Sciences, Budapest.

R. Byrnes is Director of the Russian and East European Institute, Department of History, Indiana University, Bloomington, USA.

E.O. Czempiel is Professor of International Relations, Johann Wolfgang-Goethe Universität, Frankfurt/Main.

M. Dobrosielski is Professor and Director of the Polish Institute of International Affairs, Warsaw.

A. Fontaine is Editor-in-Chief of "Le Monde", Paris.

V.-Y. Ghébali is Research-Associate at the Centre de Recherches sur les Institutions Internationales, Geneva.

W.E. Griffith is Professor of Political Science, Center for International Studies, Massachusetts Institute of Technology, Cambridge, USA.

L. Mates is Professor at the Institute of International Politics and Economics, Belgrade.

J. Pinder is Director of Political and Economic Planning, PEP, London.

I.L. Sheidina is Head of Section at the Institute of US and Canadian Studies, Moscow.

P.J. Teunissen is Professor of International Relations at the Polemological Institute, Groningen.

Z.A.B. Zeman is Professor of Central and South Eastern European Studies, Lonsdale College, University of Lancaster, Bailrigg.

ABBREVIATIONS

ABC	American Broadcasting Corporation
ACDA	Arms Control and Disarmament Agency
ALA	American Library Association
CBM's	Confidence Building Measures
CBS	Central Broadcasting System
CEE	see EEC
CEP	Circular Error Probable
CIES	Conference on International Economic Cooperation
CMEA	Council of Mutual Economic Assistance
COMECON	see CMEA
CSCE	Conference on Security and Cooperation in Europe
CM's	Cruise Missiles
CPSU	Communist Party of the Soviet Union
ECE	Economic Commission for Europe (UN)
ECM	Electronic Counter Measures
EEC	European Economic Community
ELINT	Electronic Intelligence
ERRB	Enhanced Radiation Reduced Blast
FBI	Federal Bureau of Investigation
FBS	Forward Based Systems
GATT	General Agreement on Tariffs and Trade
GDR	German Democratic Republic
GFR	German Federal Republic
GNP	Gross National Product
ICBM's	Intercontinental Ballistic Missiles
ICEM	Intergovernmental Committee for European Migration
IRBM's	Intermediate Range Ballistic Missiles
LSI	Large Scale Integration
MaRV	Multiple Manoeuvrable Re-Entry Vehicles
MBFR	Mutual and Balanced Force Reductions
MFN	Most Favoured Nations (clause)
MFR	Mutual Force Reductions

MLF	Multilateral Force
MPLA	Marxist Popular Liberation Army, Angola
MRCA	Multi-role Combat Aircraft
MIRV	Multiple Independently Targettable Re-entry Vehicles
MRP	Mouvement Républicain Populaire
NATO	North Atlantic Treaty Organization
NBC	National Broadcasting Corporation
NGO	Non-governmental Organization
OECD	Organization for Economic Cooperation and Development
OPEC	Oil Producing and Exporting Countries
OTAN	see NATO
PCF	Parti Communiste Français
PCUS	see CPSU
PGM'S	Precision Guided Munitions
RDA	République Démocratique d'Allemagne
RFA	République Fédérale d'Allemagne
RFE	Radio Free Europe
RL	Radio Liberty
RPV's	Remotely Piloted Vehicles
SALT	Strategic Arms Limitations Talks
SED	Sozialistische Einheitspartei Deutschlands
SIPRI	Swedish International Peace Research Institute
SLBM's	Sea-Launched Ballistic Missiles
TERCOM	Terrain-matching Guidance System
TNW's	Theatre (tactical) Nuclear Weapons
UDR	Union de Démocrates pour la République
UK	United Kingdom
UN	United Nations
UNCTAD	United Nations Conference on Trade and Development
UNESCO	United Nations Education, Scientific and Cultural Organization
URSS	See USSR
US(A)	United States of America
USIA	United States Information Agency
USIS	United States Information Service
USSR	Union of Socialist Soviet Republics

PROLOGUE

by *Frans A.M. Alting von Geusau*

UNCERTAIN DÉTENTE—so we have been told by a variety of observers and politicians—is inappropriate as a title for an evaluation of East–West relations more than two years after the conclusion of the Final Act of the Conference on Security and Cooperation in Europe (CSCE). At best the title expresses unwarranted pessimism. All States participating in the Conference, though, have committed themselves to "broaden, deepen and make continuing and lasting the process of détente". Official opinions in several Western countries are cautiously positive. Although a final evaluation of the process initiated with the CSCE cannot as yet be made after two years, the interim assessment may, on the whole, be a positive one.[1] The US Congress Commission on Security and Cooperation in Europe: "remains confident of the constructive potential of the 35-nations agreement. It finds, however, that much of the potential is yet to be realized."[2]

Official opinion in the Soviet Union and other Warsaw-pact countries has challenged the title as an expression of the opponents of détente in the West. In their view the process of détente is an irreversible one, indicating the shifting correlation of forces in favour of the ultimate and unavoidable victory of "socialism". For observers from non-aligned countries, Helsinki marked a positive trend towards expanding the process of détente.[3]

---

1. Günther von Well, Secretary of State at the Foreign Office in Bonn in his article: "Belgrad 1977. Das KSZE—Folgetreffen und seine Bedeutung für den Entspannungsprozess". *Europa-Archiv.* Folge 18/1977, p. 577.

2. Report to the Congress of the United States on Implementation of the Final Act of the Conference on Security and Cooperation in Europe: *Findings and Recommendations Two Years after Helsinki.* Washington D.C. August 1, 1977, p. 3/4.

3. See, e.g., Osmo Apunen, "The Principles of Relations between the States of Europe". *Yearbook of Finnish Foreign Policy.* 1975; Djura Ninčić, "The Spirit and Letter of Helsinki". *Review of International Affairs.* Belgrade, vol. XXVII, number 626. May 5, 1976. Also: this author's: "Détente After Helsinki. Attitudes and Perspectives". *Yearbook of World Affairs.* 1978, vol. 32. London, 1978.

For a number of expelled or "dissident" Soviet authors and scholars, our title is likely to sound dangerously optimistic and imprecise. Soviet historian Andrei Amalrik said: "The movement for the rights of man in the Soviet Union is for détente. But we are for détente which will really facilitate and ameliorate relations between East and West. Détente as conceived and represented by Kissinger, which consists simply of consolidating all that is bad in the East and in the West, can only lead the world to catastrophe".[4]

Similar warnings have been voiced by Andrei Sakharov and Alexander Solzhenitsyn. These men not only have a right to speak, it is our obligation to listen to them. They know from bitter experience and suffering what it means when they warn us of the "ever constant global threat posed by the totalitarian nations".[5]

Détente thus means very different things to many persons and policy-makers. As the CSCE has shown so far, the negotiators have agreed on little else than détente as an acceptable term for indicating the present state of East–West relations. For each government represented, it has not measurably changed the course and conduct of its foreign policies. When one reads through the variety of diverging interpretations of the principles and provisions of the Final Act, one observes an enhanced sensitivity about divergent policies rather than an emerging common view on the future of Europe.

The contributions to this volume cannot but underline this basic lack of progress in East–West relations. The analyses, sometimes statements, presented here—whether on problems and principles, on arms control and forces reductions, on economic cooperation or on human rights and humanitarian concerns—hardly offer any new proposals or perspectives. At best they contribute to a better mutual understanding of persistent differences.

Détente, the reader will become increasingly aware, is most uncertain indeed. It has not provided us with a key towards better solving the international, political problems we face. The carefully drafted ten principles have not enlightened the path for nations towards an agreed common code of conduct. And, as will be shown, the declared complementarity of political and military détente has done next to nothing to foster agreement on curbing the arms race and to fulfil the hopes of mankind in disarmament.

The process of economic cooperation continues to suffer from the

4. Speech before the Anglo-American Press Association in Paris. In *U.S. News and World Report*. Oct. 25, 1976.
5. Andrei D. Sakharov, *My Country and the World*. New York 1975, p. 89.

security problems; it has hardly—if at all—benefited from the very long series of provisions written into the Final Act. Whoever may think that détente favours the aspirations of man to move around more freely, to express his thoughts, to emigrate or simply to be reunited with his kin, will probably cry out in despair after having worked himself through the contributions on cooperation in humanitarian and other fields.

Uncertain détente not only is discouragingly adequate a label for the European situation today, it points above all to a situation we are required to change, and change profoundly. Where so little progress has been made—since the Second World War—towards genuine reconciliation and mutual trust and tolerance, a far more fundamental re-appraisal of political attitudes than has been made so far appears to be the most urgent requirement for future action. To such a re-appraisal, this volume hopes to challenge its readers.

Part One

DÉTENTE: PROBLEMS AND PRINCIPLES

INTRODUCTION

The Final Act of the Conference on Security and Cooperation in Europe (CSCE) expresses the determination of the participating States "to broaden, deepen and make continuing and lasting the process of détente" (preamble, 5th paragraph). Its conclusion, in fact, marked the multilateralization of a process begun—according to many observers—with Soviet–American détente in the early sixties.

The four contributions included in this first part indicate that the actual process of détente, and its possible outcome, is far less certain than the pre-cited preamble suggests.

Griffith in his broad survey and Ghébali in his detailed analysis of the "Declaration on Principles Guiding Relations Between Participating States" both underline the persistent divergencies in the concepts of détente held in the Soviet Union and the Western Alliance. A Soviet contribution—had we been able to include it—would certainly have emphasized such divergencies. As Brezhnev told the 25th Congress of the CPSU in February 1976:

> "Détente and peaceful coexistence have to do with interstate relations ... Détente does not in the slightest abolish, nor can it alter, the laws of the class struggle ... We make no secret of the fact that we see détente as the way to create more favourable conditions for peaceful socialist and communist construction".

Concepts of détente, however, do not only diverge between East and West. As Fontaine explains, consecutive French Presidents have pursued a dream of their own: to elevate France to the role of a balancing power between the Soviet Union and the USA and thus liberate France (and Europe) from the constraints of a Soviet–American condominium. Mates expects *détente* to promote the concept of non-alignment in Europe, by shifting emphasis from inter-bloc and inter-ideology confrontation to inter-state competitions.

Whereas Ghébali concludes that the Ten Principles of the Final

Act have done more to evoke tension than to facilitate détente, Griffith expects that the factors likely to destabilize détente can be counterbalanced by mutual Soviet and US interests to pursue policies of détente.

Chapter 1

EAST–WEST DÉTENTE IN EUROPE

by *William E. Griffith*

In the last few years Western views about East–West détente in Europe[1] have been increasingly overtaken by malaise. The Soviet and East European leaders, on the other hand, have not faltered in their support of their version of détente. To understand this divergence, we must consider the nature and causes of East–West détente and the causes of the Western malaise about it. Finally, we must try to draw up a balance-sheet on its present and future.

Definitions

What is détente? The West and East have viewed it quite differently. To oversimplify, the East views it minimally as relaxation of tension in order to lower the risk of nuclear war and maximally as an instrument to expand its influence. The West has viewed it as avoiding nuclear war and leading to what Dr. Kissinger called "a stable structure of peace." But to expect that the Soviet Union will agree so to define détente flies in the face of modern Russian history, of Marxist–Leninist ideology, and the theory and practice of the Soviet Union in international affairs.

The United States, Western Europe, and Japan are political and military status quo powers, albeit economically expansionist ones. The Soviet Union, like Imperial Russia before it, is a politically and militarily expansionist power in a young imperial phase, largely comparable to Imperial Germany before World War I. It feels that it deserves, and it is determined to get, its "place in the sun"—to be equal to the other super-power, the United States.

---

1. For general background, see William E. Griffith, ed., *The Soviet Empire: Expansion and Détente* (Lexington, Mass.: Lexington Books, 1976); David S. Landes, ed., *Western Europe: The Trials of Partnership* (Lexington, Mass.: Lexington Books, 1977); and Nils Andrén and Karl E. Birnbaum, eds., *Beyond Détente: Prospects for East–West Cooperation and Security in Europe* (Leyden: Sijthoff, 1976).

Moreover, because of the organic interaction between its perceptions of its national interest and its ideology, the Soviet Union wants to "make the world safe for communism": e.g. to give arms and money to "national liberation movements." Moscow therefore sees détente as not only lowering the risk of nuclear war but also favouring such aid, since it makes it less likely that the United States will try to prevent it by military means. Finally, Marxism, Soviet and elsewhere, views history as moving inexorably and progressively, by contradictions and conflict, toward an ultimate perfect society. Status quo and stability are not only contrary to Marxist goals but in the Marxist view do not, and cannot, exist.

Causes

Soviet and American desire to limit the risk of nuclear war was the principle cause of East–West détente. There were others: the East–West stalemate in Europe and Asia, the death of Stalin, and the Sino-Soviet split. Khrushchev and Brezhnev wanted credits and technology from the West and Japan. They wanted to recognize the Soviet sphere of influence in Central and Eastern Europe. They wanted to limit their own arms expenditure. Finally, they wanted to avoid more political unity and nuclear weapons in Western Europe, and most of all—for them, probably, their worst nightmare—a nuclear Western Germany (and a nuclear Japan) allied with a (nuclear) China against Moscow. However, they followed a more expansionist policy than Stalin in the underdeveloped world and tried to use détente to expand their influence there.

The United States' and Western Europe's perception of Soviet threat has declined because of the Sino-Soviet split, communist pluralism in Eastern and now in Western Europe[2] and Soviet détente policy itself. The West has become less committed to the Cold War and wants to cut the spiralling costs of weapons systems and increase trade with the East. West German *Ostpolitik* recognized the status quo in order to change it (*Wandel durch*

---

2. William E. Griffith, "Eurocommunism: The Third Great Communist Schism?" (M.I.T. Center for International Studies C/76-19, mimeo., November 1976), of which a revised version has been published in a collective volume edited by Karl Kaiser and Hans-Peter Schwartz for the Deutsche Gesellschaft für Auswärtige Politik and "The Diplomacy of Eurocommunism" (MS., March 1977), later published in a collective volume edited by Rudolf Tökés for the Council on Foreign Relations.

Annäherung). Finally, autonomist Yugoslavia and Romania have pushed détente in Europe to insure themselves against Soviet pressure and military intervention.

The German Settlement[3]

The German treaties have been the major results of East–West détente in Europe. They resulted, in my view, from East–West compromise. Their basic causes were two. West German public opinion had become increasingly resigned to the indefinite partition of Germany and had concluded that some *modus vivendi* with the East must therefore be found, inter alia to prevent East Germans from losing contact with West Germany and the sense of belonging to one common German nation. The Soviet leadership was willing to compromise on this basis, i.e. to abandon its attempts to change the status of West Berlin to its favour and therefore potentially to destabilize the Federal Republic and move toward detaching it from its alliance with the United States. The Soviet Union, Poland, and the other East European States also wanted to get massive German credits and technology transfers. East Germany was alone opposed to the treaties, which for it sacrificed its interests to Moscow's desire for agreements with Bonn and Washington, but Moscow removed Ulbricht and forced East Berlin to accept them.

Their consequences remain in dispute. Bonn's professed principal aim, "change through rapprochement" in East Germany, has so far had nothing like major success. Yet the massive inflow of West German tourists, the impact of the Helsinki Final Act, the East Berlin communist conference declaration, and the recent intellectual dissent in the DDR seem to indicate that *Ostpolitik* may have some long-term impact in the DDR. West German economic relations with the Soviet Union and Eastern Europe have continued to increase. East Berlin has continued to attempt to limit any progress by West Germany, with varying results. Finally, the replacement of Brandt by Schmidt as Chancellor has lowered Bonn's priority for *Ostpolitik*.

On balance, *Ostpolitik* has in my view so far been more successful

---

3. Karl Birnbaum, *Peace in Europe* (New York: Oxford University Press, 1970) and his *East and West Germany: A Modus Vivendi* (Lexington, Mass: Lexington Books, 1973); Lawrence Whetten, *Germany's Ostpolitik* (New York: Oxford University Press, 1971); and Helga Haftendorn, "Ostpolitik Revisited 1976," *The World Today*, June 1976.

for the West, and particularly for Bonn, than for the East. It gave away, as Brandt said, nothing which Hitler had not thrown away before, and it has at least slowed down, if not reversed, the isolation of East Germany from the West—which was, after all, its principal objective.

CSCE

The initial proposal for what became a Conference on Security and Cooperation in Europe (CSCE)[4] was a Soviet one—enough to

---

4. By far the best recent analysis, based on extensive interviewing of CSCE delegates, is Karl Birnbaum, "East-West Diplomacy in the Era of Multilateral Negotiations: The Case of the Conference on Security and Cooperation in Europe (CSCE)" in Andrén and Birnbaum, *Beyond Détente*, op. cit. An earlier German version was published as Karl Birnbaum, *Die Konferenz über Sicherheit und Zusammenarbeit in Europa: eine Zwischenbilanz der Genfer Kommissionsphase* (Bonn: Forschungsinstitut der Deutschen Gesselschaft für Auswärtige Politik, Arbeitspapiere zur Internationale Politik, no. 2, May 1974). Dr. Birnbaum, of the Swedish Institute of International Affairs, is completing a book on the CSCE. See also Uwe Nerlich, "Zur Struktur und Dynamik, europäischer Sicherheitspolitik," *Europa Archiv*, July 25, 1971; Paul Frank, "Zielsetzungen der Bundesrepublik Deutschland im Rahmen europäischer Sicherheitsverhandlungen," *Europa Archiv*, March 10, 1972; Hans-Georg Wieck, "Überlegungen zur Sicherheit in Europa," *Aussenpolitik*, July 1972; Götz von Groll, "East-West Talks in Helsinki," *Aussenpolitik* (English ed.), no. 4, 1972; Hans-Peter Schwarz, "Sicherheitskonferenz und westliche Sicherheitsgemeinschaft," *Europa Archiv*, Dec. 25, 1972; Guido Brunner, "Das Ergebnis von Helsinki," ibid., July 10, 1973; Götz von Groll, "The Foreign Ministers in Helsinki," *Aussenpolitik* (English ed.), no. 3, 1973, "The Geneva CSCE Negotiations," ibid., no. 2, 1974, and "The Geneva Final Act of the CSCE," ibid., no. 3, 1975; Wolfgang Wagner, "Eine Station auf einem langen Wege. Zur geschichtlichen Einordnung der Konferenz über Sicherheit und Zusammenarbeit in Europa (KSZE)," and Otto Graf Schwerin, "Die Solidarität der EG-Staaten in der KSZE," *Europa Archiv*, Aug. 10, 1975; Gerhard Henze, "Neue Aufgaben der Entspannungspolitik," ibid., Sept. 25, 1975; Klaus Blech, "Die KSZE als Schritt im Entspannungsprozess," ibid., Nov. 25, 1975; Leo Mates, "Europa nach der KSZE," ibid., Nov. 25, 1976. Gregory A. Flynn, "The Content of European Détente," *Orbis*, Summer 1976. See also in general Timothy W. Stanley and Darnell M. Whitt, *Détente Diplomacy: The United States and European Security in the 1970s* (New York: Dunellen, 1970).

For Soviet policy toward CSCE, see Marshall D. Shulman, "A European Security Conference," *Survival*, Dec. 1969 and *Europa Archiv*, no. 19, 1969; Robert Legvold, "European Security Conference," *Survey*, Summer 1970; Boris Meissner, "The Soviet Union and Collective Security" and Gerhard Wettig, "Soviet Shifts make the West, and especially Washington and Bonn, determined to have nothing to do with it. The initial Soviet aims were two: minimally, to get multilateral Western ratification of Soviet hegemony over Eastern Europe and to increase East–West trade and technology transfers; and maximally, to use the CSCE (in which, Moscow proposed, only European States, i.e. not the United States, would participate) to disengage the United States gradually from Europe, limits the rise of West German influence, and increase tensions in the Western alliance.

Moscow first proposed a European security conference in 1954.

---

in European Security Policy," *Aussenpolitik* (English ed.), no. 3, 1970; Wettig, *Gesamteuropäische kollektive Sicherheit und osteuropäische kollektive Souveränität als Elemente des sowjetischen Europa-Programms*, Berichte des Bundesinstituts für ostwissenschaftliche und internationale Studien, no. 25, 1972; Lilita Dzirkals and A. Ross Johnson, eds., *Soviet and East European Forecasts of European Security: Papers from the 1972 Varna Conference*, RAND R-1272-PR, June 1973; Ye. A. Boltin, *Sovetskaya Vneshnaya Politika i Evropeiskaya Bezopasnost* (Moscow, 1972), tr. in JPRS 57815, Dec. 20, 1972; Charles Andras, "East–West Cooperation and Ideological Conflict," *Radio Free Europe Research*, Sept. 5, 1973; Wettig, *Etappen der sowjetischen Europa-Politik im Blick auf KSZE und MBFR*, Berichte des Bundesinstituts für ostwissenschaftliche und internationale Studien, no. 39, 1973 and *Sowjetische Vorstellungen über eine Neuordnung der zwischenstaatlichen Beziehungen in Europa*, ibid., no. 40, 1974: Philippe Devillers, "La conférence sur la sécurité et la coopération en Europe," *Défense nationale*, no. 3, 1973; Mojmir Povolny, "The Soviet Union and the European Security Conference," *Orbis*, Spring 1974; Wettig, "Freiere Begegnungen und Dialoge zwischen Ost und West," *Aus Politik und Zeitgeschichte*, March 15, 1975; Andras, "European Security and 'Social Process,'" *Radio Free Europe Research*, July 21, 1975; Wettig, "Zum Ergebnis der KSZE," *Osteuropa*, Dec. 1975 and *Frieden und Sicherheit in Europa* (Stuttgart, 1975.)

For East European attitudes, see Peter Bender, *East Europe in Search of Security* (London: Chatto and Windus, 1972); Robert R. King and Robert L. Dean, eds., *East European Perspectives on European Security and Cooperation* (New York: Praeger, 1974); John C. Campbell, "European Security: Prospects and Possibilities for East Europe," *East Europe*, November 1970; Robin Alison Remington, "Yugoslavia and European Security," *Orbis*, Spring 1973; Adam Bromke, "The CSCE and Eastern Europe," *The World Today*, May 1973.

For assessments of Soviet policy since Helsinki, see F. Stephen Larrabee, "Soviet Attitudes and Policy towards 'Basket Three' since Helsinki," *Radio Liberty Research*, March 15, 1976 and "Soviet Implementation of the Helsinki Agreement: The Military Dimension," ibid., Jan. 1, 1977; Ignacy Szenfeld, "Cooperation in the Field of Cultural Exchanges since the Helsinki Conference," ibid., Jan. 5, 1977; Marshall Goldman, "Cooperation in the Field of Economics: The Soviet Side and Basket Two," ibid., Jan. 10, 1977.

It reinforced its effort in 1969 just before the negotiation of the German treaties. By then, however, the situation had changed greatly and Soviet aims had therefore become limited to their minimal ones. Global and European détente was intensifying, the Vietnam War was ending, and the American rapprochement with China was under way. Most importantly, by the end of 1972 the West–East German Basic Treaty had been signed, in part, like the other German treaties, because Bonn and later Washington had successfully established linkage (*Junktim*) between them and Western agreement to a CSCE.

Because of Senator Mansfield's pressure for unilateral US troop withdrawals from Germany Washington had two motives for agreeing to a CSCE: to signal its determination to remain involved in European affairs and to use it to bring about East–West negotiations on mutual balanced troop withdrawals, thus countering Mansfield's pressure. The Nixon administration embraced the "Chinese connection" and East–West détente. It also became convinced, after initial and in my view unwarranted skepticism, that Brandt's *Ostpolitik* was defusing the German question, notably in Berlin. However, because of what I have always thought to be his overly pessimistic estimate of its prospects, Dr. Kissinger remained skeptical about CSCE. He did not want it. He reluctantly agreed to it. He was uninterested in when not actively hostile to it. Once it met, he wanted it to end as soon as possible.

The principal minimum West European objective in CSCE was to prevent the Soviets from limiting what West European unity the EEC had achieved. The West Europeans also wanted in part to compensate for rising Soviet military power and to encourage contacts with and more human rights in the Soviet Union and Eastern Europe. West Germany was determined to hold open a legal option for the peaceful reunification of Germany. The smaller West European States and the European neutrals wanted to play a role.

The two non- or semi-aligned states in Eastern Europe, Yugoslavia and Romania, wanted to use the CSCE to deter the Soviets from invading or putting irresistible pressure on them. Poland and Hungary may well have wanted to use CSCE to strengthen détente *per se*, but if so, Soviet pressure kept them on the same loyally pro-Soviet line as the DDR, Czechoslovakia, and Bulgaria.

During the long CSCE negotiations at Geneva the Soviets (and their East European allies) and the nine EEC members played the main roles. The United States was largely passive. The non-aligned and the neutrals[5] tried to assert themselves, with some success. This was easier because the Conference operated by "consensus"—all decisions by unanimous vote only.

The CSCE negotiations were essentially a struggle between Moscow, which wanted multilateral *ratification* of the status quo and increased East–West trade plus non-interference in internal affairs ("baskets" 1 and 2), and the EEC States which, with some but not strong US support, pushed for increased East–West contacts and guarantee for human rights ("basket" 3), i.e. to *change* the status quo. From the Western viewpoint, CSCE's most positive aspect was the successful daily coordination of the policy of the EEC States (the "Nine")—just the contrary of what Moscow had hoped to achieve in the conference.

The inevitable result was a compromise which East and West could—and did—quote and use for their own purposes. The Soviets accepted provisions on human rights in basket 3 which they probably later regretted. Moreover, although the CSCE Final Act reaffirmed the territorial status quo, the same reservation was added to authorize peaceful change which had been in the German treaties—i.e. the Final Act made no legal change in the already existing situation. Yet the Soviets could cite basket 1 to justify their rejection of any interference in their internal affairs—i.e. they refused to implement basket 3 to any major extent.

The Final Act provided for a review conference in Belgrade in 1977. This "follow-up" procedure had originally been pushed by the Soviets, who hoped thereby to be able to influence Western affairs while preventing Western influence in their own sphere. At first the Americans were opposed to "follow-up" out of fear that the Soviets would achieve these objectives. However, as CSCE went on and the EEC States became confident that they were making progress on basket 3, the Soviets became correspondingly less interested in institutionalizing the conference and willingly modified their proposals to meet the initial Western objections to them. The military aspects of CSCE were reduced, by the separation of MBFR from it, to purely confidence-building measures (CBMs) such as mutual notification of and exchange of observers at military manoeuvres.

---

5. See the earlier analysis by a Yugoslav CSCE delegate, Ljubivoje Aćimović, "Die blockfreien Länder und die europäische Sicherheit," *Europa Archiv*, Dec. 10, 1969.

CSCE's Aftermath

When the CSCE Final Act—it was not a treaty binding in international law—was signed in Helsinki in 1975, there was much criticism in the United States and Western Europe that the West was thereby ratifying the division of Europe and Soviet domination over its eastern half. But since then events in the Soviet Union and Eastern Europe have showed that the Final Act encouraged dissidence rather than discouraged it. It has therefore become an embarrassment to the Soviets, not to the West. Moreover, the fact of Helsinki and the Final Act, plus the subsequent Soviet and East European intensification of repression, further sensitized Western public opinion to this repression and therefore made it more skeptical about détente. Soviet and East European dissidents have tried to use the Final Act vis-à-vis regime pressures against them. Many of the perhaps 100,000 East Germans who have applied to emigrate to West Germany have cited the Final Act as justification. As was to be expected, however, the Soviet Union and its East European allies, and even Yugoslavia, have on balance increased their repressive measures against dissidents.[6] The autumn 1977 Belgrade follow-up conference will provide a forum for discussions on how well the Final Act has been carried out. The Soviets now seem to want to have the Belgrade follow-up conference as brief as possible and to agree on conferences on transportation and the environment. The West is not striving for an East–West confrontation there. Yet the highlighting of human rights by President Carter and the increased Soviet and East European repression of dissidents make it doubtful that an East–West confrontation there can be avoided.

President Carter's recent declarations on human rights have brought the Final Act, and particularly basket 3 into the news. It is still too early to know what the results of this new American initiative will be. Initial Soviet reaction has been, predictably, strongly hostile. Yet past experience would indicate that Moscow may well implicitly tolerate what it become convinced that it cannot stop. For Moscow détente has always been a combination of arms control agreements, increased East–West trade and technology transfer, and the "continuation of the ideological struggle," i.e. setting forth abroad its own values and goals. Moscow would of

---

6. See in general Curt Gasteyger, "Europa zwischen Helsinki und Belgrade," *Europa Archiv*, Jan. 10, 1977.

course prefer that the West not do the same, but, rather, that it tacitly accept something close to unilateral Western ideological disarmament—which the last Administration came close to doing. The new Administration seems to be trying to carry on détente in a manner more symmetrical with the Soviet practice—i.e. arms control plus "ideological struggle."

MBFR

MBFR[7] was a 1968 Western initiative; the Soviets first re-

---

7. By far the best recent analysis is Christoph Bertram, "European Arms Control" in Andrén and Birnbaum, *Beyond Détente*, op. cit. See also John Yochelson, "MBFR: The Search for an American Approach" and J.I. Coffey, "Arms Control and the Military Balance in Europe," *Orbis*, Spring 1973; Alfons Pawelczyk, "Möglichkeiten eines Streitkräfte-Abbaus in Europa," *Europa Archiv*, Jan. 25, 1977; Johan Jørgen Holst, "East–West Negotiations, Arms Control and West European Security," Norsk Utenrikspolitisk Institutt (Oslo), NUPI-N-91, April 1975. "Brezhnev's Inch," *The Economist*, Feb. 28, 1976; Jacques Huntzinger, "Les interrogations de Vienne," *Le Monde*, June 20–21, 1976, May 7, 1976; J.I. Coffey, "Détente, Arms Control and European Security," *International Affairs* (London), Jan. 1976; Gerhard Wettig, *Die sowjetische MBFR—Politik als Problem der Ost–West-Entspannung in Europa* (Cologne: Bundesinstitut für ostwissenschaftliche und internationale Studien, mimeo., no. 4, Dec. 1975); Christoph Bertram, "The Politics of MBFR," *The World Today*, Jan. 1973 and *Mutual Force Reductions in Europe: The Political Aspects*, Adelphi Papers, no. 84 (London: IISS, Jan. 1972); Lothar Ruehl, "Beiderseitige Truppenverminderung in Europa," *Europa Archiv*, May 25, 1973 and "Die Wiener Verhandlungen über Truppenverminderung im Ost und West," ibid., Aug. 10, 1974; Uwe Nerlich, "Die Rolle beiderseitiger Truppenverminderung in der europäischen Sicherheitspolitik," *Europa Archiv*, March 10, 1972; and "Continuity and Change: The Political Context of Western Europe's Defense" in Holst and Nerlich, eds., *Beyond Nuclear Deterrence* (New York: Crane, Russak, 1977). I also benefited from participation in a Harvard Program for Science and International Affairs Workshop on Force Restructuring and Force Reduction in Europe, November 1974, and particularly from the papers by Steven L. Canby, Colin Gray, and Gen. Andrew Goodpaster. For the Soviet position on MBFR, see Yu. Kostko, "'The Balance of Fear' or the Safeguarding of Genuine Security," *Mirovaya ekonomika i mezhdunarodniye otnosheniya*, June 1972, tr. in *Survival*, Sept.–Oct. 1972. See also John Erickson, "Soviet Theatre-Warfare Capability: Doctrines, Deployments and Objectives" (MS., mimeo., Edinburgh, March 1975). For general background, see John Newhouse, *U.S. Troops in Europe* (Washington, D.C.: Brookings, 1971) and Robert Lucas Fischer, *Defending the Central Front: The Balance of Forces*, Adelphi Paper no. 127 (London: IISS, Autumn 1976.)

ciprocated in 1971. The United States had two main reasons for proposing it: to try to diminish the Soviet asymmetrical military advantage on the Central European front and to head off Senator Mansfield's pressure for unilateral US troop reductions there. Indeed, from the American viewpoint, Soviet agreement to MBFR negotiations was a precondition for US agreement to CSCE.

The other major Western power concerned, West Germany, wanted to avoid unilateral US troop withdrawals and to prevent the Soviets from getting any control over the level and armament of the Bundeswehr. Its MBFR strategy was therefore one of damage limitation. The French refused to participate in the MBFR negotiations: they wanted to avoid any international agreements limiting their military independence and any reduction, unilateral or otherwise, of US military strength in Europe, which would lower their own security and therefore their military independence. In short, the West's MBFR strategy gave priority to constraining the Soviets and keeping US troops in Europe rather than to reducing military forces.

The Soviets wanted, minimally, to insure through MBFR that any US troop withdrawals from Europe would be symmetrical (i.e. that the Soviet military advantage be maintained), gradual, not compensated for by increase in or greater integration of West European, and particularly West German, forces, and not politically destabilizing. The Soviets also hoped to participate in multilateral limitations and/or controls which would limit or prevent any increase in the Bundeswehr and thereby establish a Soviet *droit de regard* on it. Moscow wanted to preserve its asymmetrical military superiority in Europe and to get it ratified by the West. Finally, by 1971 Moscow was deploying large forces on the Chinese border and wanted détente to its west. Maximally, the Soviets hoped to further Soviet–US bilateralism, thereby worsen NATO cohesion, slow down West European integration, especially military, and encourage a controlled US military withdrawal from Western Europe.

MBFR negotiations began in 1973 in Vienna. Both sides aimed more at negotiations *per se* than at actual reductions. They have produced no results to date, basically because Moscow insists on symmetrical reductions (i.e. preserving its superiority) while the West insists on asymmetrical ones in its favour. After a long deadlock, in December 1975 the NATO powers proposed that not only ground troops, as they had until then insisted, but also planes, missiles, and tactical nuclear weapons be reduced—which Moscow had been demanding. However, the West still insisted on asymmetrical ("balanced") reductions, to NATO's advantage. In January 1976 the Soviets for the first time agreed to accept initial reductions only in "stationed forces," i.e. primarily Soviet and American, rather than indigenous ones, e.g. West German, as well, a position which the West had consistently taken. However, the West still insisted that all reductions be symmetrical and that there be national force sub-ceilings (i.e. including on Bonn instead of general East–West, as NATO insisted). In June 1976 Moscow for the first time gave figures on Warsaw Pact force strengths and proposed a second stage of small symmetrical troop and nuclear reductions of stationed and indigenous forces.

These were only small steps forward. At this writing agreement still remained far away. Some changes in attitudes, primarily on the Western side, have occurred. Unilateral US troop reduction is much less likely. Now Great Britain, rather than West Germany, favours cuts in indigenous forces. The West Europeans, particularly the West Germans, are more determined to prevent the Soviets using MBFR to constrain their own political and military unity. The general Western malaise about détente, of which more below, has lowered expectations in general. In short, incentives for agreement remain few—particularly since the conclusion of the German treaties and CSCE deprived the West of much of its linkage potential vis-à-vis the Soviets. It seemed likely, if only because Moscow usually has difficulty carrying on simultaneously two major negotiations with the West, that significant progress would probably occur only after a SALT II agreement. Indeed, MBFR may end up with little more than some further confidence-building measures (CBMs).

One reason why this may be the outcome is that the MBFR negotiations involve highly complex technical problems. They are made more difficult by the technological revolution now under way in strategic and conventional weapons systems, the resultant greater problems of verification, the asymmetrical advantages of the Soviets in ground troop strength, tank forces, weapons standardization, and nearness of home bases, and the Western asymmetrical advantage in tactical nuclear weapons and perhaps in precision-guided munitions (PGMs) and cruise missiles (CMs). Moreover, most of the Western and Soviet non-tactical nuclear weapons systems were not in the Central European area but in the UK, the Sixth Fleet in the Mediterranean, or in Western Russia.

The Western Malaise about Détente

The major cause of the malaise about détente in the West,[8] in my view, has been the West's and particularly the United States' misperception of what it is and what it can and cannot be. Moscow has never interpreted, or intended, détente to mean recognition of the status quo. Indeed, it has constantly said just the contrary: that détente helps to change the status quo in favour of socialism. Only wishful thinking hindered taking the Soviets at their word.

There are other reasons why détente cannot be stable. They may best be divided into those which are the results of détente and those which exist independently from it.

By increasing East–West contacts détente destabilizes itself. Pierre Hassner has put this so well that I need only quote his penetrating analysis:

> ... In this new phase [détente] characterized by ambiguity and contradiction, the isolation can be broken, but in favour of a penetration which is asymmetrical and not equilibriated rather than by reconciliation. There can always be enough fermentation to prevent stability by freezing, enough separation and divergence to stop stability by integration. The essential characteristic of "hot peace" is neither force nor cooperation, but the constant reciprocal influence of societies within a competition whose aims are less and less tangible, whose means are less and less direct, whose consequences are less and less calculable, precisely because these activities will be as important for their effects on what societies *are* as on what they *do*.
>
> ... What characterizes all negotiations in the age of hot peace is the importance of the time dimension and therefore of uncertainty and betting: rarely has diplomacy (as also the use of force) so been based on implicit bets about its effect on long-term processes ... about which no one can know to what point troops and treaties can manipulate, reverse, influence, control, or limit them ...
>
> ... Hot peace does not necessarily break the equilibrium between alliances and societies, but it tends to make each more vulnerable to the other. From the moment when the existence and legitimacy of the structure are confirmed, the real competition, intentional or involuntary, begins ...[9]

---

8. F. Stephen Larrabee, "Détente Enfeebled: Soviet–U.S. Relations in 1976," *Radio Liberty Research*, Dec. 17, 1976 and "The Problematic Honeymoon: One Month of Soviet–U.S. Relations," ibid., Feb. 28, 1977.

9. Tr. from his seminal article, "L'Europe de la guerre froide à la paix chaude," *Défense nationale*, vol. 29 (March 1973), pp. 35–54, at pp. 45–47. See also the earlier version of this article, "The New Europe: From Cold War to Hot

I shall only mention, for space precludes analyzing them at any length, the internal problems of Western and Soviet societies. The former, many observers feel, is grappling, or rather *not* grappling, with social, cultural, and spiritual problems of major proportions. These include an explosion of transnationalism (e.g. in US-controlled multinational corporations), technological change, ethnic particularism, mass migration of poor workers, and their frustrated aspirations plus those of the new professional classes—all increased by the explosion of mass communications, the de-legitimization of ruling political elites, and a more negative attitude toward force and its use. The latter is also *not* grappling—with slow economic and technological growth, intellectual dissidence, nationalities tensions, and East European rebelliousness, and bureaucratic stagnation.[10]

There are other specific political and economic and military causes of global and regional instability. Soviet quantitative military build-up and US qualitative response plus the asymmetry on Soviet and US military doctrines are destabilizing.[11] The rise in petroleum prices has further economically destabilized such "fourth world" countries as India and Bangla Desh and, in Western Europe, Great Britain and Italy. It is beginning to have similar serious effects, because of Moscow's rising oil export prices, in several East European countries, which are now massively indebted to the OECD countries.[12] North–South antagonism is increasing.

Finally, there is the crisis in Southern Europe. Although from the NATO viewpoint two years ago this seemed more critical and more destabilizing and for Moscow more promising, in Portugal and potentially in Spain, it now seems more serious in France and Italy. The decline of Gaullism in France and of the Christian Democrats in Italy, a result of length of power, the economic crisis, and the rising aspirations of the lower half of the population and deepening

---

Peace," *International Journal* (Toronto), Winter 1971–1972; his *Change and Security in Europe*, Adelphi Papers nos. 45 and 49 (London: IISS, Feb. and July 1968); and Alvin Z. Rubinstein, "The Elusive Parameters of Détente," *Orbis*, Winter 1976.

10. Zbigniew Brzezinski, ed., *Dilemmas of Change in Soviet Politics* New York: Columbia, 1969).

11. Banjamin S. Lambeth, "Selective Nuclear Operations and Soviet Strategy," in Holst and Nerlich, eds., *Beyond Nuclear Deterrence*, op. cit.

12. Thomas E. Heneghan, "Latente Krise in Polen," *Europa Archiv*, Dec. 10, 1976; Robert J. Lieber, *Oil and the Middle East War: Europe in the Energy Crisis* (Cambridge, Mass.: Harvard Center for International Affairs, 1976).

intellectual alienation, and the rising popularity, nationalism, and reformism of the Italian and French communist parties make their—probably minority—participation in power, unlike the Spanish or Portuguese communists, an increasing possibility. But while this is probably still viewed favourably in Moscow, one wonders, given these parties' deviations from the Soviet line, how long it still will be.

The Middle East[13] remains a crisis area and southern Africa[14] has recently become one. Both inevitably affect détente in Europe, and the former also affects the West European economic situation. Indeed, much of the disillusionment about détente among formerly left-wing intellectuals in the United States, and particularly among Jewish intellectuals, arises from their belief[15]—contrary to the evidence, in the view of most experts[16]—that Moscow planned and started the 1973 Middle Eastern war or at least encouraged its outbreak. When added to Moscow's harassment of Soviet Jews and to domestic factors (e.g. resentment against reverse discrimination),[17] this has pushed many intellectuals to a more conservative, anti-Soviet, pro-Israeli position.[18] It also contributed to the Jackson–Vanik amendment and Moscow's subsequent denunciation of the Soviet–US trade treaty. Yet I hasten to add, this is not, as many Soviets would like us to think, the key factor in the rising unpopularity of détente in the United States—the other,

---

13. William E. Griffith, "The Middle East and the Great Powers" (M.I.T. Center for International Studies C/76–20, mimeo., November 1976), published in *Europa Archiv*, no. 6, 1977 and *Politique Etrangère*, March 1977.

14. William E. Griffith, "The Soviet–U.S. Confrontation in Southern Africa" (M.I.T. Center for International Studies C/76–21, mimeo., November 1976), published in *Europa Archiv*, no. 2, 1977.

15. Eugene V. Rostow, "America, Europe, and the Middle East," *Commentary*, Feb. 1974.

16. Galia Golan, "Soviet Aims and the Middle East War," *Survival*, May–June 1974; Alvin Z. Rubinstein, *Red Star on the Nile* (Princeton, New Jersey: Princeton, 1977); William E. Griffith, "Soviet Influence in the Middle East," *Survival*, vol. 18, no. 1, Jan.–Feb. 1976. For the contrary view, see Uri Ra'anan, "The USSR and the Middle East: Some Reflections on the Soviet Decision-Making Process," *Orbis*, Fall 1973.

17. See the special bicentennial issue of *The Public Interest*, Fall 1975.

18. Norman Podhoretz, "Is It Good for the Jews?" *Commentary*, Feb. 1972, his "School Integration and Liberal Opinion," ibid., March 1972, and "Making the World Safe for Communism," ibid., April 1976.

broader ones I have discussed have been that. However, because this reaction to Middle Eastern events has not been nearly so strong in Western Europe, it has increased the Atlantic gap in thinking about détente.

Although Peking has refused to reciprocate Moscow's post-Mao offensive for Sino-Soviet détente and Sino-Soviet relations have recently worsened again,[19] Sino-Soviet détente, although in my view unlikely, might occur. The results for détente in Europe would be unfavourable for it would relieve Moscow's concern about the East and allow it to adopt a more forward policy to its left.

The Revolution in Weapons Systems

An important independent destabilizing factor in détente in Europe is the recent rapid, primarily Western development of new, technologically advanced weapons systems,[20] whose verification is difficult. The most important common characteristic of these new weapons systems—MIRVed and MaRVed strategic missiles, cruise missiles (CMs), and precision-guided munitions (PGMs)—is the much greater accuracy of their delivery systems, primarily as a result of advanced microelectronic information and retargetting systems. There has also been rapid Western technological progress in electronic intelligence (ELINT) and electronic countermeasures (ECM).

The Soviets are trying to overcome this increasing United States lead by quantitatively increasing their weapons production. This in turn causes the United States to try for more qualitative

---

19. "Observer," "Anti-Soviet Fabrications," *Pravda*, Feb. 10, 1977; departure of Soviet border negotiator Ilyichev from Peking; "New Tsars Push a National Annexation Policy" and "Exploitation and Oppression of Non-Russian People in Central Asia," *Peking Review*, March 4, 1977.

20. The three best recent analyses, in my view, with extensive bibliographies, are Johan J. Holst and Uwe Nerlich, eds., *Beyond Nuclear Deterrence*, op. cit., and Richard Burt, *New Weapons Technologies*, Adelphi Papers, No. 126 (London: IISS, Summer 1976), and especially his "Technology and East–West Arms Control," *International Affairs*, Jan. 1977. See also Kosta Tsipis, "Cruise Missiles," *Scientific American*, Feb. 1977 and James F. Digby, *Precision Guided Weapons*, Adelphi Papers, No. 118 (London: IISS, Summer 1975). I am also grateful to Messrs. Tsipis and Digby and to Profs. John Deutsch and W.W. Kaufmann for discussions on these matters.

superiority. Thus the asymmetrical qualitative revolution in the arms race destabilizes détente.

It is beyond the scope of this paper to go into this subject in any detail. I shall therefore only try to point out its importance for the military situation in Europe and therefore for détente.

Western public discussion has centred on the massive Soviet arms build-up on the central front in Europe, particularly in tanks and IRBMs (e.g. the SS-20), within the context of a general modernization of the Soviet ground and air forces and the growth of Soviet naval power in the Norwegian seas and the Mediterranean. I intend neither to dismiss nor to downgrade their importance. It has been rapid and massive. It has changed the military balance in Europe to Moscow's advantage. It is not in accord with the West's image of détente. Were it to continue without adequate Western military response, it would result in political destabilization in Western Europe—which is the main Soviet objective in this military build-up.

Less Western attention has been paid to the new US technological developments in weapons systems. They mark a major US leap forward in weapons technology, perhaps comparable to the introduction of the machine gun and of missile warfare. In strategic (thermonuclear) weapons these have been primarily in MIRV and the much more advanced MaRV, now under development: separable reentry vehicles, with MaRV retargettable in flight for greater terminal accuracy. In conventional non-strategic nuclear warfare they centre in the sea- or air-launched cruise missile (CM), whose trajectory is adjustable in flight, e.g. by a terrain-matching guidance system (TERCOM), and which has a CEP accuracy of c. 100 m. The other aspects of this technological revolution are much longer ranges (up to 2,000 miles) for much smaller vehicles by means of more efficient small jet engines; miniaturization of conventional and nuclear warheads; for cruise missiles, low-altitude flight and low radar reflectability, which degrade hostile air defenses; small remotely piloted vehicles (RPVs) for television target acquisition and designation; and the whole technology of sensors and large-scale integration (LSI) of electronic circuits. The development of air- and ground-launched PGMs, with a CEP of 10 m., has greatly increased tank and airplane vulnerability.

US cruise missile deployment will be slowed down by two factors: the obstacle it presents to SALT II, because of Soviet pressure against US deployment of it, and its bureaucratic threat to US manned bombers and large attack carriers, those missions CMs are seen by their proponents as threatening. Historically, bureaucratic resistance to new weapons has caused long delays in their deployment; arms control negotiations may delay them still further.[21]

The implications for détente and the military balance in Europe of the deployment of CMs and PGMs are considerable. Long-range air- or sea-launched CMs blur the distinction between strategic and conventional arms—i.e. between SALT and MBFR. Theatre CMs and PGMs make theatre nuclear weapons more accurate and also less necessary, because of the longer range greater accuracy of non-nuclear CMs and PGMs. The difficulty of their verifiability and the fact that they could operate from launching sites outside regional areas such as Central Europe make such arms control negotiations as MBFR more difficult. So does the US asymmetrical technological advantage.

Cruise missiles also raise problems for Soviet and American relations with Western Europe, and particularly with West Germany. They have such increased range and accuracy for delivery of conventional explosives, through technologies which the West European States can acquire, that they could enable the West Europeans to compensate considerably, cheaply, and rapidly for the Soviet military build-up on the Central European front, particularly if the United States would transfer CM technology to the West Europeans.

The potential advantage of CMs is the greatest for non-nuclear West Germany, which could target large numbers of relatively invulnerable, very accurate CMs on Soviet forces in East Germany, thus partially compensating for its non-nuclear status and increasing its deterrence against Soviet attack. (CM conventional warheads accurately targetted on European Russia would be too small to be an effective deterrent.) CM deployment would thus enable West Germany to convert its technological power into military power cheaply, rapidly, and effectively—something which the Soviet Union has always tried to prevent or at least to limit.

It is not surprising that Moscow has tried so hard in the SALT II negotiations to prevent US deployment. Moscow is now also trying to prevent West European, and particularly West German, CM deployment as well, and US technological aid to it. Moscow has another motive in this: US agreement to this in SALT, where its

21. Richard Burt, "Technological Change and Arms Control: The Cruise Missile Case" and Graham T. Allison and Frederic A. Morris, "Precision Guidance for NATO: Justification and Constraint" in Holst and Nerlich, eds., *Beyond Nuclear Deterrence*, op. cit.

West European allies are not represented, would probably worsen its relations with them. CMs could worsen Western alliance relations by Soviet–US arms control negotiations preventing their deployment. Indeed, London and Bonn reportedly have already intervened in Washington against any such Soviet–US agreement.[22] Finally, because CMs are strategic and tactical, nuclear and conventional, they logically require merging of SALT and MBFR.[23]

Regional Destabilizing Factors

Détente is also destabilized by specific factors in European politics itself: reviving intellectual dissidence in Eastern Europe, interacting with the rise in autonomist and reformist tendencies in West European communism ("Eurocommunism"), which bring forth repressive Soviet and East European regime reactions.[24] These in turn favour anti-détente sentiment in the West and escalate communist ideological and inter-party tensions. While the Soviet Union had hoped that the Helsinki Declaration would stabilize its hold on Eastern Europe, recent developments in East Germany, Czechoslovakia, and Poland show that it has if anything stimulated intellectual dissidence and attempts by more than one hundred thousand East Germans to emigrate legally to West Germany.

In two instances, the two Germanies and Yugoslavia, there are the additional factors of multiethnic and irredentist tensions. While West German *Ostpolitik*, and Moscow's forcing East Germany to reciprocate, did result in the *de facto* recognition of division of Germany, it also opened up East Germany to millions of West German and West Berlin visitors. This plus the enormous East audience there of West German television led to some unrest. The 1971 Croatian crisis showed how vulnerable Yugoslavia[25] is to

---

22. William Beecher from Washington, "Allies Oppose Limits on Cruise Missiles," *The Boston Globe*, March 27, 1977, p. 21; Michael Getler from Bonn, "Moscow, Bonn Differ on Cruise Missile," *The Washington Post*, March 31, 1977.

23. For a stimulating review article on SALT and recent books concerning it, see Colin S. Gray, "Détente, Arms Control and Strategy: Perspectives on SALT," *American Political Science Review*, Dec. 1976. See also the excellent analysis from a European perspective by Johan J. Holst, "SALT and East–West Relations in Europe," in Andrén and Birnbaum, eds., *Beyond Détente*, op. cit.

24. For an excellent, very brief analysis, see Pierre Hassner in Holst and Nerlich, *Beyond Nuclear Deterrence*, op. cit., pp. 44–45.

25. Carl Gustaf Ströhm, *Ohne Tito* (Graz: Styria, 1976.)

ethnic tensions. They are likely to increase after Tito. While it seems unlikely that the Soviets will invade Yugoslavia or that the country will fall apart, Moscow will continue to try to get more influence over it. Insofar as it succeeds, the East–West balance of power in the Balkans and the Mediterranean will be destabilized.

In sum, there are in Europe tendencies toward stabilization and also toward destabilization. Which will prevail, when, and for how long, one cannot predict. Yet because they interact and because détente does reflect certain minimal stabilizing tendencies particularly with respect to limiting the risk of nuclear war and, despite Soviet–US trade problems, a relatively high level of West–East trade, credits, and technology transfer, a minimal level of détente is likely to remain. Even so, destabilization is likely to limit détente and to make it in the future more symmetrical. The West and particularly the United States will probably move closer to the Soviet definition of détente: relaxation of tensions combined with continued ideological-political struggle.

Kissinger and Détente in Europe

Kissinger saw détente as aiding the establishment of a conservative, stable, and largely bilateral world order—a "stable structure of peace"—and increased US influence over its allies. The Soviets have seen it as a slow, controlled instrument to change the "correlation of forces" to their advantage and to increase their control over their allies. The smaller powers hoped that it would change the correlation to *their* advantage, and with their participation. Thus Kissinger's fundamental and insoluble problem was that his adversaries and his allies opposed his policy. East–West détente in Europe could not have been so extensive had it not been intensified by, and been a part of, global East–West détente. For global intensification of détente Henry Kissinger did very much. His greatest achievement was the Sino-American rapprochement, which, as he intended, put more pressure on the Soviets, to intensify détente with the West. (That Kissinger was initially unenthusiastic about *Ostpolitik* and continually so about CSCE did not have much effect.) Kissinger's post-1973 Middle Eastern policy at least postponed another war there and thus also contributed to global and European détente.

Yet until 1973 his policies did not improve US–West European relations; on the contrary. Kissinger's preference for secret bilateral negotiations with the Soviets made many West Europeans think that their interests were being sacrificed to a Soviet–American *double hégémonie*.²⁶ They exaggerated—but there was something in it. Nor was this new: all recent American presidents and secretaries of state have proclaimed that they will give priority to America's relations with its allies over those with its adversaries, but none of them has consistently done so. Indeed, none of them has resisted the temptation to deal bilaterally with Moscow instead. Great powers and their statesmen, after all, usually suffer from great-power chauvinism, and the United States and Henry Kissinger have been no exceptions.

Yet men do learn from their mistakes and they are often saved, despite themselves, from their consequences. By 1973 Kissinger had realized to some extent the negative and unnecessary results of his neglect of Western Europe. Pompidou and even more Giscard d'Estaing were less anti-American than de Gaulle. The 1973 quadrupling of oil prices weakened most West European countries financially and strengthened the US position, which was further aided by the end of the Vietnam War and of Watergate. By the beginning of 1977, when Kissinger left office, American–West European relations had considerably improved. Many problems still remained, however, most of them economic. Neither Soviet–Western relations nor détente in Europe were doing as well. The Middle Eastern truce remained precarious. Kissinger's successes in Southern Africa seemed likely to be temporary and that area to remain an aggravating factor in Soviet–US relations.

The Carter Administration and Détente in Europe

As of this writing (October 1977) Carter has been President for only nine months. It is still too early to predict how his foreign policy will turn out. The pre-election statements made by him and his principal advisors were strongly "trilateralist": they echoed the aim of the Trilateral Commission to give priority in US foreign policy to relations with Western Europe and Japan. That the Carter Administration intends to do this seems to me clear. That it will do so is less so. Democratic Administrations, because of their priority for negotiations with the Soviet Union about arms control and non-proliferation, have usually neglected Western European sensitivities. The Carter Administration's priority for non-proliferation has strained US relations with Federal Republic

26. For a penetrating West German view, see Uwe Nerlich, "Westeuropa und die Entwicklung des amerikanisch-sowjetischen Bilateralismus," *Europa Archiv*, Oct. 25, 1972.

because of the West German–Brazilian nuclear deal. There is a serious potential conflict looming between the US and its principal West European allies on deployment and transfer limits on the cruise missile, which the Soviets favour and many West Europeans (and Americans) oppose.

Yet I see little reason to be very pessimistic about East–West détente or US–West European relations. The reason why, to use Marxist terminology, are both objective and subjective. To begin with the objective ones: the mutual Soviet and US interest in arms control agreements remains. The Soviets have the more reason to try to achieve them because they lag behind in the qualitative revolution in weapons technology. The Carter Administration gives higher priority to arms control agreements than its predecessors did. The Soviets are trying to convince the US Administration and public that Carter's public declarations on human rights will prevent arms control. After he persisted in them and in his arms control efforts, however, Moscow appeared in early autumn 1977 to be more likely to reciprocate on the latter.

As to subjective reasons: the Warnke confirmation vote made clear that, as public opinion polls demonstrate,[27] there has been a major change in US public opinion concerning relations with the Soviet Union, one considerably larger and deeper than in Western Europe. Disillusionment with détente and with Soviet policies now characterizes the attitude of most Americans. The human rights issue intensifies it.

The Carter Administration seems to share this view. However, that this will seriously interfere with the limited definition of détente which I have set forth above is in my view unlikely. Indeed, by early autumn 1977 SALT negotiations seemed rather promising. What it may do, however, is to limit Soviet–US bilateralism. This will certainly be the case if, as seems likely, Washington makes a major effort at economic policy coordination within OECD.

Thus while it is too early to make any reliable predictions about the effect in Western Europe of the Carter Administration's détente policy, it bids fair to be at least as successful, and as favourably regarded by the West Europeans, as Kissinger's—and quite likely more so.

---

27. Lloyd A. Free and William Watts, "Nationalism, not Isolationism," *Foreign Policy*, Fall, 1976.

Chapter 2

DÉTENTE—ENTENTE—COOPÉRATION

by *André Fontaine*

(Summary in English)

General de Gaulle conceived the notion of détente—entente—cooperation to indicate the continuing progress to be achieved in East–West relations. Détente—since the Cuban missile crisis—was to be followed by durable understanding and active cooperation. Such a development would enable France to enhance its role by acting as a balancing force between the two superpowers: the USA and the USSR, and might also serve his goal of a Europe from the Atlantic to the Urals. This line of thinking explains his decision in 1966 to withdraw from NATO, his solitary policies in the late sixties and his efforts to find support for an independently operating Europe. Following the events in May 1968 in France and the Soviet invasion of Czechoslovakia in August 1968, de Gaulle abandoned his European dream, despite his declarations to the contrary.

Whatever differences in political style may be observed, Pompidou and Giscard d'Estaing essentially pursued de Gaulle's détente policies, including the special relationship with the Soviet leaders. Jobert, while being foreign minister again denounced the Soviet–American condominium. The Soviet leaders, for a while, preferred Chaban-Delmas as their favourite for president. Giscard accepted a summit meeting to conclude the CSCE.

The Final Act of Helsinki contains little more than repetitions, whether on the consolidation of the *status quo* or the principle of non-intervention, without in any way restricting interference in the affairs of other States. It was the various movements of contestation in the Socialist countries that focused attention on the significance of the Final Act and in particular on its "third basket". These movements do embarrass the Kremlin leaders, as also in the past, détente produced crises in Eastern Europe.

In the future, these developments, the evolution of the Atlantic Alliance and events outside Europe are likely to have a major influence on East–West relations.

As power at present seems in the Kremlin to be disputed

between the gerontocrats and the army, major policy changes or adventures would be surprising. The Soviet bureaucracy does not know quite how to deal with Carter's emphasis on human rights. It also faces increasing debts in trading with the West. It seems to be approaching a crucial choice between more arms-control and more economic development versus a return to cold-war economic policies. Carter's support for the dissidents and the assumed crisis in the Western world may strengthen the hands of the hard-liners in the Kremlin. Evidence, however, suggests that the line of coexistence still prevails.

*   *   *

C'est le général de Gaulle qui est l'auteur du triptyque: "détente-entente-coopération". Dans son esprit, il s'agissait d'une progression continue. Du fait constaté de la "détente" — après la crise des fusées de Cuba et la signature des premiers accords est-ouest: téléphone rouge, traité de Moscou de 1963 sur l'arrêt partiel des essais nucléaires — il s'agissait de parvenir à une "entente" plus durable, celle-ci débouchant elle-même sur une active "coopération". A aucun moment le gouvernement français ne s'est depuis lors écarté de cette ligne, même dans les moments de tension comme celui qui a suivi l'invasion de la Tchécoslovaquie. Les divers échanges de visites qui ont marqué, depuis le voyage de de Gaulle, en 1966, les relations franco-soviétiques, ont été pour ainsi dire à chaque fois l'occasion, pour l'Elysée, de réaffirmer son attachement au fameux triptyque. M. Giscard d'Estaing, notamment, n'y a jamais manqué. C'est pour lui un moyen de rassurer des interlocuteurs naturellement enclins à le soupçonner "d'européisme", ou "d'atlantisme", et qui, pour cette raison, seraient facilement tentés de voir dans le moindre changement de vocabulaire l'indice d'un changement de politique à leur égard. Il ne faut pas se dissimuler cependant que la formule, pour être répétée, s'applique aujourd'hui à un contexte très différent de celui dans lequel elle a été conçue.

De Gaulle n'était pas un juriste, et la précision du vocabulaire n'était pas son fort. Les mots, pour lui, étaient avant tout le moyen de frapper les imaginations et, ce faisant, de façonner une politique. Il lui en a suffi d'un, parfois, pour changer le cours du destin. En réduisant à un "quarteron", en 1962, les généraux insurgés d'Alger, il les a ridiculisés, tout en les vouant à l'exécration des Français et, pour commencer, de leurs propres troupes. Ce faisant, il a consommé leur perte. En prenant à partie M. Jean Monnet, en ne le désignant que comme "l'*inspirateur*" et en accusant les partisans de l'intégration européenne de ne parler que le "volapük", il a provoqué le retrait du gouvernement Debré des ministres MRP, la mise en minorité à l'Assemblée nationale de ce gouvernement, la dissolution de l'Assemblée et de nouvelles élections dont il devait sortir vainqueur.

L'Europe de l'Atlantique à l'Oural

Quand il parlait de "*détente, d'entente et de coopération*", le général avait également en tête un autre dessein, le plus vaste à la vérité de tous ceux qu'il ait conçus. Il espérait contribuer ainsi à la naissance de cette "*Europe de l'Atlantique à l'Oural*" dont il avait tant parlé et qui devait être essentiellement, dans son esprit, une Europe "européenne", c'est-à-dire sans Américains. L'expression était mystérieuse et il est mort avant d'avoir écrit le passage des *Mémoires d'Avenir* qui seul aurait permis d'expliciter tout à fait sa pensée sur ce point. L'URSS, en effet, ne s'arrête pas à l'Oural. Sous-entendait-il qu'au-delà elle n'avait que des possessions en quelque sorte coloniales, et que ce ne serait que justice, au siècle de la décolonisation, qu'elle les abandonne à son tour? Peut-être bien, car il serait tout de même assez surprenant que, pour exprimer son ambition politique, de Gaulle se soit contenté de la définition purement géographique de l'Europe que tous les enfants de France ont apprise sur les bancs de l'école. Mais on ne saurait cependant exclure qu'il y ait eu chez lui, au départ, une certaine méconnaissance des réalités géographiques soviétiques: à preuve les circonstances dans lesquelles il substitua, dans ses propos, l' "Union soviétique" à la "Russie", et abandonna la formule de l'Europe de l'Atlantique à l'Oural.

C'était en mai 1966, à l'issue d'un voyage en URSS que les dirigeants du Kremlin avaient tout fait pour rendre triomphal. L'accueil qui lui a été réservé, devait nous dire un politologue soviétique, effaça, sur les lieux mêmes de l'événement, le pire affront qu'il ait jamais reçu: le refus de Staline, en décembre 1944, de la prendre au sérieux.

Le général fut conduit jusqu'à Novosibirsk, métropole de plus d'un million d'habitants, au coeur de la Sibérie. Novosibirsk est située sur le méridien de Calcutta: c'est donc indiscutablement une ville d'Asie. Mais elle n'est peuplée que de Russes, et son paysage rappelle plutôt les immensités de l'Europe du Nord ou du Canada que l'exotisme de l'Orient. Quant à l'Oural, ses sommets paraissent si modestes, vus d'avion, qu'on a peine à admettre qu'il puisse séparer deux continents, ou même partager en deux une nation.

Est-ce la leçon qu'il tira de cette expédition lointaine? Au moment des adieux, dans la somptueuse salle Saint Georges du Kremlin, le président de la République leva son verre non à la Russie, mais à l'Union soviétique, pour la première fois appelée par son nom, et à "l'*Europe* ... — il marqua une seconde d'hésitation — *d'un bout à l'autre*". On ne devait plus jamais entendre parler de l'Europe de l'Atlantique à l'Oural. Mais le général ne devait pas pour autant préciser où se trouvaient ces "deux bouts" du continent, même si son admirateur et ami Coudenhove-Kalergi, président du Mouvement paneuropéen, se hasardait pour sa part à envisager une Europe ... "de San Francisco à Vladivostok".

Au cours de ce voyage de Gaulle s'était enhardi jusqu'à parler — une seule fois, au cours d'un discours à l'université Lomonossov — "d'*alliance*" entre la France et l'URSS. Le mot, curieusement, fut à peine relevé. Mais le fait est que les rapports des deux pays étaient alors à leur zénith. Le temps était loin où le général poussait à la résistance, dans l'affaire de Berlin, un Eisenhower hésitant et un Macmillan défaitiste, avant d'assurer Kennedy, dans la crise de Cuba, de son total appui. L'affaire de la "*force multilatérale*", où il voyait une tentative pour établir durablement sur l'Europe l'hégémonie américaine, la vivacité de la réaction de Washington à la conclusion du traité franco-allemand de 1963, l'engagement croissant des Etats-Unis dans le conflit vietnamien, dont il craignait les répercussions pour la paix mondiale, l'avaient convaincu que le moment était venu de prendre ses distances avec la puissance dirigeante du monde libre.

Le retrait de la France de l'OTAN

Il l'avait toujours désiré. "*Toute ma vie*, devait-il écrire au comte de Paris en 1969, après son départ du pouvoir, *je me suis efforcé de faire la politique des Capétiens*". La politique des Capétiens, qui fut aussi celle de la révolution de 1789, de Napoléon et de la IIIe République, c'est la priorité absolue donnée à l'indépendance nationale, le refus de toute supranationalité qu'elle fût à coloration britannique, germanique ou américaine, à forme impériale ou fédérale, voire simplement communautaire.

A peine revenu aux affaires, à l'été 1958, il déclare à l'un de ses plus proches collaborateurs: "*il va falloir que nous quittions l'OTAN*" et son plan de "directoire occidental" soumis à Eisenhower et Macmillan en septembre de cette même année, en allant au-devant d'un inévitable refus, n'a sans doute d'autre objet que de fournir la raison d'un retrait ultérieur. Aussi bien lorsque Kennedy passe par Paris, en mai 1961, est-il officiellement averti par le général que la France se retirera de l'organisation militaire intégrée du pacte atlantique lorsque la tension internationale sera retombée.

Retrait ne veut pas dire rupture. Dans l'esprit de de Gaulle c'est seulement en jouant l'une contre l'autre "les deux hégémonies" que la France peut préserver son indépendance. Il ne s'en est jamais expliqué si clairement que devant M. Brejnev, à Moscou, en mai 1966: *"Je voulais vous dire, monsieur le secrétaire général,* commença-t-il, *à quel point la France est heureuse de trouver l'Union soviétique pour l'aider à équilibrer le poids souvent trop considérable des Etats-Unis ..."* Et, comme le visage de son interlocuteur s'illuminait: *"de même que nous sommes bien heureux de trouver les Etats-Unis pour nous aider à équilibrer le poids souvent excessif de l'URSS ..."*

Mais pour de Gaulle, *"être grand c'est épouser une grande querelle"*. Il a horreur du neutralisme, dans la mesure où celui-ci signifie repli sur soi, refus de se mêler des grandes affaires de ce temps. C'est tout le contraire: la France, *"princesse des contes"* au destin exemplaire, se doit de montrer aux autres le chemin d'un monde meilleur. Et pour cela il lui faut d'abord se faire prendre au sérieux. Elle se dote d'une arme nucléaire, même si celle-ci, au début, fait sourire. Elle ferme la porte du Marché commun à une Grande-Bretagne trop visiblement encouragée à poser sa candidature par les Etats-Unis. Mais ce n'est pas assez pour impressionner les Soviétiques, pour qui de Gaulle n'est alors qu'un satellite américain parmi d'autres. Pour qu'ils changent d'avis, il faudra le combat obstiné du général contre le force multilatérale et plus encore la reconnaissance de la Chine populaire.

De Gaulle fait cavalier seul

De toute, façon, à partir du début de 1966, le doute n'est plus permis. De Gaulle fait cavalier seul. La tension internationale étant retombée, il retire la France du commandement intégré atlantique et invite les Etats-Unis et le Canada, qui obtempèrent, à rappeler leurs unités stationnées en France. Il va à Moscou, invite, de Phnom-Penh, les Américains à quitter l'Indochine, avant de s'écrier à Montréal: *"Vive le Québec libre!"* Il habitue chacun à attendre ses discours, ses conférences de presse, comme des coups de théâtre. La France a les mains libres et entend s'en servir. Il le montrera une nouvelle fois, en 1967, au moment de la guerre de six jours, en condamnant l'initiative d'Israël et en plaçant l'embargo sur les expéditions d'armes à destination de ce pays.

Son dessein, pour l'Europe, de Gaulle ne l'exprime qu'à demi-voix, mais il est bien clair. Il voudrait rallier les autres nations d'Europe occidentale à la notion d'Europe indépendante -d'où le plan Fouchet de coopération européenne abandonné en 1962, mais qu'en diverses occasions il cherche à relancer sous une autre forme. Mais il escompte aussi qu'en contrepartie les pays d'Europe orientale se détacheront petit à petit de l'URSS. Celle-ci doit comprendre, en effet, qu'une fois la détente muée en entente, sa domination sur ses voisines n'a plus d'objet, ou du moins devrait prendre des formes plus humaines. Nous n'avons aucun élément d'information particulier sur le sujet, mais il nous semble qu'entre ce que pouvaient être alors les vues du général et ce qu'on a appelé, dix ans plus tard, la doctrine Sonnenfeld, impliquant tout à la fois la reconnaissance d'une certaine mainmise permanente de l'URSS sur sa sphère d'influence et un assouplissement de cette mainmise, il n'y a, à tout bien prendre, que des nuances.

C'est à cela qu'était censée conduire la politique de "détente, d'entente et de coopération." Et sans doute, si les résultats avaient été à la mesure de ses espoirs, le général aurait-il été disposé à payer un prix supplémentaire: tel que le retrait pur et simple de la France du pacte atlantique ou la conclusion avec l'URSS d'un nouveau traité destiné à remplacer celui que Moscou avait dénoncé, en 1955, pour protester contre le réarmement de la République fédérale. Mais le destin devait en disposer autrement.

Dès l'été 1967, à Varsovie, où il se rend en visite officielle, de Gaulle mesure comme il sera difficile d'amener les dirigeants de l'Est à partager ses vues. Gomulka, invité à prendre ses distances vis-à-vis du Kremlin, répond par un sec *"non possumus"*. L'espoir survit cependant, parce qu'il y a la Roumanie, *"la France de l'Est"*, qui rue de plus en plus dans les brancards du pacte de Varsovie. De Gaulle attache tellement d'importance à cette évolution, il est tellement déterminé à l'encourager, que les événements de mai 1968 en France ne l'empêchent pas de répondre à l'invitation de Bucarest, que lui a adressée le président Ceausescu. Comme à Varsovie, l'accueil est triomphal, et, selon tous les témoignages, largement spontané: preuve que la politique d'ouverture à l'Est du chef de l'Etat français rencontre l'approbation de populations qui croient, comme lui, qu'elle aidera à leur émancipation.

L'invasion de la Tchécoslovaquie

Nulle part sans doute à ce moment-là, de Gaulle ne serait mieux reçu, s'il y allait, qu'à Prague, alors tout enivrée de son éphémère "printemps", impensable sans la "détente". La volonté des Tchécoslovaques de vivre plus libres, tout en restant fidèles à l'alliance avec Moscou, correspond tout à fait aux espoirs de l'Elysée. Très vite cependant celui-ci s'alarme. Dès le mois de juillet l'intervention des troupes du pacte de Varsovie est tenue, à Paris, pour une probabilité. Lorsqu'elle se produit, le 21 août, M. Michel Debré est depuis quelques semaines ministre des affaires étrangères. Il a toujours démenti avoir réduit la portée de l'invasion à celle d'un *"accident de parcours"*. Le mot, s'il est apocryphe, résume cependant assez bien la philosophie de de Gaulle et de son disciple préféré, pour qui il n'est pas de politique de rechange à celle qui vise à conduire, grâce à la détente, au relâchement de l'emprise des grandes puissances sur les nations de leur zone d'influence. Henry Kissinger répétera lui-même, quelques années plus tard, qu'il n'est *"pas d'alternative à la détente"*. Le drame de Prague signifie que la partie est remise, non qu'elle est perdue.

Mais il n'y a pas eu que Prague, il y a eu le mouvement quasi insurrectionnel de mai, qui a imprimé une rude secousse à l'économie française, mettant à mal le matelas d'or et de devises sur lequel de Gaulle s'appuyait pour faire la guerre au dollar. Les capitaux fuient à qui mieux mieux, et la dévaluation du franc, à la rentrée, n'est évitée que de justesse. L'attitude de la République fédérale, qui se refuse à tout geste de solidarité, conduit Debré à préconiser un rapprochement avec la Grande-Bretagne. En même temps, les craintes qui subsistent, après l'invasion de la Tchécoslovaquie, quant aux intentions de l'URSS, poussent à la détente avec les Etats-Unis. Ceux-ci viennent de mettre fin aux bombardements du Vietnam et d'engager des négociations avec Hanoï ; en suivant ainsi les conseils du général, ils facilitent son désir de reprendre le dialogue. A peine élu, Richard Nixon sera reçu avec chaleur par le président de la République qui lui sait gré, au demeurant, de se refuser de prendre parti dans la querelle avec Londres, ouverte par l'affaire Soames.

Le dégel avec les alliés traditionnels n'implique pas de refroidissement avec Moscou. Au début de 1969, Kirilline, vice-président du conseil soviétique, vient à Paris pour la réunion de la *"grande commission"* chargée de veiller au développement des échanges entre les deux pays. De Gaulle le reçoit à déjeuner et se garde bien, dans son toast, de toute allusion un peu nette à la Tchécoslovaquie. Néanmoins l'esprit n'est plus le même, quand ce ne serait que parce que le général a été très affecté par mai 1968, et qu'il se sent condamné à plus ou moins brève échéance. Si jamais il a pu espérer voir de son vivant la réalisation de son rêve d'une Europe desserrant la double tutelle qu'elle subit depuis 1945, à ce moment-là il y a renoncé. Les dirigeants soviétiques ont trop clairement exposé la doctrine Brejnev, qui leur ouvre le droit d'intervenir dans tout pays du pacte de Varsovie afin d'y consolider, voire d'y rétablir l'ordre "socialiste", pour que l'on puisse nourrir le moindre doute à ce sujet.

Pompidou et le "condominium"

De toute façon, en avril 1969, de Gaulle, après son désaveu par le referendum, quitte le pouvoir sans le moindre testament politique. Georges Pompidou, qui lui succède, est plus conservateur et donc plus "européen" et plus anticommuniste que lui. Mais il n'est pas moins attaché à l'idée de l'indépendance française, S'il fait entrer la Grande-Bretagne dans la CEE, c'est pour équilibrer une Allemagne dont il redoute la puissance. C'est ce même désir d'équilibrage qui lui fait insister en de nombreuses occasions sur la nécessité de maintenir avec l'URSS des liens étroits de coopération. A Moscou, où l'on a craint que l'éclipse du général ne signifie un retour au bercail atlantique, on poursuit d'autant plus volontiers dans cette voie que l'on a la Tchécoslovaquie à se faire pardonner et que l'on a de plus en plus besoin, pour maintenir l'économie à flot, du concours des biens et des capitaux de l'Occident. Et puis il est bon, pour les bilans politiques, notamment à l'occasion des sessions du plenum du comité central du soviet suprême ou des congrès du parti, de pouvoir faire état des relations en quelque sorte privilégiées qu'on entretient avec un grand pays capitaliste: manière de dire aux autres, et pour commencer aux Etats-Unis qu'il ne tient qu'à eux d'en entretenir d'aussi bonnes.

La difficulté consiste cependant à trouver les moyens d'aller de l'avant dans le domaine politique. Moscou pousse à la conclusion d'un pacte d'amitié. Pompidou refuse d'en entendre parler. De même ne manifeste-t-il qu'en enthousiasme limité devant l'idée relancée par le Kremlin d'une conférence sur la sécurité européenne. S'il finit par en accepter le principe, il manifeste clairement qu'il s'oppose à toute tentative de la réunir, comme le veulent les Soviétiques, au "sommet".

De toute façon, on s'agace sans trop le dire, à Paris, de voir d'autres reprendre à leur compte la politique de détente. Que Willy Brandt aille à Moscou conclure un pacte avec Brejnev, et voilà l'ombre de Rapallo qui resurgit. Que le même Brejnev traverse l'Atlantique pour signer avec Richard Nixon un traité sur la prévention de la guerre nucléaire, et Michel Jobert, devenu ministre des affaires étrangères, dénonce le *"condominium"* soviéto-américain. Plus que jamais le salut est dans l'Europe "européenne", sous forme de confédération ou d'union politique et monétaire. Mais c'est seulement à Pékin, où Pompidou se rend malgré la gravité de son état de santé, que ce projet rencontre un appui complet. Brejnev réserve à Jobert, en Crimée, un accueil plutôt froid, et Kissinger ne laisse rien ignorer de son hostilité à tout ce qui soustrairait le vieux continent au *leadership* américain.

Eclate sur ces entrefaites la guerre du Kippour, qui fait apparaître l'Europe pour ce que Jobert appelle une "non-personne", totalement ignorée par les Grands qui négocient par-dessus sa tête, et tristement dépendante pour ses approvisionnements en énergie d'un monde arabe qui la traite pratiquement en otage. L'occasion ne serait-elle pas bonne pour l'Europe ainsi humiliée, d'imposer enfin à Washington et à Moscou la reconnaissance de son existence en tant qu'entité distincte? Pompidou le pense, mais un discours des plus secs de Kissinger, à Londres, au banquet des Pilgrims, marque un brutal coup d'arrêt.

Le président de la République n'a plus que quelques mois à vivre. Son dernier voyage sera pour Pitsounda, en Géorgie soviétique, où il rencontrera Brejnev. Il arrive épuisé, ayant souffert d'une hémorragie dans l'avion. Au secrétaire général du PCUS, il confie qu'il devra bientôt quitter le pouvoir, mais il assure que son départ ne changera rien et que le peuple français demeurera toujours fidèle à l'amitié soviétique.

Le Kremlin et la campagne présidentielle en France

Ces paroles ne sont pas oubliées à Moscou où l'on fait l'équation: de Gaulle, Pompidou, UDR = bons rapports avec l'URSS. Lorsque s'ouvre la campagne pour l'Elysée, les Soviétiques ne font pas mystère des voeux qu'ils forment pour le candidat de l'UDR: Jacques Chaban-Delmas. De Valéry Giscard d'Estaing, membre du Comité d'action pour les Etats-Unis d'Europe de Jean Monnet, ils redoutent que s'il devient président, il ne ramène la France dans l'organisation intégrée du pacte atlantique. Et ils ne font aucune confiance à François Mitterrand, lui-même "européen" affirmé, et de surcroît ami d'Israël, malgré le soutien, à leurs yeux bien imprudent, que lui donnent les communistes français.

Lorsque Chaban est éliminé au premier tour, ils se gardent d'exprimer une préférence en faveur de l'un ou de l'autre des deux candidats restants. Mais le PCF proteste lorsque l'ambassadeur soviétique à Paris, M. Tchervonenko, rend une visite, entre les deux tours, à Giscard. Il est vrai que l'entrevue se situe à un moment où la campagne n'est pas officiellement rouverte, et qu'elle a pour objet de préparer la prochaine réunion de la grande commission franco-soviétique, dont Giscard d'Estaing, qui a conservé la direction du ministère des Finances, est le co-président. Il n'empêche qu'il y a des photographes lorsqu'arrive le diplomate et que sa venue fait sensation. Il est difficile de ne pas avoir le sentiment qu'entre Mitterrand, qu'ils ne connaissent pas et dont ils se méfient comme de la peste, et Giscard, grâce auquel les échanges franco-soviétiques ont quadruplé en quelques années, ils préfèrent encore celui-ci.

Aussi bien Giscard, devenu président, multiplie-t-il les gestes pour persuader les Soviétiques de sa bonne volonté à leur endroit. Il reçoit Brejnev avant d'aller rencontrer à la Martinique le président Ford. Et, lorsqu'il va lui-même à Moscou en visite officielle, il n'hésite pas, lui, l'"anticollectiviste" déclaré, à aller poser une gerbe au mausolée de Lénine sur la place Rouge. Rien ne prouve, bien au contraire, que le Kremlin ait beaucoup apprécié cet hommage, plutôt incongru de la part d'un homme aussi éloigné des idéaux professés par Wladimir Illyitch. En revanche, Giscard leur avait fait un beau cadeau en se ralliant à l'idée combattue, on l'a vu, par Pompidou, de réunir au "sommet" la conférence sur la sécurité européenne, devenue entretemps la conférence sur la sécurité et les échanges en Europe. Pourquoi ce ralliement? Le président de la République ne s'en est jamais très clairement expliqué. Mais il ne fait pas de doute que dans son esprit il s'agissait ainsi de renforcer le courant qui, en URSS, était favorable à la coexistence. *"Je préfère, devait-il dire un jour en privé, que le XXVe Congrès du PCUS soit celui de l'apothéose de la détente plutôt que celui du retour à la guerre froide"*.

Une fois de plus, en effet, des nuages planaient sur les rapports Est–Ouest. Les Etats-Unis s'inquiétaient du réarmement massif de l'URSS. Les accords de Paris sur le Vietnam n'étaient plus qu'un souvenir. La négociation SALT piétinait. La tension persistait au Proche–Orient. Et tout indique que lorsque Brejnev était venu en France, il avait dit à Giscard qu'avant de quitter la scène, il souhaitait voir la détente consacrée par les trois grandes réunions auxquelles il se préparait: conférence de sécurité, rencontre européenne des partis communistes, et enfin congrès du parti soviétique.

Le sommet d'Helsinki

Il ne faut pas se dissimuler, de toute façon, que le sommet paneuropéen que s'est réuni à Helsinki le 31 juillet et le 1er août 1975, était loin d'avoir la portée que lui ont donnée tant ses thuriféraires que ses contempteurs. Lorsque les Soviétiques en avaient parlé la première fois — au cours de la conférence des quatre ministres des affaires étrangères, à Berlin, au début de 1954 — son but essentiel était le consécration du *statu quo* territorial issu de la deuxième guerre mondiale. Et tel était toujours le propos de la relance, bien des années plus tard, de ce projet. Mais lorsque les trente-cinq se sont enfin réunis à Helsinki, le *statu quo* avait été consolidé de toutes les manières possibles: par la signature de traités entre RFA et ses voisins de l'Est, y compris la RDA, par la reconnaissance par Bonn de la ligne Oder Neisse, par la conclusion d'un accord à quatre sur le statut de Berlin, et enfin par l'entrée des deux Allemagnes aux Nations Unies. Le poids de l'"acte final" d'Helsinki, qui ne porte aucune signature, et qui relève de la déclaration d'intentions plus que de l'engagement formel, ne peut être mis en balance avec celui de tous ces accords diplomatiques en bonne et due forme, tous plus "*contraignants*" les uns que les autres. Aussi bien a-t-on quelque peine à comprendre ceux qui ont dénoncé les "abandons" que l'Occident aurait, selon eux, commis à Helsinki. Si abandons il y a eu, à supposer qu'ils aient pu être évités, il faut remonter bien avant Helsinki.

A parcourir l'énorme "acte final", dont la lecture est si fastidieuse que nul ne se l'est imposée, sans doute, qui n'y ait été professionnellement obligé, on se rend compte que les bonnes paroles, pour ne pas dire les mots creux, en constituent l'essentiel. Or, là aussi, il s'agit de la répétition, non contraignante, d'engagements solennels pris auparavant, notamment aux termes de la charte des Nations Unies et de la Déclaration universelle des Droits de l'Homme. Il en va ainsi notamment de tout ce qui concerne la non-ingérence, "*sous quelque prétexte que ce soit*", dans les affaires des autres. On a mesuré la valeur de cette clause à la manière dont l'Est et l'Ouest ont alimenté les caisses des partis politiques rivaux du Portugal, à la signature entre la RDA et l'URSS, quelques semaines plus tard d'un traité d'"amitié" qui reconnaît pratiquement à celle-ci le droit d'intervenir chez celle-là, sans même l'accord de son gouvernement, aux mises en garde réitérées de l'administration Ford contre la participation des communistes à des gouvernements ouest-européens, et plus récemment, à la lettre du président Carter à Andrei Sakharov et au soutien qu'il donne à la cause des droits de l'homme en Union soviétique.

La contestation à l'Est

Au lendemain de la conférence d'Helsinki, on aurait été tenté de dire qu'elle n'avait été qu'une péripétie modeste, ne méritant certes pas que tant de chefs d'Etat se dérangent, alors que ses seuls résultats pratiques se résument, pour l'essentiel, à quelques échanges d'informations sur les manoeuvres militaires des deux camps et à une modeste amélioration du sort des correspondants étrangers dans les pays de l'Est comme des familles séparées. Mais le développement pris par la contestation dans plusieurs pays du pacte de Varsovie amène à formuler aujourd'hui un jugement plus nuancé.

Tout se passe en effet comme si les dispositions de l'"acte final", relatives aux diverses libertés fondamentales, sur la portée desquelles on ne se faisait guère d'illusions à l'Ouest, avaient été prises au sérieux par des milliers et des milliers de dissidents, à l'intérieur du monde communiste, et qu'ils étaient décidés à faire le meilleur usage possible de l'arme qui leur a été ainsi, bien involontairement, fournie. Ce n'est pas le moindre paradoxe de l'affaire que de constater que c'est la "troisième corbeille" d'Helsinki, celle qui portait sur les échanges de personnes et d'idées, qui avait paru apporter les résultats les plus modestes, les plus décevants, et que c'est elle qui se révèle finalement la plus chargée d'espoir, pour ne pas dire de dynamite. Le fait est, en tout cas, qu'en Tchécoslovaquie, avec la "charte 77", en Pologne, en RDA, en URSS avec les comités Sakharov et Orlov, on ne compte plus les manifestations d'intellectuels et de scientifiques qui dénoncent la contradiction entre la pratique soviétique en matière de droits de l'homme et les accords d'Helsinki.

Face au développement de la contestation, on sent le pouvoir soviétique embarrassé. Répéter sur tous les tons que la détente ne doit à aucun prix s'étendre au domaine idéologique ne sert exactement à rien. La preuve est faite maintenant que contrairement à ce que croient certains esprits chagrins d'Occident, la détente conduit toujours à un relâchement idéologique. Il est vrai que, malheureusement, jusqu'à présent ce relâchement a souvent conduit lui-même à une intervention armée soviétique. La détente consécutive à la mort de Staline a amené le soulèvement est-allemand de juin 1953 qui a été réprimé par l'Armée rouge;

l'octobre polonais de 1956, qui a été à un cheveu d'entraîner une invasion russe; l'insurrection hongroise de la même année dont personne n'a oublié comment elle a été écrasée. De même la détente qui a suivi la crise de Cuba a-t-elle entraîné le printemps de Prague, lui aussi liquidé par les chars du pacte de Varsovie. La vérité est que les dirigeants du Kremlin ne peuvent pas à la fois chanter quotidiennement des hymnes à la coexistence et prêcher le durcissement idéologique. Maintenant que l'Amérique s'en mêle, contrairement à ce qui avait été le pratique constante de l'administration Ford, dont Paris et Bonn, apparemment, continuent de suivre l'exemple, la direction collégiale hésite visiblement devant la route à suivre.

Beaucoup de facteurs, dans l'avenir, vont continuer de peser sur les relations Est–Ouest. Une reprise des hostilités au Proche-Orient, par exemple, porterait sans doute un rude coup à la détente, et pourrait faire reprendre à l'URSS, dans cette région, une partie du terrain perdu au cours des dernières années. Le conflit pour l'Afrique australe, du fait de ses répercussions stratégiques, place les Etats-Unis devant un dilemme des plus embarrassants. La possible participation au pouvoir de communistes en France ou en Italie, l'effacement progressif de la Grande-Bretagne, risquent de réduire l'alliance atlantique, pour l'essentiel, à un *partnership* germano-américain, ce qui bouleverserait les données du jeu politique européen. L'éventualité d'une extension des membres du club nucléaire risque, de son côté, de bouleverser les données du jeu stratégique mondial.

Beaucoup de choses dépendront d'autre part de ce que fera ou ne fera pas la Chine, comme de ce que l'URSS entend faire ou ne pas faire avec elle. Mais si tous ces nuages sont solidement campés à l'horizon, il n'est au pouvoir de personne de dire si le vent les emportera ou si, au contraire, ils amèneront de nouveaux orages. En revanche, il paraît évident que, pour les mois et les années qui viennent, l'avenir de la détente et de la coopération Est–Ouest, sera étroitement lié à l'analyse du rapport que l'on fera, à Moscou, entre trois éléments: l'évolution des armements, celle des échanges, et la question des droits de l'homme.

Entre la gérontocratie et l'armée

Un des principaux dirigeants de l'Europe de l'Est, recevant un important homme politique occidental lui disait il y a quelque temps que le pouvoir à Moscou est, en fait, disputé "*entre la gérontocratie et l'armée*". Ce n'est pas pour rien que Léonide Brejnev s'est fait nommer maréchal et que son soixante-dixième anniversaire, en 1976, a été l'occasion de célébrer son éternelle jeunesse. La moyenne d'âge du praesidium se situe maintenant autour de 69 ans, et son benjamin a cinquante-quatre ans. De la part d'une équipe aussi vieille, dans un régime bureaucratique à direction collégiale, une initiative aventureuse serait surprenante.

Il est tout aussi difficile d'attendre d'elle un changement profond dans quelque domaine que ce soit, à commencer par celui de l'idéologie. Même si elle répugne à montrer une brutalité excessive, quand ce ne serait que parce qu'elle ne sait pas très bien ce que pourraient en être à terme les effets, elle est évidemment décidée à ne pas laisser la contestation remettre en question la toute puissance de la bureaucratie. Jusqu'à présent certes, elle a jeté du lest, et de façon parfois fort imprudente: c'est ainsi par exemple qu'en expulsant Pliouchtch, elle a signé un aveu monumental: plus personne ne peut croire que les asiles psychiâtriques, en URSS, n'abritent que des malades mentaux. Sans doute a-t-elle cru qu'en laissant partir quelques dissidents célèbres, elle apaiserait l'opinion occidentale à bon compte; elle n'a fait qu'encourager les contestataires en puissance à reprendre un combat dont ils savaient désormais qu'il n'était pas vain. Dans ces conditions, la tentation doit être forte pour les dirigeants soviétiques de donner un net coup d'arrêt. L'armée, qui avait pesé d'un grand poids dans la décision d'intervention en Tchécoslovaquie, n'est sans doute pas la dernière à le réclamer.

Le problème pour l'URSS c'est l'interférence de la question des droits de l'homme avec l'ensemble de ses relations avec l'Occident, c'est-à-dire essentiellement avec les Etats-Unis. Jusqu'à présent, grâce à Henry Kissinger, il avait été possible de séparer ces problèmes. Les dirigeants soviétiques savaient bien que leurs *opposite numbers* américains avaient tout fait pour empêcher l'adoption de l'amendement Jackson. Aujourd'hui la situation est différente. Au nom d'un moralisme sur la sincérité duquel des gens aussi cyniques que ceux qui gouvernent l'URSS n'ont sans doute pas fini de s'interroger, c'est M. Carter lui-même qui se permet de les rappeler au respect des droits de l'homme. Le président le ferait-il s'il n'était pas convaincu que pour Moscou aussi *"there is no alternative to détente"*? On peut au moins se poser la question. Mais si l'on dispose pour y répondre d'une certitude, à savoir que l'URSS a besoin du concours économique de l'Occident, les conclusions que l'on peut tirer de l'évolution de la balance des forces est malheureusement plus hypothétique.

Pour nourrir sa population, développer ses richesses naturelles et notamment celles de la Sibérie, pour se doter d'une industrie compétitive, pour faire face au désir de consommation grandissant des pays "alliés", où l'idéologie n'a guère pris et qu'on ne peut espérer faire tenir tranquilles que grâce au *"communisme du goulash"* — de la tartine beurrée — sans pour autant se laisser distancer dans la course aux armements, à l'espace et aux faveurs du tiers monde, l'URSS a dû faire appel de plus en plus aux importations, au crédit et à la technologie de l'Occident. Résultat : les achats à l'Ouest des pays membres du Comecon ont été multipliés par sept en dix ans, mais les ventes n'ont pu être multipliées que par cinq. D'où un déficit qui, vis à vis de l'ensemble des pays de l'OCDE, atteignait 11 milliards de dollars en 1975, à mettre en rapport avec un endettement supérieur, à l'heure actuelle, à quarante milliards de dollars.

L'Occident a tout intérêt au développement de ces échanges qui vient à point nommé, en période de récession, ouvrir des marchés à son industrie. Et c'est bien pourquoi il consent aux pays de l'Est des conditions de crédit impensables dans le cadre national. Mais l'insistance des pays de l'Est à conclure des accords de troc, afin d'alléger le déficit de leur balance commerciale, la possibilité de voir certains Etats communistes développer, grâce à l'aide de l'Ouest, une industrie qui risque de concurrencer la leur dans l'avenir avec des prix de dumping, enfin et surtout l'endettement excessif de l'URSS et de ses partenaires, amènent certains à se poser des questions. Aussi bien un consortium de banques dirigé par la *Bank of America* a-t-il repoussé, la requête qui lui était présentée par le Comecon, au nom de la Pologne, en vue du placement d'un emprunt de 200 millions de dollars.

Le choix de la direction soviétique

Arrivée à ce point, la direction soviétique a clairement le choix entre deux directions : ou bien, ce qui serait la sagesse, elle se prête à un accord qui réduit le coût de la course aux armements et libère des crédits budgétaires pour le développement économique de l'URSS et des pays de sa sphère d'influence. Ou bien elle retourne à l'économie de guerre froide, et se prépare à une confrontation aux conséquences imprévisibles. C'est dire l'importance des conversations SALT, qui se déroulent alors que les progrès de la technique des armements amènent les superpuissances au seuil d'une situation dans laquelle la volonté politique de parvenir à un accord risque de buter sur l'impossibilité technique d'en contrôler l'exécution. Les satellites artificiels sont en effet incapables de distinguer un *Cruise* classique d'un *Cruise* nucléaire comme de repérer une installation de lancement du nouveau missile soviétique SS 20. Certes, cette arme n'est pas "stratégique" dans la mesure où elle ne peut atteindre le sol américain. Elle n'en fait pas moins peser sur la sécurité de l'Europe occidentale une menace dont il est difficile de ne pas tenir compte et qui devrait en bonne logique conduire à une extension de la négociation SALT, comme les Soviétiques l'ont d'ailleurs toujours souhaité, aux armes stratégiques et tactiques stationnées de part et d'autre du rideau de fer. Ce qui implique nécessairement la participation de la France et de la Grande-Bretagne.

La question que l'on est en droit de se poser aujourd'hui est de savoir si le soutien ouvert donné par Washington à la dissidence des pays de l'Est ne va pas fournir un argument aux éléments durs de la direction soviétique, à ceux qui s'alarment de l'érosion pratiquée dans le système communiste par la coexistence et qui préfèrent miser à la fois sur la recherche d'une supériorité stratégique et sur l'aggravation inéluctable, à leurs yeux de communistes, de la crise économique et intellectuelle du monde occidental: la capacité de résistance de celui-ci à une offensive politique un peu forte est en effet rien moins que démontrée. Jusqu'à preuve du contraire, Léonide Brejnev, Kossyguine, Gromyko, demeurent attachés à la ligne de la coexistence. Mais il ne faut pas s'étonner que tel ou tel gouvernement d'Europe occidentale préférerait en même temps qu'on chatouille un peu moins brutalement l'amour propre du Kremlin et qu'on y regarde à deux fois avant de lui faire, en matière de contrôle des armements, des concessions sans contrepartie immédiate.

Chapter 3

THE FUTURE OF NON-ALIGNMENT IN EUROPE

by *Prof. Leo Mates*

Using the term *non-alignment* for European countries and in the context of intra-European relations could be misleading, since the term has come into general usage denoting the group of countries working together on the world scene on the basis of a platform which is not applicable to intra-European relations. The Non-aligned Countries represent on the world scene the claims and aspirations of the Third World, the less developed countries, and they have a much more developed common platform, than the term "non-aligned" would normally indicate.

In Europe, the position of countries not belonging to either military alliance and/or economic integration, are in fact not aligned, and have no more specific common interest among themselves than influencing European developments towards de-emphasizing alignment. Even in this respect, one could easily define differences among the European non-aligned countries. In a wider sense of political behaviour, beyond the confines of Europe and in less politically determined fields, the differences among these countries are still greater. Nevertheless, the preparations, then the course of debates of the Helsinki Conference, and the follow-up, caused a somewhat livelier cooperation and consultation among this third group of European countries.

Nevertheless, it would be exaggerating to view this group as in any way comparable to the two coherent and formally established sides which emerged during the Cold War in Europe. There are no special links among them in the sphere of interstate activities, or in the sense of an elaborated political platform, not to say anything about cooperation in the military field. If they are mentioned and did really begin to function as a group during the long debates of the Helsinki Conference, particularly in Geneva, this was on a narrowly defined common interest concerning European cooperation and security viewed from the point of view of countries not belonging to either military alliance.

It should also be remembered that, with the exception of

Yugoslavia, all countries belonging to this group belong to the Western world. In basic concepts, political systems and ideology, they are a part of that world and they have similar economic interests. Yugoslavia is the only one among them which belongs to the movement of non-aligned countries and has a developed view on non-alignment. It is also the only one among these countries which is socialist.

The Helsinki Conference, thus, rather than de-emphasizing, did in fact emphasize group contacts and cooperation in Europe. This, of course does not mean that the Conference did not, or will not in the follow-up process, contribute to de-emphasizing the bipolar constellation in Europe. As a matter of fact this paper, as its main topic, discusses exactly this side of the Conference and of developments after Helsinki.

Developments in the West after Helsinki

Already, before the beginning of the debate in Geneva, the Western countries approached the Helsinki Conference with the aim of acting in full consonance and standing as one unified partner against the Warsaw Pact countries. This position was in the first place adopted on the basis of the determination of the Western countries of Europe to proceed with their efforts of unifying Western Europe. The core of this endeavour was and remains the development towards higher forms of integration in the European Communities, and the plan for direct elections of representatives in a Western European Parliament.

Besides incentives derived from aspirations for more integration and unity, coordination in the West on the eve, during and after Helsinki, was also prompted by a strictly coordinated and uniform position of the Warsaw Pact countries. The only exception on the Eastern European side was the behaviour of Rumania in regard of a great number of items discussed in Geneva. Thus the stage for the Helsinki Conference was set along lines of a typical East–West dialogue.

The not aligned countries had no choice but to accept the bipolar setting and could do no more than adapt their behaviour to this pattern. This induced them in the first place to develop regular contact and consultations with the not aligned countries at the Conference. This was then continued after Helsinki and in the beginning of February 1977 a consultative meeting of representatives of eight not aligned countries of Europe was held in Belgrade. The role of this cooperative effort could only be to try to avoid at least hard clashes between the two sides and to induce as much as possible a multilateral debate instead of a bipolar dialogue.

The revolution in Portugal, with the emergence of the Portuguese Communist Party as an important element of the newly structured political establishment, created considerable apprehension in Western Europe. The reaction to the developments in Portugal were particularly articulate and intransigent in the United States. At one moment it appeared that a crisis in the Western alliance might develop. The excitement, however, subsided in 1975 with the stabilization of the political situation in Portugal after the elections. But, soon thereafter, developments in Spain and the successes of the Italian and French Communist Parties again brought up the issue of communism in the West to first class prominence.

In fact the rise in political influence and the changes in attitudes and policies of the communist parties in Western Europe already began some time before the Helsinki Conference, but the importance and full impact of this evolution became visible only after Helsinki. This applies in particular to the communist parties of Italy and France, but also increasingly to that of Spain.

The most significant changes can be summarized under two headings, internal developments and relations with other parties and international relations.

Concerning the internal development of their own countries the parties in question have emphatically and most authoritatively declared that they had abandoned the Soviet model as an example to be followed. Moreover, they have strongly criticized many aspects of political life in the Soviet Union and in other Eastern European countries. Furthermore, they have declared their readiness to respect the constitutional framework of their own country and in particular they have accepted the principles of pluralism, parliamentary democracy and democratic freedoms as defined in the West.

In the field of international relations, these parties have declared that they accept the continued membership of their countries in NATO and have rejected any foreign influence based on the concept of discipline and obedience to any centre outside their country. Concerning European affairs, these parties have begun to participate together with other parties in the carrying out of the integration in the Communities, although in foreign policies, as well as in internal, they continue to express the traditional demands and positions of the European Left.

Finally, in 1976 and in the beginning of 1977 a general debate on what was called Eurocommunism developed in the West, mainly in Western Europe. The United States was at that time in a period of transition from the Ford–Kissinger Administration to the Carter Administration. In this transition period, of course, controversial voices were heard. The voice of the outgoing administration could not carry much weight, particularly after the verdict of the American electorate in November. The voice of the new administration was not quite unisonant and reflected, still some time after the inauguration, more intentions and aspirations than determined policies and attitudes.

The debate on Eurocommunism in Western Europe also demonstrated changes in emphasis and evaluations of most of the partners in it. Attitudes and arguments were, quite naturally, coloured very much by national origins of the protagonists and by their basic political profiles. There was, however, a general pattern emerging and reducing the debate to a bipolar dialogue. With a great number of shades and differing accents, the two views can be reduced to the belief that all communist parties are at all times a danger to Western cooperation and an opportunity for the Soviet Union to subvert the Western security system. This view was opposed by another, that the strengthening of the left, if it is not following outside guidance, is an internal affair of each country, not necessarily affecting the credibility of the alliance as the balancing factor to the Warsaw Pact.

This debate is relevant to the examination of the future of non-alignment in Europe, since it is raising issues connected with the stability and credibility of an existing nature and pattern of alignment in Europe. This is not the place, however, to enter into a more detailed discussion of the debate on Eurocommunism. For the purpose of this paper, and the prospects of non-alignment, it is enough to point out that the debate turned mostly around the problem of cohesion in Western Europe. In this way the debate had a certain unsettling effect, although it would be too much to say that it affected cohesion. Furthermore, it appears that the original shock and fear of regarding the strengthened communist parties of the south as an agency of Moscow, gave way more and more to a calmer appraisal.

In fact it might be said without much risk and incertitude that the emergence of Eurocommunism demonstrated how unfounded were the hopes, respectively fears, of the one or the other side that communist parties could at some future time upset the bipolar pattern giving supremacy, if not complete ascendancy, to the East in Europe. Furthermore, another effect of this phenomenon is likely to be the strengthening of the already rising trend of emphasizing the peace-preserving role of the Western alliance and the pursuing with more vigour of détente and cooperation with the other side.

This trend in Europe was supplemented by the continuing endeavours of the United States and the Soviet Union, the two global powers, to continue the increasingly delicate and difficult dialogue on the reduction of strategic armaments. The dialogue was greatly handicapped by inherent problems, new developments of arms and by the presidential problems in the United States. It appears, however, that the Carter Administration will reopen the talks and that the Soviet Union is ready and even impatient to do so. This should be borne in mind when considering the prospects of cohesion within a wider framework of the West, including both the United States and Western Europe.

In this wider framework, however, we can discern the shaping up of the European element on the Western side more distinctly than in the past. It does reflect certain differences of opinion, interests and also policies, with the United States, but it reflects still more the aspirations of the European members of the alliance to integrate more closely into a body with more united foreign attitudes and policies. It also expresses the desire of the countries of Western Europe to play a more autonomous role in world affairs, and naturally in European affairs. Thus, in the Helsinki Conference, the Western European countries acted with particularly close coordination and in the post-Helsinki period continued to emphasize this West-European coordination and cooperation. They had also their caucus in February of 1977 on a ministerial level, preparing for the meeting in Belgrade.

Summarizing the developments in the West we can say that the Helsinki Conference and the events unfolding simultaneously did not produce visible or substantial destabilizing effects on the cohesion of the West, but emphasized a close cooperation in Western Europe and enhanced the general inclination of the West to pursue détente and to emphasize the peace preserving and balancing functions of the Western alliance.

Developments in the East after Helsinki

As well as in the case of the West, the Eastern alliance prepared for Helsinki with the accent on close coordination and cooperation. This did not appear to pose special problems, with the exception of Rumania. There is not much known about the functioning of the coordinating mechanism, except press handouts giving only vague and general information. The same would apply to the activities during the long debate in Geneva. Only after the debate moved into the final and decisive stage in 1974 was a new initiative aiming at the coordination of political attitudes on European problems launched. It was a consultative meeting in Warsaw, formally sponsored by the Communist Parties of Italy and Poland. The aim of it was to explore the desirability and the content and procedures of a conference of Communist parties of Europe.

At the meeting it was agreed to hold a conference and it was planned to convene it before the expected date of the final stage of the Helsinki Conference. The original plan for this conference was to work out a detailed and concrete platform uniting the policies of Eastern European States and the communist parties in the West. The time and proposed platform for the conference leaves little doubt that the aim was to give a parallel political platform to the more general, and by a general consensus, accepted platform of the Helsinki Conference.

As official statements and releases to the press show, the meeting ultimately agreed on a much wider, and in fact very broad, approach to European security and cooperation which was originally submitted by the representative of Yugoslavia. This proposal was based not only on a general expression of intention, avoiding any specific policy definition, but also defined the purpose of the conference as an exchange of views without binding decisions. Thus, a debate opened which delayed the holding of the conference until well after Helsinki.

The Berlin Conference of the communist parties of Europe (end of June 1976) therefore cannot be considered as giving a binding and concrete policy guidance to the communist parties attending it. Policy coordination with regard to the formulation of the Final Act of Helsinki and of follow-up activities could not include the Western communist parties, but had to remain within the framework of the Eastern alliance. In fact, concerning some of the problem areas discussed in a lively manner in Geneva, substantial differences developed between Western communist parties and the East-European media of public information.

This debate gradually gained in scope and emphasis of differences. In fact, it would seem that on both sides a further drifting apart developed. The one side was more and more articulate in criticizing certain practices and views prevailing in Eastern Europe and the other side responded by rejecting them and by intensifying the criticized practices. The main debate related to what was known in Geneva as the Basket No. 3, but it was by no means limited to these problem areas only.

The coordinating and cooperating framework of the Eastern-European alliance was intensified, but the influence on policies and attitudes of the most important communist parties of Western Europe practically disappeared. Thus the post-Helsinki debate in Europe was not carried out along the line of confrontation of Communism versus Anticommunism, it was reduced to the interstate framework. In fact relations in Europe after Helsinki are much more of a State to State nature, than based on ideological grounds. Of course the separate grouping of States on both sides in Europe is now obviously as much emphasized as ever, but it is based mainly on relations between interstate alliances.

As distinct from the Western side, in the East the major power remains closely linked with other Eastern European countries. In fact the link would appear rather to be tighter than before Helsinki. Finally, it should be observed that this account of developments was given more as a relationship in time, rather than as a causal one. There can be no doubt that the various events and trends were linked causally, but it is not always easy to establish these causal links with certainty. It is much simpler, and can be stated with more certainty, what happened at what time. Finally, the task of this chapter was wisely defined as an analysis of developments within a sequence of time, not necessarily insisting on causal links.

The Effects of Developments in the East and the West on Non-alignment in Europe

It may be best to immediately underline the fact that the continued existence of two sides in Europe re-emphasizes the need of continued activity of the not aligned countries of Europe along the general lines which they had followed in Helsinki and in Geneva. Neither is it likely that the ranks of the aligned countries will falter or that substantial defections will occur, nor could it be assumed that the not aligned countries will give way and abandon their distinct and separate position in the debate and in actual relations among European countries.

This would also mean that there is little cause to expect any appreciable growth of the spirit, not to say political actions, along the lines of non-alignment in Europe. This, of course, should not mean that the cause of the not aligned countries has no hope in a more distant future. But, leaving this attempt to look into the future aside for a moment, we may return to the more immediate and close at hand consequences of the described developments in the East and in the West.

First of all, the hope for overcoming the existing bipolar and antagonistic pattern in Europe, or reducing it to the minimum requires a further diminishing of tensions and a much more developed cooperation irrespective of the lines of division. One particular and most significant element is the reduction of ideologically burdened antagonism. In other words, not aligned countries could hope to come nearer to their goal and advance their cause best by converting the confrontation of communism and anti-communism into a confrontation between two groups of States, governed by State interests and aspirations.

The development of Eurocommunism, which means in the first place autonomy for the Western communist parties and then also their acceptance of the constitutional framework for their political action, contributed greatly to the blurring of the ideological overtones in the East–West confrontation. This is, perhaps, as in most other cases, better visible in the West than in the East. Furthermore, in the East, persistent efforts were made after the Berlin Conference of communist parties to play down the differences, and in particular the insistence of the Western parties on full freedom of action and their questioning of the Soviet interpretations of *socialist internationalism*.

For the Western alliance, that means for NATO as well as for other Western organizations and institutions, the question arose with all its consequences, whether they stand against any form of radical leftism, even if it is pursued within constitutional limits, or whether they have rallied to combat a threat to their independence and national interests from an opposed alliance. In the past this distinction was never brought out into the open, as the two things, communism and the Warsaw Pact, were thought to be one and the same thing. The military threat and the aims of actions at preserving the national interest were seen as directed against a "Moscow centred international conspiracy". It was uncritically assumed that any communist movement anywhere must always be the "extended hand of Moscow". Even the break of 1948 between Yugoslavia and the Soviet bloc did not essentially change this attitude, with the exception of direct relations with Yugoslavia. The Yugoslav case was taken as an exception which confirms the rule.

Later, after the breakaway by China and Albania, the theory was developed that parties in power could be governed by State interests, whilst parties in opposition or in a pluralistic society are still bound to follow the lead from Moscow and must remain hostile to the pluralistic system of Western democracies, which was thought to be an additional reason for their close ties with the Soviet Union.

Taking all this together, it would appear that the mentioned development did bring about the necessity of distinguishing between the aims of the communist parties in the West and the confrontation between the two military alliances. Consequently, the road towards a Europe not dominated by the bipolar pattern of two military alliances was no longer blocked by a distinct division based solidly on the ideological controversy between pro- and anti-communism as in the past.

Interstate developments in the period after Helsinki, and in particular in the economic field, also give rise to hopes that the hesitatingly undertaken development of economic relations across the dividing lines between East and West, may further develop and become a stabilizing factor. In this respect, however, significant political spill-over can be expected only if economic links were to develop to such a degree that any disturbance or threat of breakdown would cause such great disadvantages, that it could influence political behaviour and thinking. Disappointment about the lack of stabilizing effects of economic activities so far in East–West relations should not be taken as proof to the contrary. These economic interactions are still of marginal significance to both sides, although they have generated more desire to continue along the road of détente.

Generally speaking, the Helsinki Conference and other developments which more or less coincided in time, did contribute towards creating and strengthening a general trend towards East–West cooperation which was desired and promoted by the not aligned countries of Europe. The two military alliances still exist and are relevant for the overall constellation in Europe. The détente is therefore continuing gradually under the shadow of the antagonism, such as was formulated during the Cold War, but without the vehemence and acrimony of the past years. It is now much less burdened with a total confrontation, nor is it or can it remain for long, an ideologically determined confrontation, and there is no economic warfare.

In view of these developments and their consequences, the not aligned countries of Europe could be satisfied. If anything, their role in Helsinki and Geneva were vindicated by post-Helsinki developments. Hence the likelihood that these countries will in the future, and in the first place at the Belgrade meeting, continue to play the role of catalysts, mediators and active creators of an atmosphere of tolerance and cooperation between the two sides of the divided continent. With the waning of the irreconciliability of clear-cut ideological positions of the two alliances, these efforts have a better prospect, and the actors may certainly feel encouraged.

As the Belgrade meeting approaches, it seems that it might well be dominated by reproaches and counter-reproaches concerning the problems of the free flow of ideas, information and people, the well-known Basket 3 of Geneva and Helsinki. It may, however, also be hoped that the atmosphere would calm down before the meeting, and that the discussions could reopen on a more constructive note than would be possible under the pressure of sharp East–West polemics as they occurred at the beginning of 1977, and in the last part of 1976. After all, it was shown amply that pressures exercised by States or groups of States concerning internal affairs, do not produce expected results, but lead only to the exacerbation of general relations.

One further important element is the controversy on these issues between the Eastern European countries and the Western communist parties. The dispute is no longer just a Cold War disagreement on important principles and concerning concrete cases of behaviour, it is a dispute between the two alliances. All efforts notwithstanding of presenting it still as a Cold War issue, are bound to lose ground. This domain, which was in Helsinki and in Geneva rightly regarded as the most distinctly defined ideological controversy, now assumes more of the nature of criticism of the behaviour of some States. Ideologically differing political groups and parties now act along similar lines of criticism of inadequate applications of the relevant parts of the Final Act of Helsinki.

Taking all developments together, it may be said that the not aligned countries of Europe might share the general view that the intentions proclaimed in the Final Act of Helsinki were not carried out to a degree which could be accepted as satisfactory, but they could also point to more encouraging developments in other fields, and also towards the shrinking of the front of friction and controversy between East and West, which appears now to be much more manageable.

Prospects for a Non-aligned Europe in the World

The short-term developments in Europe were as inconclusive as such short experiences usually are, but they were not discouraging for the not aligned countries of Europe. This is particularly so if one takes the view that in the long run it matters much more how the atmosphere develops, than how concrete resolutions are carried out. With all the ups and downs connected with the double change in the White House during this short period, and the strains of a number of developments in Europe and in Africa, the prospects are still favourable for the meeting in Belgrade.

It would seem that slowly, but nevertheless continually, Europe is moving in the direction of dismantling the Cold War. We have noted above mostly the changes in the ideological and political constellation, but also trends in economic interaction. The military aspect is, of course, dominated by Soviet–American relations, which also do not give cause for dissatisfaction, if compared with developments preceding Helsinki.

With all this said, the important and crucial question arises: is the gradual dismantling of the Cold War and the blurring of ideological lines of division between East and West, really leading towards the state of a bloc-free multilateral pattern of relations in Europe. Even with the greatest optimism, one cannot give a clear positive answer to this question. Of course, one reason for this is the futility of predicting anything for the distant future, but there is also good reason to have doubts based on already discernible developments in Europe and in the world.

Transition from a bipolar pattern to a bloc-free Europe could, of course, be seen as beginning with the de-emphasizing of ideological antagonism, and in the first place by separating ideological issues from relations between States, and also by better economic relations. But the bipolar pattern is governed not only by antagonism and hostility between the two sides, but also by policies aiming at the creation and maintenance of separate regional groupings of countries. It is not likely that the Economic Communities of Western Europe would accept to dismantle any of the institutions or agreements which were attained during the process of integration, just because there is no longer a controversy between East and West.

The same, perhaps with more emphasis, would be true for the East. In fact the processes of growing together between the States on both sides continued throughout the détente and the events of the few past years. After the debate on Eurocommunism will have faded away, and the new status which the Western communist parties accepted generally, the integrating processes in the West may even gain new momentum. Full political representation and participation in Western institutions will in fact facilitate and enhance their viability and efficiency, as much as it is likely to reduce the antagonistic aspect in intra-European relations, taking the Cold War sting out of them.

The very same development, the debate on Eurocommunism in the West, and the polemics of the East with Western communist parties, led so far to moves aiming at still closer links in the Warsaw Pact area. One could say that the lack of political influence of the East in Western countries led to the reinforcement and tightening of relations within Eastern Europe. This development may, probably on a temporary basis, affect adversely the carrying out of the intentions proclaimed in Helsinki in Basket 3, but they quite apparently do not stand in the way of continuing the discussions concerning SALT 2 and it so happened that the Vienna conference on the Mutual Reduction of Forces, just recently had its first impulse from the East in the direction of a businesslike debate.

For all these reasons it is hard to see how even the most propitious development of East–West relations could lead automatically to the disappearance of the separate organizations, institutions and relationships in the one or the other part of Europe. The Cold War brought about the creation and the growth of these groupings, but the ending of the Cold War and of East–West tension, can hardly be expected to make them disappear.

In that sense the future of non-alignment in Europe cannot be described as bright and hopeful. On the other hand this does not mean that any activity or advocacy in this direction was or would be in the future useless and unjustified. It is beyond doubt that activities inspired by the vision of a Europe without blocs had contributed greatly to whatever modest results were so far achieved in normalizing relations on the continent. In this case, as in most human endeavours, one must aim higher in order to attain at least some worthwhile goal.

In fact it would be far fetched to assume that all the not aligned countries in Europe were at any time aiming consciously and systematically at non-alignment as a general pattern of relations on the continent. There can, however, be no doubt that a bloc-free Europe would correspond to their choice in international relations. The distinction may be subtle, but it must be made when the effect of recent developments is assessed from the point of view of the countries outside the alliances.

This means, that even from the point of view of at least most of the not aligned countries, the development is not necessarily disappointing. They did not advocate or aim at a fundamental change in the bipolar pattern of relations. For those interested in the reduction of tension and increase in cooperation and growing cooperation among countries irrespective of their alignments, progress is important even if it does not promise complete change. This progress can perhaps be also defined as increased transgroup interaction without requiring the disintegration of groups on either side.

In other words, it appears to be feasible and even probable that advantages expected from separate regional associations could be combined with the intensification and extension of interaction with partners outside the association, or the integrative organization to which a country may belong. Economically this would mean relying more on the effect of positive cooperation than on advantages gained by the exclusion of competition or cooperation with outside actors. In the military, i.e., the strategic, field it would be possible to expect more contact with outside countries only if the stability of peace is perceived as assured and if political, rather than military, elements are in the first place relied on for safeguarding the national interest. Finally, more interaction in the sphere of ideology and a free exchange of ideas and persons would have to be founded on the feeling that there is on neither side a serious interest in stimulating subversion and that there is little prospect of it that could become a real threat to internal security.

Finally, there is another aspect of non-alignment which must be brought into the picture. It is the role of Europe in world affairs. What is the possible development of the relationship of European countries to the movement of the non-aligned countries acting on the world scene. Before discussing this it is necessary to indicate the main complexes of problems which are the basic components of the movement. They can be summarized in three points: (1) standing outside of the field of gravity of any major power or group of powers; (2) promoting the economic interests of the member countries, practically all of which are less developed (although there are differences in the level of development among them); (3) safeguarding and protecting national independence from pressures coming from more powerful States or groups of States.

With the prospect and possibility of reducing the role of East–West antagonism as the main stimulant for intragroup cohesion, even a divided Europe might develop better and closer relations with the non-aligned movement. In particular this might become feasible if the dominant presence of the two super powers was mitigated by more autonomy of the countries on both sides of the dividing line. In fact political relations between some European countries and the movement of the non-aligned have improved already. It is, though, most unlikely that European countries other than those who now participate, could join the movement.

This would remain so even in the case of very radical political changes in Europe, because of the differences in the level of economic development, and basic economic and political goals and aspirations arising out of it. The economically developed countries participate in the competition on the world scene trying to make the best out of the existing rules of the game. The less-developed countries have hardly any hope to do so successfully.

They are essentially interested in changing the rules, that means changing the international economic order. The complex economic programme is at present and probably will remain in the foreseeable future, the strongest cohesive force of the movement of the non-aligned countries. This has become so partly because of the diminished threat of a general war and even of other political pressures, including the end of the decolonization and of colonial wars and armed conflicts with liberation movements in the area of former colonial empires. Even the one exception, the unresolved confrontation in the Middle East, appears to be much more under control, than ever before, and is not likely to grow into a major conflict.

In view of the gulf in economic development dividing most European countries from the bulk of the non-aligned countries, there can be nothing more than more or less an understanding for their demands and aspirations. Even a radical change of the European political constellation, the dissolution of the two blocs, could not overcome the gap in economic development. On the other hand changes in the economies cannot be but slow and incremental, and therefore not relevant within the near future, which can be reasonably discussed.

On this ground again, nothing more than cooperation can be expected. It is unlikely that opposing interests could be completely eliminated even in the case of countries which have in the recent past demonstrated a very deep understanding for the problems and the aspiration of the less-developed countries. Non-alignment as a world movement, and as it shaped up during the postwar period will remain an essentially extra-European body and will not influence to any greater degree internal developments on the continent. Still, a more outward looking attitude, even with the preservation of the European regional integrations, could reduce the strain in relations and bring more positive and constructive interaction between the Third World and the two groupings in Europe.

In conclusion, the problem concerning the future of non-alignment in Europe could be summarized in the following three points:

(1) There is no prospect of Europe becoming non-aligned in the sense of the word as it applies to the movement of the non-aligned countries. It is neither likely that new participants, certainly not a larger number of new participants, could join the movement from Europe. As a whole, Europe, irrespective of the future development in East–West relations on the continent, can develop more cooperative relationships with the Third World, which would also mean better relations with the non-aligned countries.

(2) The overcoming of the division in Europe cannot be expected in the near future, in spite of the continuing improvement in East–West relations. It is, first, unlikely that past antagonisms and differences could be sufficiently overcome through intensified interaction, although stability of peace and cooperation can be strengthened. Secondly, advantages and other considerations of a regional nature are likely to cause the continuation of separate integrative and political regional groupings, even if the East–West antagonism were to disappear completely.

(3) The changes in attitudes and concepts of the major Western communist parties and their new relationship with the East, as well as their readiness to accept the division, contributes greatly to the blunting of ideological overtones in the East–West relations in Europe. Although the Western communist parties may prefer the dissolution of the alliances, and as much as they may seek change and innovation within their own countries, the East–West relationship is moving into the sphere of nation-to-nation relations, based primarily on differences in goals and aspirations of States and groups of States. This might be a development making the transition to a bloc-free constellation more likely, but should not be considered as introducing a change of this nature automatically.

Chapter 4

LES DIX PRINCIPES D'HELSINKI: INTERPRÉTATIONS ET MISE EN OEUVRE

by *Victor-Yves Ghébali*

(summary in English)

Although the Final Act is forming an indivisible whole, a certain pre-eminence of its ten principles calls for their separate analysis. This chapter deals systematically with the five main issues contained in them.

The compromises reached on the wording of the first, third and fourth principles, dealing with the *problem of borders*, disguise two different interpretations: the Soviet interpretation of the immutability of post-war East–West borders; the Western interpretation of the inviolability of all interstate borders in Europe, which, however, can be changed—but only—peacefully and by mutual consent.

The wording of the first, second, fourth, sixth and eighth principles also disguise different interpretations on the so-called *Brezhnev doctrine*. According to Western interpretations, these principles exclude its application, according to the USSR, they codify the principle of peaceful coexistence only.

With respect to the *third basket*, the West sees its foundation in the seventh principle on respect for human rights. The East emphasizes the principles of State sovereignty and non-interference in internal affairs.

The non-aligned and neutral countries insisted on the *democratization of pan-European relations* and claim to have obtained support for it in the first principle and several others.

Especially Yugoslavia has insisted on the "universal dimension of CSCE". Several principles have re-affirmed their wider-than-European importance.

As the Final Act is the outcome primarily of a compromise between States and systems with fundamentally opposed values, its *implementation* should be examined in reference to the divergent interpretations given. In view of the character of the principles, their implementation can be examined only in terms of their violation.

As such, reference has in particular been made: by the East to violations of the principles of sovereign equality, non-intervention and cooperation between States; and by the West to violations of the principle of respect for human rights.

Beyond specific petitions, the ten principles have been central to the debates on the Soviet–GDR Treaty of Friendship (1975) and the relations among the Socialist States.

One must conclude that the ten principles have done more to maintain tension than to favour détente, reflecting the fundamentally opposite conceptions in East and West underlying détente.

* * *

L'Acte final de la CSCE forme un tout indivisible dont les différentes parties sont d'égale valeur et entre lesquelles ne saurait donc exister de hiérarchie politico-juridique. D'un point de vue purement logique pourtant, une certaine prééminence de fait semble revenir à la Déclaration sur les principes régissant les relations mutuelles des Etats participants. Ce texte énonce dix règles fondamentales (d'où l'appellation de "Décalogue") que les 35 pays de la CSCE se sont engagés à respecter et à appliquer dans leurs rapports mutuels sous toutes les formes, à tous les niveaux et dans tous les secteurs de coopération couverts par l'Acte final. Il possède par conséquent le privilège unique de régir la mise en oeuvre des trois corbeilles à la fois,[1] c'est-à-dire d'être en somme la loi fondamentale de la CSCE.

Nous nous proposons ici d'analyser les diverses interprétations du Décalogue et de dresser un bilan de sa mise en oeuvre entre Helsinki et Belgrade.

Les interprétations du Décalogue

Pour exposer le contenu du Décalogue, la méthode la plus simple serait sans doute d'examiner les principes dans leur ordre initial successif et en comparant le cas échéant chacun d'eux aux principes correspondants des Nations Unies. Mais nous lui préférerons ici une approche plus systématique tendant à mettre mieux en relief les cinq grands enjeux du Décalogue: les frontières, la doctrine Brejnev, les fondements de la troisième corbeille, la démocratisation des relations paneuropéennes et la dimension mondiale de la CSCE.

---

1. Les préambules respectifs des deuxième et troisième corbeilles prévoient expressément le plein respect des principes du Décalogue.

Le problème des frontières: immutabilité ou intangibilité?

La consécration de la situation territoriale et politique née des bouleversements de la seconde guerre mondiale en Europe était pour l'URSS l'objectif prioritaire, non seulement au niveau particulier du Décalogue, mais en réalité au niveau global de la CSCE elle-même. On peut ainsi estimer que les concessions principales faites par l'Est dans l'ensemble des trois corbeilles le furent très souvent en fonction de cet objectif. Il s'agissait de faire poser que les frontières existantes sont, dès à présent et pour l'avenir, immutables de manière à obtenir, d'une part, la légitimation du statu quo et, d'autre part, la garantie contre toute remise en question de ce statu quo. Le principe de l'inviolabilité des frontières était donc perçu comme la pierre angulaire de l'édifice de la sécurité en Europe. Etant donné que sa reconnaissance solennelle par la CSCE aurait pour effet de rendre la détente "irréversible", l'Est estimait qu'il devait avoir primauté sur les autres principes du Décalogue. En un mot, l'Est espérait étendre au plan multilatéral des 35, les bénéfices politiques et juridiques découlant des traités de l'Ostpolitik allemande selon l'interprétation restrictive qui était la sienne.

Mais l'Ouest ne se trouvait aucunement disposé à faire des concessions aussi considérables sur un tel terrain. Accorder une reconnaissance, même formelle, aux frontières européennes de l'URSS et à celles de ses alliés du Pacte de Varsovie était une éventualité politiquement inacceptable sur le plan des opinions publiques comme des gouvernements.[2] D'ailleurs la CSCE n'avait aucun titre pour agir comme une conférence générale de la paix. Enfin, et surtout, il fallait tenir compte de la possibilité d'un changement pacifique des frontières, c'est-à-dire de modifications territoriales sans recours à la force, par voie d'accord mutuel et conformément au droit des peuples à disposer d'eux-mêmes. Cette possibilité n'intéressait pas seulement l'Espagne (Gibraltar), l'Irlande (Ulster) ou Chypre. Elle touchait aussi aux perspectives d'unification politique de la Communauté européenne et de réunification de l'Allemagne.

Le compromis enregistré dans l'Acte final comporte deux éléments principaux:

— *Protection de l'inviolabilité des frontières et de l'intégrité territoriale contre tout recours à la menace ou l'emploi de la force.* Le *principe III* sur

---

2. Rappelons, à titre d'exemple, que l'annexion des pays baltes n'a jamais été reconnue par les Etats-Unis.

l'inviolabilité des frontières stipule que les Etats participants "tiennent mutuellement pour inviolables toutes leurs frontières ainsi que celles de tous les Etats d'Europe et s'abstiennent donc maintenant et à l'avenir de tout *attentat* contre ces frontières" (*"assaulting frontiers"*). En conséquence, "ils s'abstiennent de toute exigence ou de tout acte de mainmise (*"demand for, or act of, seizure or usurpation"*) sur tout ou partie du territoire d'un autre Etat participant". L'inviolabilité a été définie, ainsi que le font ressortir nos italiques, comme une protection contre tout changement par l'illégalité et la violence. La protection s'étend à toutes les frontières des Etats participants (donc y compris celles des Etats-Unis et du Canada) et de tous les Etats d'Europe (inclusion de l'Albanie, Etat non participant) quel qu'en soit le statut juridique. Ce statut demeure donc inchangé par rapport à la situation d'avant Helsinki. D'autre part, l'inviolabilité ne saurait équivaloir à l'immutabilité car une modification librement effectuée par voie pacifique et dans la légalité ne porterait en aucune façon atteinte au principe.

Des remarques similaires peuvent être faites au sujet du *principe IV* sur l'intégrité territoriale des Etats. Le fondement de ce principe réside dans l'interdiction de recours à la menace ou à l'emploi de la force. Les Etats participants se sont engagés à *respecter* leur intégrité territoriale mutuelle mais non à reconnaître le statut juridique des territoires concernés.[3] Le même principe prohibe notamment toute acquisition territoriale résultant d'un recours, direct ou indirect, à la menace ou à l'usage de la force et précise qu'"aucune occupation ou acquisition de cette nature ne sera reconnue comme légale" (paragr. 3). Le verbe "sera" ("will" dans le texte anglais), retenu à la demande expresse de l'URSS, semble indiquer qu'une telle sanction ne s'appliquera qu'aux situations postérieures à Helsinki. En fait, pour les Occidentaux, l'engagement a une portée retroactive, ce qui encore une fois signifie que l'intangibilité des frontières n'implique pas leur reconnaissance.

— *Admissibilité du changement pacifique des frontières*. L'Acte final stipule sans ambiguïté que les Etats participants "considèrent que leurs frontières peuvent être modifiées, conformément au droit

---

3. Les Etats participants "s'abstiennent de tout acte incompatible avec les buts et principes de la Charte des Nations Unies contre l'intégrité territoriale, l'indépendance politique ou l'*unité* de tout Etat participant, et, en particulier de toute action de ce genre représentant une menace ou un emploi à la force" (Paragr. 2 du Principe IV). Etant donné que la protection inclut celle de l'"unité" de tout Etat participant, le principe IV se trouve ainsi relié au principe VIII de l'auto-détermination.

international, par des moyens pacifiques et par voie d'accord". L'URSS n'a accepté cette idée qu'à condition qu'elle fût, d'une part, dépourvue de toute allusion au principe de l'autodétermination et, d'autre part, insérée ailleurs que dans le principe de l'inviolabilité des frontières ou de l'intégrité territoriale. La "phrase flottante" fut finalement glissée dans l'énoncé du *Principe Ier* sur l'égalité souveraine. Cette greffe un peu artificielle n'en a pas pour autant affaibli la force. L'idée du changement pacifique a été formulée d'une façon satisfaisante. Elle est présentée comme une règle générale du droit international soumise à deux conditions précises: le recours à des moyens pacifiques et l'accord mutuel des parties intéressées.[4] De plus, elle constitue un corollaire certain au principe de l'inviolabilité des frontières puisque les Clauses finales du Décalogue stipulent, comme l'avait voulu l'Ouest, que *tous* les principes du Décalogue "sont dotés d'une importance primordiale et en conséquence ils s'appliquent également et sans réserve, chacun d'eux s'interprétant en tenant compte des autres" (paragr. 1er).

Malgré sa netteté, ce compromis global entre l'immutabilité et l'intégrité des frontières n'a rien résolu. L'Ouest estime que l'Acte final n'a eu pour autre résultat que de réaffirmer les réalités d'une situation préexistante: l'illégalité et l'impossibilité matérielle — d'une modification des frontières par la force. Quant à l'Est, il considère que l'Acte final établit l'immutabilité fondamentale des frontières, étant cependant entendu que des rectifications *mineures* de frontières peuvent être effectuées conformément à l'idée du changement pacifique.[5]

---

4. Au cours des négociations de Genève, il avait d'abord été envisagé que les frontières des Etats participants "ne peuvent être modifiées *que* conformément au droit international par des moyens pacifiques et par voie d'accord" (doc. CSCE/II/A/126). Cette formulation, souhaitée par l'URSS, aurait signifié qu'une modification territoriale n'aurait pu intervenir par voie pacifique et d'accord que dans tous les cas où le droit international public prévoit spécifiquement une telle possibilité. La phrase actuelle attribue le fardeau de la preuve aux Etats opposés à une telle modification et non pas à ceux qui la souhaitent.

5. Selon Y. Rakhmaninov, le Principe III sur l'inviolabilité des frontières "allows for no exceptions, and cannot be made dependent upon *any* other principle, for instance the refraining from the use of force, or upon a substantive change of circumstances" ("Europe: Principles of Security and Cooperation", *International Affairs*, Moscow, 1976/2, p. 45). Le même auteur déclare au sujet de l'idée sur le changement pacifique que "though this provision is a vital element of preserving peace it would be unjustified, however, to absolutise it a 'new principle' opposing the principle of the inviolability of frontiers, just as what some people in the West want to do" (*ibid.*, p. 43).

La "doctrine Brejnev"

L'un des objectifs principaux poursuivis par les Occidentaux lors de la négociation du Décalogue, et soutenu par certains pays comme la Roumanie et la Yougoslavie, était de rendre illicite toute nouvelle intervention du genre de l'invasion de la Tchécoslovaquie en 1968. En d'autres termes, il s'agissait de s'attaquer au fondement de ce qu'à l'Ouest on appelle la doctrine Brejnev de la souveraineté limitée et de ce que l'Est considère comme étant une déformation malveillante du principe socialiste de l'internationalisme prolétarien.[6]

L'Acte final ne mentionne évidemment pas plus l'idée de souveraineté limitée que celle d'internationalisme prolétarien. Il contient cependant de nombreuses dispositions qui peuvent s'y rapporter:

— Le *préambule* du Décalogue exprime la résolution de chaque Etat participant de respecter et de mettre en pratique les dix principes dans ses relations avec tous les autres Etats participants, et cela nonobstant leur système politique, économique et social (paragr. 5). Le paragraphe 2 des *Clauses finales* du Décalogue contient un engagement similaire motivé par la nécessité d'assurer à chaque Etat participant pris individuellement "les avantages résultant du respect et de l'application de ces principes par tous".

— Le *principe Ier* énonce, dans le contexte de l'égalité souveraine, le droit de chaque Etat participant au libre choix et développement de son système politique, social, économique et culturel interne (paragr. ler) ainsi que le droit de conduire à son gré ses relations extérieures (paragr. 2).

— Le *principe II* déclare qu'aucune considération ne peut être invoquée pour justifier un recours à la menace ou à l'emploi de la force (paragr. ler). Tout acte constituant une menace d'emploi de la force ou un recours direct ou indirect à la force contre un Etat participant est interdit de même que "toute manifestation de force visant à faire renoncer un autre Etat participant au plein exercice de ses droits souverains" (paragr. 2).

— Le *principe IV* interdit, en relation avec l'intégrité territoriale, toute occupation militaire ou d'autres mesures prises à l'encontre d'un Etat participant et comportant un recours direct ou indirect à la force en contravention avec le droit international — une telle

---

6. Pour plus de détails, voir Mario Bettati, "Souveraineté limitée ou internationalisme prolétarien? Les liens fondamentaux de la communauté des Etats Socialistes", *Revue belge de droit international*, 1972, pp. 455–481.

occupation ne pourra, en outre, être tenue pour légale (paragr. 3).
— Le principe VI est sans doute plus limpide que les precédents à cet égard. Il condamne sans appel "toute intervention, directe ou indirecte, individuelle ou collective, dans les affaires intérieures ou extérieures relevant de la compétence nationale d'un autre Etat participant, quelles que soient leurs relations mutuelles" (paragr. ler). Les deux paragraphes suivants du même principe renforcent cette disposition.
— Le *principe VIII*, qui concerne l'autodétermination des peuples, affirme en termes vigoureux que "tous les peuples ont toujours le droit, en toute liberté, de déterminer, lorsqu'ils le désirent et comme ils le désirent, leur statut politique interne et externe, sans ingérence extérieure, et de poursuivre à leur gré leur développement politique, économique, social et culturel" (paragr. 2).

De toutes ces dispositions séparées ou réunies, les pays occidentaux tirent la conclusion — logique et raisonnable — qu'une nouvelle application de la doctrine de la souveraineté limitée serait entièrement contraire à l'esprit comme à la lettre de l'Acte final d'Helsinki. Tel ne semble pas l'avis de l'URSS, laquelle, grâce à une interprétation particulière des concepts ambigus de détente et de coexistence pacifique, parvient à une conclusion différente. Pour l'Est, le Décalogue est une codification des principes de la détente ou, ce qui revient au même, de la coexistence pacifique. Or la coexistence pacifique sert de base de conduite fondamentale pour pays à systèmes politiques, économiques et sociaux différents; n'étant que l'une des formes de la lutte internationale des classes, elle ne saurait de toute évidence régir les rapports entre pays socialistes qui appliquent entre eux les règles adéquates et plus avancées de l'internationalisme prolétarien.[7] Il n'en reste pas moins que la netteté des dispositions du Décalogue rend difficile une invocation unilatérale par un Etat donné de la doctrine Brejnev. C'est pourquoi il était prévisible que l'URSS tenterait au lendemain d'Helsinki de légitimer juridiquement le droit d'intervention qu'elle inclue dans des traités bilatéraux avec certains de ses partenaires du Pacte de Varsovie.[8]

---

7. Voir Robert Charvin, "La souveraineté et la Conférence sur la sécurité et la coopération en Europe", in *Mélanges offerts à Georges Burdeau. Le pouvoir*. Paris, L.G.D.J., 1977, p. 1017 et 1030. Voir aussi Konstantin Chernenko, "Principles of Peaceful Coexistence", *Soviet Weekly*, September 18, 1976, p. 6.

8. Voir Harold Russell, "The Helsinki Declaration: Brobdignac or Lilliput", *American Journal of International Law*, 1976/2, pp. 256–257.

Les fondements de la troisième corbeille

Parmi les concessions capitales réclamées par les pays occidentaux comme "prix" à l'exercice global de la CSCE, figurait surtout l'inclusion à l'ordre du jour de la conférence des questions touchant à la libre circulation des personnes, de l'information et des idées. Principal cheval de bataille de l'Ouest, le troisième corbeille ne pouvait être perçue par l'Est que comme le "cheval de Troie de la détente". Plus qu'ailleurs peut-être, les conceptions en présence étaient séparées par un abîme: car au-delà des divergences politiques, le débat mettait en cause deux *weltanschauung* et leurs valeurs philosophiques. Au nom des droits fondamentaux de l'individu, l'Ouest demandait un *libre-échange* d'hommes et d'idées; au nom de la préservation de la société socialiste, l'Est ne pouvait admettre que des *échanges contingentés* fixés discrétionairement par les Etats sur la base du plein respect des principes de l'égalité souveraine et de la non-intervention dans les affaires intérieures. L'Acte final a réalisé à cet égard un compromis minimum en posant que la coopération dans les domaines de la troisième corbeille aurait pour fondement la totalité des principes du Décalogue.

Pour les pays socialistes, cela signifie le couple souveraineté/non-intervention. Dans le cadre de l'égalité souveraine, le *Ier principe* établit en effet le droit de chaque Etat "de déterminer ses lois et ses règlements".[9] Ce droit n'est pas illimité. Le *Xème principe* précise que "dans l'exercice de leurs droits souverains, dont le droit de déterminer leurs lois et règlements (...) ils (les Etats participants) tiennent dûment compte des dispositions de l'Acte final (...) et les appliquent" (paragr. 2). Le principe de la bonne foi constitue donc une clause de sauvegarde. Quant au *principe VI* de la non-intervention, son paragraphe 1er est formulé de façon telle qu'il peut être lu aussi bien, comme on l'a dit, dans une optique anti-doctrine Brejnev que dans la perspective d'une défense contre l'utilisation abusive de la troisième corbeille par les Occidentaux.[10]

Mais pour l'Ouest, le fondement de la troisième corbeille se trouve dans le *principe VII* sur les droits de l'homme. La formulation de ce principe, dans ses éléments essentiels, correspond en effet bien à la philosophie occidentale. Ainsi, il pose que les libertés et droits civils, économiques, sociaux, culturels et autres "découlent tous de la dignité inhérente à la personne humaine" (paragr. 2), ce qui

---

9. Contrairement au souhait de l'URSS, la notion de "coutumes" et de "fondements culturels" n'a pas été admise.

10. Voir Russell, op. cit., p. 267.

implique que ces libertés et droits ne peuvent être des privilèges accordés d'une façon discrétionnaire par l'Etat à ses ressortissants. Il affirme en outre que le respect général des droits de l'homme est un facteur essentiel "pour assurer le développement de relations amicales et de la coopération" entre les 35 Etats participants (paragr. 5): les Occidentaux ont donc imposé ici l'idée que la détente devait avoir une dimension qualitative de façon à exercer ses effets au niveau des réalités concrètes de la vie quotidienne du simple citoyen. Il ouvre sans ambiguïté un niveau de communication et de coopération nouveau en posant que les Etats participants "respectent constamment ces droits et libertés dans leurs relations mutuelles et s'efforcent conjointement et séparément (...) d'en promouvoir le respect universel et effectif" (paragr. 6). Allant encore plus loin, il confirme "le droit de l'individu de connaître ses droits et devoirs dans ce domaine et d'agir en conséquence" (paragr. 7) — disposition novatrice dont on appréciera la valeur à la lumière des pratiques socialistes où le concept de "secret d'Etat" a souvent pour effet de laisser l'individu dans l'incertitude quant à l'étendue ou aux conditions d'exercice de certains de ces droits fondamentaux. En marge de ces dispositions fondamentales, l'Ouest peut aussi invoquer le *principe IX* qui reconnaît non seulement aux gouvernements, aux institutions et aux organisations, mais aussi aux personnes, "un rôle propre et positif à jouer" (paragr. 3) dans la coopération paneuropéenne.

En définitive, ce compromis n'a, là encore, véritablement rien réglé: si l'Ouest est fondé à réclamer le respect des droits de l'homme dans des circonstances particulières, l'Est se trouve non moins fondé — en vertu de l'égalité des principes — à s'abriter derrière les remparts de la souveraineté et de la non-intervention dans les limites de la bonne foi.

La démocratisation des relations paneuropéennes
Les sept pays Neutres et Non-alignés de la CSCE ne semblaient pas de prime abord devoir constituer un groupe cohérent. Il y avait parmi eux des Etats dotés d'un statut de neutralité permanente (Suisse, Autriche), d'autres qui pratiquaient un neutralisme authentique (Suède) ou parfois moins reconnu comme authentique (Finlande) et d'autres encore qui se considéraient solidaires du Tiers-Monde (Yougoslavie, Chypre et Malte). Ces pays sont pourtant parvenus, surtout dans le cadre de la négociation sur le Décalogue (et sur les suites de la Conférence) à définir une approche commune à partir de trois idées-force: l'opportunité de continuer à assurer leur sécurité individuelle en dehors des al-

liances militaires, la nécessité de tenter de favoriser le dépassement progressif de la division en blocs et, enfin, l'aspiration à une démocratisation des relations internationales. La troisième idée, qui résume en les complétant les deux premières, procède d'un réflexe typique des petites puissances. Le but principal des Neutres et Non-alignés (auxquels il faut joindre la Roumanie) était en effet l'établissement d'un système paneuropéen où tous les Etats, quel que soit leur ordre de grandeur, auraient le droit d'exister, de s'exprimer et de participer aux affaires de l'Europe (et du monde) dans des conditions de pleine égalité.

L'un des mérites principaux du Décalogue est de refléter assez bien ces diverses préoccupations. Les Neutres et les Non-alignés ont ainsi obtenu une formulation aussi explicite que possible du *principe Ier* de l'égalité souveraine et du respect des droits inhérents à la souveraineté des Etats. Chaque Etat participant s'est vu formellement reconnaître le droit de définir et de conduire à son gré ses relations avec les autres Etats, et notamment le droit d'appartenir ou non à des organisations internationales, d'être partie ou non à des traités bilatéraux ou multilatéraux (y compris les traités d'alliances) ou encore à la neutralité. Touchant ce dernier point, on peut estimer qu'il y a là une reconnaissance à la fois du rôle actif que certains Neutres ont joué dans la préparation de la CSCE, et de la contribution que les Neutres et les Non-alignés en général peuvent apporter dans les relations Est–Ouest. L'idée de la neutralité comme facteur de paix dans les relations internationales n'est certes pas neuve. Mais, jusqu'alors, elle n'avait reçu qu'une application limitée à des cas spécifiques concrets; or, désormais, on admet un droit *général* à la neutralité.

Quant au *principe IX*, il prévoit que le développement de la coopération entre les 35 se fera de façon à permettre à chaque Etat participant d'apporter une contribution propre "dans des conditions de pleine égalité" (paragr. ler).

Les principes restants peuvent également faire l'objet d'une lecture favorable aux intérêts des Neutres et des Non-alignés. Tel est sans doute le cas de certaines dispositions relatives au non-recours à la force (*principe II*), au règlement pacifique des différends (*principe V*),[11] à la non-intervention (*principe VI*), à l'inviolabilité des frontières et à l'intégrité territoriale (*principles III et IV*).

---

11. Rappelons que la Suisse avait proposé à la CSCE un projet de convention instituant un système européen de règlement pacifique obligatoire des différends (doc. CSCE/II/B/1), mais qui fera l'objet d'un examen par une réunion d'experts après Belgrade. Sur le problème du règlement pacifique des différends, voir

La "dimension mondiale" de la CSCE[12]

Soutenue par les Non-alignés et la Roumanie, la Yougoslavie mena un combat incessant en faveur de l'ouverture de la CSCE sur le monde extérieur, à partir de l'idée de l'indivisibilité de la coopération et de la sécurité en Europe et dans le monde entier.[13]

L'Acte final reconnaît cette indivisibilité dans le paragraphe 6 du préambule général de la première corbeille. Quant au Décalogue, il lui fait place de deux façons différentes:

— D'une part, à travers les dispositions de certains principes. Ainsi, le *principe II* déclare que l'interdiction du recours à la menace ou à l'emploi de la force est valable non seulement dans les relations mutuelles des Etats participants, mais aussi dans leurs relations internationales (paragr. 1er). Le *principe VII* envisage le respect effectif des droits de l'homme dans le contexte universel aussi bien que paneuropéen (paragr. 6). Le *principe VIII* réaffirme également l'importance universelle du respect et de l'exercice effectif par les peuples de droits égaux et de leur droit à disposer d'eux-mêmes (paragr. 3). Le *principe IX* énonce que dans leur coopération, les Etats participants prennent en considération notamment l'intérêt des pays en voie de développement du monde entier (paragr. 2). Enfin, l'une des Clauses finales du Décalogue stipule que les Etats participants s'inspirent de ces dix principes dans leurs relations avec tous les autres pays non participants (paragr. 5).

— D'autre part, en proclamant son appui au renforcement des Nations Unies et la conformité de ses dispositions avec les principes de la Charte.[14]

L'Acte final a été négocié par des Etats à systèmes de valeurs fondamentalement opposés, mais que la règle du consensus

---

F.A.M. Alting Von Geusau, "CSCE and the Peaceful Settlement of Disputes", *Review of International Affairs*, No. 643, 20.1.77, pp. 12–15. Du même auteur, voir "Conflict Structures and Modes of Conflict Resolution—A Post-CSCE Perspective", *Co-existence*, vol. 14 No. 1, Special Issue (1977), pp. 60–62.

12. Expression empruntée à l'excellent article de Ljubivoje Acimovic, "European Principles", *Review of International Affairs*, No. 612, 5.1.77, p. 7.

13. C'est en application de cette même idée que la Yougoslavie fut également l'un des pays les plus attachés au dialogue euroméditerranéen dans le cadre de la CSCE.

14. Pour plus de détails sur ce point, voir notre étude: "L'Acte final de la Conférence sur la sécurité et la coopération en Europe et les Nations Unies", *Annuaire français de droit international*, 1957, pp. 73–127.

condamnait à trouver au moins un vocabulaire formel commun. Or, abstraction faite des pays neutres et non-alignés, la CSCE mettait en présence deux mondes qui, ou bien ne parlaient pas le même langage, ou bien utilisaient les mêmes mots pour viser des réalités différentes. L'Est et l'Ouest ne sont parvenus à des compromis mutuellement acceptables qu'au prix de formulations ambigües sauvegardant, souvent dans une même disposition, leurs positions ou conceptions de base respectives. Pour compliquer davantage la situation, on relèvera que les six versions de l'Acte d'Helsinki (toutes d'égale foi) ne sont pas toujours de la plus parfaite concordance — défaut très sensible dans le cas particulier du texte russe où l'on trouve d'importantes différences de sens. De tout cela, il découle que l'Acte final est sans doute plus qu'aucun autre document multilatéral de ce genre susceptible d'une pluralité de "lectures" politico-juridiques divergentes et contradictoires, mais souvent également soutenables. Dans ces conditions, il serait partial de parler d'infractions ou de violations sans préciser, en même temps, par rapport à quel système de référence on se situe. Pour obtenir un bilan aussi objectif que possible, il faudrait systématiquement s'efforcer d'examiner la pratique à la lumière de la pluralité des "lectures" possibles des textes.

La mise en oeuvre du Décalogue[15]

Si bien des dispositions de l'Acte final réclament une action opérationnelle concrète et spécifique, il en est d'autres qui ne s'y prêtent pas en raison de leur caractère abstrait et général. Tel est le cas du Décalogue. Sa mise en oeuvre ne peut surtout être appréciée que sur un plan négatif, c'est-à-dire à partir de son infraction. La pratique du Décalogue entre Helsinki et Belgrade confirme ce point de vue.

Ainsi, le principe de l'*égalité souveraine* a été évoqué à l'Est pour dénoncer de supposées tentatives de l'OTAN visant à priver Chypre de sa souveraineté.[16] Pour leur part, les pays occidentaux ont décliné la proposition socialiste de non-élargissement de l'OTAN et du Pacte de Varsovie en rappelant que "le droit des Etats à participer ou non à des traités d'alliance a été confirmé

---

15. Ces développements sont empruntés à notre article "Le bilan intérimaire de la CSCE à la veille de Belgrade", *Politique Etrangère*, 1977/2, pp. 113 et ss.

16. Voir Oleg Stroganov, "La troisième corbeille: composante naturelle ou 'Cheval de Troie' de la détente", *Etudes soviétiques*, No. 338, mai 1976, p. 17.

dans l'Acte d'Helsinki",[17] c'est-à-dire dans le principe Ier du Décalogue.

Le principe de la *non-intervention dans les affaires intérieures* est celui auquel les gouvernements ont fait le plus souvent référence. Il a, par exemple, été invoqué par l'Espagne à l'occasion des vives réactions suscitées en Europe par l'execution des militants de l'ETA après le procès de Burgos,[18] par l'Ouest pour stigmatiser l'ingérence soviétique dans les affaires portugaises et angolaises,[19] par l'Est pour condamner les pressions de l'OTAN et de la CEE vis-à-vis du Portugal (conditions préalables posées par les Occidentaux pour toute aide à ce pays, en août 1975) et de l'Italie (déclaration tapageuse du chancelier Schmidt sur l'opposition des Occidentaux à une éventuelle participation des communistes italiens au gouvernement),[20] par la CEE pour repousser les attaques soviétiques concernant la partie du Rapport Tindemans consacrée aux questions de défense,[21] ou encore par l'Est pour s'élever avec vigueur contre l'interventionnisme moralisant de l'Administration Carter.

Le principe du *respect des droits de l'homme et des libertés fondamentales* n'est pas non plus demeuré en reste. Il a été constamment invoqué par la presse occidentale en rapport avec la nouvelle vague de contestation (et de répression) en URSS, RDA, Pologne ou en Tchécoslovaquie. L'Est s'en est aussi servi pour rappeler aux pays de l'Ouest qu'ils devaient d'abord l'appliquer dans leurs rapports réciproques avant de protester contre sa prétendue violation dans le reste de l'Europe: les droits de l'homme ne sont-ils pas bafoués de façon constante en Ulster et à Chypre? L'attitude réservée à l'égard de la ratification des deux Pactes des Nations Unies n'est-elle pas le fait exclusif des Occidentaux?[22] Du côté des Neutres et des Non-alignés, la Yougoslavie a reproché à l'Autriche

---

17. OTAN, communiqué de presse M2(76)19, 2ème alinéa du paragr. 3.
18. *Le Monde*, 28–29 septembre 1975.
19. *Nouvelles atlantiques*, No. 799, 6 février 1976.
20. *Le Monde*, 16 août 1975, *Izvestia*, 21 juillet 1976, *Pravda*, 30 juillet 1976.
21. *Nouvelles atlantiques*, No. 792, 14 janvier 1976.
22. Stroganov, op. cit., p. 17. Si le premier argument n'est pas entièrement injustifié, le second mérite réponse. La ratification des Pactes par les pays socialistes ne s'est pas accompagnée de la signature du Protocole facultatif au Pacte relatif aux droits divils et politiques qui donne son plein sens à la protection des droits envisagés. D'autre part, les deux Pactes en question vont *moins loin* que la Convention (ouest-européenne) de sauvegarde des droits de l'homme et des libertés fondamentales du 4 novembre 1950 et de ses 5 protocoles additionnels.

d'appliquer un traitement discriminatoire à ses minorités croates et slovènes.[23]

Enfin, signalons que l'Est continue à dénoncer la politique de "discrimination commerciale" de la CEE, présentée comme une violation du principe de la *coopération entre les Etats* et de celui de l'exécution de *bonne foi* des obligations internationales.[24]

Au-delà de ces pétitions courantes de principe, le Décalogue s'est trouvé surtout au centre de deux débats particuliers comme suite au traité signé entre l'URSS et la RDA le 7 octobre 1975, deux mois à peine après le sommet d'Helsinki.

Le premier débat porte sur l'égalité des dix principes. Le paragraphe premier des Clauses finales du Décalogue stipule que tous les principes "sont dotés d'une importance primordiale" et qu'"en conséquence ils s'appliquent également et sans réserve, chacun d'eux s'interprétant en tenant compte des autres". Le but d'une telle disposition était d'éviter qu'un Etat ou un groupe d'Etats puisse se constituer un "menu à la carte" limité à certains éléments du Décalogue. Or, le traité de 1975 affirme dans son article 6 que les deux parties "considèrent l'inviolabilité des frontières en Europe comme la condition essentielle de la sécurité européenne et expriment leur ferme intention de défendre, conjointement ou en alliance avec les autres Etats signataires du Pacte de Varsovie (...) et conformément à ce dernier, l'inviolabilité des frontières des Etats membres dudit Pacte, telles qu'elles se sont fixées à l'issue de la 2e guerre mondiale et de l'après-guerre, notamment entre la R.D.A. et la R.F.A.". Ne faisant aucune référence à l'Acte final et ignorant, contrairement aux accords germano-soviétiques antérieurs (1959 et 1964), toute éventuelle réunification de l'Allemagne par voie pacifique, il pose l'idée implicite que l'intangibilité des frontières équivaut à leur immutabilité. Les Allemands de l'Est ne s'en cachent même pas : peu avant la conclusion du traité, un membre du bureau politique du S.E.D. affirmait sans ambages que la CSCE était la première véritable conférence de paix européenne et qu'à ce titre elle avait légalisé les problèmes en suspens depuis 1945.[25] Dans l'optique occidentale, le traité porte atteinte au Décalogue en ce qu'il privilégie le principe

---

23. Voir Bogdan Osolnik, "International Aspects of Austrian Responsibility for Nonfulfillment and Violation of the State Treaty", *Review of International Affairs*, No. 639, 20 novembre 1976.

24. Stroganov, op. cit., p. 17; voir aussi l'article de Janos Nyerges dans *Népszabadsàg* du 6 février 1977.

25. *Le Monde*, 23 octobre 1975.

III sur l'inviolabilité des frontières au détriment du principe Ier sur l'égalité souveraine (où apparaît la notion du changement pacifique des frontières) et du principe VIII sur l'autodétermination des peuples. L'examen du traité de 1975 à travers la "lecture" socialiste du Décalogue aboutit à un résultat tout différent. L'URSS affirme reconnaître l'égalité des principes mais conteste que le traité en question établisse entre eux une hiérarchisation indue; elle rappelle qu'à la CSCE elle n'avait admis la perspective d'un changement pacifique que pour les rectifications mineures de frontières.

Le second débat concerne l'applicabilité du Décalogue aux rapports entre pays socialistes. Rappelons à cet égard que le Décalogue proclame la résolution de chaque Etat participant pris individuellement de respecter et de mettre en pratique les principes du Décalogue dans ses relations avec tous les autres Etats participants "indépendamment de leur système politique, économique ou social ..." (paragr. 5 du préambule) et qu'il précise aussi sans équivoque la nécessité d'"assurer à chaque Etat participant les avantages résultant du respect et de l'application de ces principes par tous" (paragr. 2 des Clauses finales). Appuyés par les Neutres et les Non-alignés, les Occidentaux voulaient par ces précisions mettre en valeur l'idée que le Décalogue n'était pas une codification pure et simple des principes de la coexistence pacifique lesquels, selon la conception socialiste, sont uniquement valables dans les rapports entre pays à régimes économiques, politiques et sociaux différents. En d'autres termes, le Décalogue de la CSCE se présente bien comme un code de bonne conduite global, applicable au niveau des relations intra-systémiques aussi bien qu'inter-systémiques. Mais là aussi, le traité URSS-RDA de 1975 est venu jeter des ombres au tableau. Ce traité est, de fait, plus dualiste que moniste; il expose avec ostensibilité la position classique des pays de l'Est (la Roumanie exceptée): entraide fraternelle entre pays socialistes (paragr. 7 du préambule et art. 4) et coexistence pacifique avec les pays capitalistes (paragr. 9 du préambule et art. 5). L'Ouest y voit là une réaffirmation directe de la validité de la doctrine Brejnev. L'URSS, qui nie jusqu'à l'existence d'une telle doctrine, se retranche derrière des considérations d'ordre idéologique d'après lesquelles la finalité des relations interétatiques est conditionnée par les structures internes des Etats concernés.

Pour alléger en quelque sorte les aspects négatifs du bilan, il serait tentant de prendre en considération le règlement, définitif semble-t-il, du litige italo-yougoslave sur le statut de Trieste réalisé par les accords d'Osimo du 10 novembre 1975. Ceux-ci, qui constituent sans doute une application spécifique du changement pacifique des frontières, du respect des droits de l'homme (par leurs dispositions relatives à la protection des minórités) et de la coopération ont été présentés par les deux parties comme une conséquence de la CSCE et une contribution à l'esprit d'Helsinki.[26] Mais l'affaire de Trieste nous paraît être le type même de développement qui doit davantage à la détente et dont la CSCE n'aurait à la rigueur fait qu'accélérer la matérialisation.

De tout ce qui précède, on se trouve amené à conclure un peu abruptement peut-être que le Décalogue — en dehors de ses avantages unilatéraux pour tel ou tel groupe d'Etats — aura plus contribué à éveiller une certaine tension qu'à favoriser la détente. Ne sont en cause ici ni la nature ou le contenu intrinsèque des principes, ni la bonne foi des Etats participants. La tare congénitale du Décalogue est de passer pour une codification de l'incodifiable: la détente telle qu'elle est à la fois conçue par l'Ouest et par l'Est.

L'Ouest analyse la détente comme un processus dynamique (exigeant des efforts continus), global (couvrant les relations internationales sous tous leurs aspects humains), indivisible (ne connaissant pas de zone de prédilection géopolitique) et qui, enfin, implique une relaxation des tensions sur tous les fronts y compris celui de la lutte idéologique.[27] Pour l'URSS, c'est plutôt un état stationnaire car "irréversible" (du moment que le statu quo territorial et politique de l'Europe n'est pas remis en question). Cette définition entraîne les corollaires suivants: la détente se limite fondamentalement à la sphère des relations intergouvernementales; elle est divisible en secteurs bien distincts (politique, militaire, économique, etc.) et plutôt étanches; elle ne postule en aucune façon — bien au contraire — qu'une sourdine soit mise à la confrontation idélogique.[28] L'antinomie des conceptions Est–Ouest nous paraît avoir été aggravée par la CSCE en ce sens que l'Acte final a introduit le mirage d'une définition générale commune et

---

26. Voir Vladimir Vugdelic, "Yugoslavia's and Italy's Contribution to the CSCE", *Review of International Affairs*, No. 641, 20 décembre 1976, pp. 25–27, et Union interparlementaire, doc. EUROPE/INF/11 ANNEXE I/Add. 4.

27. Voir Max van der Stoel, "Les relations Est–Ouest: limites et possibilités", *Revue de l'OTAN*, décembre 1976, pp. 3–5.

28. Voir Vadim K. Sobakine, "L'Union soviétique et la détente. Réalisations, obstacles, perspectives", *Studia diplomatica*, 1976/6, pp. 731–741.

d'une codification des principes qui en découleraient.[29] Les remous de l'affaire angolaise offrent une illustration exemplaire d'une telle affirmation. Le soutien actif accordé par l'URSS au MPLA n'a pas été seulement ressenti comme une tentative d'extension de la sphère d'influence soviétique en Afrique, mais aussi comme une violation du Décalogue: à quoi sert, fit-on valoir, de prêcher la non-intervention en Europe et, en même temps, de pratiquer sans gêne l'intervention en Angola? La réponse soviétique ne manque pas non plus de logique interne: la détente ne signifie et ne signifiera jamais l'abandon du combat pour la victoire mondiale du socialisme, laquelle passe notamment par le succès — et donc l'appui — des mouvements de libération nationale. Avant Helsinki, le fond du débat n'aurait guère été différent, mais à coup sûr, se serait-il deroulé avec moins d'ambiguité et aussi d'illusions réciproques.

Le Décalogue énumère les règles formelles d'un jeu dont la finalité se trouve, sinon indéterminée, du moins interprétée de façon différente selon les acteurs en présence. Le mérite essentiel qu'on pourrait malgré tout lui attribuer serait peut-être de mettre en lumière la nature foncièrement insatisfaisante du concept même de détente, c'est-à-dire de poser a contrario que la sécurité devrait reposer sur des bases plus claires et plus fermes.

---

29. Le 2ème paragraphe du préambule de la Ière corbeille contient une définition générale de la détente assez proche de la conception occidentale. Il dispose que les Etats participants sont convaincus de la nécessité de déployer des efforts pour "faire de la détente un *processus* tout à la fois *continu*, de plus en plus *viable* et *global*, de *portée* universelle ..." (nos italiques).

Part Two

DÉTENTE AND DISARMAMENT

INTRODUCTION

According to the Final Act of the CSCE, "the participating States recognize the interest of all of them in efforts aimed at lessening military confrontation and promoting disarmament which are designed to complement political détente in Europe and to strengthen their security".

A pious wish? Or a genuine commitment to complement détente with agreements on arms-control and disarmament?

The four authors, who have contributed on this subject, agree on at least one point: no progress of any significance has so far been made towards the stated objective. An exception may be, as Aćimović points out, the implementation of certain confidence building measures. The chances for agreement on new and more such measures are not promising, however.

Dobrosielski, who reviews the whole field of present East–West negotiations—on nuclear weapons and the reduction of forces and armaments—maintains that the Western States are to be blamed for this lack of progress.

Teunissen gives a detailed account of the Vienna negotiations on the Mutual Reduction of Forces and Armaments and Associated Measures in Central Europe (MURFAAMCE), and the disagreements hampering a successful outcome. In his opinion, NATO should be able to display unilateral restraints, in particular with respect to advanced weapons and weapons of mass-destruction, if compromises continue to be out of reach. Czempiel takes a look at the domestic situation in the United States to identify the forces which produce both a trend towards further détente and a trend towards continuing the arms race. His "case" study is instructive and discouraging. If economic interests, public opinion and an independently minded Congress have as yet not prevailed over the bureaucratically entrenched military community in the US, a comparable "case" study of the Soviet Union would certainly yield even bleaker a prospect. There does not even exist a societal, political or economic counterweight against the Soviet military, which might restrain its considerable power in the Kremlin bureaucracy. In the Soviet Union—as in the US—the arms race goes on, and the official ideology sees to it that the contradiction with détente is conveniently explained away.

Chapter 5

ARMS REDUCTION IN EUROPE AND THE PROBLEM OF NUCLEAR WEAPONS

by *Prof. Marian Dobrosielski*

On August 1, 1975, in Helsinki at the CSCE, leaders of 35 States from the east and west, north and south of Europe as well as from North America pledged to broaden, deepen and make continuing and lasting the policy of détente and cooperation. They emphasized also that the further consolidation of this policy demands marked progress in the area of military détente, i.e., on halting and abandoning the arms race and concluding concrete disarmament agreements, especially in the Vienna negotiations concerning Mutual Force Reductions in Central Europe. Regretfully, in the period that has elapsed since the Helsinki summit, major progress has not been accomplished in this sphere.

The arms race has become a global phenomenon and has reached absurd dimensions. According to UN statistics the world spends daily on armaments over 1,000 million dollars, or as much as the GNP of 65 countries of Latin America and Africa, or the total national income of countries whose population makes up more than half of mankind. Nearly 100 million people are linked, directly or indirectly, to military projects. Over 400 thousand highly qualified scientists and engineers are working to improve and multiply means of destruction, although the existing stockpiles would suffice to destroy completely—many times over—mankind and our entire planet. An equivalent of over 15 tons of TNT has been prepared for every inhabitant of our globe, and more than 60 tons for every person living in the Warsaw Treaty and NATO areas. If we realize that this vast quantitative and qualitative potential of human intelligence and energy, the enormous sums of money, the tremendous amounts of raw materials and other material resources are allotted and wasted for the purposes of devastation, destruction, annihilation of life and all cultural and civilizational heritage of mankind, at a time when the whole world, individual countries or continents, are facing urgent, unsolved and complex socio-economic and other problems demanding the concentration of all resources of intelligence, imagination and material means the world can afford, then I believe the word "absurd" used at the outset will not seem exaggerated.

Contrary to various Western "theories", attempting to prove that armaments and pursuance of the policy of strength safeguard peace best, the continuation of the arms race creates a serious danger of the outbreak of wars, including a global nuclear war. In the long run, détente, cooperation and peaceful coexistence cannot develop parallel to the arms race. If an end is not put to the arms race, then it will put an end to the policy of détente, international security, world peace. The checking and halting of the arms race is the most vital problem of the contemporary world—one which has to be solved as promptly as possible. This is the prerequisite for saving mankind from a nuclear holocaust, of maintaining and building a durable peace and international security.

The questions of disarmament are very difficult and complex. At the same time, they are too important and affect too much the life and prosperity of every man, wherever he might be living in the world, to leave them solely in the hands of experts and politicians. The world public opinion must be aware of the consequences and effects of the arms race and must do its utmost to bring about its discontinuation, pursuing concrete disarmament agreements and— in perspective—general and complete disarmament.

There is not enough imagination in the world to realize the destructive power of the existing supply of weapons, the terrible waste of human intelligence, energy and material resources allocated for the purposes of destruction. Nor is there full understanding of the creative potentialities of means furnished by science and technology for attaining man's age-old ideal—a world without wars, a world of peace, freedom, justice, dignity, prosperity for all societies and for every man.

Armaments have never before solved a single political, social, or economic problem and will never solve one in the future. Armaments only give rise to and fan mutual distrust. Despite this we are witnessing a steep increase in the process of militarization of the economy in non-socialist countries. "The working machinery of preparations for war, as Leonid Brezhnev said at the World Congress of Peace Forces in Moscow in October of 1973, poisons the political atmosphere in the world with fumes of hatred, fear, constraint. To justify its existence, myths are being invented about the 'Soviet threat', about the necessity of defending the so-called Western democracies. Militarism, however, is caressing—like a beloved child—reactionary, despotic, fascist régimes and devouring democratic freedoms". I mention this in order to demonstrate that the problem of the arms race and disarmament has not only military and economic implications and cannot be considered apart from its political, social, moral, psychological and other aspects.

The Problem of Nuclear Weapons

Throughout the millenia of man's history, wars and threats of war have frequently been regarded as "continuation of policy by other means". Nuclear weapons have created an entirely new situation. No positive political or any other aim can justify the use of these weapons. However—as Einstein apparently said after atomic bombs had been dropped on Hiroshima and Nagasaki—nuclear weapons have changed everything except our ways of thinking. Averting the threat of nuclear war is today the most burning, top-priority task of mankind.

The question of "theatre nuclear weapons" (TNW) reduction in Europe is an essential component of the overall effort to have military détente in Europe materialize. It is today more topical than ever before, since the development of technology has been obliterating the boundary line between those weapons and conventional weapons. Western strategic concepts, which favour a flexible use of TNW, aim at making nuclear war more thinkable and, in effect, more probable.

Already some twenty years ago, Poland submitted in the UN General Assembly a proposal for setting up an atom-free zone in Central Europe, combined with a reduction of conventional forces. Between 1958 and 1964 she modified her proposal many a time to render it acceptable to all parties concerned, limiting it to a freeze of nuclear armaments in Central Europe. The Polish initiative, which received full support from all socialist countries, aroused considerable interest and affected the thinking of many politicians and experts in various parts of the world. The firm opposition of the then FRG and US Governments prevented serious negotiations for putting these proposals into being. However, the initiatives had a profound effect on both theoretical thought in the area of arms control and disarmament and on international politics.

The notion of nuclear-free zones has today become a universal idea. This concept is contained in a number of international treaties concluded in the past dozen or so years, such as the Antarctic Treaty of 1959, the 1967 Treaty of Tlatelolco for Latin America, the 1967 Outer Space Treaty, the 1971 Sea-Bed Treaty. Some elements of the Polish denuclearization plans were utilized in the provisions of the Non-Proliferation Treaty of 1968. Meanwhile, a number of concrete proposals were made for setting up nuclear-weapon-free zones in various regions of the world: in the south (Balkans, Mediterranean Sea) and north (Kekkonen Plan) of Europe, in the Indian Ocean and South Pacific, in the Middle East, South Asia and Africa. Scientific circles (Pugwash) put forward ideas to create a European and, recently, also a global nuclear-weapon-free zone. In 1974 the UN General Assembly decided to carry out a comprehensive study of the question of nuclear-weapon-free zones in all of its aspects.

Reverting to Europe, it must be said that a number of elements of the Polish proposals of 1957–1964 have instigated concrete projects for mutual reduction of armed forces and armaments in Central Europe. It is a source of great satisfaction for us that for the first time we can note a major turn in the attitude of the USA and other NATO States, which, taking into consideration the socialist countries' position in the Vienna talks, have included in the Western reduction schemes a certain part of their TNW potential stationed in Central Europe. This is a weighty political fact although the way to achieve denuclearization of Central Europe, as provided for in the Polish plans, still seems long under the existing conditions. The current situation, however, in no way impairs the political and moral significance of the Polish initiatives. The plans remain one of the sources of inspiration for finding solutions to concrete problems of military détente in Europe.

The premise for realistic discussion of the question of reduction and gradual elimination of nuclear weapons from the territory of Europe is the concentration of efforts on solving priority problems which have already become the subject of exchange of views between governments:

— the proposal to conclude a treaty between the 35 States—signatories of the CSCE Final Act in which they would pledge not to use nuclear weapons as the first party;
— nuclear weapons reduction within the framework of agreements on mutual reduction of armed forces and armaments in Central Europe.

Theatre Nuclear Weapons

The question of the role of TNW in Europe is not only extremely complicated per se, but is also the axis of unending controversy even within NATO, not to mention the entirely different approach in the East and West. The situation is further complicated by the fact that both the NATO military doctrine and the vast Western literature on this subject present these problems, first and foremost, from the viewpoint of the West's military interests, from the angle of war confrontation with the socialist countries and the inevitability of using nuclear weapons. What is being overlooked is the situation which has taken shape in effect of political détente and the mutually agreed principles governing relations between the States participating in the CSCE.

We have recently noted an increased interest in the problem of TNW in Europe. Among the major sources of this phenomenon, mention is due to:

— the emergence of new trends in the arms race in Europe (combination of precision with destructive force and miniaturization of nuclear weapons);
— evolution of the US doctrine concerning the "threshold" on nuclear weapons' use in Europe;
— discussions on the question of TNW in East–West negotiations.

In pointing to the significance of the détente dialogue for solving the TNW problem, I adopt the optimistic assumption of the durable character of the process of détente. Without such an assumption, discussion would be useless since it would put us on the track of considerations: what to do in case of war? how to get ready for it? It would lead us to ponder over the ways of improving the bellicose postures, in which the problem of using nuclear weapons would be one of the central questions. This would be in contravention to the spirit and letter of the Final Act. It is therefore necessary to examine the present state and prospects for the solution of the TNW problem in the context of the indispensability of the further development of détente and cooperation in Europe, including active cooperation of States in the domain of military relations with a view to lowering the level of the arms stockpiled, the level of confrontation.

The actual state of affairs concerning TNW in Europe is rather well known, although evaluations are often controversial, incomplete, or even misleading. On the whole, the TNW question is considered from a qualitative, quantitative, definitional and doctrinal angle. The problem is in large measure approached statically in the sense of appraisal of the stockpiled potential and its destructive force. Recent SIPRI publications point to the dynamics of the long-term development of TNW in effect of combining new technological accomplishments in the area of precision of attack with the destructive force of nuclear explosives, warheads, bombs and mines of new types. More and more facts are being revealed, concerning "miniaturization" of nuclear weapons and the consequences of introduction by the USA in Europe of modified kinds of nuclear weapon systems.

The dissemination of publications showing the actual state in both quantitative-static and qualitative-dynamic terms plays an important part. We thereby receive a synthetic picture of the threat posed by TNW to European security and perceive better the lines of development of those weapons, which have to be counteracted.

A picture of disastrous consequences of the use of the nuclear arsenal stockpiled in Europe in the past 25 years can be found in the already classical studies: the report of the UN Secretary-General on the effects of nuclear weapons' proliferation, many publications by Soviet and US experts, the studies conducted under the guidance of Professor von Weizsäcker, the works of SIPRI and other institutes. The conclusions stemming from these studies are univocal: should only several hundreds of the over 13 thousand nuclear warheads stationed in Europe be used, which, according to some estimates, have a total force of 400 megatons (i.e., the destructive force of 20 thousand bombs dropped on Hiroshima) and a range of attack covering the whole Continent, Europe would cease to exist as a geopolitical and civilizational region. It is also believed that even a limited exchange of nuclear blows in Europe would result in direct and genetic destruction of many millions of people even in adjacent regions. Moreover, the conviction prevails that the use of TNW in Europe would irrevocably bring about escalation of the use of nuclear weapons on a strategic, and thus global scale. It is impossible to predict the end of such a conflict or envision which sanctuaries outside Europe would resist nuclear blows. This is perhaps why military circles are making desperate attempts to substantiate the advisability of using those weapons in smaller areas and demonstrate that both sides could tolerate losses within certain limits. The adoption of such a way of thinking is tantamount to embarking upon the road of global nuclear conflict.

It is difficult to resist the reflection that it was the West which initiated the introduction of TNW in Europe in the early 1950s and their subsequent stockpiling and improvement. The socialist countries naturally had to adopt appropriate steps to strengthen their defences. In doing so they retained a sense of restraint. In effect, the NATO nuclear theatre superiority over the Warsaw

Treaty countries—according to a majority of Western experts—is now 2 or 3 to 1, posing a serious menace to the socialist countries.

Definitional approaches to the TNW problem proceed along two lines: according to the traditional definition, the nuclear weapons maintained by the US in Europe were referred to as "tactical", a term intended to convey the idea of smaller destructive force, shorter range and limited combat applications in comparison with other kinds of nuclear weapons in the possession of the USA, Great Britain and France, and described as "strategic".

From the viewpoint of the socialist States, the nuclear weapons brought by the USA to Europe have never had tactical significance. They were operational or even strategic weapons. In fact, they transcended all imagination of tactical advantages. For example, by using "Pershing" missiles against the socialist countries, NATO units could cause destruction which, as seen by military experts from such countries as Poland, would wipe out most of our country's industrial and urban regions. In other words, TNW make possible the attainment of strategic military goals. The above reflections lead to the conclusion that TNW are, firstly, offensive weapons, secondly, weapons which transcend the boundaries of limited use and pose the inevitable danger of escalation of the conflict and, thirdly, weapons which are particularly conducive to the spread of nuclear weapon systems in contravention to the Non-Proliferation Treaty.

From a doctrinal viewpoint, TNW were introduced in Europe and later developed and improved by the NATO States in order to offset the alleged superiority of the USSR and the Warsaw Treaty States in conventional forces. They have been assigned the function of a deterrent supporting conventional capabilities.

The NATO political-military doctrine developed under the impact of "cold war" conditions. Its evolution from "massive retaliation" to "flexible response" and "forward defence" was based each time on false, cold-war-infected perceptions of the intentions of the USSR and the socialist countries. Our States were being constantly charged with aggressive intentions of assaulting Western Europe. The NATO military system was described as defensive, while the character of the armed forces of the socialist States was referred to as "offensive". Contrary to realities, the improvement and modernization of the NATO forces in every new generation of armaments was described as "necessary" in the face of the alleged threat on the part of the Warsaw Treaty. The continuing attempts at reviving the long-refuted myth about "communist aggression" serve only the acceleration of the arms race, poison the political atmosphere and thus diminish mutual security.

The West's doctrinal posture on military questions, including the TNW problem, fails to take notice of the progress made to date in the area of political relations on the European continent. This progress was possible owing to, among other things, the recognition of the nuclear-strategic parity between the USSR and the US and the equilibrium of military forces in East–West relations. However, the Western doctrine is based on the "inborn" hostility of the two parts of Europe. Inherent in this doctrine are political, formal and material contradictions, and, briefly speaking, it does not take account of the actually existing reality.

The conclusion of the US–USSR agreement on the preventing of a threat of nuclear conflict was the first harbinger of rejection also by the USA of the possibility of an armed conflict on our Continent. The US–USSR agreement and the Helsinki Final Act provide a good basis for establishing a developed system of safeguards for European security also in the military domain, including a gradual elimination of nuclear weapons from Europe. From a military point of view, TNW do not offer guarantees of security to any State. We have mentioned that their use could lead to the destruction of the whole Continent rather than to the defence of any European State.

It is being maintained that TNW possess an autonomous combat function. They are either to have a limiting effect on the conflict or to serve as a fuse for launching strategic weapons. Characteristic are the hesitations of Western strategists and experts in these matters. In 1971–1974 we saw attempts by US strategists to induce NATO to accept the concept of "counter-force" at the TNW level in Europe.

It is not fully clear what political, military-technical and doctrinal implications the implementation of such a concept would have. Widely known is the critical assessment of these plans by the French side, which fears another phase of subordination of the French forces to the NATO. On the other hand, there are pronouncements by FRG generals appealing for turning "mini-nukes" into conventional means of combat, whose use would not require the US President's decision.

The Pentagon's official posture seems to be oscillating between these two standpoints. It seeks to introduce new, "clean" and more precise means for nuclear attack. It speaks about a "selective" approach to targets, especially typically military ones, though allegedly raising the threshold of the TNW use. At the same time, it attempts to secure for the USA, the FRG and the other NATO States operations superiority by means of a whole spectrum of those weapons.

The dynamism of the development of TNW, demonstrated by SIPRI, should be credited, above all, to the armaments industries of the USA, Great Britain and, to some extent, France. It poses the threat of a new escalation of the arms race. In fact, technological continuance of TNW modernization in the territory of Europe may lead in the 1980s—according to Western experts—to abolishing the threshold distinguishing nuclear from conventional weapons. Diversification of TNW aggravates the asymmetry in the NATO and Warsaw Treaty armaments. This, in turn, makes comparisons and evaluation of the balance of forces difficult. Generally speaking, it is a direction which contradicts the trends of strengthening the sense of security in Europe. It also denies the concepts of arms sufficiency and limitation which lay at the root of the SALT and Vienna negotiations.

No-first Use of Nuclear Weapons

The initiative put forward by the Warsaw Treaty States in the autumn of 1976 to conclude a treaty between the 35 States participating in the CSCE on no-first use of nuclear weapons was discarded at the NATO ministerial session as aimed at consolidating the Warsaw Treaty's alleged superiority in conventional weapons. The session also referred to the existing prohibition of the use of force contained in the CSCE Final Act. Some speakers went so far as to say that the proposal of the Warsaw Treaty States was set forth for propaganda purposes before the Belgrade meeting.

None of these arguments holds the test of reality. Rather, they are an attempt, artificial and unthoughtful, at discrediting in the eyes of public opinion in the NATO States an initiative aimed at a real strengthening of the détente process and European security.

The introduction of the prohibition of the use of nuclear weapons as the first party in Europe would have a profound meaning as a step toward thinking in new political-military categories as regards the role of TNW in both the NATO and Warsaw Treaty States. Firstly, it would raise an international legal obstacle to the development by NATO militarist circles of erroneous and dangerous concepts of obliterating the boundary line between nuclear and conventional weapons. It would reduce to reasonable dimensions nuclear defence planning in NATO and the Warsaw Treaty, the dimensions adapted to the demands of peacetime. Secondly, it would be a significant act of political will to prevent a deeper division of Europe. The agreement would be a concretization of the UN Charter and Final Act provisions, especially of the principle of refraining from the threat or use of force, and would constitute an instrument of international law which imposes concrete restrictions on States possessing nuclear weapons. Thirdly, such an agreement would be a major political-moral obstacle to attempts at acquiring nuclear weapons by States which do not have them so far. It would provide a good incentive for concrete steps in the field of mutual reduction of armed forces and armaments in Europe, including nuclear weapons reduction and the implementation of the idea of regional denuclearized zones.

It should also be noted that the Bucharest proposal provoked contradictory reactions in government circles of the NATO States and among some segments of societies, including certain ruling parties in West European countries. Moreover we have welcomed the views of neutral States which assessed the rejection of the Warsaw Treaty's proposal as too hasty and unwise, badly substantiated and undermining the possibility of a rational East-West dialogue on nuclear weapons in the territory of Europe.

The differences of opinion in the West enable us to hope that the Warsaw Treaty's proposal will be re-examined by official authorities with greater insight. An encouragement for such reconsideration has been provided by Minister Gromyko's suggestion, made during the visit in Moscow of the Polish Minister of Foreign Affairs in January of 1977, to hold a conference or a series of meetings of the States concerned, with a view to carefully examining the proposal and concluding an agreement. This would be the right approach to the problems of military détente in Europe. It should be assumed that a number of controversies on a whole range of problems would be adjusted in the course of a frank dialogue between representatives of NATO, the Warsaw Treaty, and neutral and non-aligned States.

Mutual Reduction of Armed Forces and Armaments

The negotiations on mutual reduction of armed forces and armaments and associated measures in Central Europe have a set of strictly agreed principles (mutuality, equality, respect for the security of the parties, refraining from seeking unilateral advantages); a clearly defined objective (increase of the sense of security and stability); a definite subject-matter (armed forces and armaments reduction and related measures) and an agreed zone of future reductions in Central Europe (the territories of Poland, Czechoslovakia, the GDR as well as the FRG, Belgium, Holland and Luxembourg).

Each of the above understandings must apply not only to conventional, but also to nuclear weapons in Central Europe. This is the prerequisite of a real and effective reduction of the military potentials and of lowering the level of confrontation. By making the proposal of December 16, 1975 the NATO countries admitted that a future agreement should also encompass nuclear weapons reduction. They did so belatedly, to a minimum extent and putting many conditions, but they doubtlessly recognized in some measure the rightness of the position of the Warsaw Treaty States.

The socialist countries, ever since the submission of the draft "Agreement on Mutual Reduction of Armed Forces and Armaments in Central Europe" on November 8, 1973 have represented the view that the proposal for a 15 per cent reduction of all forces and armaments in the agreed region should embrace the same number and types of units armed with nuclear weapons.

On February 19, 1976 Poland, the USSR, Czechoslovakia and the GDR suggested a first stage agreement on reductions of US and Soviet forces, along with the specific quantities and kinds of nuclear weapons.

Such an agreement would be the first, but not the last measure. The second step should embrace more radical reductions with the participation of both the two big powers and the remaining States taking part in the Vienna negotiations. The socialist countries postulate the attainment of the 15 per cent. reduction of the ground and air forces in Central Europe by the end of 1978.

This programme encompasses substantial quantities of nuclear weapons and imposes post-reduction limits on the remaining ones.

An essential element of the socialist countries' plan is the proposed method of reduction—by whole units. Personnel is to be reduced along with armaments and military equipment. This leads to a simplification of the approach to the question of nuclear weapons reduction. For within the fixed quotas concrete units would be reduced, including units equipped with nuclear weapons. The units withdrawn from the reduction zone are to be disbanded, i.e., they cannot be moved as combat units to regions adjoining the zone.

As is known, the Western side has so far refused to accept this plan of compromise even for the first phase agreement.

The American proposal to reduce 56 US "Phantoms", 36

"Pershing" launchers and 1,000 nuclear warheads is contained within the whole of the Western scheme of asymmetric armed forces reduction. They are being offered as a "price" for the withdrawal of a 68-thousand-strong Soviet armoured army, 1,700 tanks and major types of its equipment, which—as specialists know—comprises a considerable amount of artillery rockets and air missiles capable of delivering nuclear warheads.

Moreover, the NATO proposal is conditioned by the postulate to fix the ceilings for NATO and Warsaw Treaty land and air forces at the level of 900 thousand soldiers, these ceilings being collective for the military blocs. Thus, it would be possible to increase some national forces even in the course of general reduction agreement.

The Western approach to reduction would permit a restructuring of the NATO potential, with the global ceilings being retained. This would permit not only an increase of the conventional combat strength, but also modernization of the nuclear potential, numerically smaller but more effective in terms of combat capabilities. In view of the present situation and possibilities, this would obviously involve, first of all, the armed forces and conventional weapons as well as nuclear delivery vehicles of the FRG. The socialist countries reject such reduction schemes as dangerous and as bringing unilateral advantages to the NATO States.

The search for compromise solutions is going on in Vienna. Comprehension of the problems essential for overcoming the differences in standpoints and attaining a reduction agreement is as important as it is time-consuming. Since the negotiations are taking place against the background of broader détente efforts, it can be hoped that the difficulties will be gradually eliminated.

Let us take a look at some of the basic difficulties that have to be settled. Problem number one, which determines further progress in negotiations, seems to be the question of evaluation of the force relation between the NATO and Warsaw Treaty States in Central Europe.

The Western side is constantly accusing the Warsaw Treaty States of having overwhelming superiority in ground forces, which expresses itself in the number of soldiers and basic combat tanks. The figures reported by the NATO delegations in December 1976 continue to be based on this thesis, indicating an alleged superiority by over 150 thousand soldiers on the Warsaw Treaty side. The socialist countries reported the strength of their forces in June of last year.

As of January 1, 1976 NATO had in Central Europe 791 thousand soldiers in land forces, while the Warsaw Treaty States had 805 thousand. The strength of the air forces is similar and, according to Western delegations, does not affect the equilibrium.

In view of the Western denials that there exists an approximate force equilibrium in Central Europe, the Vienna negotiations will have to focus on correcting the mistaken estimates of the Warsaw Treaty ground forces which appear in NATO declarations. Such a discussion will explain a lot and will be highly instructive also for solving the problem of mutual nuclear weapons reduction.

The second basic difficulty, directly related to the question of nuclear weapons reduction, lies in the attempts of the Western delegations in Vienna to exclude from future reduction agreements the nuclear delivery vehicles in the possession of the West European participants at the Vienna negotiations, and especially the FRG, Great Britain, Belgium and Holland.

These attempts meet with criticism by the socialist countries, since they assume that, while the US reduces a certain amount of nuclear weapons, the FRG will be able to replenish its stock of Pershing or Lance missiles, or delivery aircraft, taking advantage of the fact that no restrictions will be imposed in this field.

The posture of Poland and other socialist countries on this question is clear. The proportional reductions proposed by the socialist countries should eventually lead to an equal lowering of the conventional and nuclear potentials in the zone. Those who have more arms and forces must reduce proportionally more of them.

The third essential problem which gives rise to much difficulty in the Vienna negotiations is the question of comparability of the various types of units, arms and combat equipment. Practice has failed to furnish testable, adequate standards of conversion: a soldier for equipment, a tank for a nuclear warhead, a ground unit for an air force unit, etc.

Under such circumstances, the socialist countries' approach is more rational, being based on equal reduction quotas which should be made up of whole units together with their complete armament. In this way nuclear weapons would also be included. An annex to the reduction agreement will list the names of units, their strength and equipment.

As regards the socialist countries' offer of February 19, 1976, which provides for a compromise reduction of the US and USSR forces, including the above-mentioned numbers of American and Soviet nuclear delivery vehicles, the same quota and generation indices were applied to balance the offer.

This offer of the socialist countries in Vienna has never been treated by them as the last word. It was and remains an invitation to negotiate an agreement on an equal basis convenient for both sides.

I have presented only some of the difficulties, taken out of the context of complex problems which have to be solved in Vienna. Their solution would contribute toward reaching agreement on the most vital questions of security of every European nation. Also essential is understanding of the significance of the Vienna agreement on mutual reduction of armed forces and armaments in Central Europe as a model for more complex solutions on an all-European scale.

Further Problems

Going beyond the scope of the Vienna talks, mention should be made of two categories of problems: (1) attempts to take up the question of the so-called "TNW grey zone"[1] by including it in the SALT talks or the Vienna negotiations, or opening a third channel for talks; (2) efforts connected with the implementation of the concept of denuclearized zones in the various regions of Europe.

At the present stage, it is difficult to express views on the advisability of including some operational missile systems stationed outside the Central European zone in the subject-matter of the strategic arms limitation talks, or assigning this problem to the competence of the Vienna negotiations. The complexity of the problems to be coped with in each of the two channels of negotiations is so evident that it now seems most logical to avoid burdening them with additional aspects. In the long run, however, it may become necessary to take a closer look at these problems.

As regards the various proposals for setting up denuclearized zones in Northern Europe, in the Balkans and in the seas surrounding Europe, we greatly appreciate and have much sympathy for these projects. Poland extends far-going support to each of these proposals. We are also of the opinion that it is necessary to continue the work on general principles governing the establishment of denuclearized zones, since the experience in this field possessed by Europe can serve well the cause of strengthening international peace and security.

---

1. Types of nuclear weapons stationed outside Central Europe, which are not the subject of the SALT talks or the Vienna negotiations.

Chapter 6

THE VIENNA NEGOTIATIONS ON MUTUAL REDUCTION OF FORCES AND ARMAMENTS AND ASSOCIATED MEASURES IN CENTRAL EUROPE (MURFAAMCE)

by *Paul J.M. Teunissen*

Negotiations on arms control and disarmament in Europe have been conducted since the division of Germany became a fact.[1] However, up till the middle of the 1960s these negotiations were without any prospect of success.

During this period the West German Government made arms control and disarmament in Europe conditional on progress towards the reunification of Germany. This policy—which remained a corner-stone of West German foreign policy until 1966—was closely linked with the priority the West German Government gave to the inclusion of the Federal Republic in the system of Western cooperation and Western defence.[2]

Arms control did not start at the European level. The first steps towards it were set by the super powers, in their bilateral relations and at a world level: the Antarctica Treaty and, after the Cuba crisis of 1962, the "hot line", the partial test ban and the opening of negotiations on the non-proliferation treaty.

The years 1966–1968 were a period of transition, during which the ideas of peaceful coexistence, recognition of the territorial status quo, and arms control and disarmament became influential in Europe. Two main approaches to arms control and disarmament in Europe became opposed to each other:

— The Warsaw Pact approach, which aimed in particular at nuclear arms control and disarmament as well as elimination of the US presence in Europe. This had to be achieved within the framework of political arrangements for European security and

---

1. See: Heinrich Siegler, *Dokumentation zur Deutschlandfrage, Von der Atlantic Charta 1941 bis zur Berlin-Sperre 1961*, 2e Auflage, Bonn, 1961. Charles R. Planck, *Sicherheit in Europa, Die Vorschläge für Rüstungsbeschränkung und Abrüstung 1955–1965*, München, 1968.
2. Helga Haftendorn, *Abrüstungs — und Entspannungspolitik zwischen Sicherheitsbefriedigung und Friedenssicherung — Zur Aussenpolitik der BRD 1955–1973*, Düsseldorf, 1974, p. 29 ff. Charles R. Planck, op. cit., p. 15 ff., chapters II and IV.

recognition of the territorial status quo. In this context steps could also be taken towards conventional arms control and disarmament among European States, such as disarmament between the two German States. In view of the ongoing unilateral Western reductions and US troop withdrawals from Europe agreements on conventional disarmament were not a top priority to the Warsaw Pact, however.[3]

— The NATO approach, which mainly intended to counter unilateral Western force reductions and to maintain solidarity among the members of the alliance.[4] Force reductions had to be mutual; the existing balance of forces had to be maintained, but at a lower level.

To this end and to counter the Warsaw Pact countries' renewed drive for a European Security Conference, NATO countries launched the proposal for mutual and balanced force reductions.

Prelude to the Talks

On June 25, 1968 the Foreign Ministers and Representatives of countries participating in the NATO Defence Programme called for mutual and balanced force reductions, "particularly in Central Europe", stating *inter alia:* "Mutual reductions should represent a substantial and significant step, which will serve to maintain the present degree of security at reduced cost, but should not be such as to risk to destabilize the situation in Europe".[5] According to a preparatory study by the Federal Republic mutual reductions of stationed forces should amount to some 25 per cent.[6]

Initially the Warsaw Pact countries did not react to this NATO declaration. Apparently they did not feel inclined to help NATO in solving its internal problems. They continued to launch their appeals for a European security conference which was intended for the political scene in Europe and to establish conditions propitious to measures of arms control. The latter were to be achieved through specific agreements, not at the European security con-

   3. Yuri Kostko, "Military Détente in Europe: Concepts and Problems", in: *Instant Research on Peace and Violence*, 1/1977, p. 11 ff.
   4. Gerd Schmückle, "Die NATO-Strategie und die Truppenverminderungen. Eine Betrachtung über denkbare Entwicklungen im Westlichen Sicherheitssystem", in: *Europa-Archiv*, 1967, pp. 551–557. Helga Haftendorn, op. cit., p. 271 ff.
   5. *NATO Facts and Figures*, Brussels, 1971, p. 368.
   6. Helga Haftendorn, op. cit., p. 247.

ference itself, and not necessarily in a multilateral context. The Prague communiqué of October 1969, which contained the first formal agenda proposal for a European security conference, did not include the question of arms control.[7] However, for a number of reasons, this attitude of the Warsaw Pact changed gradually.

The NATO countries refused to participate in a conference on security and cooperation in Europe unless the Warsaw Pact proved ready to enter into negotiations on force reductions.[8]

NATO's MBFR proposals were modified and became more interesting to the Warsaw Pact. The NATO communiqué of Rome, May 1970, stated that "Reductions should include stationed and indigenous forces and their weapons systems in the area concerned".[9] There has been some difference of opinion on the meaning of the term "weapons systems" in this phrase. According to Lothar Ruehl[10] the Governments of Wilson and Brandt in Great Britain and West Germany had meant to include tactical nuclear weapons in this offer, but at that time the US were still against negotiating on nuclear weapons through MBFR. Thus the question had been left open. The same applied to NATO's air forces. But in fact the Warsaw Pact countries could claim that they had been given an argument to insist on the inclusion of nuclear weapons and air forces in negotiations on force reductions.

In June 1970 the Warsaw Pact answered that "a study of the question of reducing *foreign* armed forces on the territory of European States would serve the interests of détente and security in Europe". It could be discussed "in the body which it is proposed to set up at the all-European conference or in another manner acceptable to interested States".[11] The Warsaw Pact countries still wanted to separate arms control from the European security conference, while giving priority to the latter.

In 1971 both sides came somewhat closer to each other again. At the 24th Party Congress of the CPSU Secretary-General Brezhnev unfolded a six-point programme for peace, in connection with

---

7. Declaration of the Consultative Meeting of the Ministers of Foreign Affairs of the Warsaw Treaty Member States. Prague, October 30–31, 1969. *Survival:* December 1969.

8. Helga Haftendorn, op. cit., p. 316 ff.

9. *NATO Facts and Figures*, op. cit., p. 380.

10. Lothar Ruehl, "Die Wiener Verhandlungen über Truppenverminderung in Ost und West", in: *Europa-Archiv*, 1974, pp. 507–518, p. 514.

11. Warsaw Pact Memorandum. Budapest, June 21–22, 1970. *Survival:* September 1970.

SALT. It included among other things a conference of the five nuclear powers and a world disarmament conference. Furthermore Brezhnev stated: "We stand for the dismantling of foreign military bases. We stand for a reduction of armed forces and armaments in areas where military confrontation is especially dangerous, and above all in Central Europe".[12]

At that time Brezhnev's remarks went largely unnoticed by the public opinion in the West. But Western Governments asked further information: what forces and armaments were included in the Soviet proposals? Were reductions to be effected bilaterally or multilaterally? In his well-known speech in Tiflis, on May 14, 1971, Brezhnev still evaded these questions: "... we are perfectly ready to give the necessary clarification ... you should start negotiations".[13] On June 11, he affirmed that the Soviet Union was ready to negotiate on national as well as on foreign forces.[14]

According to US sources this Soviet readiness to enter into negotiations on force reductions in Europe had been obtained through a compromise in the preliminary SALT I agreement of May 1971, according to which only "some offensive strategic weapons" were to be included in a first SALT agreement.[15] Thus the Soviet Union was allowed to reduce her arrears in offensive strategic weapons with respect to the US. At the same time Soviet interest in these negotiations had been raised because the US—complying with a strong demand by their Western European allies—had excluded their nuclear weapons in Europe from SALT. Negotiations on arms control in Europe might open up additional perspectives to the Soviet Union.

From the Soviet point of view several reasons may have converged for this interest to enter into such negotiations. If the Soviet Union were to accept a ceiling for strategic weapons in SALT, such a ceiling had to be fixed at a level high enough to avoid the risk of a conflict leading to nuclear war with a third

---

12. *Keesing's Contemporary Archives*, 1971, p. 24656.
13. Rede des Generalsekretärs des ZK der Kommunistischen Partei der Sowjetunion Leonid Breshnjew, in Tiflis, zum 50. Jahrestag der Georgischen Sowjetrepublik, in: *Europa-Archiv*, 1971, p. D 348.
14. Rede des Generalsekretärs des ZK der Kommunistischen Partei der Sowjetunion, Leonid Breshnjew, auf einer Wahlkundgebung in Moskau, in: *Europa-Archiv*, 1971, p. D 354.
15. *Keesings Historisch Archief*, 1971, p. 390.

nuclear power or alliance.[16] A more general stabilization of political and military relations in areas directly bordering upon the Soviet Union was a corrolary interest. Moreover US senator Mansfield's proposal for a 50 per cent. reduction of American forces in Europe, together with West-European uneasiness about Soviet-American bilateralism, might induce the West European States to closer military cooperation, involving a central role for the military forces of Western Germany. The readiness of the Soviet Union to enter into negotiations may well have been spurred by these reasons, as is indicated, i.e., by the increased Soviet attention to the Bundeswehr since that time.

During the next two years a tug of war arose, because of East–West divergencies and lack of agreement among the NATO allies. — In May and June 1971 the US wanted to speed up negotiations. In the US calls for a withdrawal of forces from Europe were continuing. In Moscow ambassador Beam had obtained information that the Soviet Union was ready rapidly to start negotiations on "force reductions in Central Europe". Western European studies on reduction models were considered inadequate by US Secretary of Defence Laird, who announced more comprehensive US proposals.[17] But the Western European allies wanted a delay. They insisted on further clarification by the Soviet Union that negotiations were to aim at *balanced* reductions, including indigenous forces as well.[18] The West German Government, in particular, wanted the question of Berlin to be settled before any agreement on force reductions.

On June 11, Secretary-General Brezhnev declared that the Soviet Union was ready to negotiate on reductions of both stationed and national forces.

After the conclusion of the preliminary Four Power Agreement on Berlin, on September 3, 1971, Federal Chancellor Brandt paid a visit to Brezhnev at Oreanda. According to the communiqué both sides outlined their views on the question of "the reduction of armed forces and armaments in Europe without detriment to the

---

16. Paul H. Nitze, "Assuring Strategic Stability in an Era of Détente", in: *Foreign Affairs*, January 1976, p. 207 ff., pp. 216–217.

17. *Keesings Historisch Archief*, 1971, pp. 387, 388. See also: Helga Haftendorn, op. cit., p. 264 ff.

18. Final Communiqué of the Ministerial Meeting of the North Atlantic Council, 3rd and 4th June 1971, par. 13, in: *NATO Facts and Figures* op. cit., p. 391 ff.

participating States".[19] After his return home Brandt explained that this was to mean "balanced" reductions.[20] But the Western European allies reproached Brandt that he had consented—and without sufficient consultation of the NATO allies at that—to a formula which, according to the Soviet standpoint, implied symmetrical reductions, i.e., reductions by an equal percentage or by equal numbers.

— In October 1971 the NATO countries participating in the talks on force reductions appointed former Secretary-General Brosio as their common envoy to Moscow. This was both in order to start talks at an official level and to make an end to bilateralism in the East–West negotiations on this issue. Within NATO serious differences of opinion existed. The US preferred not to delay the negotiations until the questions of Berlin and the preparation of the Conference on Security and Cooperation in Europe would have been settled. They were sceptical, if not about the possibility of multilateral negotiations on reductions, then at least about the prospects of their leading to rapid results. The US were only ready to accept the NATO concept of phased reductions if the US forces were allowed to reduce first.

The Soviet Union refused to receive Brosio. At the end of January 1972 a forum of experts of Radio Moscow declared that negotiations on force reductions should not be conducted on a bloc to bloc basis; "balanced" reductions should be rejected; negotiations on force reductions had to be kept apart from the European security conference.

— In May 1972 the US and the Soviet Union agreed on a package deal, within the framework of SALT I. The American–Soviet

---

19. *Keesing's Contemporary Archives*, 1971, p. 24857.

According to West German Government sources four "common elements" existed in the West German and Soviet views:

(1) In any negotiations on disarmament not only the "super-Powers" should be involved but other countries as well.

(2) In an eventual agreement not only forces stationed on foreign territory should be taken into consideration but also national forces.

(3) Disengagement should be carried out over a wider area than that of the two Germanies.

(4) The balance of power should be maintained. (This point was alluded to in the communiqué as reduction "without detriment to the participating States").

The second common element was mistakably seen by Brandt as a new Soviet concession; in reality this concession had been made in Brezhnev's speech of June 11, 1971.

20. *Europa-Archiv*, 1971, pp. D 473, 474.

communiqué announced that a "conference on security and cooperation in Europe" was to take place "without undue delay"; negotiations on a "reciprocal reduction of armed forces and armaments, first of all in Central Europe", were to take place "in a special forum". "Any agreement on this question should not diminish the security of any of the sides".[21] Soviet expert Y. Kostko published an extensive comment in which he rejected "balanced" or "asymmetrical" reductions. "Arguments about 'military inequality' in the spheres of conventional forces ... do not stand up to criticism". The balance of conventional forces could not be separated from that of nuclear forces, the regional balance in Central Europe was part of the all-European and global balances. He rejected the relevance of the argument that NATO was dependent on forces from the US. The Soviet Union was confronted with a similar problem. She had not only to maintain troops on her Western frontier, but in the south and the east as well. The distances to be covered on their transport to Europe exceeded those between the US and Western Europe.[22]

At the NATO Council of May 30 and 31, 1972 the Western European NATO allies stressed that President Nixon had not been their spokesman in Moscow. He was criticized for having accepted the principle of peaceful coexistence, while shortly before he had insisted that the Western European allies should not make this concession to the Soviet Union. Disappointment existed that the American–Soviet communiqué did not speak of "balanced" force reductions. It was not clear which countries were to take part in the negotiations. The Scandinavian and the Mediterranean NATO countries feared that they would be kept out. They insisted on non-circumvention measures in order to secure themselves against Soviet troop replacements towards their borders. It was agreed that negotiations on force reductions had to take place before or parallel with CSCE, as political détente was considered impossible without military détente. Reductions in Central Europe should not diminish security in other parts of Europe.

— From June 1972 on the Soviet Union urged France to take part in the negotiations on force reductions. The French Government stuck to its refusal, however. The formal argument was that France was opposed to any bloc to bloc negotiations. In reality the French Government was concerned that force reductions in Europe would

---

21. *Keesing's Contemporary Archives*, 1972, p. 25315.
22. See: *Force Reductions in Europe*, SIPRI, Stockholm, 1974, pp. 56–60.

weaken the security of Western Europe. This French refusal made the Warsaw Pact countries continue to insist on priority for CSCE.
— In September 1972 Dr. Kissinger, on a visit to Moscow, succeeded in fixing a time-schedule for both CSCE and MFR with the Soviet leaders. The preliminary negotiations of CSCE were to begin on November 22, 1972; those of MFR on January 30, 1973. CSCE was to be opened at the end of June 1973, MFR not later than October 1973. This agreement once again revealed to what extent East–West relations were dominated by US–Soviet bilateralism.
— The last phase before the opening of the preliminary MFR negotiations was marked by mutual confusion and manoeuvring.

On October 23, 1972 the NATO allies agreed on the question of participants and observers to the negotiations. Participants were to be the States having forces in the reductions area. On the side of NATO: the US, Canada, Great Britain, West Germany, the Benelux countries. The Northern and the Southern flank countries were each as a group to be represented by one observer, to be appointed on a rotation basis. In particular the Federal Republic insisted that the negotiations should concentrate on Central Europe. The flank countries gave in to this position. On November 15 the participating NATO countries sent invitations to the Soviet Union, Poland, the GDR, Czechoslovakia and Hungary to open negotiations on January 31, 1973. Again complications arose. On a visit to Hungary, from November 27 to December 2, 1972, Brezhnev discussed the problem of force reductions. He declared that "the sovereign rights and interests of the States concerned" had to be respected.

On January 11 and 12, 1973, Brezhnev and Pompidou had talks at Minsk. Notwithstanding very strong insistence by Brezhnev Pompidou remained opposed to French participation in MFR. Instead he complained that the Soviet Union kept France insufficiently informed about American–Soviet negotiations, which were of vital interest to Europe. In this respect Pompidou referred to the data scheme for CSCE and MFR, fixed by the US and the Soviet Union. This was in contradiction to earlier agreements between France and the Soviet Union and to Soviet practice before SALT I.

The Soviet reaction was outspoken. On January 18 the Warsaw Pact declared that MFR negotiations should not take place in Geneva but in Vienna. They should not be conducted on a bloc to bloc basis and had to be open to all European States having a "justified interest" in participation. Romania and Bulgaria made it known that they refused to be excluded from the negotiations.

According to press sources the US induced the Western European NATO allies to give in. The negotiations were moved to Vienna. Romania and Bulgaria were allowed to be present at the preliminary talks, as well as all NATO flank countries. During the talks the question of participation by all interested European States was to be discussed.

On January 31, the preliminary talks were opened. No agreement existed on the agenda and the participants in the negotiations. It was decided to adjourn the plenary meeting until these problems had been solved. The Warsaw Pact delegates removed indications in the conference room that the negotiations were dealing with mutual and *balanced* force reductions. The plenary meeting was resumed on May 14.

Preliminary Talks

These talks fell into two periods. The first one lasted from January 31 up till and including May 14. During this period the question of participants and observers was dealt with.

The Soviet Union made known that Hungary refused to be a participant. On the other hand the Soviet Union wanted to keep open the possibility of—at least partial—French participation. Romania wanted to be a full participant.

On May 14 a partial solution was agreed upon. Full participants were to be: the US, Canada, Great Britain, West Germany, the Benelux countries; the Soviet Union, Poland, the GDR, Czechoslovakia. By the consensus of all full participants other States could be included in decisions on general as well as specific reduction measures.

Observers ("participants with a special status") were to be: all flank countries of NATO as well as Romania and Bulgaria. No agreement was reached on Hungary. According to the Warsaw Pact countries Hungary could only consider participation in possible agreements "if the appropriate conditions are fulfilled". According to official explanations this meant: if Italy was made a full participant too.[23] But NATO excluded full participation by Italy. On the other hand it stressed that the question of the status of

---

23. Italy is adjacent to Yugoslavia and the Balkan area; US nuclear weapons are stationed on its territory. These factors may explain the Soviet standpoint.

Hungary remained open. During the second period, from May 15 up to and including June 28, the basic goals and principles of the negotiations were treated. Again no definitive result was reached.

According to the final communiqué the negotiations were to deal with "mutual reduction of forces and armaments and associated measures in Central Europe". The general objective of the negotiations was "to contribute to a more stable relationship and to the strengthening of peace and security in Europe". Reductions had to be "carefully worked out in scope and timing in such a way that they will in all respects and at every point conform to the principle of undiminished security for each party".

No agreement was reached on an agenda for the negotiations.

In a press statement on the final communiqué Jhr Mr. B.E. Quarles van Ufford, leader of the Dutch delegation and spokesman of the NATO participants, declared that "the elements of the NATO concept of 'balanced' are satisfactorily covered in the communiqué agreed today, and we would also say that there is a substantial measure of agreement between the two sides as regards the underlying content of the 'balance' concept, even though the Eastern authorities have been unwilling to accept the word itself".[24] He explained that "in our view the term 'balanced' comprehends the ideas that any future measure should be reciprocal, should provide for enhanced stability at a lower level of forces, and should not diminish the security of any party". Furthermore he referred to the communiqué of the NATO Council in Copenhagen, on June 15, which spoke of "practical arrangements which ensure undiminished security for all parties at a lower level of forces in Central Europe".

It should be noted, however, that the Copenhagen communiqué—due to differences of opinion between the US and the Western European allies—did not speak of reductions leading to "enhanced stability at a lower level of forces", i.e., to asymmetrical reductions. From the Warsaw Pact side Quarles van Ufford's interpretation of the communiqué was rejected. The forthcoming negotiations were to bring the existing balance of forces to a lower level, with "undiminished security" for all parties; reductions should be symmetrical, i.e., in equal numbers or percentages for both sides.

---

24. Press statement on final communiqué by Ambassador Quarles van Ufford, June 28, 1973, pp. 4, 5.

In the matter of this debate on the principles of reduction it is relevant to note that the NATO participants had accepted, if not introduced, the concept of "undiminished security". In the NATO declaration of May 1970 it was stated that "mutual force reductions should ... not operate to the military disadvantage of either side, having regard to the differences arising from geographical and other considerations".[25] This was a formula of "undiminished security", with some vague reservations. NATO's conceptions of "differences arising from geographical and other considerations could be challenged by those of the Warsaw Pact, as was made clear by Y. Kostko. This was the more so since even at the time of the beginning of the preliminary negotiations the NATO participants had not yet been able to agree on elaborate plans and principles of reduction. This was notably pointed out by President Nixon in his report on US Foreign Policy for the 1970s, of May 3, 1973, published two weeks before the second round of the preliminary MFR talks in Vienna, which was to deal with the principles of reduction: "We will need an unprecedented degree of unity on fundamental military and political security questions"[26] ..."The Alliance is committed to 'undiminished security' in the MBFR process, but we must agree on what this means in concrete terms".[27] On proportionately equal reductions he stated: "This appears to be a simple but equitable approach. If applied to all forces, however, it could create an imbalance because it would favour the offence and because of the geographical advantages of the Warsaw Pact".[28] The implications *a contrario* were unmistakable: proportional reductions could be acceptable to the US if only a part of NATO's forces—e.g., the US forces in Europe—were concerned, or if additional measures were taken to restrict potentially offensive movements or deployments of forces by both sides.

Nixon's report analysed various reduction methods and gave some general indications on the reduction proposals which the US at that time presented to their NATO allies; afterwards they were leaked through the press.[29] These proposals have been of essential

---

25. See: "Final communiqué of the ministerial meeting of the North Atlantic Council, May 26th and 27th, 1970, Declaration on Mutual and Balanced Force Reductions", par. 3, in: *NATO Facts and Figures*, 1971, p. 377 ff., p. 380.

26. *US Foreign Policy for the 1970s, Shaping a Durable Peace*. A Report To The Congress by Richard Nixon, President of the United States, May 3, 1973, p. 90.

27. *Ibidem*, p. 206.

28. *Ibidem*, p. 205.

29. See, e.g., the Dutch newspaper *NRC Handelsblad* of June 8, 1973, pp. 1 and 5.

significance to the further development of the MFR negotiations. They provided reductions in two phases. In the first phase foreign (non-European) forces were to reduce, in the second phase the national (European) forces. Three options were offered:

(1) Under certain circumstances the non-European forces might reduce symmetrically while the European forces were to reduce asymmetrically. This was to depend among other things on the possibility of agreement on associated measures, notably on constraints with respect to movements and deployment of forces.
(2) A second option implied asymmetrical reductions by the non-European, as well as the European forces.
(3) According to the third option the West would be ready to exchange tactical nuclear weapons against offensive potential of the Warsaw Pact (tanks, preponderance in ground forces). The US Government indicated that this option would probably meet with interest by the side of the Warsaw Pact countries.

Clearly the US did not in all circumstances insist on asymmetrical reductions; they had created an option on proportionately equal reductions between the two super powers. Dr. Kissinger is reported to have expressed his doubts about the preference for asymmetrical conventional reductions among the Western European allies. But in the majority the Western European allies stuck to their position. Equally they rejected the inclusion of tactical nuclear weapons in the negotiations, at least for the time being. The communiqué of the NATO Council in Copenhagen, on June 14 and 15, 1973, was nebulous: "it will be the aim of the Allied Governments concerned, bearing in mind the indivisibility of the security of the Alliance, to secure step to step practical arrangements which ensure undiminished security for all parties at a lower level of forces in Central Europe. The readiness of the Warsaw Pact countries to contribute to balanced results would, together with a successful outcome of the parallel negotiations in CSCE open the way to a more fruitful and stable relationship in Europe.[30] Surely this was more of an invitation to the Warsaw Pact, than a strict demand of balanced reductions.

The American proposals to NATO were part of a broader policy. In June 1973 indications were given that the US might include their Forward Based Systems in the negotiations on SALT

---

30. *Keesing's Contemporary Archives*, 1973, p. 25969.

II.[31] With the tactical nuclear weapons *stricto sensu* included in MFR the whole American nuclear arsenal would be covered by East–West negotiations on arms control. In order to strengthen the political basis of SALT the two superpowers concluded the Agreement on the Prevention of Nuclear War of June 22, 1973. Both sides were to refrain from aggression against each other as well as against their respective allies; they were to prevent situations that might endanger international peace and security; in case the danger of nuclear war would arise, either between the two sides directly, or between one of them and a third nuclear power, they were to enter into urgent consultations in order to remove this danger.

In Western Europe fears arose that in case of a war in Europe the US would not only refrain from a first use of nuclear weapons, but also resist a possible first use of Western European (French, British) nuclear weapons. But didn't this announce the end of NATO? The French Government opposed the agreement in the most outspoken way. Hadn't Kissinger in the foregoing month of April—without prior consultation—announced "the year of Europe" and called for a new Atlantic Charter? What exactly did US foreign policy aim at? Kissinger explained that in case of war the agreement did no longer apply. At the end of June 1973 Brezhnev visited Pompidou in order to explain personally the intention of the superpowers to prevent a nuclear holocaust. But scepsis remained among the US allies.

In May 1973 Lothar Ruehl had pointed out that on the question of force reductions no more than a formal agreement existed between the US and their allies. It was agreed that there should be MBFR negotiations, but no agreement existed on common reduction proposals. However, the US no longer wanted to remain the nucleus of the defence of Western Europe now that the European Community was becoming stronger. Western European governments were in doubt about the real meaning of SALT. If it was the beginning of a real partnership between the US and the Soviet Union, Western Europe would have less reason to fear Soviet power. But if no partnership was to come about, the American forces in Europe would be the more important, or they would have to be replaced by a Western European deterrent.[32]

---

31. See a.o.: "Ein neues Jalta in Washington?", in: *Die Zeit*, 29. Juni 1973, p. 3.
32. Lothar Ruehl. "Beiderseitige Truppenverminderungen in Europa. Grundlagen, Möglichkeiten und Grenzen von MBFR-Verhandlungen", in: *Europa-Archiv*, 1973, pp. 325–340.

The NATO allies worked out a compromise, as usual. The Atlantic Declaration of June 1974 stated that "while ... a major aim of their policies is to seek agreements that will reduce the risk of war, they also state that such agreements will not limit their freedom to use all force at their disposal for the common defence in case of armed attack". The strategic relationship between the two superpowers had become one of parity: "The Alliance problems in the defence of Europe have thus assumed a different and more distinct character". In view of this the French and British nuclear forces were declared to be "capable of a deterrent role of their own contributing to the overall strengthening of the deterrence of the Alliance".[33]

In the matter of mutual force reductions a compromise between the interests of the allies was also effected.

Initial Proposals: the Warsaw Pact Draft-agreement

The MFR negotiations were opened on October 30, 1973. During the first round both sides presented their proposals. The Warsaw Pact submitted a draft treaty, dated November 8, 1973. Its contents have in essence been made known by the Bulgarian party organ *Rabotnitchesko Delo*.[34] It is summarized below.

Article 1. The participating States on both sides reduce by equal numbers and percentages without detriment to the security of any of the contracting parties.

Article 2. The ground forces, as well as the air forces, are to be reduced, including their nuclear weapons; they are to be reduced along with an equivalent part of their armament and other equipment.

— In 1975 a first reduction of 20,000 men on each side, along with their armament and other equipment.

— In 1976 on each side a reduction of 5 per cent. of the remaining strengths.

— In 1977 on each side a further reduction of 10 per cent.

33. *Keesing's Contemporary Archives*, 1974, pp. 26607, 26608.
34. *Rabotnitschesko Delo* of March 3, 1974. See: Lothar Ruehl, "Die Wiener Verhandlungen über Truppenverminderung in Ost und West", op. cit., p. 511 ff. Lothar Ruehl, "The Negotiations on Force Reductions in Central Europe", in: *NATO Review*, October 1976. Gerhard Wettig, *Frieden und Sicherheit in Europa*, Stuttgart-Degerloch, 1975, p. 176 ff.

Article 3. The reductions will be put into effect by the withdrawal of whole units including their armament and other equipment.

The equality of reductions on both sides is to be ensured by the approximate similarity in weapons and types of units.

The units to be reduced, along with their armament and equipment, will be listed in a supplementary protocol which constitutes an integral part of the agreement. They will be specified down to the level of battalions and squadrons.

Article 4. The foreign units to be reduced will have to be withdrawn from the reductions area to their national territories, along with their armament and other equipment. They are not allowed to leave stores in the reductions area.

Article 5. The units of national forces which are to be reduced have to be disbanded, their personnel demobilized, their armament and other equipment decommissioned. Their replacement by other units is not allowed.

Article 6. Regulates the definition of the size, structure, armament and equipment of all remaining national and foreign forces in the reductions area. These forces are equally to be listed in the supplementary protocol.

Exchanges of forces, armament and equipment are free, provided they are for routine purposes and do not exceed the agreed force levels.

Article 7. Provides among other things consultations among the contracting parties for the execution of their obligations, as well as a verification conference. All parties to the treaty have the right to demand that the conference be convoked.

Article 8. No party to the treaty is allowed to enter into international obligations that are contrary to the present treaty.

Article 10. Refers to Article 102 of the UN Charter concerning the registration of treaties by the UN Secretariat.

Although both sides have developed their standpoint in later proposals they have not essentially moved from their original positions. Therefore an analysis of them remains relevant.

The Warsaw Pact draft treaty represents a comprehensive approach in two respects. The reductions agreement should comprehend all forces, armaments and equipment in the reductions area. All obligations of all participants should be specified from the outset. This precludes the need of renewed negotiations for each successive stage. Furthermore all participants are to take part in each stage of the reductions.

The proposed reductions amount to about 15 per cent. of the

total strength on each side. This may seem rational from the point of view of reducing "overarmament".

According to the IISS Western estimates[35] the combined strength of the ground and air forces of NATO in the reductions area was 1,010,000 men, while that of the Warsaw Pact was 1,100,000 men. Calculated on this basis the Warsaw Pact proposals would lead to the following new force levels: NATO 841,500 men; Warsaw Pact 918,000 men. NATO's ground forces would have to be reduced from 777,000 men to 644,000; those of the Warsaw Pact from 925,000 men to 775,000. The US forces in Central Europe would have to be reduced from 193,000 men to 161,000 ($= -32,000$); the Soviet troops from 460,000 men to 382,000 ($= -78,000$).

Foreign troops would have to be withdrawn along with their armament and equipment. This would conflict with NATO's system of the dual basing of overseas forces[36] which is considered essential to the rapid reinforcement of NATO in case of a crisis or armed conflict. The Soviet Union would have to withdraw her forces, armament and equipment by no more than some 600–700 kms. They could be brought back in a few days, by land or air transport; all necessary transports would take place on friendly territory. NATO's reinforcements would have to cross the Atlantic Ocean or the Atlantic airspace. These lines of communication have become highly vulnerable in time of crisis or war, in view of the changing balance between the US and Soviet maritime and air forces.[37] Article 5, too, is considered to imply a disadvantage to NATO. While the Soviet Union would only have to withdraw 15 per cent. of her forces, armaments and other equipment from the reductions area to her adjacent national territory, her main Western European counterpart, the FRG would have to *curtail* her forces by the same percentage, i.e., by about 75,000 men.

The Western European countries in particular have underlined from the beginning that asymmetrical reductions would contractualize the existing imbalance in ground forces and would be to the disadvantage of the weaker party, i.e., NATO. They might cost

---

35. *The Military Balance 1975–1976*, The International Institute for Strategic Studies 1975, p. 102.

36. The US have $2\frac{1}{2}$ divisions earmarked for NATO with heavy equipment stockpiled in West Germany.

37. See a.o.: *Strategic Survey 1976*, The International Institute for Strategic Studies, London, 1977, p. 1 ff. *West German White Paper on Defence* 1975/1976, p. 30 ff.

the alliance too many troops in absolute numbers. It has been estimated that NATO needs at least about 700,000 ground troops for a coherent defence of the central front line.[38] A second argument in this context was formulated by Ambassador Quarles van Ufford: "if one side has an advantage of 150,000 men and 9,500 tanks, as the East has, and if reductions are calculated on the basis of this present relationship of forces, as the East would have us do, then the existing margin in favour of the East is not only maintained, it is augmented. This is because a smaller number of NATO forces are spread more thinly over the same area against a potential adversary who retains the same margin of superiority and who could pick and choose the point where he could use his tank preponderance against that thin line".[39] These arguments are probably also used in order to conceal a more complicated problem. NATO's forces in the reductions area are less combat ready and have less equipment than those of the Warsaw Pact. This holds, in particular, true for the forces of the Benelux countries. Disbanding combat ready units and decommissioning their armament and equipment would oblige NATO to do away with a number of its best trained and equipped units and with badly needed material. NATO has insisted that it should be allowed to reduce by individual soldiers and that it should not be obliged to decommission material. This would enable the alliance to effectuate a military reorganization concomitant to force reductions. In this context NATO would like to thin out logistic units and to reinforce combat units. Furthermore logistic functions could be committed to civilian personnel.[40]

Articles 3 and 6 taken together imply that on both sides the defence structures in the reductions area would be fixed to a very high extent. This would pose no particular problems to the Warsaw Pact, which has already a highly integrated military organization. But NATO's military organization needs to adapt to the realities of the actual balance of forces between East and West, which demand

---

38. General Ulrich de Maizière, *Rational deployment of forces on the central front*, Assembly of Western European Union, Document 663, 2nd April 1975, p. 41.

39. Press briefing by Ambassador Quarles van Ufford, January 14, 1974, pp. 2, 3. According to the Warsaw Pact proposal NATO's ground forces would be reduced from 777,000 to 644,000; the Warsaw Pact superiority would be reduced from 150,000 to 133,000.

40. Yuri Kostko, *Military Détente in Europe*, op. cit., p. 20, criticizes NATO for this replacement of military personnel by civilians, as it would undermine the objective of arms control in Europe.

a stronger emphasis on conventional forces. NATO wants to reform command structures and to eliminate problems of maldeployment of forces and armaments. It wants to be free to effectuate a specialization in tasks among the allies, a redivision of the defence burden within the alliance (either between the US and Western Europe, or among Western European allies), a change of the ratio between ground and air forces. The Western European allies maintain an option to develop further defence cooperation. According to the Warsaw Pact draft treaty such measures would be excluded or become dependent on Warsaw Pact consent. In fact both sides would obtain a *droit de regard* on the defence organization of their counterpart. But which side would be in the best position to make this right effective? NATO's military organization is notorious for its intractability. A Warsaw Pact's right to intervene in it would further complicate matters. Article 6 forbids both sides to exceed the agreed force ceilings, even if only temporarily, for manoeuvres and other routine activities. This would constitute a particular handicap to NATO, as it would impede exercises including reinforcements from oversea. Units and material could only be replaced after their withdrawal from the reductions area. NATO would like to allow temporary routine exceedings with advance notification.

Fixation of the total number of nuclear weapons in the reductions area might complicate future Western European nuclear defence cooperation. French nuclear weapons could only be deployed in the Western reductions area after the withdrawal of an equal number of US nuclear weapons. Surely the FRG would try to avoid this security dilemma.

The draft treaty does not provide nuclear-free zones or areas in Central Europe,[41] neither measures concerning the no first use of nuclear weapons. However, on November 26, 1976, the Warsaw Pact countries called upon all signatory parties to the Helsinki Declaration to adopt a treaty obligating them not to be the first to use nuclear weapons against each other, either on land, on sea, in the air or in the cosmic space. This would include France, but exclude China.

---

41. It is not altogether clear to what extent the Warsaw Pact advocates the idea of nuclear free zones in Central Europe. During the CCD meeting in Geneva, in the beginning of 1975, the Polish delegate stated that "the establishment of such a zone has to reconcile many interests and resolve a host of political, military and technical difficulties". The Warsaw Pact forces themselves have been trained and organized for fighting a nuclear as well as a conventional war in Europe.

From the outset the Warsaw Pact countries have been very averse to associated measures other than in the field of verification. Even in this respect the draft treaty provides only a verification conference. The absence of any further mutual verification measures is a serious handicap for the control of smaller reductions or minor exceedings of the agreed ceilings. In the long run it will undermine the treaty.

Initial NATO Proposals

The NATO participants did not accept the Warsaw Pact draft treaty. On November 22, 1973 they presented their own proposal, which was in fact more a set of general guidelines than a concretely elaborated plan;[42] it was elaborate mainly as far as the first stage of reductions was concerned. Notwithstanding very intensive preparatory studies—dating back to 1967—which had resulted in 25 reduction models, the NATO participants had achieved no more than a limited agreement. The US wanted MFR to lead to at least some rapid results. They were ready to negotiate on symmetrical reductions, as far as their own part was concerned, and could even accept the reductions percentage of 15 which had been proposed by the Warsaw Pact. In July 1973 the US Government had persuaded the Federal Republic to stay out of the first stage of reductions as it would complicate the negotiations. The Western European participants continued to insist on balanced reductions; they considered the first stage of reductions an experimental one, during which the intentions of the Warsaw Pact had to be clarified. As a result of the partly converging, partly diverging, views NATO's two-stage reductions proposal emerged.

1. In the first stage the US and the Soviet Union were to withdraw 15 per cent. of their ground forces in the reductions area. According to Western estimates the US were to withdraw 29,000 troops, the Soviet Union 68,000. The US were to be allowed to reduce by thinning out individual soldiers from their logistic forces, the Soviet Union would have to withdraw one tank army, including 1,700 tanks.

   This first reduction would have to be arranged in a separate agreement. It would have to include associated measures,

---

42. Statement by Ambassador Quarles van Ufford, October 31, 1973, pp. 8–10. "Declaration by US Ambassador Stanley R. Resor on October 30, 1973", in: James F. Sattler, *MBFR, its origins and perspectives*, Atlantic Treaty Organization.

consisting of constraints with respect to potentially offensive troop movements and deployments, non-circumvention clauses and adequate verification measures.
2. After this first stage had been implemented and mutual confidence established negotiations were to be opened on a second stage of reductions, in which European forces were to be reduced.[43] This stage was to lead to a common collective ceiling of about 700,000 troops each for NATO and the Warsaw Pact. To NATO this would mean an additional reduction of 48,000 men, to the Warsaw Pact a further reduction of 157,000 men.

NATO's reductions plan was by and large based on the first option of the reductions plans which the US had presented to the NATO allies in June 1973. There were some asymmetrical elements in the proposed first stage of reductions, however. The Soviet Union would have to withdraw a tank army, i.e., to withdraw a complete unit with 1,700 tanks.[44] The US were to be allowed to withdraw individual soldiers from logistic units, without armament and equipment.

The plan clearly deviated from the NATO declaration of Rome, May 1970, as well as the conclusions of the preliminary MFR negotiations, in that only reductions of Soviet material were demanded. NATO felt quantitatively inferior in armaments and its qualitative lead was shrinking. The alliance felt a need to reallocate matériel and to maintain the logistic infrastructure for the dual basing of overseas forces ($2\frac{1}{2}$ US divisions). No air forces were included in the plan, nor nuclear weapons. The Western European allies wanted to refrain from any measure which might impair NATO's air power and nuclear deterrence in a period in which the balance of forces in Europe was changing in favour of the Soviet Union.

NATO's common collective ceiling plan implied that in fact

43. NATO's guidelines keep open the possibility of additional US reductions in the second stage. Such reductions would underline the principle of asymmetrical reductions.

44. In the course of the negotiations the NATO participants have specified this proposal by demanding the withdrawal of the 1st Soviet tank army in the region Dresden-Cottbus. This is the only Soviet tank army deployed west of the Soviet Union. See: Lothar Ruehl, "Die Wiener Verhandlungen über einen Truppenabbau", *Europa Archiv*, 1977, pp. 399–409, p. 400. Ruehl points at Soviet criticism that NATO is demanding withdrawal of the strongest and most modern equipped Soviet unit. He is sceptical as to whether NATO will be able to carry this claim through, at least in this form.

national ceilings were imposed on the ground forces of the two superpowers in the reductions area, as well as on the number of Soviet tanks. For these were to be reduced on a national basis during the first stage. The European participants were to reduce on a collective basis and consequently not to be bound by national ceilings.

The NATO plan was based on the philosophy that MFR had to contribute to enhanced stability in Europe by eliminating existing imbalances in ground forces and by such constraints with respect to troop movements and deployments as to exclude the possibility of military surprise action.[45] Both sides had to renounce the capacity, as well as the opportunity, for surprise and offensive military action and thus virtually to preclude a war in Europe. This approach was clearly different from the Warsaw Pact proposal of arms control through symmetrical reductions of forces and armaments.

For the same reasons NATO insisted on non-circumvention measures. NATO was not only interested in preventing a redeployment of Warsaw Pact forces close to the borders of the flank countries, but in particular in non-circumvention measures with respect to Hungary. Hungary borders on the reductions area. At the same time it occupies a central position in the Warsaw Pact area and it is also bordering on Yugoslavia and Romania. It can serve as a basis for offensive military action against Western Europe and the southern flank of NATO. In 1973 Soviet military aid to the Arab States went via Hungary and the Yugoslavian airspace. The effects of reductions in Central Europe would be undermined very seriously if the Warsaw Pact were allowed to reinforce its troops and armaments in this country. At least a redeployment of Soviet forces or a deployment of new Soviet forces would have to be excluded. This implies that in fact Hungary would have to participate in a ceiling agreement.

Further Course of the Negotiations

At present 12 rounds of negotiations have taken place. They can roughly be divided into three periods:
Rounds 1–6: no agreement on reductions, neither on freeze.
Rounds 7–8: vain efforts to achieve a breakthrough.
Rounds 9–12: debate on data concerning force levels.

---

45. In this context the confidence-building measures should also be taken into account. These measures have a more limited significance, however. They do not forbid the movement of forces and are on a voluntary basis.

The main developments of the negotiations can be summarized as follows:[46]

From the very outset the Warsaw Pact countries have criticized the NATO proposal on the grounds that it was based on the principle of asymmetrical reductions; that reductions of matériel, air forces and nuclear weapons were excluded, with the exception of Soviet tanks; that NATO was allowed to reduce by individual soldiers, even of logistic forces, while the Soviet Union was to withdraw a tank army; that the system of collective ceilings would allow the Federal Republic to develop the Bundeswehr into the most powerful army in Europe, while the Soviet troops in the reductions area (allegedly 460,000) had to be reduced by 15 per cent.; that each stage of reductions required special negotiations and a separate treaty: after the Soviet Union had withdrawn her tank army during the first stage, negotiations on the second stage had to begin, with an uncertain outcome; in the meantime the conventional balance of forces could shift in favour of the Federal Republic, while France and Great Britain could concentrate their defence efforts on nuclear armaments.

In the course of 1974 and 1975 the NATO participants accepted links between the two reduction stages. Negotiations on the second stage should begin within a fixed time span (18 months) after agreement had been reached on the first stage. In the meantime both sides were to freeze their overall levels of active duty military personnel in the reductions area, air forces as well as ground forces. In the second stage all European participants were to participate in the reductions. The first stage agreement might be reviewed if within a given time span no agreement would be reached on the second stage.

Although NATO rejected national ceilings it was ready to give assurance to the Warsaw Pact that the Bundeswehr would clearly remain below the level of 700,000 ground troops. In fact NATO was willing to accept a certain conception of national ceilings on an intra-alliance basis, but not formally binding with respect to the

---

46. For this analysis the present writer has in particular drawn from the press conferences by the spokesmen of NATO and the Warsaw Pact as well as from: Lothar Ruehl, "Die Wiener Verhandlungen über Truppenverminderung in Ost und West", op. cit.; Idem, "Die Wiener Verhandlungen über einen Truppenabbau", op. cit.; Idem, "The Negotiations on Force Reductions in Central Europe", in: *NATO Review*, October 1976, pp. 18–25. Alfons Pawelczyk, "Möglichkeiten eines Streitkräfte-Abbaus in Europa. Grundpositionen und Bewegungen in den Wiener MBFR-Gesprächen", in: *Europa-Archiv*, 1977, pp. 41–47.

Warsaw Pact. NATO's "national ceilings" would be established within the framework of its common defence concept.

Because of the controversies on the reduction proposals the Warsaw Pact presented some proposals for a weapons freeze.

The first proposal was worked out in the course of 1974 and presented on October 31 of that year. Both sides should reduce by 20,000 men as a symbolic first step, committing themselves to further reductions. It was not explicitly stated that reductions should be in units. A two-stage element was built in in that the Soviet Union and the US were to reduce first, 10,000 men each. Subsequently the FRG and Poland were to reduce by 5,000 men each, while the other participants on both sides would each as a group reduce by 5,000 men.[47]

This proposal was rejected by NATO because it came down to acceptance of symmetric reductions, codification of the existing imbalance in ground forces between NATO and the Warsaw Pact as well as national ceilings.

On December 5, 1974 the Warsaw Pact countries proposed a freeze without any prior reductions. This was rejected by NATO in the beginning of 1975. The NATO participants declared that they could not know what the Warsaw Pact implied materially, as the Warsaw Pact refused any discussion on force levels before an agreement on the principles of reduction had been reached. According to NATO's own estimates the proposal would codify an existing imbalance in ground forces.

During the 5th and 6th round the two sides engaged in a discussion on the definition of ground and air forces. This served to give them more insight into the criteria on the basis of which the reduction proposals had been drafted, to clarify the position of nuclear weapons systems, etc. However, this discussion could not bridge the fundamental antagonisms. In the summer of 1975 it was generally felt that the negotiations were in an impasse.[48]

The most important development on the Western side was NATO's offer of December 16, 1975.

---

47. In connection with this proposal the Warsaw Pact adapted its original reductions proposal of November 1973 in the beginning of 1975.

In the first stage the participants were to reduce as set out above in the text. In the second stage (5 per cent. reductions) the US and the Soviet Union were to reduce in the first half of the year, the other participants in the second half. In the third stage all participants were to reduce at the same time.

48. See press briefing by Ambassador De Vos van Steenwijk on July 17, 1975, p. 1.

In the first place it included an additional offer to NATO's original proposal for the first stage: additionally the US would withdraw 1,000 nuclear warheads, 54 Phantom combat aircraft and 36 Pershing weapons systems.

A 900,000 men combined collective common ceiling would be acceptable for both ground and air forces. This would include the 700,000 men ceiling for the ground troops. Both sides would be free to increase their air force personnel in the reductions area, but only at the expense of their ground forces.

With this offer NATO shifted from the first to the third option of the US proposals of June 1973. Although it has been stated that no specific meaning should be attributed to the numbers of the proposed reductions it should be noted that 1,000 nuclear warheads represent about 15 per cent. of the total of US nuclear warheads in Europe and a somewhat higher percentage of the nuclear warheads in the Western reductions area.[49]

By this offer NATO tried to make asymmetrical reductions more acceptable to the Warsaw Pact. Now NATO would have to reduce 110,000 men (about 11 per cent.), the Warsaw Pact 200,000 men (about 18 per cent.). According to NATO's original proposal NATO would only have had to reduce 10 per cent. of its ground forces in the reductions area, the Warsaw Pact 25 per cent. The NATO offer was based on three conditions:

— That the Warsaw Pact would accept asymmetrical reductions of the ground forces within the reductions area to a collective common ceiling of 700,000 men.
— That the Warsaw Pact would accept NATO's two-phase concept.
— That the Warsaw Pact would withdraw a complete tank army, including 1,700 tanks, in exchange for a withdrawal of 29,000 US soldiers (NATO's original offer for the first stage).

NATO's offer was a one-time offer, to be accepted or rejected, but the alliance did not set a time-limit. This could imply that the alliance might further develop its proposal when the Warsaw Pact gave a sufficiently positive response without accepting NATO's offer as such.

The NATO offer should be seen in the context of the new US policy with respect to nuclear weapons in Europe since the Schlesinger report, which aimed at a thinning out of the US

---

49. See: Jeffrey Record, *US Nuclear Weapons in Europe*, The Brookings Institution, Washington, 1974, p. 19 ff.*

nuclear arsenal in Europe by withdrawing the heavier TNW's as well as those deployed in forward positions.[50] NATO's offer also served Western European efforts to prevent a unilateral withdrawal of the weapons concerned. The means of delivery (Phantom combat aircraft, Pershing weapons systems) belonged to the most powerful ones of NATO, the Forward Based Systems, which are able to reach the territory of the Soviet Union. The Soviet Union has always insisted on the inclusion of these weapons in SALT. But the Western European allies have opposed this. On their insistence the US kept the FBS out of the SALT agreement of Wladiwostok (1974).[51] At the same time the Western European allies refused to include these weapons in MFR, since they stood averse to anything which might be interpreted as a weakening of the strategic part of NATO's nuclear deterrent. This policy had become hazardous, however, because the Soviet Union continued to press the US for negotiations on the FBS.

NATO's offer had the twofold effect of corroborating the exclusion of FBS from SALT and strengthening the link between MFR and SALT. This was considered an advantage to the Western European NATO partners; now they participated again in the strategic dialogue between the two super powers.

In principle NATO's offer could have been strengthened by a non-circumvention clause excluding the introduction of any nuclear weapons above the ceiling to be agreed on into the reductions area. This would restrict possibilities for future Western European nuclear defence cooperation. Such restriction would be in the line of Dutch foreign policy. However, up till now, the majority of Western European governments, in particular that of West Germany, have rejected any measures to this effect. In their opinion MFR should not prejudice Western European inte-

---

50. *The Theater Nuclear Force Posture in Europe, A Report to the US Congress*, Washington, 1975 (unclassified version).

51. "Throughout the SALT Two negotiations, our negotiators strove for the following objectives:
— One, to achieve a ceiling on the number of total delivery vehicles.
— Second, to achieve a ceiling on the number of MIRV'ed delivery vehicles.
— Third, to have these ceilings equal.
— Fourth, not to count forward-based systems.
— Fifth, not to count the British and French nuclear forces.
— Sixth, not to give compensation to any other geographic factors."
See: Secretary Kissinger's News Conference of December 7, 1974, in: *The Department of State Bulletin*, December 30, 1974, p. 910.

gration.[52] In his press conference of April 8, 1976, the Western spokesman, Ambassador De Vos van Steenwijk, made it clear that the NATO participants were only ready to accept a non-circumvention clause excluding the introduction of new *US* nuclear weapons above the ceiling to be agreed on. The offer did not include Western European aircraft and nuclear delivery systems. Formally this could be based on the argument that in the first stage only the US and the Soviet Union were to reduce. But NATO spokesmen have made clear that the Western European participants refuse to reduce their air forces. At best they will freeze their air force personnel, or accept a combined collective ceiling of 900,000 men for both ground and air forces. In view of deficiencies in its military organization (lack of mobilization capacity, maldeployment of forces and matériel, etc.) NATO is highly dependent on its air forces from the very beginning of combat operations. Reductions of Western European aircraft would accentuate an asymmetry with respect to Warsaw Pact air forces from outside the reductions area. Soviet air forces deployed on national territory could reach Central Europe within half an hour.[53] Moreover, Western Europe is developing cooperation for the production of military aircraft (MRCA, etc.). This would be hampered by ceilings for air force matériel in the reductions area.

Contrary to expectations that had been raised unofficially the Warsaw Pact participants did not accept the NATO offer of December 1975, although it met with "appreciation" in Warsaw Pact circles.[54] Western commentators supposed that NATO's offer had been insufficient, since NATO could have reduced 1,000 nuclear warheads anyhow, even unilaterally. Reference was made to a study by the Brookings Institution, which had come to the conclusion that some 2,000 TNW's or even a few hundreds, would suffice for NATO's nuclear deterrent.[55]

However, this interpretation was not supported by the comments of Ambassador Dabrowa in his press conference of January 30, 1976. Dabrowa explained the position of the Warsaw Pact by declaring that the Pact participants stuck to two demands: reductions should be symmetrical and should not only have to

52. Statement by Ambassador Quarles van Ufford, October 31, 1971, p. 10.
53. Press conference by Ambassador De Vos van Steenwijk, April 15, 1977, Questions and Answers, p. 16.
54. Press statement by Ambassador Dr. Slawomir Dabrowa, January 30, 1976, in particular p. 4.
55. Jeffrey Record, *US Nuclear Weapons in Europe*, op. cit.

include troops, but armaments and equipment as well; all obligations of all participants should be defined from the outset, before any reductions were to take place.[56] Thus a NATO offer would also have to include aircraft and nuclear weapons and delivery systems in the hands of the Western European participants. In any case any increase of these had to be excluded.

This position of the Warsaw Pact countries was again confirmed by the Warsaw Pact proposal of February 19, 1976. This offer was presented as a supplementary proposal to the draft agreement of November 8, 1973.

— In 1976 the US and the Soviet Union would reduce their forces in the reductions area by 2 to 3 per cent. of the total personnel strength of the respective alliances in the reductions area. Both participants would further reduce by 300 tanks, one Army Corps headquarters, 54 nuclear capable F-4 equalling SU 17/20 A and C combat aircraft, 36 Pershing equalling Scud B missile systems. Furthermore: the customary conventional and nuclear armament of those units, including ground to air defence systems, in particular an unspecified number of Nike-Hercules equalling SAM-2 air defence systems.

In 1977 both sides would not increase their forces in the reductions area.

In 1978 the European forces would be reduced by 2 to 3 per cent. of the total forces of the alliances in the reductions area.

— Reductions would be effected in complete units, including their armaments and equipment.

— All reduced units, those of the US and the Soviet Union included, would be disbanded and their armaments and equipment decommissioned. However, the US and the Soviet Union would be allowed to add the personnel of their withdrawn and disbanded units to existing units outside the reductions area.

— National ceilings would have to be fixed in the reductions area. With this proposal the Warsaw Pact accepted to a large extent the NATO concept of two-stage reductions, with reductions by the superpowers in the first stage, reductions by the European participants in the second stage and a mutual freeze of forces between the two stages. More specifically the Warsaw Pact accepted some of the numbers of aircraft and nuclear weapons systems of the NATO offer of December 1975.

---

56. Press statement by Ambassador Dr. Slawomir Dabrowa, January 30, 1976, p. 2.

For each stage of reductions a special agreement was to be concluded, but in fact the second agreement was essentially contained in the first one, as the Warsaw countries stuck to their demand of prior definition of all reduction obligations by all participants. They equally stuck to the principle of symmetrical reductions with the inclusion of all forces and armaments in the reductions area. The formula "2 to 3 per cent. of the total number of forces in the reductions area" implied in fact that the level of reductions of all participants would be about the same as that of the draft treaty of November 1973: 13–15 per cent.

NATO rejected this proposal as it insisted on symmetrical reductions. According to Western sources[57] the proposal was unfavourable to NATO in some specific respects. A reduction of 300 tanks would mean a 5 per cent. reduction to NATO (official estimate of tanks: 6,000), as opposed to a 2 per cent. reduction to the Warsaw Pact (on the basis of 15,500 estimated tanks).

A reduction of 54 tactical aircraft would mean a 47 per cent. reduction by the US, since they have 114 nuclear capable F-4s in the reductions area. To the Soviet Union it would mean a 17 per cent. reduction, since she possesses 270 to 280 combat aircraft of the SU 17/20 Fitter type in the reductions area, and about 320 other nuclear-capable tactical aircraft.

The proposed reduction of aeroplanes would be qualitatively unequal. The F-4 is estimated to have a much longer range and more than double the combat weight (and thus about double the carrying capacity and throw-weight) of its Soviet counterpart.

The proposed reduction of missiles would be less unbalanced, since the US have 108 Pershing weapons systems in the reductions area and the Soviet forces 120 Scud launchers.

A final question with respect to the Warsaw Pact proposal is, that it is not clear how US and Soviet armaments and equipment could effectively be decommissioned after their withdrawal as long as both super powers reject any ceilings to the levels of armament and equipment on their national territory and on allied territory outside the reductions area.

On June 10, 1976 the Warsaw Pact participants presented data on their force levels in the reductions area, in reaction to continuous criticism from the West: 987,300 men, of which 805,000

---

57. See: Lothar Ruehl, "The Negotiations on Force Reductions in Europe", op. cit., p. 24. The Warsaw Pact proposal underlined the principle of symmetrical reductions in that Soviet aircraft and missiles were offered in reply, although these had not been demanded in NATO's proposal of December 1975.

ground forces. Thus in their opinion approximate parity did already exist between the forces on both sides, and the debate on symmetrical versus asymmetrical reductions was by and large irrelevant. The NATO participants were invited to review their data. The revised Western data were presented towards the end of the 10th round. According to these NATO had 791,000 ground forces in the reductions area, the Warsaw Pact 962,000. The air forces had already been estimated by NATO in 1976: on both sides about 200,000 men. According to its own data the Warsaw Pact had 182,300.[58]

Interim assessment

At the time of writing this (October 1977) no agreement appears as yet to be in sight, although negotiations are likely to go on. It may be useful, therefore, to make an interim assessment with respect to: areas where some progress has been made; areas where disagreement persists; and underlying differences as between the NATO and Warsaw Pact members' approach to the negotiations.

Progress first of all has been made towards solving the question that MFR should be one operation, in which the obligations of all participants are defined in advance. NATO has been ready to link the reduction stages. The time interval between the first stage and the beginning of negotiations on the second should not exceed 18 months. The parties reducing in the first stage should be allowed to review their positions if within a given time-span no agreement on the second phase would be reached. In the second stage all European participants would be included in the reductions. Between the two stages the European ground forces and air forces personnel would be frozen. The European ground forces would be frozen for five years.[59]

The Warsaw Pact countries insist that all reduction obligations of all participants should be defined in advance. But in their proposal of February 19, 1976 they have to some extent accepted NATO's concept of two-stage reductions, with a freeze of forces in between.

NATO participants furthermore have suggested unilaterally to establish—within the framework of NATO's common defence

58. See: Lothar Ruehl: "Die Wiener Verhandlungen über einen Truppenabbau", op. cit.; Press Statement by Soviet Delegation Spokesman, July 21, 1977; Press statement by Ambassador De Vos van Steenwijk, July 21, 1977, Questions and Answers, p. 10.
59. See: Alfons Pawelczyk, op. cit., p. 45.

system—national ceilings which could be made known to the other side. Thus the Bundeswehr would remain substantially below the total ceiling to be allowed to NATO. NATO participants also have proposed to include nuclear weapons and air forces in the negotiations. The number of nuclear weapons offered surely falls within the terms of the Warsaw Pact's reduction principles. US Phantom aeroplanes and Pershing weapons systems have been offered for reduction. Western European participants are willing to freeze their air force personnel and US nuclear weapons; they refuse to reduce or freeze air force matériel and to renounce their option on conventional and nuclear defence cooperation. However, the Warsaw Pact insists on a freeze of Western European air force matériel.

Warsaw Pact participants finally have presented data on their force levels. This has enabled an East–West discussion on a better definition of the military balance in Europe.

Progress in these areas, however, has not yet produced any substantial agreement, mainly because of the persistent disagreement on two crucial issues: the one of symmetrical versus asymmetrical reductions; and the other one pertaining to the method of reductions. NATO participants continue to favour reductions of numbers of troops coupled with selective reductions of matériel. Warsaw Pact participants continue to favour reductions of units together with their armaments and equipment. Differences with respect to the so-called associated measures (constraints, non-circumvention measures, verification problems) have so far hardly been discussed.

The underlying approach to negotiations also continues to differ. NATO's principal objectives are to redress military relations in Europe in such a way that each side no longer has the capability to undertake surprise military action or to gain substantial military advantage in the case of an armed conflict. By renouncing these capabilities, the risk of war in Europe would become remote, if not practically excluded. To these ends the conventional balance in Europe should be one of approximate parity. It would have to be embedded in a network of cooperative measures, such as several associated measures, confidence-building measures and measures towards further East–West cooperation in general (the latter two being part of CSCE). The Warsaw Pact's principal objective is to leave the existing balance essentially as it stands. Both sides should reduce their military strength by equal numbers and percentages. No further cooperative measures, aiming at structural changes in East–West relations, are envisaged.

At first sight NATO's proposals may seem clearly superior from the point of view of promoting military stability in Europe, but they have their weak sides as well. According to NATO's most recent data NATO would have to reduce by 91,000 ground troops (11.5 per cent.), the Warsaw Pact 262,000 (27.2 per cent.). This claim is not easy to carry through, even when in the interest of peace. NATO would be less sensitive to the conventional preponderance of the Warsaw Pact if the alliance were better organized; if less mutual distrust existed among the Western allies about their alliance solidarity. The Warsaw Pact's superiority of 170,000 men would be less potentially destabilizing and NATO would be less dependent on warning time, constraints and confidence-building measures, if the alliance had a more effective mobilization potential in Western Europe that would eliminate its problems of maldeployment.

Furthermore two imbalances in favour of NATO should be taken into account. The more NATO's and the Warsaw Pact's forces are made equal in numbers, the more NATO may try to take advantage of its capacities to maintain a technological lead in the arms race. Although this capacity has been dwindling in the past decennia is still exists. This has become clear among other things by the recent development of precision-guided weapons and cruise missiles.[60] Furthermore, any reduction of the risk of war in Europe through measures of arms control and disarmament will strengthen the political and economic position of the Western world vis-à-vis the Warsaw Pact. The more the West feels secure from military action by the Warsaw Pact, the more it can tighten up its conditions for political, economic and cultural cooperation.

Given the inaptitude of the Soviet Union bureaucratic mind to accept cooperation and openness in matters of security and defence, arms-control may pose serious political problems to the Soviet system, thus evoking new East–West tensions. NATO might therefore do well to display moderation in pursuing its arms-control objectives.

Some Broader Considerations (1): Differing Perspectives on Security

For an analysis of the broader strategic context of the MFR negotiations it is useful to start with the perspective of the two super powers on arms control. In the 1960s, when East–West

60. See, e.g., Western European Union: Symposium on a European Armaments Policy, Paris, March 3 and 4, 1977.

détente set in, arms control could still be considered in a mainly bipolar context. When SALT and MFR got under way it became clear that this was no longer the case. Both superpowers wanted to see SALT in the context of a world that had become multipolar; to the Soviet leadership in particular arms control had become a multipolar problem. This Soviet view was notably exposed in the reports of Secretary-General Brezhnev to the 24th and 25th Party Congresses of the CPSU. The Soviet Union feels first of all confronted by the US. But in a second order of magnitude a number of other threats pose themselves to her: NATO with its theatre nuclear weapons and Forward Based Systems, the nuclear forces of Great Britain, France and China, the danger of a nuclear confrontation in the Middle East (detonated perhaps by Israel), the future military potentials of Japan and India. The Soviet Union feels surrounded by inimical powers, with the danger of nuclear war looming at her from all sides.

In reaction the Soviet leaders have developed a concentric peace policy. This aims in the first place at a more stable strategic relationship with the US. In the second place it seeks to limit all third nuclear powers or alliances, because these can destabilize a strategic equation between the two superpowers. To this end the Soviet Union has launched her appeals for a world disarmament conference and a special conference of the five nuclear powers. In connection with this she has been propagating international treaties banning the use of nuclear weapons.[61] Furthermore she has been pursuing regional security arrangements: for Europe, the Middle East and South-East Asia. To the Soviet Union a halt of the global arms race is a precondition to her being able to agree on a strategic balance with the US. On the US side a similar view has existed with respect to China.[62] Thus it was convened in the SALT I agreements that: "each Party shall, in exercising its national sovereignty, have the right to withdraw from this [Interim Agreement] [Treaty] if it decides that extraordinary developments

---

61. Wolfgang Heisenberg, "Verbot des Ersteinsatzes von Kernwaffen: Fesselung oder Entfesselung des modernen Krieges?", in: *Europa-Archiv*, 1974, pp. 729–737.

62. In December 1970 US Ambassador G. Smith declared that the US and the Soviet Union were to reconsider the strategic situation when China would become a strategic threat to the US. "In this respect we foresee that every SALT agreement will contain a clause of periodical reappraisal of the strategic situation". Quoted from: Michel Tatu, *Le Triangle Washington–Moscou–Peking et les deux Europe(s)*, Paris, 1972, pp. 63, 64.

related to [its] subject-matter have jeopardized its supreme interest".[63]

In the meantime it has become clear that both superpowers stand highly ambiguous regarding arms control and to equality as the basis for arms control agreements. The Nixon–Kissinger administration had great difficulty to make the US Congress, the Pentagon and the NATO allies accept the principle of strategic parity with the Soviet Union. The desire to maintain at least a qualitative lead is persistent. At his first press conference, on February 8, 1977, President Carter reassured his audience that the US nuclear forces were superior to those of the Soviet Union.[64] For her part the Soviet Union feels faced with the necessity that in an all-out war she will not only have to withstand the US, but the US allies and China as well. She wants to be able to match not only any single opponent, but any combination of opponents as well. In this way Soviet strategic thinking has become similar to that of the US as exposed by McNamara in 1966. But isn't this the same as striving for superiority? Experts are divided on this question.[65] Soviet security policy is based on the primacy of the principle of peaceful coexistence, which means that war at the inter-state level should be avoided. But if a war should break out the Soviet Union would have to win, or at least to obtain a relative advantage. In the 1970s the Soviet Union has built up the potential and organization for a Blitzkrieg type of war enabling her to force a rapid decision. She should be able either to outmanoeuvre NATO at the conventional level, leaving minimal time to the US President to consider the possibility of resort to nuclear weapons, or to decide a nuclear conflict in Europe to her advantage, with a minimal risk of

---

63. Art. VIII Interim Agreement on Certain Measures with respect to the Limitation of Strategic Offensive Arms, Article XV, ABM Treaty. Arms Control and Disarmament Agreements. US/ACDA Washington DC., 1975.

64. See: President Carter's News Conference of February 8, 1977, in: *The Department of State Bulletin*, February 28, 1977, p. 158.

65. Paul H. Nitze, op. cit., supports the thesis that the Soviet Union aims at strategic superiority. In the same sense: Clarence A. Robinson Jr., "Soviets Grasping Strategic Lead" in: *Aviation Week and Space Technology*, August 30, 1976. An opposite view has been given by Les Aspin, "How To Look at the Soviet–American Balance", in: *Foreign Policy*, Number 22, pp. 96–107. See also: Rede des Amerikanischen *Verteidigungsministers*, Robert McNamara, vor der American Society of Newspaper Editors am 18 Mai 1966 in Montreal, in: *Europa Archiv*, 1966, p. D 325.

escalation to the strategic level by the US.[66] Rapid decisions would also reduce the risk of a war on two or more flanks.

Essential to the Soviet negotiating posture in MFR has been that her military preponderance and offensive potential should be preserved. The existing balance of forces in Europe should not be changed, but brought down to a somewhat lower level. For it is this balance which is to her the guarantee of peace and the political status quo in Europe.

In the opinion of the Western European governments this Soviet military policy has been far from comforting. Since the end of the 1950s the position of Western Europe has changed fundamentally. The Soviet Union has indisputably become the dominant military power on the Euro-Asiatic Continent. The US nuclear guarantee has been weakened because the US have become vulnerable to Soviet nuclear weapons. Until the beginning of the 1970s the position of NATO was weakened furthermore by unilateral US force reductions and continuous calls in the US Senate for further reductions.

For these reasons the attitude of the NATO allies to MFR was also ambivalent. To the US Government MFR negotiations were not only an instrument of arms control, but also a means to reduce pressures at home for further unilateral troop withdrawals and to exert pressure on the Western European allies to increase their defence efforts.[67] In the same way the Western European participants considered MFR equally, if not more, a framework of negotiations to maintain the security of Western Europe in a period of rapidly changing strategic relationships. It was the Western European participants who insisted most on asymmetrical reductions, associated measures, a common ceiling for the European participants and no-prejudication of future Western European defence cooperation. They wanted to redress the conventional balance and leave aside—at least initially—the air forces and nuclear weapons. NATO's air forces and nuclear deterrent had to

66. See: *United States Military Posture for FY 1978*, By Chairman of the Joint Chiefs of Staff, General George S. Brown, USAF, p. 37. Steven Canby, "The Alliance and Europe: Part IV, Military Doctrine and Technology", *Adelphi Papers* No. 109, p. 9 ff. A.A.. Sidorenko, "The Offensive, Moscow, 1970" published under the auspices of the USAF in the series *Soviet Military Thought*.

67. *The Defense Monitor*, Washington D.C., December 1975, p. 3, quotes Louis Michael, Director of the Defense Department's MBFR Task Force: "Essentially, we are ... applying MBFR, or participation in MBFR, in support of the basic objectives ... namely, strengthening of our conventional defenses, and getting our Allies to do more in terms of supporting their share of the burden".

be kept intact; Western Europe had to keep open the option to build up a strategic deterrent of her own now that the US were forced to reduce their role in the world.

The Western European participants have been able to stick to their position because from 1973 on the pressures for unilateral US troop withdrawals ceased and NATO's solidarity was strengthened again. The oil embargo of 1973 and the increase of oil prices by OPEC changed the balance of payments problem between the US and Western Europe and made an end to intra-alliance disputes on the division of the defence burden. During the subsequent negotiations in the UN, UNCTAD and CIES on a new international economic order the Western countries became aware of their interdependence in the economic field. In particular the FRG proved to be a close ally of the US. In NATO the idea that a stronger conventional defence was both necessary and possible was given new impulses.[68] Reinforcement programmes were effectuated and France decided to co-ordinate her defence with NATO's forward defence.[69]

Some Broader Considerations (2): the Continuing Strategic Arms Race

At the same time it has become clear that the strategic arms race has been continuing with the problems of SALT and the "Eurostrategic balance"[70] complicating each other. During the SALT I negotiations the Soviet Union wanted to extend the object of the negotiations as much as possible by including NATO's nuclear weapons—at least the Forward Based Systems—and those of Great Britain and France. This was rejected by the Western powers, in particular by the Western European NATO allies.[71]

---

68. The possibility and necessity of an adequate conventional defense for NATO has been underlined in recent years by the studies of Steven Canby and by the US Secretaries of Defense Schlesinger and Rumsfield in their annual reports. See also R.O. Lawrence and J. Record, *US Force Structure in NATO*, the Brookings Institution, Washington 1974. Leon Sloss, "NATO Reform: Prospects and Priorities", *The Washington Papers*, No. 30, London, 1975.

69. See: Lothar Ruehl, "Ansätze zu einer Revision der Strategie und des militärpolitischen Konzepts Frankreichs", in: *Europa-Archiv*, 1976, pp. 767–779. "Zur Revision der französischen Verteidigungskonzeption", in: *Europa-Archiv*, 1976, pp. D 655–D 664.

70. See also: Richard Burt, "The SS-20 and the Eurostrategic balance", in: *The World Today*, February 1977, pp. 43–51.

71. See: *The Department of State Bulletin*, July 3, 1972, p. 14.

This rejection was motivated with the argument that the Soviet Union refused to include her intermediate range (Euro-strategic) nuclear weapons in SALT, on the ground that these were not strategic weapons in the sense of SALT. In reality France and Great Britain rejected negotiations with respect to their nuclear forces; NATO wanted to preserve the strategic part of its nuclear weapons. In the SALT I agreements the problem could be dealt with more or less implicitly in that the Soviet Union was allowed a numerical superiority in ICBM's and SLBM's.[72] This quantitative difference was officially motivated with the qualitative lead of the US, but one could argue as well that in the long run the Soviet Union would arrive at a more or less equal technological level with the US, so that the quantitative differences would become more important.

This more or less "Atlantic" SALT I posture of the US Government was rejected by the US Senate, however. In September 1972 the Senate in fact rejected the SALT I agreements by adopting the Jackson amendment, according to which the US Government had to ensure equality in levels of strategic armaments in future SALT negotiations. As a consequence the Soviet Union continued her efforts to include the nuclear weapons of NATO, Great Britain and France in arms control negotiations. By mid 1973 the US appeared to be willing to meet some Soviet demands, by including NATO's theatre nuclear weapons in MFR (option III) and inclusion of the Forward Based Systems in SALT. Again the Western European allies resisted. In reaction to the American–Soviet agreement on the prevention of nuclear war of June 22, 1973 it was underlined that this did not imply an obligation of no first use of nuclear weapons. In the Atlantic Declaration of 1974 the contribution of the British and French nuclear forces was emphasized.[73] The European allies pressed the US to avoid negotiations on the western part of the Eurostrategic balance. This objective was carried through in the Wladiwostok agreement of 1974, but at the price of a considerable enhancement of the ceilings to be set for the strategic weapons. Each side was to be allowed 2,400 strategic delivery vehicles, of which 1,320 MIRVed. In his press conference of April 1, 1977, Brzezinsky gave as his opinion

---

72. The US were permitted 1,054 ICBM's and 656 SLBM's (41 submarines), the Soviet Union 1,618 ICBM's and 740 SLBM's (56 nuclear-powered submarines).

73. *Keesing's Contemporary Archives*, 1974, p. 26607.

"that it comes close to a misstatement to call any such arrangement arms limitations".[74]

At the present moment of writing the prospects of arms control have become still more sobering, however. President Carter's efforts to go beyond Wladiwostok by substantial reduction obligations have been rejected by the Soviet Union, among other things on the ground that they do not take into account the Eurostrategic balance.[75] In the meantime the US–Soviet and the Eurostrategic balances have been changing by the development of new weapons on both sides. The SS-X-20 missile and the Backfire bomber on the Soviet side, the MX, the Mark 12-A, the cruise missiles and the neutron bomb on the US side.

In view of these developments the prospects of a successful outcome of MFR are remote, if not non-existent. Surely NATO and the Warsaw Pact are not working towards a broader agreement that reflects a common interest of both. NATO no longer feels an urgent need for arms control negotiations for Central Europe. In the early 1970s the Soviet Union was ready to enter into MFR negotiations as proposed by NATO in order to obtain Western participation in CSCE and a more moderate US posture in SALT. However, CSCE has ceased to be of great interest to her, since it has had counterproductive effects in the fields of human rights and cultural cooperation. A more moderate US posture in SALT is hardly to be expected now that the strategic arms race between the two super powers has got a new impetus and the new Chinese leadership has resolved to make China a modern and advanced military power. An MFR agreement might even sharpen the tensions between the Soviet Union and China.

In fact there is only a small number of factors that might eventually lead to arms control agreements for Europe, but they are still weak: the increasing economic burden of the arms race; the idea that the arms race as a whole does not lead to more security, that it has even become counter-productive in many respects; the increasing importance of regional arms control and security arrangements now that at a world level no effective arms control seems possible; the idea that in the long run the absence of

---

74. See: Presidential Assistant Brzezinski's News Conference of April 1, 1974, in: *The Department of State Bulletin*, April 25, p. 420.

75. Jacques Amalric, "M. Gromyko reproche aux dirigeants américains de ne pas tenir compte des intérêts soviétiques", in: *Le Monde*, 2 avril 1977, p. 3. An excellent account of the Carter proposals has been given by Herbert Scoville Jr., "The SALT Negotiations", in: *Scientific American*, August 1977, pp. 24–31.

any military détente would seem incompatible with political détente, or at least contrary to it. These ideas and factors seem more relevant to the smaller partners in the East–West negotiations than to the greater powers; we may expect that mainly the former will continue to press for political and military rapprochement. Such indication was given, e.g., by the Polish Ambassador Dr. Slawomir Dabrowa in the very press conference in which he rejected on behalf of the Warsaw Pact the NATO offer of December 1975: "From the very outset permit me to underline that problems discussed in Vienna belong to the top priorities of the foreign policy of Poland".[76]

The Need for a New Approach

Analyzing the course of MFR and SALT we have to come to the conclusion that arms control and disarmament can only be attained if traditional conceptions of arms control and strategy are abandoned. This applies most of all to the concept of equality in armaments.

In a classic bipolar world the two sides may agree on a common ceiling for their armaments as a basis of arms control. Although this may be difficult to effectuate in practice it is surely conceivable in principle. In a multipolar world the situation is fundamentally different. If at least one State wants to be able to match a combination of opponents, while the other ones also insist on equality, it becomes impossible to find an equilibrium acceptable to which all parties can agree. Instead a centrifugal development sets in which will become stronger according to the level of industrial and technological development of the States concerned. In the world of today the arms race thus becomes practically impossible to stop. Under modern circumstances equality in armaments is no longer necessarily a guarantee of military stability between two parties, however.

Military stability might be achieved when at least some parties take the initiative to refrain from the pursuit of equality and restrict themselves to a defence posture of "sufficiency" or "minimum deterrent".[77] To this end the following conditions should be met:

---

76. Press statement by Ambassador Dr. Slawomir Dobrowa, January 30, 1976, p. 1.
77. In the same sense: Richard Burt, "Technology and East–West arms control", in: *International Affairs*, January 1977, pp. 51–72, p. 72. Alva Myrdal,

— States (alliances) adopting a military posture of sufficiency should first of all have a realistic conventional threshold against armed attack. The costs of aggression would in any case have to be much higher than the gains, so that even in periods of international tension aggression does not seem a rational option. This does not require strict equality in levels of conventional armaments. The attacking party has to outnumber the defendant, provided the latter's defence forces are well organized.

— In the relationship between nuclear States (alliances) the State (alliance) being attacked with nuclear weapons should have a capacity to retaliate. This does not require equality in numbers and quality of nuclear weapons either, because even under circumstances of modern precision warfare it will practically always be possible to secure a certain capacity to retaliate.

— A sufficiency posture should be strengthened by political security agreements among States (or alliances) aiming at reducing or eliminating the danger of aggression.

States or military alliances adopting such a policy take a certain risk: the risk that their counterpart may nevertheless undertake military action, because he feels stronger. However, if no States or alliances are willing to take these risks the arms race will continue, without any improvement of international security. Furthermore it should be taken into account that in East–West relations the level of armaments has become such as to make military action only thinkable out of anxiety or irrationality.

A breakthrough in MFR is only thinkable if the NATO participants are willing to include the whole of the non-European and European forces in the reductions area in the negotiations; if NATO and the Warsaw Pact are ready to discuss the future of the Eurostrategic balance; if some compromise can be achieved on the question of symmetrical versus asymmetrical reductions. If, nonetheless, no agreement or series of partial agreements would be within reach NATO should be able to display unilateral restraint, in particular with respect to advanced weapons and weapons of mass destruction.

The Game of Disarmament, New York, 1976, who pleads for the concept of minimum deterrent and unilateral restraint in addition to arms control through international treaties. See in particular Chapters IV and XI.

Chapter 7

THE CSCE AND THE MILITARY ASPECTS OF EUROPEAN SECURITY

by *Ljubivoje Aćimović*

The growing significance of the external i.e. international factor of national security of States has become a characteristic feature of contemporary world developments. This international aspect of security has two complementary and closely related components—political and military. The military component of international security, however, is also undergoing an evolution: whereas the cold war, naturally, insisted exclusively on increasing military power as a form of strengthening national security, the process of lessening tension has gradually emphasized the indispensability of restricting the military factor on the international plane, i.e., of exerting an organized international effort aimed at checking unbridled armament and recourse to arms. In our age, in the presence of modern, one might say absolute weapons, the primary interest of any State is to avoid war. In other words, the strengthening of security means above all the removal of any possibility of an armed conflict, especially in one's neighbourhood, and most certainly on one's own borders. The way to achieve this is, on the one hand, a gradual transformation of international relations along the line of overcoming the consequences of the cold war and introducing a more democratic pattern of these relations (the political component), and on the other the limitation of the military factor in terms of arms limitation and disarmament (the military component).

During the postwar period, in fact, treatment of the problem of armament versus disarmament has experienced a noticeable evolution: from a rather simplified concept it has become a complex one composed of several components: in addition to general and complete disarmament, being the ultimate, long-term objective, new notions have been introduced, such as arms control, arms limitation, reduction of forces, collateral measures and, finally, the notion of confidence-building measures. The complexity of the situation in the field of disarmament and the urgent need realistically to approach this problem in terms of moving gradually towards its solution and thus achieving an early check on the uncontrolled arms race, have led to this broader and diversified notion of disarmament, understood as a complex and gradual process. Indeed, the traditional notion of general and complete disarmament is merely one of the components in the complex effort to control this unbridled arms race, which at the same time constitutes the final, desired overall result, while other aforementioned components serve its function.

In connection with these tendencies it is worthwhile emphasizing that if we agree that long-term solutions of the security problem lie in the substantial transformation of the existing system of international relations, then it would seem logical to assume that in this system the power factor, i.e., the military one, would have to have an essentially different role. As far as the entirety of this process is concerned, one might say that the interrelation of the political and military factor in the process of lessening international tension and strengthening security bears the following implications: firstly, progress achieved in the political sphere makes not only possible, but also indispensable, the materialization of positive results in the military field as well (otherwise détente becomes unstable, limited and even bound to come to a deadlock); secondly, measures to restrain armament and achieve disarmament are not merely a result of political developments, but also a factor which stimulates and promotes them; and finally, as a consequence of what has been just said, it would seem only natural that international efforts to strengthen security should develop side by side—both in the political and military field.

Consequently, if this line of thought on international security and détente is accepted—and in my opinion it is the only one that is tenable—it becomes clear that it was both natural and necessary that the military component of security should find its place at the Conference on Security and Cooperation in Europe. All the more so if the armament situation is borne in mind, which is not only in full discord with positive developments in the political sphere, but also occasionally disturbs, or, even, slows them down. Is it really possible, in the presence of a gigantic armament race, to confine the issue of European security merely to the political field, leaving aside its military component? In the opinion of a number of participating States, mostly small ones and in particular those not belonging to either of the two blocs, this is impossible. Believing that the political and military aspects of security are closely related and starting from an awareness of the very unsatisfactory situation and unfavourable trends in the military sphere, especially in

Europe, these countries held that it was absolutely vital for this issue to be given an adequate place at the Conference. And this not only implies, as many people often believe, confidence-building measures, but also a series of measures involving the military aspects of security.

Different Approaches to the Problem

Views on the issue of the military aspects of European security at the Conference differed widely.

The most restrictive attitude was that of the USSR and of other Warsaw Pact countries which at the beginning held that the Conference should not deal with the military aspects of European security (with the exception of some general attitudes regarding the disarmament subject); later on, when the USSR, in an arrangement with the United States, accepted parallel talks on the mutual reduction of forces (MFR), thus achieving that the issue be taken out of the Conference, these States agreed, on the insistence of other participants, to introduce the issue of military aspects of European security into the Conference agenda. Nonetheless, the Warsaw Pact countries continued to believe that the final result would boil down to symbolic solutions—to some more or less general, declarative statements on the military aspects of security in the Final Act. This was quite obvious from the proposal which the USSR submitted during the first phase of the Conference.[1]

In the West there was the common attitude of NATO as a whole and the attitude of some small member States.

The attitude of NATO as a whole was determined by a combination of tactical and practical considerations and was in fact confined to the issue of prior notification of major military manoeuvres and exchange of observers. (This was how far the United States and France seemed prepared to go.) Tactical motives were shared by all NATO member States and were aimed at intensifying their pressure on the USSR and its allies during the negotiations at the Conference by insisting on introducing this item and related far-reaching demands into the agenda. It was mostly on these lines that they also supported the Swedish proposal (revealing data on military budgets) and the Spanish proposal (exchange of military personnel, and so forth). Smaller countries of this group were also guided by practical reasons because it was in these measures (including prior notification of major military move-

---

1. CSCE/I/1 of July 3, 1973, *CSCE—Stage I, Documents*, Helsinki, p. 4.

ments) that they saw useful instruments for additional strengthening of their security. Secondly, they wanted to be directly included in a general system of military measures involving European security, as they were excluded from the MFR talks in Vienna. The basic difference among NATO member States was related to the issue of prior notification of military movements, in which particularly Norway, Denmark and the Netherlands were keenly interested, while the United States was against. These smaller NATO States also took a more flexible attitude towards some other proposals submitted by bloc-free (neutral and non-aligned) countries.[2]

These neutral and non-aligned countries took the most ambitious and comprehensive approach. According to them, the Conference on Security and Cooperation in Europe should, in an appropriate way, comprise the entire subject-matter, the whole spectrum of security measures in the military field—from confidence-building measures to general and complete disarmament. In other words, all issues within this field should be dealt with at this gathering, in keeping with their nature, so as to produce decisions ranging from statements of principle or intent to concrete and operative measures.

Accordingly, bloc-free countries, as well as Romania, developed a large-scale joint action in the field of the military aspects of security with a view to achieving the best possible results at the CSCE. As an expression and instrument of this collective effort, six non-block countries—Austria, Cyprus, Finland, Sweden, Switzerland and Yugoslavia—submitted their joint proposal of a draft document on the military aspects of European security (the so-called proposal of the six),[3] which was also fully backed by Malta (which for its own specific reasons did not formally joint the group) and by Romania. In this action these countries accomplished *ad hoc*

---

2. These differences in attitudes are illustrated also by the plurality of proposals on this issue on the part of NATO member States: Norway—CSCE/II/C/4; Belgium—CSCE/II/C/10; Federal Republic of Germany—CSCE/II/C/11; Great Britain—CSCE/II/C/12 and CSCE/II/C/17.

3. This draft contained all basic aspects of the military measures of security: (*a*) confidence-building measures (notification of military manoeuvres and movements; exchange of observers by invitation); (*b*) measures intended to restrain military activities which might cause misunderstanding or tension; (*c*) attitudes of principle regarding the military aspects of security and especially the reduction of armed forces; (*d*) attitude of principle regarding contribution to efforts aimed at general and complete disarmament—CSCE/II/C/13 Rev. 1.

collaboration with some smaller States, members of NATO, especially with the Netherlands.

Basic Problems and Results of the Conference

The subcommittee for the military aspects of security faced four complex issues to be agreed upon: (1) Confidence-building measures; (2) Measures designed to restrain military activities which might cause misunderstanding or tension; (3) General considerations concerning the conduct of negotiations on the reduction of forces and armaments; (4) General considerations concerning disarmament.

The latter issue did not cause major difficulties and was solved first, as early as in the summer of 1974. Since this document contains a very general and simple statement on the disarmament subject, there is no need to discuss it in this chapter.

Confidence-building measures

To understand better and evaluate what has been achieved at the Conference it seems necessary to scrutinize each aspect of this complex issue:

Prior notification of major military manoeuvres

During negotiations at the second phase in Geneva there was much discord about how this measure was to be formulated in the Final Act—above all, to what degree it should be compulsory and how far the Final Act should go to make them concrete. Accordingly, agreement was to be reached, on the one hand, on the nature of the manoeuvres' notification system, that is, on the question of its compelling nature, and on the other, on the issue of its parameters:

The voluntary basis issue at one point became a key issue in reaching agreement on this matter. At the beginning the Soviet Union, as we all know, was not very enthusiastic about the inclusion of the military measures of security in the Conference agenda and when it had to accept it to some extent at Helsinki, it afterwards made every effort to make the measure of prior notification of military manoeuvres less difficult for itself. When it finally realized, after much resistance, that it would have to accept more realistically set parameters, the USSR resorted to mitigating the effects of notification measures by insisting on the voluntary basis. This attitude was the result of two circumstances: first, a genuine reluctance to reveal something (i.e., measures of building-up defence power, military manoeuvres being a part of this) which has been traditionally treated as top secret, and, secondly, the asymmetric position of its main rival, the United States, whose territory was *via facti* exempted from the application of this measure (because security in Europe is at issue). This Soviet move, however, met with an unfavourable reaction among most of the other countries which feared that in this way the measure would become arbitrary and thus lose its efficacy substantially.

A rather happy solution was finally found within the preamble of the document, which combines the above Soviet attitude with phrases emphasizing the importance and need of regular and consistent implementation of this political agreement on prior notification of major military manoeuvres.[4] It could be maintained, however, that an obligatory system of notification of major military manoeuvres was set up. It is clear, however, that what is at issue here, as elsewhere in the document, is a political obligation.

Parameters for the notification of major military manoeuvres referred to the following specifications of this measure: firstly, the size of forces engaged in the manoeuvres; secondly, the area of application; thirdly, the time when notification must be given in advance of the start of the manoeuvre; and fourthly, the contents of the notification (data about the manoeuvre).

The starting positions differed very widely:

— *Size:* Western attitude—one division, or 12,000 troops and more; the Eastern attitude: one army or army corps, or 45,000 to 50,000 troops and more (the USSR was always reluctant to state these figures accurately).

— *Area:* Western attitude—the initial proposal referred to the whole territory of all European States which took part at the Conference and later on to an area within a 600 kilometres limit from the frontier only for the USSR and Turkey (States whose territories spread to Asia); the Eastern attitude—the initial proposal referred to a frontier area within 100 kilometres for all European countries, and later this solution was offered to refer only to the USSR and Turkey, while for other countries the area would cover the whole territory.

— *Time:* West—notification to be given 60 days in advance; East—5 days.

— *Contents of notification:* West—detailed data on manoeuvres (in addition to basic general data on the time, place and designation of the manoeuvre; there should also be information regarding the

4. *Final Act*, p. 85.

time of introductory and conclusive military movements, numerical strength and structure of forces, level of command as well as the general purpose of the manoeuvre); East—merely basic general data.

A compromise solution was also found on this subject: the size of forces—25,000 troops (and more), independently or combined with any possible air or naval components; territory—for the USSR and Turkey—an area within 250 kilometres from the frontier, for other European countries the whole territory; notification should be given 21 days or more in advance; the contents of notification—the information should contain the designation, the general purpose of the manoeuvre, the States involved, the type and numerical strength of the forces engaged, the area and estimated time-frame of its conduct.[5]

Thus the Conference on Security and Cooperation in Europe agreed upon the first all-European military security measure in history. To be more precise, this is an operative measure. Its significance is manifold—truly, rather political and psychological than military in practical terms. Prior notification of military manoeuvres, when carried out regularly, has, in fact, a triple effect: firstly, it increases mutual confidence (the very act of notification is both an expression of confidence in others on the part of those who do the notifying, and a factor of increasing confidence on the part of those to whom the notification is addressed); secondly, it helps to avoid eventual misunderstandings and their damaging effects; and thirdly, it removes the practice of misusing manoeuvres—their utilization for the purpose of exerting pressure or even as a prelude to aggression.

It should be mentioned, however, that the importance of this measure is of a relative nature, especially if one bears in mind what could have been in fact accomplished, or what non-aligned and neutral countries were striving for (for instance, the introduction of a provision on the reduction of the frequency of manoeuvres as well as their scope; the introduction of the naval component, that is,

---

5. *Final Act*, pp. 85–86. The bloc-free countries proved most realistic in their proposals which contained the following parameters: level—one reinforced army division or 18,000 people (in the last phase as a compromise they offered 25,000 troops); territory—this issue was not specified in the original proposal because the text implied whole territories in Europe; later on it was proposed that the frontier area for the USSR and Turkey should be 300 kilometres; the deadline for notification 30 days; contents of notification—roughly on the lines that were accepted.

manoeuvres of naval forces; a substantially lower level of combined manoeuvres performed by military alliances and so forth). In addition, there are some gaps left in the system of notification (for instance, the parameter involving the size of forces can be evaded by dividing major military manoeuvres into smaller ones, carried out either in succession or simultaneously in different places).

In spite of all this, however, the measure of prior notification of major military manoeuvres occupies an important place within international efforts to strengthen European security. So far it is the first and sole practical, operative measure of this kind, which may have a beneficial impact on both the promotion of international relations in Europe and on the further development of the system of military security measures. It should be looked upon as the first step and in this sense its implementation deserves full attention.

Prior notification of other military manoeuvres

The introduction of this provision was motivated by two objectives: to encourage, on a completely voluntary basis, the expansion of this measure by also embracing those manoeuvres which are not explicitly referred to in the document and thus to introduce a dynamic component into the implementation of confidence-building measures; and secondly, partially to satisfy those participating States which desired a smaller scale of manoeuvres for advanced notification (specifically the manoeuvres taking place in the vicinity of borders), and those that stood for the inclusion of other kinds of manoeuvres too, for instance naval manoeuvres. Indeed, the wording of this provision is very modest: it indirectly expresses the desire to notify other manoeuvres, too.[6]

In this respect, as an expression of desirability to go beyond what has been stated for major military manoeuvres, this decision is useful. It has been proved already in practice to some extent, because some States have so far mutually notified each other on even much smaller scale manoeuvres, especially those that took place in border areas.[7]

Exchange of observers at military manoeuvres

The practice of inviting observers to attend military manoeuvres has been known for some time now, but so far it has mostly involved an exchange of observers among allies. This is the first

6. *Final Act*, p. 86.
7. In this respect the Yugoslav-Italian practice based on a special bilateral agreement is especially instructive.

time that this measure covers the whole of Europe, so that invitations are to be sent even across the borders of antagonistic military alliances.

In the document on the military aspects of security the measure of exchange of observers at manoeuvres is of a voluntary character; it is presented explicitly as an act of good will, which means that States will carry out this measure according to their own will whenever they consider it appropriate.[8] This, if properly implemented, might also be an effective confidence-building measure.

Prior notification of major military movements

It is to be regretted that this important measure, designed to promote confidence, could not have been realized in the same way as major military manoeuvres. Nevertheless something was accomplished,[9] more as a possibility for the future than as an effective measure. To tell the truth, the value of this modest result lies in the fact that it formally provides for a basis to continue efforts in this particular field. Moreover, the issue of prior notification of major military movements has been thus officially recognized. It is unlikely that it will be successfully solved in the near future, but it would be also rather difficult to remove it from the European agenda.

Other confidence-building measures

Following the initiative of Sweden and Spain, the Conference discussed two other measures intended to strengthen confidence. These include the publication of data on military budgets (Sweden) and exchanges by invitation of military personnel (Spain). Unfortunately the Swedish initiative was met with a host of difficulties and resistance, especially on the part of the USSR and other Warsaw Pact countries, so that its final version, which was made very palliative and general, met with ill success.[10]

This is why only one measure was adopted under this heading—the exchange of military personnel.

Measures intended to restrain military activities that might cause misunderstanding or tension

Due to the unbending resistance on the part of blocs, especially on the part of the United States, the USSR and France, it was

8. *Final Act*, p. 86.
9. *Final Act*, p. 86.
10. CSCE/II/C/9.

impossible to achieve more than a general statement expressing this idea in an indirect way and rather unintelligibly.[11]

The solution adopted by the Conference, however inadequate and unsatisfactory it may seem, constitutes the most that could have been achieved under the existing conditions and certainly is significant as a breach in the wall of resistance, thus opening up very modest, but genuine room for further efforts in this direction. If a concrete measure to restrain military activities which might cause misunderstanding or tension could not be accepted, an affirmative political attitude regarding the desirability of such behaviour was certainly taken. It would be inadmissible—considering the spread and frequency of activities of this kind in the postwar period and their unfavourable effects on international relations—for the Conference to have ignored the problem. If the result of the initiative is rather disappointing, a political point was, nonetheless, certainly made. This must not be ignored, especially in the context of the follow-up to the CSCE, because, besides the notification of military movements, this is the least elaborated issue in the document on the military aspects of European security.

General considerations

First of all, it should be made clear that general considerations refer to the question of reducing armed forces in Europe, and, particularly, to negotiations held to this end.

Bloc-free countries in approaching the problems of the military aspects of security in Europe, pursued the following line of thought: the Conference on Security and Cooperation in Europe is certainly not the place to conduct talks or make decisions on the reduction of forces and disarmament in Europe, nor was it entitled to interfere in such negotiations held elsewhere. However, this Conference, dealing essentially with the problems of European security, could not neglect this issue entirely because it concerns one of the basic factors of security and because agreements and negotiations in this field may, in terms of their effects, take an unfavourable course for individual countries not participating in them.

These considerations suggested, firstly, that the solution is to be sought in the field of principles, and secondly, that the purpose and meaning of this solution lie in the reaffirmation, within a general European agreement, of the idea of the necessity of reducing armed forces, and in the establishment of political standards to be

11. *Final Act*, p. 87.

observed by participants in negotiations on this matter, with a view to protecting the interests of other European countries and of Europe as a whole.

To ensure a desirable conduct of negotiations on the reduction of forces, which would suit general interests, in fact means to thwart certain—potential or already manifested—deviations in this field, such as, in the first place: the attempt to separate the political from the military aspects of security (at the expense of the latter, by resisting or even refusing to make efforts aimed at promoting these aspects); tendencies to treat diversely the European geo-political space by concentrating efforts to strengthen security merely in individual areas (such as Central Europe), neglecting other, usually peripheral parts of this continent; eventual agreements at the expense of States not participating in negotiations, or in other words solving problems vital for the interests of these States without consulting them; and finally, unwillingness to inform other States participating in the CSCE about the progress and results achieved in the respective negotiations, thus depriving them not only of the right to be informed about matters important to their security, but also of the possibility for a timely answer to such challenges.

Accordingly, the following essential considerations were proposed and later adopted, reflecting four interests bound to be protected:

— The complementary nature of the political and military aspects of security;
— The inseparable character of European security, including its Mediterranean dimension and the world context;
— Compatibility between the agreed measures aimed at reducing armed forces and the security interests of all States participating in the CSCE;
— Information to be provided to all other States participating in the CSCE on the situation in the given negotiations.

It was extremely difficult to reach agreement on adequate formulations related to these items, because both the interests and corresponding attitudes differed widely.

The interests of bloc-free countries on this subject are well known and fully understandable and there is no need to elaborate on them any further.

Two super powers, the United States and the USSR, were opposed because they feared that acceptance of these considerations could, in fact, induce some third countries to interfere in their otherwise very difficult and complicated negotiations on the reduction of forces and that it could make a breach from the outside in the whole complex of military security issues which they consider to be their exclusive domain. France, on the contrary, feared that such acceptance could involve her in the arrangements of the super powers which she is boycotting; in other words, she was reluctant to compromise her position of keeping aloof and of preserving full independence in the field of military efforts to strengthen national security, denying any support to ongoing negotiations in the field of disarmament and arms limitation.

The road to agreement was a very difficult one but a text was, nonetheless, adopted which, generally speaking, quite properly defines these general considerations. This is why, in spite of some of its inevitable weaknesses, this chapter of the document on the military aspects of security is of extraordinary importance for its political image.

Generally speaking, the value of this document lies, above all, in its specific political effect, particularly because its adoption demonstrates that the attitude on the complementary nature, or mutual relationship of the political and military aspects of security, has been, on the European scale, recognized in principle and applied in concrete terms; a new step was made towards creating an all-European multilateral system of military security measures and the first, albeit modest, mechanism was created to build up confidence (in the first place the measure of prior notification of major military manoeuvres); and finally, the monopoly of the blocs in the field of military security was seriously challenged and a new all-European track of efforts was traced aimed at controlling and restraining the effects of the military factor in Europe. This achievement, as an initial step and a basis for further developments, is no doubt important and deserves attention. Yet, viewed as a move towards the ultimate goal, it is extremely modest, almost negligible; moreover, it is disproportionate to what was accomplished in other domains at the Conference, especially in the political field. This critical note, needless to say, should not be understood as a negation of what has been achieved, but rather as recognition of the realities which call for new, increased efforts on the road that has just commenced.

Implementation of the Document on the Military Aspects of European Security

The system of notifying military manoeuvres, along with the inviting of observers, has been, on the whole, functioning rather satisfactorily. According to information at my disposal, notification of twenty-one military manoeuvres has been given so far: thirteen of them organized within NATO, three within the Warsaw Pact and five in neutral (Switzerland, Sweden) and non-aligned countries (Yugoslavia). This entirely new practice in Europe becomes still more significant if some additional facts are taken into account: the system of prior notification has functioned regularly despite the fact that the Final Act suggests, in a way, its voluntary basis; a large proportion of the notified manoeuvres has been of a level lower than 25,000 troops; invitations to observers have been issued in nine cases; in addition to the above-mentioned notifications on large-scale military manoeuvres there have been quite a few notifications of smaller-scale military manoeuvres given on a bilateral basis (for instance, between Yugoslavia and Italy).

However, in the functioning of this system there have been certain weaknesses. Some instances of evading notification of major military manoeuvres have been reported, by breaking them into several smaller-scale, mutually coordinated ones, developing either in succession, or simultaneously at different places but in one geostrategic area. In addition, there have been some complaints about the way in which exchanges of observers were implemented because in some instances the observers were not offered adequate possibilities properly to fulfil their functions.

As to the other measures, however, very little has been accomplished so far: there has been no notification of major military movements; the already existing exchanges of military personnel have, in fact, little changed within the Follow-up to the CSCE—either in qualitative or in quantitative terms; no visible self-restraint has been displayed in military activities liable to cause misunderstanding or tension; no information about relevant developments in the MFR negotiations has been provided to other States by the negotiating forum in Vienna; the whole concept of the complementary nature of the political and military aspects of security, as set forth above, has not been genuinely applied in practice.

Finally, as far as the present military context of European security is concerned, the situation is, no doubt, unsatisfactory: nothing has changed from the Cold War days regarding either the military structure or the level of arms and forces deployed in

Europe. Moreover, from the point of view of the modernization of armies and qualitative improvements of weapons the situation has even worsened. It goes without saying that this state of affairs affects the process of promoting security and cooperation in Europe. It, in fact, sets limits to this process.

Future Tasks

First of all, let me make a preliminary remark: in discussing the implementation of the Final Act everyone eloquently emphasizes the necessity of its integral application; in practice, however, many have a rather selective approach and de facto treat individual portions of the document quite differently. Furthermore, deficiency lies in a tendency amongst many to alleviate the concessions they made at the Conference for the sake of compromises by interpreting certain provisions of the Final Act in a way which actually means a retreat to their original, i.e., starting positions; finally, the third deficiency lies in the fact that the implementation of the Final Act has been approached in a static way in spite of its in-built dynamic concept.

These three deficiencies figure very prominently in the domain of the military aspects of security. This has been manifested so far first because individual provisions of the Final Act have been either neglected or interpreted in "one's own way" and secondly, many States have made it known that they consider these measures to be definite and final, refusing further to develop them at all (and this is precisely the subject of our interest in this chapter).

A genuine realization of the concept of European security built into the Final Act calls for serious efforts to further promote the military measures of security. The more so if one bears in mind the continuing unsatisfactory situation in the military field, where there is a very high level of military potentials and the armament race is still progressing. Indeed, it is precisely this state of affairs which, among other factors, caused a certain setback in détente in the period between Helsinki and Belgrade.

In this light the issue of ensuring the proper place and adequate treatment of the military aspects of European security at the Belgrade Meeting has become increasingly important.

The Belgrade meeting 1977, being the first stage within the Follow-up to the CSCE and an expression of the generally accepted view that the initiated multilateral process must be continued, should discuss "the implementation of the provisions of the Final Act and of the tasks defined by the Conference" and "the deepening of their mutual relations, the improvement of security and the development of cooperation in Europe, and the development of the process of détente in the future".[12] In accordance with this, the function of the Belgrade meeting would be to reaffirm the objectives, commitments and tasks undertaken in Helsinki, to evaluate the implementation of the Final Act hitherto and take steps to further develop the measures of the Final Act. In short: all that was agreed upon must be reaffirmed and evaluated, and new efforts to reach an all-European détente should be initiated.

To be very specific, the tasks of the Belgrade meeting regarding the military aspects of security could be as follows: (1) reaffirmation of the concept of interrelation between the political and military aspects of security and of the corresponding commitments taken in Helsinki; (2) a thorough exchange of views on the European situation in this domain and especially the implementation of the respective provisions of the Final Act; and (3) discussion of future efforts and initiation of new measures. The realization of these three basic tasks—which are closely mutually related—should include the following:

1. The *reaffirmation* of relevant general considerations of principle implies, first, that the question of the military aspects of security—by the place and importance it will get at the meeting, by the broadness and profoundness of discussion on this issue, as well as by the results achieved—should be given its full political weight; secondly, the discussion should embrace the problem of the military situation in Europe in its totality, and it should insist on exerting efforts towards solving the whole complex, including the issue of reducing armed forces and armaments; thirdly, the meeting should note the very unsatisfactory situation in this field in general, which is in vast discord with the results achieved in the political sphere and, accordingly, it should imperatively insist on the progressive alternation of this state of affairs.

This general objective of reaffirmation of the importance of the military component of security and of adequate commitments will be present throughout the entire course of the Belgrade meeting, especially in the opening and concluding debate at its plenary sessions. The outcome, needless to say, should be reflected in the final document as adequately as possible.

2. The *evaluation* of the implementation of the Helsinki provisions should be comprehensive and must, on the one hand, make use of positive experience, and on the other, point to negative

12. *Final Act*, pp. 133–134.

experiences. In general, the discussion on this subject should serve the promotion of the very practice of implementing the adopted measures, as well as their further development. In accordance with this, in the political-psychological sphere, it should act both as a pressure towards a consistent implementation of obligations and as an impetus for new efforts. It also should be clearly reflected in the final document of the meeting.

3. *New measures* or efforts to further develop the system of measures for the strengthening of security and promoting cooperation in Europe will no doubt be an important component of the action of bloc-free and some other, mostly smaller, countries at the Belgrade meeting. The reasons for insisting on this dynamic component of the Follow-up to the CSCE are manifold. First of all, if the Final Act adopted in Helsinki recognizes the Conference as a multilateral all-European process or as a continuing effort, then it necessarily presupposes a permanent advancement of the action, i.e., the taking of new measures. In some way this was stated in the Final Act. Further, the Helsinki document is undoubtedly an important, but only the first, step made so far, which means that many issues are still pending. Finally, not only was the Final Act unable to solve everything adequately and efficiently, but the time factor should also be taken into account; if there were no continuous and progressive development of the Final Act, it would shortly become obsolete—not so much in terms of general considerations but in terms of practical-operative issues.

Efforts along the line of adopting new measures could be realized in three ways, that is according to three types of decisions: (1) declarations of intent to adopt new measures and guidelines for their elaboration; (2) procedural decisions to this end (the setting up of working groups or groups of experts, convening of diplomatic conferences and so forth); and (3) new measures.

The character and the contents of these three kinds of potential decisions of the Belgrade meeting are clearly denoted in the above headings: the declarations of intent would in fact express the orientation for future action regarding a measure and commitment (explicit or tacit) to consider or eventually adopt this measure at the next meeting; the decisions on procedural issues should include not only those involving the setting up of working bodies but also their mandates; the decision on concrete measures would contain more or less elaborated elements of these measures, rather as was done in the Final Act.

As for *new measures*, they could include the following in general terms:

— Confidence-building measures
1. Notification of major military movements—concrete elaboration of the system.
2. Notification of major military manoeuvres and exchange of observers—the removal of deficiencies (including the elaboration of a code of conduct governing exchange of observers).
3. Naval component—an expansion of confidence-building measures to this area as well.

— Measures designed to restrain military activities that may cause misunderstanding or tension—concrete determination of both the content of the measures and their obligatory nature.
— Force reductions (General consideration)—the commitment contained in the Final Act regarding information on the negotiations in Vienna to be provided to other States, should be made more specific.

This is only a list of potentially feasible, and in the opinion of a number of States, desirable measures that might be considered. True, they are not entirely new, because they are already embodied in the Final Act (in a certain way and partially); one should rather say that the above proposals are aimed at making these ideas more operational and better elaborated. They, however, do not include the improvement of parameters for notification of major military manoeuvres (size, territory), as such an attempt would be fully unrealistic at present and as it is not of urgent importance.

Each of the above measures would be useful while some of them, such as notification of major military movements and measures intended to restrain military activities which might cause misunderstandings or tension, seem especially important at the moment. It would be of major importance also, considering the limited possibilities of the Belgrade meeting, to set up a group of experts to deal with military questions. The setting up of such a group would be of not only practical but also of great political significance.

However, we should not cherish illusions that the aforementioned measures can be easily realized. Resistance on the part of blocs, especially great powers, has already been manifested, suggesting that it is too early even to discuss new measures, to say nothing of introducing them; any new effort to this end would, according to these views, allegedly imply the revision of the Helsinki document. It is obvious that these arguments are untenable, because as regards certain measures, not only is it not too early for them to be realized now, but it was already time to do so in Helsinki; secondly, there can be no revision of something which was adopted as a general and programme platform for a long-term action if the innovations to be made are in accordance with the basic principles and if they are in the interest of the action and its successful materialization.

In conclusion, I would like to underline only two things. Firstly, the Belgrade meeting would obviously have a manifold function as regards the initiation and promotion of the process of military détente. Especially in the field of new measures, it should not confine itself merely to their adoption, but would have to make fresh initiatives and take appropriate steps for their future realization—so far as it would be unfeasible at this meeting.

Next, the issues of the military aspects of European security will also figure as one of the priorities of bloc-free countries in the field of European security. This stems from the significance which the military component plays in the détente process as well as from the concept of the interrelation between the political and military aspects of security, which was explicitly built into the Helsinki document at the insistence of bloc-free countries. At the same time this was the leading thought which gathered together all neutral and non-aligned countries in Helsinki and Geneva, in their joint efforts to realize this concept at the Conference. This practically means that these countries, with some support on the part of some other small States, will wholeheartedly endeavour to give this issue a prominent place at the Belgrade meeting and to accomplish an adequate result in this particular field.

Chapter 8

MILITARY AND POLITICAL DÉTENTE IN AMERICAN FOREIGN POLICY

by *Ernst-Otto Czempiel**

How will the Carter administration deal with détente? The word is back now, after Ford had banned it from political use. But what about political practice? Will Carter follow the Nixon–Kissinger policies which tried to play down the differences between the Soviet Union and the USA and to balance the relationship with the USSR and China in a sort of cooperative-competitive triangle? Or is Carter heir to the election campaign tactics of the Ford administration, which answered the conservative argument of Reagan with a hardened attitude toward the USSR?

It is, of course, very difficult to tell how the Carter administration finally will behave. The emphasis Carter gives to the Civil Rights issue in the Soviet Union (and elsewhere) might look like a renewal of cold war orientations. This must, however, not necessarily be the case. To bring back moral values to international politics is, in itself, neither bad nor aggressive. To care about Human Rights in foreign countries should be one of the most important orientations of foreign policy. Experience, on the other hand, teaches that pushing the issue of domestic conditions in foreign countries very often accompanies a hardening of conflict behaviour. It can serve to drum up public opinion for a new round of conflict, it can serve to detract public opinion from domestic deficits at home, it may be used to re-assemble tired allies around the bloc leader. In other words: emphasizing the moral and ethical issues in international politics can serve several and multiple aims. It will not be easy to find out what purposes the Carter administration really is pursuing.

There are some indications, though. Officials of the Carter administration have said several times that there is no linkage between the Human Rights issue and other substantial issues, e.g., SALT II. This leads to the assumption that Carter will not revoke

* I am indebted to the Deutsche Forschungsgemeinschaft for a grant facilitating conversations and the collecting of new material in Washington, Spring 1977.

the ideology of the cold war, that he intends nothing but to bring up one of the missing elements in the Nixon–Kissinger policies, the Human Rights. In fact, Kissinger's policies looked very much like the traditional European power politics, the interplay between governments without regard to human interests and ethical values. It is possible that President Carter intends to combine the pragmatic orientation of Kissinger with the interest in democratic legitimacy President Wilson tried to realize.

Even if this comes true, it will not be easy. To promote democratic standards in foreign countries is extremely difficult and can be done indirectly only. To use the direct approach inevitably leads to war even if it may be termed a holy war, or, to use a more modern term, a crusade for freedom.

There are other explanations for Carter's behaviour. He may look for a new frontier as Kennedy has done, fulfilling some of the promises of this campaign, mobilizing the nation for his administration. The Human Rights issue may be used as a scapegoat only, behind which sober and pragmatic policies are being pursued. Judging from the persons President Carter has appointed as his top aides his administration is not heading for a renewal of the cold war, nor for the pragmatist policies of Kissinger. Carter obviously tries to combine the continuation of American policies toward the Soviet Union with the Human Rights added. Whether this new brand will fit into the trends of the international system remains to be seen. It remains to be seen, still, whether Carter will succeed domestically and in Moscow. His success or his failure will depend on what role the Human Rights issue will play within the overall relationship between Washington and Moscow. It will depend on how détente is being understood in the two capitals. How is détente being understood in Washington?

The word is back, as mentioned. But it is a difficult word, as open to misunderstandings as the term interdependence. In its proper meaning détente describes nothing else than the reduction of tensions. International conflict can have several, and different, degrees of tensions. More precisely: one conflict can live through several degrees of tensions, the most eminent examples being the American–Chinese conflict in the sixties and the seventies and the development of the East–West conflict since 1949. Although in both cases the conflict matter has not changed, the degree of tensions varied considerably. Generally speaking: the amount of tension is not necessarily determined by the substance of the conflict. Détente, therefore, means nothing else but that the United States would be prepared to continue the lowering of tensions in her conflict-relationship with the Soviet Union.

In the long run, of course, the reduction of tensions affects the substance of the conflict. If tension is diminished to such a level that no partner of the conflict is prepared any more to use military means for its resolution, there will arise consequences for the substance of the conflict itself. It may be still the same thing, but its evaluation has changed. There exists a certain linkage between the degree of tension and the substance of conflict. It is, however, a very weak relationship, but it has to be kept in mind. It contains possibly one important clue for the American (and perhaps not only the American) attitude towards détente.

The meaning of détente can be different in different regions and different segments of international politics. In a sense détente is not indivisible as Kissinger had assumed. He should have reminded himself that he pursued détente with the Soviet Union in Europe, although he was fighting Communism in South-East Asia. Détente should not be confused with the absence of conflict. The term concerns only the means of resolving it. Obviously, one cannot combine general détente with war in a particular area. But without this extreme general détente can be combined with any degree of tension in any region of the world, if the tendency of this tension is directed downwards. We can (and probably shall) have a rather low degree of tension in Europe, and at the same time a comparatively high degree of tension between East and West in the third world. By the same token we can (and probably shall) have a considerable degree of tension between East and West in the military field, going along with a comparatively low degree of tension in the economic field. The three baskets of the Helsinki Conference contain also three different degrees of tensions going along with the substance matters involved. Add to the three the special basket of the strategic arms limitation talks between the two super powers and the basket of the mutual force reduction talks, going on between the major political units in Eastern and Western Europe. It is evident that the term détente covers a very broad complex of different substances with different patterns of tension. They include the Human Rights issue, but they are not identical with it. Human rights are only one, and perhaps a minor, factor within a whole bunch of problems which come under the range of détente.

American attitude and politics towards détente, therefore, cannot be discussed only in one dimension. The paper confines itself to the East–West conflict, predominantly in Europe. Within this region, however, it tries to come to grips with the political, the military, and the economic aspects of détente, meaning the preparedness to reduce tensions. From this vantage point a view can be taken upon the possible outcomes, the possible futures of American policy towards the East–West conflict in Europe. In order to reach that point, however, a short view back into the past of the respective American policy and into its domestic bases is unavoidable.

Détente in American Foreign Policy

When did détente become a goal in American foreign policy? The usual answer points towards Kissinger and the year of 1969. This view is not only an oversimplification, it is simply wrong. Kissinger has been one of the most eloquent architects of the détente, but he was not the only one, and he did not invent it. Détente started much earlier than 1969, it is not the result of the thinking of one mastermind. Détente must be seen as the result of a certain constellation of interests which started roughly in 1955 and lived through several stages. We have a very good witness for this early beginning of détente policy in the United States: Konrad Adenauer. He felt very deeply that the situation had changed in 1955.[1] He fought very hard to establish a "junctim" between reunification of Germany and/or disarmament on the one hand, détente on the other. He was not unsuccessful, at least as far as the formal recognition of détente was concerned. In practical political terms, however, the interest of the United States to reduce tensions in Europe after its division had come to a certain end prevailed. The developing strategic balance between the two super powers expressed in terms of the capacity of mutual deterrence was stronger than any partial political interest.

There were roadblocks, of course: the Berlin ultimatum of 1958, the U-2 incident of 1960. There was the Berlin wall in 1961, intensifying tension for a short while in order to permit its further reduction in the long run. It is important to note that during most of the Berlin crisis, interrupted only for several days, the talks between the United States and the USSR for an atom-test-stop-treaty were continued. The missile crisis of 1962 gave the final push towards détente. It demonstrated that there was no alternative left to the super powers. They could only choose between détente or confrontation with the possibility of a direct war.

After 1962 détente was stepped up and became partial coopera-

1. Konrad Adenauer: *Erinnerungen 1955–1959*, Fischer, Frankfurt, 1969, p. 155.

tion between the Soviet Union and the United States.[2] Involved in a range of conflicting interests there arose the common interest in controlling the proliferation of atomic weapons. Common control—sort of a duopol—appeared to be the best solution for the situation in Central Europe, because it could keep the peace there and at the same time keep under control the allies of both sides. It was possible to lower the tension between the two super powers as long as they succeeded in controlling their alliances. The United States used the MLF for this purpose, the Soviet Union could rely upon her military strength. President Kennedy was prepared to continue this particular policy of détente. He urged West Germany to follow suit, to accept détente as the necessary trend of the international system in Central Europe. Kennedy did not succeed, because adaptation of West Germany's politics towards détente with Eastern Europe took much more time than anticipated, and Kennedy himself was assassinated already in 1963. But the Ostpolitik of Brandt and the Social-Liberal Coalition was, in its final analysis, nothing else but the necessary and unavoidable contribution of West Germany towards the politics of détente.

President Kennedy, however, started with the intervention in Indochina the interlude to détente. It was not interrupted, it continued with Johnson in late 1964 informing the Soviet Union that he was prepared to go along with a non-proliferation treaty and with the end of the MLF-scheme. But the Vietnam War, of course, deviated American attention from détente in Europe. Washington was interested in détente as a parameter of its Asian involvement. The Russians went along, upheld détente in spite of the American war against one of their communist friends in South-East Asia. But for a couple of years détente was only of minor interest to the United States. Entangled in a land war in South-East Asia American foreign policy lost its original orientation.

It was Henry Kissinger and Richard Nixon who disentangled the United States from this involvement and re-established détente as the major goal of the United States foreign policy. This, in fact, is a historical merit the two have earned. This positive judgment does not include the means Kissinger has applied, does not justify the many human lives the retreat from South-East Asia has demanded. But to end the Vietnam tragedy, to bring back United States troops from a war which proved to be the wrong means for an ill-perceived goal, certainly was a major achievement. The war in

---

2. See for details E.-O. Czempiel: "Grundzüge der Weltpolitik", in: J. Mück (ed.), *Internationale Politik*, Wiesbaden o. J. (1970), pp. 32–98.

Vietnam was not only a military disaster, it was at the same time a political catastrophe at home. In its wake two Presidents had to step down, the political system was shaken up, consensus fell, insurrections occurred. But what is more important: the Nixon-doctrine of limitationism, which ended formally the role of the United States as world policeman Number One was a true reflex of the public opinion within the United States. Stirred up by the Vietnam war and led by the young academic elite this public opinion denied the political system the right to involve the United States in wars like that in Vietnam. It re-established the general liberal bourgeois orientation towards peace, at least non-war, as the natural precondition of foreign policy. Kissinger reflected this mood, when he re-invented détente and emphasized the word. He and Nixon managed to bring back United States foreign policy towards the traditional track, leading towards Western Europe and Japan as its main field of interest, establishing détente also in South-East Asia and re-emphasizing it in Central Europe.

It is not easy to assess the Vietnam War properly. Was it the structural behaviour of a capitalistic society, as the revisionists assume?[3] Was it nothing but a "mistake to intervene in Vietnam" as many of the then decision-makers would like to have it now?[4] In my view the Vietnam War was more or less a deviation from the traditional foreign policy behaviour of the United States, produced by a constellation of domestic forces, which was—and still is—alien to the American society. I shall come back to this point a little later on. If this explanation is true, if the Vietnam war, in fact, was nothing else but a temporary aberration then, of course, there should have been overall agreement within the United States with the Kissinger–Nixon foreign policy. But this did not occur. To be sure, there was the 1972 summit in Moscow and in its wake the landslide victory of Richard Nixon. There was, in a different realm, the war powers act,[5] the institutional expression of limitation, so to speak. The American legislative regained its position over the "imperial presidency".[6] But it seems that the war powers

---

3. Cf. Richard J. Barnet: *Roots of War*, Atheneum, New York 1972.
4. Cyrus Vance, in: *U.S. Congress 95/1, Committee on Foreign Relations, Senate:* "Vance Nomination, Hearings", Washington 1977, p. 15.
5. See *U.S. Congress, 94/2, Committee on International Relations, House:* "The War Powers Resolution, Relevant Documents", Correspondence, Report, Committee Print, January 1976 Edition, Washington 1976.
6. See the history of President–Congress relationships in: Arthur M. Schlesinger, Jr.: *The Imperial Presidency*, Popular Library Edition 1974.

resolution of November 1973 was the climax of this general acceptance of détente and limitationism. In 1974, when Kissinger tried to establish a linkage between the Most Favoured Nation Treatment of the Soviet Union and her facilitating the emigration of Soviet Jews, the conservative fraction in Congress balked. The Jackson–Vanik amendment to the Trade Reform Act of 1974 and the Stevenson amendment to the Export-Import Bank Act of 1975, tied MFN-treatment and export credits for the Soviet Union to explicit surrender to the conditions of the American Congress.[7] In the wake of these events and, of course, supporting Jackson's aspirations for the nomination to become the next American President an anti-détente campaign started in the United States. Led by the conservative wing of the Republican Party, promoted by such traditional right-wing organizations as the American Security Council and supported by a considerable number of social scientists[8] the movement gained considerable political strength. President Ford was able to dismiss Secretary of Defense Schlesinger. But Schlesinger's successor, Rumsfeld, sided very quickly with the conservative military forces and alarmed Congress permanently with new and secret information about the Soviet Union's armaments.[9] The movement finally culminated in the election campaign of Ronald Reagan, who pressed President Ford very hard for his détente orientation. Ford had to dismiss the word, if not the policy.

This conservative upsurge of an anti-détente element in the United States cannot be explained very easily. Of course, the element is not identical with those forces who promoted the Vietnam war. One must distinguish between two groups. There is one which really cares about the outcome of détente, asking whether the lowering of détente produces progress within the Soviet Union towards more Human Rights. There is another group which points towards the considerable re-armament of the Soviet Union since 1963 and discriminates against détente because of its neglect of this development. Nevertheless the two work together as an anti-détente force in the United States. Since this force did not cease to exist on the election of President Carter it must be seen as

7. *Trade Act of 1974, P. L. 93–618. Export-Import Bank Act of 1945*, as amended, P. L. 93–646.

8. See, e.g., *U.S. Congress, 93/2, Committee on Armed Services, Senate:* "Détente: An Evaluation", Washington 1974.

9. Rowland Evans and Robert Nowak: "Pentagon's 'Show and Tell'", in: *International Herald Tribunal*, 25.1.1977.

one of the important parameters of Carter's foreign policy behaviour. Therefore, a somewhat more detailed look into the domestic structure of the United States is pertinent. Hopefully it will be proof for the above-mentioned thesis at the Vietnam war was nothing but a deviation from the structure of the foreign policy behaviour of American society.

Domestic Forces and Détente Policies

One minor, but nevertheless, important element within the domestic scene of the détente period was the authoritarian style of Kissinger and Nixon. Although Nixon had considerable experience in Congress he followed Kissinger's neglect of the legislative. Given the sensitive relationship between the two branches of government some part of the anti-détente sentiment in Congress can be explained as an anti-Kissinger sentiment. Kissinger arranged his trading the MFN-treatment against Jewish emigration from the USSR without even mentioning it to Congress. Small wonder that Congress balked.

For its larger part, of course, the explanation has to look for other and more important forces. They are to be found in the considerable changes the American society has experienced during the 30 years of the cold war. The most basic change concerns the role of the military. Up to 1939 it played a minor role, was practically without political influence. After 1947 and 1949 the military establishment became one of the most eminent and dominant sectors of political decision-making in the United States. The Secretary of Defense became the most important advisor to the President for national security affairs, the President himself could relay his orders immediately via the Secretary to the military branches.[10] Or, more broadly: after the militarization of the East–West conflict since 1950 military thinking prevailed in American foreign policy decision-making. It spread towards the civilians, as is demonstrated in the Pentagon Papers.[11] The military became used to being the decisive factor in Washington, in political as well as in financial terms. With—temporarily—up to 58 per cent. of the national budget used for defence related matters, organizational interest, group interests, career interests established themselves, and became active as a tremendous political force. Its relationship with certain parts of industry, above all with the military-related

10. C.W. Borklund: *The Department of Defense*, Praeger, New York 1968.
11. The New York Times (ed.): *The Pentagon Papers*, Bantam Books 1971.

committees in Congress, gave much political power to the military establishment. Its strength is of such a quality that Carter's Secretary of State Vance in March 1977 could not offer to the Russians what he would have liked to offer: the inclusion of the cruise missile into the SALT II talks.[12]

This is not a new version of the military-industrial-complex-theory. We do know that this complex cannot explain American armaments politics.[13] Instead of this narrow theorem one has to ask what kind of perceptions and attitudes do come into foreign policy decision-making, if the military participates in such a degree as has been the case in the United States. It is unavoidable that 30 years of tremendous military impact combined with the impact of conservative orientations within the American legislative form a structural pattern, which tends to become permanent. This social pattern tends to continue its orientation and its demands, its analysis and its assessments. The social psychological mechanism which steers this process has been established long ago by Schumpeter.[14] He interprets imperialism as an orientation, which has become anachronistic because of the change of circumstances. Accordingly, the anti-détente orientation of the American military and the political conservative wing can be interpreted as the continuation of orientations and values which are outmoded, but still existent.

This does not mean that these social forces are necessarily against détente. But it does mean that they are against détente in so far as détente affects negatively their political position and their share of allocated financial values. They sense very deeply and correctly that détente after Vietnam might be combined with a reduction of armaments, with—in other words—a reduction of their potential of influence and political strength. As long as détente meant nothing else but a lowering of tensions without any consequences for the means allotted to them, these groups were not against détente, at least not very outspoken. Things are different now, after Vietnam, after Watergate, and after the on-going discussion within the United States on national priorities.[15] Kissinger was about to

12. *International Herald Tribune*, 24.3.1977.

13. Gert Krell: "Zur Theorie der Rüstungsdynamik im Ost-West-Konflikt", in: *Politische Vierteljahresschrift* 17,4, Dezember 1976, p. 437 f.

14. Joseph Schumpeter: "The Sociology of Imperialisms", in: J. Schumpeter: *Imperialism and Social Classes: Two Essays*, Meridian Books, Cleveland and New York 1965.

15. *U.S. Congress 91/2, Joint Economic Committee:* "Changing National Priorities, Hearings, Part 1", Washington 1970 ff.

establish a real working cooperation with the Soviet Union with regard to the offensive weapons. During his campaign Carter promised to cut the military budget substantially. Here we have reached the—above mentioned—point where détente begins to affect the substance of the conflict with consequences for the means involved. If détente reaches a quality which changes the aspect of the conflict the means of resolving the conflict must change accordingly. It is politically impossible to spend one-third of the national budget for armaments, if détente has proved that there is no real and present danger. The American military and the Conservatives react against this linkage between détente and their position in, and their part of, the allocation of values in the United States. They have learned that they cannot win another Vietnam—not even perhaps in Latin America. But they are not prepared to learn that détente has diminished their role. They react accordingly.

The structural problem of a détente policy is, therefore, how to balance the military. If possible, they should be diminished to the necessary and functionally correct degree. This will be a very difficult and time-consuming process, but a very necessary one. The growth of the military has changed the pattern of liberal capitalistic societies substantially. They are, so to speak, deformed. In order to regain their original and socially correct shape they have to reduce the number and the influence of the military. Economic and political considerations must be put back in their place again. Only then will liberal democracy again establish and promote the goals upon which it is traditionally and socially oriented: economic profit and peace. Where are the forces which could perform this re-forming of the American Government? There is, first, the liberal wing in the political parties and in Congress; there is, above all, the economic community, there is public opinion.

Although it is not easy to assess the flow of political attitudes within the American parties, one can note a growing liberal agglomeration of Democratic Congressmen. The Democratic Study Group, starting with regular meetings of a small group of representatives in 1953, has a membership ranging between 100 and, roughly, 200 Congressmen. It is not a political bloc, but it demonstrates considerable political cohesion and influences the outcome of voting in the House to a remarkable degree.[16] Its

16. Arthur G. Stevens, Jr. *et al.:* "Mobilization of Liberal Strength in the House, 1955-1970: The Democratic Study Group", in: *American Political Science Review*, 68, 2, June 1974, p. 667 ff.

members are not united on all items, of course, but they are sensitive against the demands of the military. The Vietnam war was a focal point in the political development of the Study Group, and although all of them are for the necessary military strength against the Soviet Union, they are not prepared to accept everything the military is saying. Above all, Representative Les Aspin has been very critical, and his critique has been successful.[17]

Structurally more important is the support for détente by the economic community in the United States. For Republican administrations economic and political issues traditionally are very close to each other. The Republicans recognized very early that the cold war policy of sharply restricted trade and of embargos against the socialist countries was counter-productive to American economic interests. The European countries profited from expanding trade with the socialist States, the American economy suffered from the lack of such a relationship. Although the balance-of-payments difficulties of the United States could not be related to the absence of trade with the Soviet Union and other bloc-countries the resumption of this trade could lead to an improving of the balance-of-payments situation. The recognition of these interests played an important role for the inauguration of the détente-politics of the American Government.[18]

In the wake of the Moscow summit in May 1972, several agreements have been concluded between the United States and the USSR, intended to facilitate trade between the two countries. Although the trade agreement could not become accomplished because of the Jackson–Vanik amendment and the Stevenson amendment, some important deals have been made, notably the grain deal. The US–USSR-Trade Economic Council is still working with its American co-chairman Donald Kendall (who is the chairman of PepsiCo) actively pleading for the continuation of détente policies. On the American side, this council is supported by more than 200 American corporations whose annual sales combined exceed 25 per cent. of the American GNP, demonstrating very markedly the substantial interest of American business in

---

17. See the exchange of views: "Soviet Strength and U.S. Purpose", in: *Foreign Policy* No. 23, Summer 1976, p. 32 ff.

18. *U.S. Congress, 95/1, Commission on Security and Cooperation in Europe:* "Basket II—Helsinki Final Act, East–West Economic Cooperation, Hearings", Washington 1977, Statement Parsky, p. 57 ff.

détente.[19] With the intention of countering anti-détente groups like the Committee on the Present Danger or the very recently formed Coalition for a New Foreign and Military Policy more than 100 American business leaders and members of the political élite founded the American Committee on US–Soviet Relations, chaired by Fred Warner Neal.[20] Even if in the public campaign the pro-détente groups should not become victorious it is evident that the economic interest of the business community in the United States point towards détente as the condition for improving economic relationships with the socialist countries. Public opinion is hard to assess. The Chicago Council on Foreign Relations found out that the American people are tired of interventions, but that they are prepared to shoulder their burden in the defence field. It seems to be that in 1976, as the Republican election campaign has borne out and certainly re-inforced, preparedness to spend more on arms has been growing again. The Democratic candidate Carter promised to cut the defence budget by at least 10 per cent. With extreme caution it can perhaps be said that public opinion is ambivalent. At present there is a certain tendency to become inward-oriented following the long-term swing of public opinion in the United States. But it will not be impossible to arouse public opinion again.

Concluding these remarks on the structural basis of American foreign policy behaviour it can be said that there is a certain division between the defence community on the one hand and the business community on the other hand. The defence community is definitely not prepared to accept détente to a point where its vested interest will be damaged. The business community, on the other hand, is substantially interested in an ongoing détente, although some qualifications have to be added (which I shall discuss later). Judging from a structural point of view, the economic community should prevail. Given the administrative position of the military and defence-related industry it will not be easy for the business community in general to re-establish their interests against the bureaucratic power of the defence branch. This dichotomy explains, in my view, the policies which the Ford administration has pursued after Helsinki. Possibly, this explanation is valid for Carter's behaviour as well.

19. Statement Kendall, *ibidem*, p. 117 ff.
20. Fred Warner Neal: "The Salvagers of Détente", in: *World Issues*, February/March 1977, p. 27 f.

Evaluating Détente

The Ford administration tried to live up to Helsinki and to détente without neglecting the interests of the defence community. Ford accepted the Helsinki accord, but stated repeatedly that United States policy towards the future developments in Europe would depend on the extent to which the specific, concrete provisions of the final document of Helsinki would be actually implemented. In its first critical review of this implementation, published in December 1976, the Ford administration was not too sceptical. It found mixed results, differing from country to country and from basket to basket. It was highly critical of Soviet interpretations of the declaration of principles guiding relations between participating States[21] and listed all deviations of the Eastern parts on these principles. The record of the confidence-building measures, however, appeared in Washington as "moderately encouraging".[22]

An even better grade was given to basket II. The Ford government found a "significant increase in US trade with the Soviet Union and individual East European States as well as some efforts by the Eastern countries to facilitate US business interest".[23] The particular interest of American business to get more economic and commercial information was responded to fairly well by Romania and Hungary, modestly improved by the Soviet Union and rather bad by Bulgaria and the GDR. Czechoslovakia was found somewhere in the middle. The Ford administration registered that trade with Eastern Europe and the Soviet Union "has increased substantially in the period since Helsinki".[24]

In basket III, by contrast, the behaviour of the socialist States was termed to be more or less insufficient. After having enacted in early 1976 a series of limited measures, Soviet implementation of basket III obligations was found to have "slowed markedly".[25]

Altogether, the Ford administration was neither disappointed nor discouraged. It was prepared to take part in the Belgrade Conference with "no wish to see the Belgrade meeting devolve into

---

21. *U.S. Congress, 94/2, Committee on International Relations:* "First Semiannual Report by the President to the Commission on Security and Cooperation in Europe", December 1976, p. 14.
22. *Ibidem*, p. 18.
23. *Ibidem*, p. 23.
24. *Ibidem*, p. 34.
25. *Ibidem*, p. 40.

an exchange of recriminations and polemics".[26] It believed that the CSCE could "contribute to a relaxation of tensions between States and to practical improvements in the daily lives of people".[27]

This moderately positive attitude towards Helsinki and Belgrade was to some extent shared by Congress. Although its Commission on Security and Cooperation in Europe was founded in the summer of 1976 primarily as a means of observing the administration and keeping it from making concessions with regard to the CSCE,[28] the commission tried to be as objective as possible. The report of its study mission, which went to Europe in November 1976, was objective and positive: the commission found that the Helsinki accords "were beginning to have a productive but limited effect on the improvement of East–West relations".[29] The study group brought home the fact that most European leaders, even those who had been critical towards Helsinki at the outset, now have a more optimistic view of the potential long-range advantage the follow-up of Helsinki could bring. With this in mind the study group recommended closer cooperation between the United States and its NATO allies in order to work out a common approach to the Belgrade Conference. It recommended further that more money should be made available to exhaust the basket III provisions.

The Ford administration was prepared to go along with the spirit of Helsinki and to cooperate in Belgrade. It followed the general line of Kissinger that there was no alternative to détente, and that the only chance in Europe to improve the situation existed in the lowering of tensions. "Détente", said Kissinger, "is the improvement of long-term relations with an emerging super power",[30] and the so-called Sonnenfeldt-doctrine did nothing else but articulate the practical consequence of the combination of two American goals in Europe: to avoid war and to improve the political and human situation in Eastern Europe.

26. *Ibidem*, p. 61.
27. *Ibidem*, pp. 61–62.
28. *U.S. Congress 94/2, Committee on International Relations, House* "Conference on Security and Cooperation in Europe: Part II, Hearings", Washington 1976.
29. *U.S. Congress, 95/1, Committee on International Relations, House:* "Report of the Study Mission to Europe to the Commission on Security and Cooperation in Europe", Committee Print, Washington 1977.
30. *U.S. Congress, 94/2, Committee on International Relations, House:* "United States National Security Policy Vis-à-Vis Eastern Europe (The 'Sonnenfeldt Doctrine'), Hearings", Washington 1976, Summary of Remarks by Henry Kissinger, S. 60.

If political insight led the Ford administration towards détente so did the interests of the business community. The Ford administration continued to oppose the Jackson–Vanik amendment and the Stevenson amendment, both of which were deemed to be inconsistent with the Helsinki accord and with American interests.[31] The administration shared in full the objectives the amendments tried to realize. But it criticized the means the amendments chose, because they did not link trade and progress in Human Rights, but provoked nothing but a confrontation.[32] While emigration from the Soviet Union generally went up, the number of Jews emigrating from the USSR was significantly lower than in the years of 1972–73, before the Jackson–Vanik amendment.[33] Secretary of Commerce Richardson tried very hard in January 1977 to convince the Commission on Security and Cooperation in Europe that the Jackson–Vanik amendment should be replaced by the relevant paragraphs of basket II and III of the Helsinki accord. In his view the United States "should lean heavily on the final act", because it contains the "kinds of relationship which all the signatories have said should characterize the standards which they apply internationally and to each other".[34] In other words: the Ford administration was prepared to give the Most Favoured Nation Treatment to the USSR and to the Eastern European countries and to rely only on the reciprocity provided for in the Helsinki accord to realize the political and the human goals in this area.

The American business community was even more outspoken. For them, "the provisions of basket II do provide a useful codification of the principles American businessmen would like to see firmly established in our commercial relations with that part of the world".[35] They accept the wording of the final act as a standard formulation which could be incorporated into any bilateral agreement between the USA and a socialist country.

This does not mean that the American business community is oriented only towards economic relations with the socialist countries and forgets completely the Human Rights issue there. On the contrary, businessmen are interested in these questions, and for this reason they criticize the Jackson–Vanik–Stevenson amendments.

31. "Basket II Hearings (note 18)", Statement Richardson, p. 94 f.
32. *Ibidem*, p. 107.
33. Statistics in: "Semiannual Report" (note 21), p. 41.
34. "Basket II Hearings" (note 18), p. 110.
35. *Ibidem*, p. 28, Statement Wilson, U.S. Chamber of Commerce.

They follow the functional approach, assuming that the growth of stable commercial relationships with countries of different social and economic systems will do a lot to promote the respect for basic human values. This is a standard assumption within liberal thought. Obviously these functional consequences do not occur automatically. Trade is no ersatz for politics. Trade is no guarantee for the growth of respect for Human Rights. But it cannot be denied that, in the absence of other means available, trade is a very pertinent means of influence. It establishes channels for the communications of ideas and goods which affect necessarily the situation in the countries involved.

The Ford administration was prepared to apply these means to the European situation. It recognized the fact that the international system had changed considerably in the seventies, that after the oil shock, the end of the Vietnam war, and the considerable rearmament of the Soviet Union a phase of the post-war era had come to an end. In the new period economic power was far more important than military power. It was more flexible and could be much better tuned to the American goals. Military power was a necessary, but no more the exclusive medium of power, not even the dominant one. The USA was able to accept a certain parity in the strategic field with the Soviet Union. To slow down the arms race was, in this view, more important than to win it. To remain number one economically was more interesting than to remain number one militarily.

Kissinger obviously was very much engaged, in January 1976, to reach an accord with the Soviet Union, which would have produced a certain pause in the production of the cruise missiles and the backfire bomber. This, perhaps, would have opened the way for a SALT II agreement, a formal codification of the Vladivostock agreement. But Kissinger failed, not because of resistance in Moscow (that was also there), but because of the resistance in Washington. The military was—and is—not prepared to include the cruise missiles into an agreement with the Soviet Union. It is obviously not a bargaining chip as it is usually termed. Otherwise Kissinger would have struck this bargain already in 1976.

In this dichotomic situation Ford did what was left to him: he tried to live with the military-conservative wing and with the business community. He fulfilled more or less the obligations of basket I and basket II of the Helsinki accord; he did not live up to the basket III demands, since he gave way to the veto of the AFL–CIO against visas for Soviet labour leaders and Italian communists. He did not struggle too hard to have the Jackson–Vanik amendment lifted, which also was against the Helsinki accords. In the broader context of Helsinki there was no progress either. SALT II was practically halted, and so were the MBFR talks.

In the economic field everything went as well as it possibly could, even the two amendments. The Secretary of the Treasury Simon and his Assistant Secretary for International Affairs Parsky took part in the third annual session of the US–USSR-Trade and Economic Council together with the Russian counterpart Patolichev. In 1977, 24 American firms had already established offices in Moscow, another 10 are waiting for accreditation. The US–USSR Commercial Commission's Working Group of Experts, established under the long-term agreement between the two States to facilitate economic, industrial, and technical cooperation, did equally well. It is not directly related to Helsinki but to the American–Soviet accord of May 1972. The same is true for the Joint American–Polish Trade Commission and the Joint American–Romanian Economic Commission. Both were established prior to Helsinki but continued to work after Helsinki to fulfil the obligations under basket II. In 1976, a long-term agreement on economic, industrial and technical cooperation with Romania was concluded.

In spite of all these activities the commerical relations between the United States and the socialist countries in Europe remain in a "holding pattern", because of the Jackson–Vanik amendment and the Stevenson amendment. Does the former prevent the broad development of economic relations which depend on the MFN-treatment, so keeps the latter a lid on the credits available in the United States. The trade agreement between the United States and the Soviet Union was not entered into force, and the lend-lease repayments were suspended. In spite of all partial successes, the momentum established in 1972 slowed down in the wake of title IV of the Trade Reform Act of 1974.

Balancing Ford's compliance with the wishes of the military-conservative wing and those of the business community, it seems that the military-conservatives prevailed. This is true, but only at the first glance. If business interests in the United States would have been seriously damaged, the influence of these groups would certainly be applied to correct the situation. This is being done, but only in a comparatively moderate way. The reason is that the American multinational corporations can realize their interest in dealing with the Soviet Union and the Eastern European countries from their affiliates in Western Europe, where they have everything: credits and no limitations. American businessmen place their Soviet orders with their overseas affiliates or subsidiaries, and take thus advantage of the more liberal policies of the Western European countries. Really suffering from the restrictions imposed by Congress is not the American business community but the American workers. The jobs which would be likely to come with the expansion of the East–West trade are not created in the United States but in Western Europe and in Japan. Since the American Labour Unions are, for political reasons, strictly against any commerical dealings with communist countries, they cannot do anything to correct the situation. Once more structurally speaking, one consequence of this situation will be that a correcting influence stemming from business interests will not appear. Since American industry, trade, and banking can realize the interests from abroad they can afford waiting until the situation in the United States changes. For this time the dichotomy will present an imbalance.

The Contradiction Remains

This is the context within which the new Carter administration had to establish its policies towards Belgrade. The impact of this context was heavily felt during the first three months of the new administration. Carter was convinced that a breakthrough in the SALT stalemate between the USSR and the USA is absolutely necessary. He succeeded in making Warnke Chief of ACDA and of the American SALT-Delegation to Moscow in March 1977. But he had to push very hard and finally must make the compromise of adding one of the close military friends of Jackson to the American delegation. As far as can be seen from the Spring of 1977, Senator Jackson still is in the position to control all American proposals for the SALT discussions. Carter's double proposal, either to cut substantially all weapons across the board or to formalize the Vladivostock agreement without mentioning the cruise missiles and the backfire bomber will probably fail. Everybody knows that the heart of the matter lies in a pause for the cruise missiles and for the backfire bomber, so that Carter's proposal necessarily must look like a scapegoat for an anticipated continuation of the stalemate. The American military obviously is not prepared to offer the cruise missiles as a bargaining chip.[36]

36. See Carter's cautious remarks in his Notre Dame address, May 22, 1977, that "American and Soviet interests, perceptions and aspirations vary", *International Herald Tribune*, May 30, 1977, p. 6.

In contrast to this it is perfectly possible that Mr. Carter will succeed in persuading Congress to eliminate the two amendments. Most Congressmen are rather unhappy with them and are looking for a way out of an impasse which was created between a Democratic Congress, a Republican Administration, and an authoritarian Secretary of State. The question here is how and how soon a solution can be worked out. After it has been found, the American economy proper and the American worker will profit from an expanding trade with the Soviet Union and the socialist countries in Eastern Europe. This will reinforce the economic interest already existing in the basket II of the Helsinki accord. Under President Carter the United States probably will continue the policies towards Helsinki which had been developed under his predecessor. Détente in Europe goes on, and so does the arms race. The contradiction remains.

Part Three

COOPERATION IN THE FIELD OF ECONOMICS

INTRODUCTION

The participating States—reads the preambular paragraph to the "second basket" of the Final Act of the CSCE—are: "*convinced* that their efforts to develop cooperation in the fields of trade, industry, science and technology, the environment and other areas of economic activity contribute to the reinforcement of peace and security in Europe and in the world as a whole".

As the provisions in this section of the Final Act recorded developments already taking place rather than breaking new ground for further promoting cooperation in those fields, the conclusions arrived at in several evaluations of their implementation, seem obvious: the Final Act has had a negligible impact, if any at all.

The two contributions in this part therefore discuss developments since rather than due to the conclusion of the Final Act. The two authors also focus on the most important aspect: the development of cooperation in the field of economics.

Bognár, in Chapter 9, emphasizes, in his first section, the reverse side of the above-quoted paragraph: the negative effect of the security system on the development of better economic conditions. He also points, thereafter, to the advantages for both the centrally planned economics, the market-economics and the developing economics, resulting from the present trends towards closer East–West economic relations. In his opinion the changes in economic policies of the socialist States are likely to improve the prospects for further cooperation.

Pinder carefully analyses the prospects and problems for improving relations between the European Communities and Comecon and its members. Political considerations and limited economic advantages for both the Soviet Union and the EEC of such a new relationship explain the slow progress of Comecon–EEC exploratory talks. In view of the major interest of the East-European—other than Soviet—Comecon States in further improving relations with the community, he offers some suggestions on how such improvements can be achieved.

Chapter 9

EAST–WEST TRADE AND THE PROCESS' OF DÉTENTE

by *József Bognár*

In this chapter we shall be concerned with problems relating to the formation and development of European economic cooperation at a time when the intertwining of political and security questions with economic ones (both in nation States and international life) has assumed unprecedented proportions. This tendency, so typical of the character and future of our era, can be demonstrated by some shifts in emphasis depending on the views taken and the focus of one's way of thinking. One should point out that the weight of international economic questions has substantially increased in relation to the problems of international politics and security, and that this process is still going on. Economists are likely to stress the latter aspect of changes. If, however, one uses the term politics in its broader sense and accordingly sets out from the focus of power where decisions are taken and to frame rational proportions of action, we may describe this tendency by saying that the economic components of political decisions are significantly strengthened.

In a traditional approach to certain problems of international trade, my task would not include the discussion of questions of politics and security. It is, however, questionable whether a traditional approach would be fruitful in a case where the world of phenomena under scrutiny manifests forms of evolution and fluctuations or oscillations that cannot be interpreted "endogenously", i.e., in terms of a resultant of purely economic forces. A traditional approach is of course feasible also in such cases, but it will be perceived as rather a circuitous approach to the system of relationships in question.

However, if the intertwining of political and security questions with economic ones and the statement concerning the growing importance of economic problems are accepted as stipulated, then it appears to be justified also to carry out the analysis and appraisal of the security system established, or about to be established, from an economic point of view. Its character considerably influences domestic and international economic relations. That it is really justified to carry out this analysis is corroborated by the fact that fundamental changes have taken place in the position and potential of the two interdependent factors. It is commonly known that the scientific and technological revolution has radically changed the earlier conditions regarding the security of nations, social systems and particular regions. (It should be noted in passing that the security aspects of the socio-political systems have been playing a very important part in international affairs since the French Revolution. This tendency has been still further strengthened by the revolutions of our century, and this system of thinking and action will retain its justifiability in the world until a collective security system acceptable to all is created.)

The Development of Economic Relations and the Security System

It is evident, that the change of era[1] in the world economy has drastically altered earlier views on the potentialities and limitations of the economy as well as on the system of conditions governing its normal operation. It is common knowledge that the security system known as equilibrium of deterrents withdraws immense resources from economic development. It is doubtful whether economies slowing down in their growth and facing such problems as the rising costs of the factors of production, the dislocation of raw-material sources, the disturbance of the ecological equilibrium, the feeding of an increasing world population, the satisfaction of basic human needs,[2] price and structural changes, and inflation, will be able to ensure and if so, by undertaking what consequences, the energies necessary to maintain that security system. The extremely high level of military expenditure has contributed in no small measure to the phenomena of the change of era in the world economy bursting into our life precisely now and under such serious conditions. This is an economic problem, and the greatest one that various economies have to cope with. The above-mentioned security system, however, affects not only domestic economies but also international economic relations.

Evidently, the indirect consequences of this security system—which incessantly add fuel to the climate of mutual suspicion—aggravate the establishment of such economic relations as are necessary in an interdependent world and which are, to a certain

1. Bognár Jósef: *Világgazdasági korszakváltás*. (*Changes of era in the world economy*), Bp. Kőzgazd. és Jogi J.—Gondolat, 1976, 225 pp.
2. *Basic Needs and national employment strategies*—June 1976, Geneva, International Labour Office, 1976, 195 pp.

extent, also possible under the present world economic mechanism. They, however, presuppose mutual confidence and goodwill.

In the world economy, however, we are experiencing a strengthening of interdependence. In respect of fundamental relationships, it means a symbiosis with nature as one of the new guiding norms of the existence of human society. It constitutes also, in its more limited sense, i.e., within the world economy, a signal warning that economic growth, economic policy and the situation of a given country or integration exert a vigorous impact on the potential development of other countries or integrations. Economic developments taking place in one constitute an economic environment for the other country.

However, the spill-over effects of this security system expressly hamper the formation of mechanisms, regulators and forms of cooperation which indirectly promote the solution of global problems, basically affecting all those who take part in the world economy. This is because these factors presuppose a high degree of mutual trust, an active community of interest and the acceptance of the idea of reciprocal dependence.

Summing up the effect of that security system on the system of internal conditions of economic growth, one can conclude that the regular withdrawal of a substantial part of economic resources from the economic sphere increases instability, which results anyway from the change of era in the world economy.

It is, however, commonly known that given growing internal instability, "external" security is inconceivable. It may therefore be assumed that the utilization of economic energies for security purposes beyond a certain limit gives birth to greater insecurity than what might arise in the military field if the same resources were used for economic purposes.

The situations, factors and consequences connected with the decay of the system of external conditions of economic growth must be assessed with great circumspection. The fact that certain countries have a lesser share in the benefits derived from the international division of labour and trade, is of course a serious problem in itself, under the aggravating conditions of economic growth. The experience also that the objective threat to the conditions of human existence makes itself felt through factors and processes whose change, or the stopping or mitigating of their dangerous elements, requires international cooperation, more economic resources and coordinated actions is another problem. Any attempt to prevent the creation of an international climate which promotes the warding off or the mitigation of these real dangers—in which a very essential role is played of course by the balance of mutual deterrence and the related system of thinking and behaviour—jeopardizes the conditions of human existence to a greater extent than it increases, if at all, the "security" of individual States or military alliances.

The conclusion logically follows from this system of interdependence between security-policy and economic factors that the economy is not a passive medium merely receiving effects, but an active power which, through its operation and mechanisms, reacts on the security sphere. Every single result of cooperation, any up-to-date method and bold initiative creating a community of interest, contributes to the lessening or dispelling of mutual distrust which, in earlier situations, led to the rise of that security system. Thus the common interests partly exert a positive effect and, beyond a certain point coming into conflict with the structure of security, partly exist side by side dooming each other to mutual impotence.

Account must also be taken of the fact that in an organized human society—and thus in international relations as well—the negative implications of the various power factors are always greater than the positive ones. To put it differently, it is considerably easier to prevent something than to get norms of behaviour that conform to a new situation accepted as a basis of action. Thus a "complete breakthrough" is hardly conceivable on behalf of the economy since, in domestic politics, the established security patterns have greatly strengthened over the decades, while in international life the structure of security (the dominant nuclear powers) and the distribution of economic power show substantial disparities.[3] As a result of this shift, the energies arising in the sphere of political power are more easily and more quickly transferred to the economy than economic energies to a political one. This is because, in the world today, political and military power is relatively concentrated, while economic power, even between States, is more widely spread, and some of its forms embody an original economic policy which is independent even of States, e.g., multinational corporations. The change of era in the world economy, however, necessitates new decisions; partly because, owing to the deterioration of the conditions of growth, the economy can feed this security system with new energies only at the expense of living conditions; partly because the mobile equilibrium

3. M. Camps: *The Management of Interdependence*, Council of Foreign Relations, New York 1974.

of certain factors appearing in the economic sphere represents today a greater danger than anything else, even if these dangers appear not in the classical, nation-state framework, but on a global or regional scale.

Weighing up the present situation, and the future, on the basis of economic factors and interconnections, the conclusion can be reached that, in the decades to come, we shall need security conceptions which: (a) do not withdraw too much energy from the economy which suffers from a scarcity of assets; (b) do not impede, but promote, the formation of a system of international political and economic relations which enables mankind to solve the problems raised by the scientific and technological revolution and the change of era in the world economy. "Solution" would mean partly the avoidance of certain imminent dangers (nuclear catastrophe, major ecological disaster, the collapse of the economic system, etc.), and partly the launching of the implementation of projects aimed at satisfying basic human needs, a more rational distribution of economic activities and the guarantee of conditions for progress in the Third World.

It is obvious that in the light of the change of era in the world economy, East–West relations cannot be treated in isolation or on a bilateral basis. These relations are part and parcel of the world's political equilibrium, which means that they must also be regarded, from the point of view of the Third World, as factors influencing a growth-determining climate. The peaceful and constructive character of this climate is beneficial both from the political and the economic point of view; if fraught with tensions, however, it is harmful from both. This is because tensions tend to change local or regional problems into international conflicts, on the one hand, and they withdraw major economic resources from world economic circulation, on the other. Therefore East–West trade is needed of a nature which is both efficient enough to bring about and develop common interests, and capable of channelling such new energies into the world economy which also promote the development of the Third World.

The structure and methods of approach of this chapter may have created the impression that the approach here exemplified is unjustifiably *normative*.

What I am explaining is what ought to be, rather than how things as established in practice could be further developed, thus serving as a starting point.

But a normative approach as a starting-point is not only right but justified and useful in cases where a change in the way of thinking which derives from given conditions is the point at issue because a new way of thinking also implies a new system of objectives, and new conditions described as optimum. The essence of the change consists exactly in the fact that in the new system of conditions something may no longer be desirable and expedient that used to be that earlier, or that such new requirements are also raised of which no account was taken before. The consequences of past pragmatic action appear today as materialized practice, but these very actions in themselves were products of some kind of conception. It is evident, of course, that the normative approach can never be the only or exclusive one, as real action derives, in its content, from interests, its "thrust" being due to economic power or power relations. If one neglects this one may easily find oneself in the realm of Utopia.

Hence, we shall, in the following section, explore the various questions on a *pragmatic basis*, trying to draw certain conclusions in that way. The simultaneous application and circumspect combination of these two approaches will enable us always to establish the relationship between objectives or postulates and the real situation.

Trends in East–West Economic Relations

An analysis of the processes and trends that evolved in the 1970s appears to suggest that East–West trade—amidst and in spite of the survival of some of the uncertainty factors that originated in an earlier period, and the emergence of new ones—has undergone substantial development in every respect. Earlier analyses, in the 1960s, established that East–West trade, that is trade between countries with differing socio-economic systems, was highly sensitive to political developments and changes. Setting out from this premise one can reach a similar conclusion arguing that détente and the abatement of the Cold War have given a new impetus to the growth of trade and economic relations.

The appreciable rise in the volume of economic and trade relations also finds expression in the fact that, by comparison with 1970, the East–West share in world trade increased from 2.6 to 3.1 per cent. Looking at it from another angle, the growth rate of East–West trade in the 1970s—including the trough of the crisis period—has surpassed the growth rate of world trade quite considerably (by 25 per cent.). The share of OECD countries in the external economic activity of CMEA countries has also risen. This proportionate share, which varies of course from country to country, now fluctuates between 30 and 35 per cent., and shows a rapid growth especially in relation to certain overseas countries like USA, Australia and Japan.

As the vigorous expansion of economic relations has taken place simultaneously with the price rises and structural shocks caused by the change of era in the world economy, with the crisis of the capitalist economy, and the switch of socialist economies from extensive to intensive growth, it has obviously also given rise to significant problems and tensions. As a result of these phenomena, that occurred as explosions, socialist countries have been unable, owing to the contraction of import markets, to expand their exports at a rate which would have been necessary to pay for their extremely high-priced imports. As a result, they have become indebted to a considerable degree, and they can offset this only by accelerating the change-over. This change-over means a consistent realization of the foreign economic orientation of the economies; that is, it requires a new strategy of external economic activity. At this stage I only wish to mention that the indebtedness of the socialist countries is far from "appalling" in view of the present international payments situation. Price rises (deterioration in the terms of trade) make themselves felt immediately, while structural changes, including the stepping up of exports which it involves, and making them more competitive, take time. Besides, the international monetary system and organization were not, and could not be, prepared for these changes.

The situation which has come about in this way must be conceived as a "thrust towards cooperation" which may play a useful role if the necessary steps are taken on both sides. The necessary steps will be determined primarily according to what mechanisms of cooperation we can establish under conditions of mutual dependence deriving from the world economy.

The impact of East–West relations on the internal economic development of countries participating in this trade has strengthened. It may be assumed that this fact is of particular importance in a period of slowing down economic growth.

In recent years, a new view has evolved in the European socialist countries on the effect and significance of international economic relations. The objective background to this new view, provided in part by the requirements of an intensive type of growth, is also related to the relaxation of international tension. In the period of extensive growth and the Cold War, imports from non-socialist countries were regarded simply as gap-filling and exports to those countries as an additional factor. To put it differently: no imports policy could be formulated which looked on imports as a component of rational economic structure, and on exports as a component of a policy of growth.

In the new view the recognition finds expression that international economic relations have and may have an economy-developing effect. In the course of its development the socialist economy cannot do without impulses derived from foreign economic activity, including of course, exports.

Benefits to the socialist countries
If this view is accepted, the benefits accruing to the socialist economies from trading with the developed capitalist countries are—besides profits—as follows:

(a) The acceleration of technical progress owing to the direct and indirect effects of imported means of production. We speak of indirect effects because technical progress achieved in one industry has, on the one hand, spill-over effects and, on the other, it has powers of attraction.

(b) The extension of the markets and, as a result, the acceleration of growth (national income, production, etc.)

(c) Increase in sophisticated production techniques, especially in the case of cooperation with technologically advanced economic units.

(d) Satisfaction of certain consumption needs at a higher level, and the indirect effects related to it.

(e) Ensuring additional development resources in certain periods.

(f) Apart from the growth and development-promoting effects, a very important role has of course been played so far, and will continue to be played hereafter as well, by imports that contribute to ensuring continuous economic activity, such as imports of raw materials and semi-manufactured goods in short supply, and agricultural products and food at times of local and temporary shortages.

It may be clear from the above list that the expansion of East–West economic relations has a growth stimulating effect from the point of view of the socialist countries.

Put somewhat differently, this statement means that the socialist countries and economies have an essential interest in the expansion of these ties. Here and now we have touched exclusively upon those ties of an economic nature, having already outlined certain factors of a system of political interests. We have no intention of discussing some further ones like the highly complex skein of problems of influences upon the internal structures of society.

Benefits to developed capitalist countries
The positive effects on the economic growth of developed capitalist countries of trade with the CMEA countries are as follows:

(a) The expansion of markets through exports promotes growth. This effect has been, and will be, of particular importance at times of slowed down economic growth. It is well known that forecasts extending to 1990 envisage a slowing down of economic growth, which raises a large number of social problems.

(b) Trade with CMEA countries promotes the further modernization of the economic and productive structure. Imports are used to restrain the activities of certain less economic industries, or to restructure their range of products. In such cases, cooperation makes possible a saving in investments, or their more concentrated use.

(c) It furthers, and cooperation could increasingly further, the diversification of the fuel and raw-materials supply. The developed capitalist countries, primarily Western Europe and Japan, but to a certain extent the United States as well, will continue to be the largest fuel and raw-material importers. A stable raw-material supply—under appropriate political and economic guarantees—will continue to remain one of the hubs of economic growth. Cooperation on their part in developing the raw-material producing capacities of the socialist countries may turn into an important aspect of the stability of their raw-material sources. Agreements of this nature have already been concluded in a significant number, and the preparation of similar agreements is under way.

(d) Imports promote the satisfaction of certain consumer and production demands on a wider scale.

I have already pointed out the national economic effects of the expansion of economic relations, but I should also like to refer to the business benefits that derive from profits, technological cooperation, greater specialization and the strengthening of dynamism. The beneficiaries of these advantages are not only the big companies well provided with capital, but also small- and medium-sized firms which have attained a high standard in manufacturing one or another product.

Benefits to developing countries
The positive effects of East–West trade, however, have not been confined to the developed world only. Tripartite production

cooperation[4] covering the Western, the socialist and the developing countries has come into being, which constitutes a most constructive approach to the problems of todays world economy. It contributes to the formation of a "genuine" world economy, allowing Eastern and Western firms to accommodate to each other, promoting technical transfer and possibly speeding up the progress of the Third World. Seventy per cent. of cooperation agreements concluded until now have concentrated on the supply of turn-key plants.[5] Most of these tripartite cooperation schemes refer to the Maghreb and the Middle East, but may well be extended to Africa South of the Sahara, India and other parts of the world.

The tripartite type of production cooperation may play an important role in the multilateralization of the payments system and in balancing the deficits arising from bilateralism. It may even promote the formation of a world economy universal in certain aspects, but in other connections made up of three blocks vigorously cooperating with each other. These problems cannot be discussed in detail within the scope of this chapter because a many sided and elaborate analysis of these intricate problems would take us too far from our subject.

In analysing the problems of East–West trade, authors often refer to the asymmetrical nature of relations. This asymmetry is reflected primarily in that the share of the developed capitalist countries in CMEA countries' foreign trade accounts for 30 to 35 per cent., while that of the socialist countries in those countries' external economic activity amounts to just 3 to 4 per cent. Asymmetry follows in the first place from the essentially diverging conception and role of external economic activity in the development of capitalist and socialist economies in the past. World economy and the world market have been a decisive driving force in the development of capitalist economies in Western Europe. Also, developments in the domestic markets only got off the ground at a time when outward expansion was impeded by factors of a political or economic nature. I use the term Western Europe because the growth model of the US has been different from the type outlined above.

In the past, domestic markets have been the main driving force

4. Patrick Gutman—Francis Arkwright: "La coopération industrielle tripartite entre pays à systèmes économiques et sociaux différents de l'Ouest, de l'Est, et du Sud", *Politique Etrangère*, 1975, No. 6, pp. 621–655.

5. Op. cit.

in the growth of socialist economies. This has determined the type of growth evolved. It follows from that difference in economic history and development that the economic energies emerging under capitalism are just about convertible energies in their very nature, while convertibility in the history of socialist economies has has been the result of a further step and special effort. However this difference in economic history and economic policy is diminishing, as in the period of intensive development the weight of external factors of growth substantially increases and, therefore, a new strategy of external economic activity is needed. The essence of this strategy lies precisely in the fact that it should make *convertible* a steadily growing proportion of the economic energies produced.

As a result one may count on a gradual diminishing of asymmetry in the future.

New forms of cooperation
The development of East–West relations is greatly promoted, and also illustrated by the new forms and methods of cooperation which first gained ground and were then realized with increasing frequency. This does not imply that further development of existing forms and methods or a more intensive utilization of the forms are no longer needed. These are of course indispensable factors of development at a time when the world economic system is undergoing far-reaching changes on the one hand, and the dimensions of East–West relations are demonstrating considerable development on the other. But even in the light of these new needs and requirements one might well say that what has happened so far in this field is far from insignificant.

Let me briefly sum up those new forms and methods of cooperation that have already led to appreciable results.

(a) Production cooperation ventures are expanding at a satisfactory rate. According to available sources,[6] there are about a thousand cooperation ventures, but their actual number is presumably higher. Hungarian enterprises alone have signed about five hundred production cooperation agreements with various capitalist firms. I do not think I have to dwell on the mutual benefits of cooperation ventures. I only wish to stress again that what we are discussing here is cooperation between firms in countries with differing social systems. In trade and economic relations with certain countries—e.g., in the trade between the

6. *L'Express*, january 16, 1977.

Hungarian People's Republic and the Federal Republic of Germany—6 to 8 per cent. of mutual deliveries already stems from production cooperation.

In addition one should mention the growth shown by tripartite undertakings in production cooperation as they will play a very important and constructive role in the development of the world economy in the years to come.

(b) The first joint ventures have come into being, though not yet in sufficient number, but in a form accepted by the legislation of socialist countries. New forms of cooperation have also been introduced for the development of raw-material production. Both forms of cooperation have already got over their infantile disorders, but the potentialities inherent in them are still far from fully exploited. It may be assumed, of course, that in the future mutually advantageous and lasting forms of cooperation will gradually develop into joint ventures. The tripartite forms of production cooperation also provide a suitable basis for the formation of joint ventures, as tasks of a more or less similar type may often be performed in several countries of the Third World. Thus a stable form of cooperation will ensure very great benefits. It is obvious that what makes the forms of occasional cooperation necessary are, first of all, mutual adaptation, the sharing of knowledge and experience, as well as the creation of mutual confidence. Various forms of cooperation in the production of raw-materials are, and will be, of particular importance partly for the growing, diversified and guaranteed raw-material supply of West European countries, partly for the expansion of East European exports.

(c) Credit and financial relations are also undergoing significant development. The socialist economies have been compelled to make use of new sources in order to finance their additional imports arising partly from the sharply increasing demand for capital in the intensive period of their development, partly as a result of the deterioration of the terms of trade and of the contraction of export outlets. In addition to commodity credits it has become possible to an increasing extent to receive medium- and long-term bank credits at more favourable interest rates, or to issue government bonds.

Banks have also played an increasingly important role in establishing business contacts.

Growing financial relations have also been underpinned in terms of organization since agencies of socialist banks in the West European countries and the representatives of various big banks in the socialist countries have become general practice.

Serious troubles arise from the world problem that the current international monetary-financial organization lacks institutions which could cope adequately with the recent international payments situation (nine out of ten countries have adverse balances of payments, and the levels of their indebtedness are relatively high). It may be assumed that the merchant banks—which have for long and far exceeded their original function—will not be able in the future to bridge the gap. Therefore, new solutions have to be found in which the individual States undertake an appropriate role, i.e., new international agreements have to be concluded.

(d) Substantial progress can also be registered in scientific and technical cooperation, which the various inter-governmental agreements and agreements between institutes often extend to production. In this way, not only an exchange of scientific values and achievements, but also cooperation in research have come to be materialized—developments which have not only enabled complex problems to be approached from different angles but have also established a transfer to the economy. It is also worth noting that the East European countries, which have built up a coherent system of research institutes, now have significant research capacities.

I should like to stress that by mutually reducing armaments to an economically reasonable level, great capacities can be released, which would make it possible to utilize them not only in the interest of solving national and European problems, but also to the benefit of the Third World. In the knowledge of the problems one can safely say—as has also been pointed out at conferences discussing the problems of the new international economic order[7]—that it would be absolutely necessary to take this step.

(e) A positive role has been played in the promotion and organization of cooperation and contacts as well as in the provision of guarantees by long-term inter-state agreements concluded at the top level.

We regard this fact as an *up-to-date element* of development as it stands to reason that the role and responsibility of States and governments will vigorously intensify in the promotion of international economic relations, in formulating the principles and priorities of cooperation in keeping with the new world situation as well as in shaping the internal and external mechanisms influencing these relations.

7. *Reshaping the International Order*, A Report To The Club of Rome. Coordinator, Jan Tinbergen, New York, Dutton, 1976.

This tendency is, by the way, in conformity with the Charter on the Economic Rights and Duties of States.[8]

Hence, these inter-state skeleton agreements have fulfilled a comprehensive and very efficient economy-organizing function by determining the principles of cooperation, since the countries concerned belong to different socio-economic systems. Both parties attach great importance to the formulation of these principles, whose political and orientating role is indisputable both in the public opinion of the individual countries and among economic experts. They specify the most important fields of possible cooperation, extending cooperation to scientific and technical fields and ensuring—according to need—guarantees by the State for inter-firm cooperation and relations. These agreements have also enriched the array of legal tools by emphasizing the organizational function of law rather than its sanctioning power. In my opinion, this trend, as the relations in question are either of an inter-state or of an economic nature, is justified and sound.

The need for CMEA–EEC discussions

Inter-state cooperation will also be enriched by those Soviet or CMEA recommendations which are aimed at discussing certain fundamental economic problems at an all-European level.

It is, however, a highly regrettable fact that the suggestions made by CMEA for a discussion of the principles of trade policy regulating cooperation between the two integrations have so far not been accepted. The reluctance and hesitation of the European Economic Community in this matter not only makes the further development of East–West relations difficult, but also hampers the realization of trilateral consultations on problems of the world economy. It is simply incomprehensible to the executives of firms, politicians and research economists who understand the serious present problems of the world economy and recognize that time is pressing that in the "era of negotiations", when any "delicate" issue ranging from the surveillance of nuclear armaments to the limitation of armed forces stationed in Central Europe can and must be discussed, why precisely the principles of trade policy have assumed a "sacred cow" character making it impossible at the very outset to approach these problems in a frank and open way.

---

8. *The Charter of Economic Rights and Duties of States.* New York, United Nations General Assembly 1975, 13 pp.

Changes in the Economic Policies of Socialist States

Parallel with the development and strengthening of East–West economic relations, important changes have taken place in economic policy and the methods of economic management in the socialist economies.

These changes are connected partly with the new requirements of intensive development, partly with the formulation of new policies of external economic activity. Reference must also be made to the fact that the principles of the intensive type of development require a new conception of external economic activity from the start. Thus a substantial part of changes would also have become necessary and rational if the set of economic phenomena here referred to as the change of era in the world economy had not emerged. These phenomena, however, require a more radical, faster and more aim-oriented adaptation.

These changes are organic parts of a reform process designed to bring about the innovation of the control system in the various socialist countries. This process is put into effect in some countries in a more spectacular, more consistent and concentrated way, while in others it materializes more slowly and with substantial setbacks. It would be a mistake to identify the essence of the reform with decentralization as is often done. Decentralization is only one important effect rather than a cause. This is because the nature of the system of management in a socialist economy depends first of all on what significance is assigned to economic categories. The centralized system of management based on plan directives had to come into being because certain economic categories were supposed not to be effective, or effective only to a limited extent, in a socialist economy. If this premise is true, then it is evident that different, but closely interconnected, processes can be directed only on a natural basis within a system of concerted directives. If, however, the economic categories referred to above exert a genuine, measurable and controllable effect in a socialist economy, then it is clear that the system of control by economic categories is the most effective.[9] It is the awareness partly of their own interests, partly of world problems as they make themselves felt in the economy which leads the socialist countries increasingly to take into account, in their control systems, the expected results, effects

9. Bognár József: "A szocialista gazdaság irányitása és müködése", Bp. *Közgazdasági és Jogi Kiadó*, Budapest, 1966. *Les Nouveaux Mécanismes de L'Economie Socialiste En Hongrie*, Paris, Pavillon, 1969, 129 pp.

and consequences of processes and new developments in the world market. This is the reason why the present economic situation leads to a further improvement of the system of economic management. In the seventies, changes were carried out in the system of control which, in the first place, were aimed at taking note of effects coming from the world economy, making the decision-making mechanisms more operative, accelerating rational structural changes, and developing and stimulating the marketing potential, as well as ensuring a necessary degree of flexibility. These changes strengthen the role of the economic categories, replacing such regulators that have not proved sufficiently efficient, subjecting the system of incentives increasingly to salesmindedness, as well as widening the margins of flexibility and risk-taking in economic action. Special attention is attached, however, to endeavours to ensure that economic decisions and actions, which prove necessary under the influence of the economic categories, should preserve their contacts, both in content and form, with the requirements of planned growth.

Efforts to improve the system of economic management

In the following I should like to comment on a few concrete changes which reflect, with relative reliability, efforts aimed at improving the system of economic management.

(a) Since the methodology of planning evolved in a period of extensive economic policy which was focused almost exclusively on the development of the domestic market, methods had to be developed which took into account, from the very beginning of the formulation of the new policy, expected world economic trends and the potential demands of external markets. If these requirements can be successfully satisfied, then socialist planning cannot be said to have the "peculiarity" of being susceptible to thinking in terms of a closed, national model. It is in the interest of this that changes, not simply methodological ones, but changes which, as shown by the method applied, can be regarded as essential, have taken place at several points.

Before the conceptual launching of the five-year plan, a forecast of the world economy for 10 to 15 years was available. Such forecasts are prepared by research institutes. Consequently, in analysing and weighing up the different development alternatives due account is taken from the very beginning of the possible external economic linkages, such as foreign-market commodity demands, cooperation possibilities, the use of alternative techniques, etc. In the process those aspects of an expansion of the development tasks are also examined, which may be improved by external participation. This means, in other words, that the whole development and investment policy is formulated with an eye to external economic activity.

Perhaps there is no need to mention that the various constructions, cooperation ventures and joint activities are firmly built into the national economic plan.

(b) External economic activities—especially exports—cannot all the same make do without initiative and risk-taking on the part of the productive enterprises. On the other hand, the utilization of quickly and sometimes surprisingly changing world-market situations as a guide to exports policy requires liquid resources, both financial and as regards skills, which had not been used yet in the original allocation system of the plan. Therefore, to quote one example, the National Bank of Hungary provides precisely in the interests of expanding commodity exports, for special credit facilities, and extends them on application to enterprises making the most favourable offers. Hence, these credits exclusively serve export purposes.

(c) In economic organization the process of taking marketing and purchasing closer to production continues. It is well known that in the first period of socialist economic development production and marketing were rigidly and consistently kept apart. This error on the part of economic organization (a discussion of the causes would take up too much space) later became the source of much trouble and difficulty. The loosening and rationalization of these rigid organizational forms has been going on since 1957, but was given a major impetus only by economic reforms. New marketing tasks are now being transferred to production, and a new system of internal and external division-of-labour relations is coming into existence (on a complex and vertical basis). Complex "export systems" are being developed which help to loosen the rigid sectoral linkages of the economy.

(d) New export-stimulating systems are being introduced to strengthen the direct interest of enterprises and producers.

(e) New forms and methods of decision making are being developed which set out from the "time system" of possible partners in cooperation and potential competitors.

The problem may be raised, which I have already touched upon, that the changes that are to be introduced are excessively concentrated on the external economy, and therefore their effect will be more limited on the other components of the mechanism already established. Other misgivings may also arise, namely that the external-economic enclave may possibly be built into the socialist economy.

In response to such misgivings I should like to emphasize that the economy is after all, a unity consisting of several blocs, and changes taking place in the focus of one activity obviously influence other activities. But setting out from the viewpoint of reform, one has to say that what really matters is not the source of a reform but its direction.

Coping with the Changes in the World Economy

The world in which mankind will have to live in future years is fraught with dangerous risks in two respects. The first risk—which has already been touched upon in the introduction—boils down to the fact that the immense possibilities created by the scientific-technological revolution have fallen out of step with the established security system. The second risk may be summed up as follows: the new postulates and needs raised by the change of era in the world economy have come into conflict with the established international economic system. These dangers are in themselves of unprecedented proportions, but are still more serious in their interdependence as communication between the two systems is present along a wide band.

In this world full of uncertainty and disequilibria one must find such relatively or potentially stable processes and relational systems on which one can rely to mitigate the dangers and establish new relations. Cooperation between East and West both on security and economic questions may become such a potentially stable process and relational system.

Significant results have been achieved in developing such contacts.

Europe is no longer a focus of dangers radiating to other parts of the world, and no longer a Continent unable to solve by itself even the elementary problems of developing mutually advantageous economic relations.

Much has been done in recent years in respect of a more realistic approach to the problems of mutual security and of developing economic links. Acting in this way one not only does not damage, but also helps each other, the Third World, and a new approach to global problems.

New steps and new initiatives are, however, needed. In one way or another one must accept the consequences of the fact that the maintenance of the established security system has become economically unbearable. At the same time one must help one another economically to an increasing extent, because the change of era has aggravated powerfully the present conditions of economic growth. One cannot thrive without cooperation nor can the necessary impulses be given to the development of the Third World. Therefore, two more things are particularly desirable: a mutually equitable settlement of the guiding principles and rules of trade policy, that is economic cooperation on the one hand, and continuous positive initiatives on the part of the responsible governments on the other. Relentless enterprise and circumspect prudence are badly needed if certain common dangers are to be recognized and prevented, and temporarily arising tensions are to be overcome. Something must be done to transfer the "centres of gravity" in government activity because immense energy is still wasted in dealing with questions which are already obsolete, or which do not derive from the imperatives of the new international security and economic situation.

Great tasks are also assigned to economists all over the world. The role of the economy is increasing in international affairs and the life of particular nations alike. But one must frankly admit that frequently in the past the economy has had negative effects as well. Economic thinking and economic development have opened up a new era in the history of mankind. They have, among other things, helped mankind, rapidly increasing in number, to take possession of practically the entire surface of the Earth, thus creating the preconditions for making available a rapidly growing quantity of material goods. They have, however, not succeeded so far in improving the distribution system so that living conditions worthy of man could be assured to all. Economic energies amassed in the hands of a few—one of the forms of modern power—promoted the oppression and subjugation of other States and the sparking off of a number of wars.

Humanity simply cannot afford today to live amidst such an immense waste of energy and such dangers!

Therefore, an economy will be needed in the future which is able not only to create new energies and to satisfy needs, but also—with the help of scientific thinking and political guidance—to curb its own harmful effects and make available a major part of its energies to those who are still suffering from want in various parts of the world.

Scientists are expected today to be prudent in realizing that in a world differing to so great an extent it is impossible to create a system which is universal in all its details. They have to be active in promoting a fruitful rapprochement between the different systems and in solving global problems as well. And it is they who must be wise enough today to recognize that in this interdependent world, despite its differences, one cannot live and do creative work without relying on one another.

I am referring to the special responsibilities of scientists because we are living at a time fraught with dangers and uncertainties, but which also includes the immense potentialities of rational and humanist action.

It follows from the dialectic nature of human action that the dangers and possibilities always appear in the handling, recognition, or non-recognition, of the same problems or in the attempts to solve them. In such historic periods, at times of long-term, decisive changes, the apperception of opportunities and dangers as well as the forecasting of the effects and consequences of the various alternatives of action constitute a scientific task in the first place as the significance of past experiences in the political and governmental fields are limited in this respect. Therefore the exclusion of emotional factors and the greatest possible intellectual courage is needed.

One can only hope that everybody, scientists, economists, politicians and those in charge of the media, will be fully aware of this great responsibility.

It is only given such conditions that one can hope that détente will really mean a further, and most important, step within European cooperation and through it towards the understanding and active adaptation of what follows from our being an interdependent world.

Chapter 10

ECONOMIC INTEGRATION AND EAST–WEST TRADE: CONFLICT OF INTERESTS OR COMEDY OF ERRORS?*

by *John Pinder*

Ironically enough, the high period for East–West negotiations, leading up to Helsinki and followed by Belgrade, has been a low period for trade negotiations between East and West in Europe. Economic integration within the two groups has not stood in the way of their negotiations with countries outside either group. The East Europeans' trading arrangements with other countries have hardly been affected by Comecon; and although trade with third countries has been much affected by the Community's common commercial and agricultural policies, this has led to more negotiating about trade with most of its partners, rather than less. Only as between the two European groups has the process of integration on each side been treated as an obstacle to trade negotiations. The aim of this paper is to investigate the reasons for this and to suggest what might be done about it.

The Slow March through Institutional Contacts towards Negotiations

Jealous of their sovereignty and afraid of disturbing their relations with the Soviet Union, the member governments of the Community delayed the final adoption of the common commercial policy up to the last moment that was legally compatible with the Treaty of Rome, and perhaps beyond. They had to hand over to the Community the right to negotiate about all aspects of commercial policy by the first of January 1975, if they were not to breach their Treaty obligations. The Commission, representing the Community for this purpose, accordingly sent a letter towards the end of 1974 to each state-trading country with which a member government had previously had a trade agreement; and this

---

* The research on which this chapter is based was undertaken with the help of a grant from the Nuffield Foundation.

included all the members of Comecon. These letters[1] contained an offer from the Community to negotiate bilaterally with each country on subjects such as most-favoured-nation tariff treatment, import quotas, agricultural trade, safeguard mechanisms, and problems of payment and financing of trade. Joint committees to supervise the application of the agreements and recommend how to attain their objectives were also proposed.

These letters evoked no replies from the members of Comecon. After an interval of over a year, however, during which there had been a meeting between representatives of the Commission and of the Secretariat of Comecon for talks about talks, but no negotiations about trade, the Chairman of the Executive Committee of Comecon conveyed in February 1976 a letter[2] to the President of the Council of the Community. This letter proposed negotiations between the two groups on trade, listing approximately the same five points that had appeared in the Community's letters (mfn, quotas, agricultural trade, safeguards and credits) as well as subjects outside commercial policy, such as standardization, environment, statistics and economic forecasts, which had arisen in the talks between representatives of the Commission and the Secretariat. The crucial issue of which subjects would be negotiated by Comecon and which by its member governments was left open by a formula that allowed for all possibilities: "certain questions on commercial and economic relations ... may be settled by bilateral and multilateral agreements between the member countries"; and "concrete questions" may be settled by "direct contacts, conventions and agreements between the member countries of Comecon and the bodies of the EEC, between the member states of the EEC and the bodies of Comecon, and between their economic and competent organizations".[3]

The Community, for its part, took nine months to answer this. Its letter,[4] delivered in November 1976 from the President of the Community's Council to the Chairman of Comecon's Executive Committee, reaffirmed that the Community envisaged trade agreements with each Comecon member country individually, and

---

1. See *Agence Europe*, Luxembourg, 28/29 October 1974. The texts of these letters and of the documents subsequently exchanged between the Community and Comecon have not been published, but it is thought that the reports in *Agence Europe* give a good approximation of their contents.
2. *Agence Europe*, Feburary 25, 1976.
3. *Agence Europe, loc. cit.*
4. *Agence Europe*, November 15/16, 1976.

proposed only the subjects outside commercial policy (environment, statistics, forecasts etc.) in its draft for an agreement to be concluded between the Community and Comecon as such.

Will these delays be prolonged indefinitely, with letters and meetings in which the two groups fail to agree on how trade negotiations are to be started? Or did the Soviet Union's negotiations with the Community early in 1977 on fish imply a change of policy on the eastern side? Could the framework of the CSCE offer an opportunity to resolve the problem? To evaluate the prospects, we need to understand why the progress towards trade negotiaions has been so slow and difficult up to now. An understanding of these difficulties will remain important, moreover, even when negotiations start; for some of them reflect issues profound enough to outlast any likely changes in the political conjuncture.

Political Obstacles

The origin of the political obstacles to trade negotiations is easy to identify. The Soviet Union decided to oppose the establishment of the Community and its further integration, on both political and ideological grounds.[5] Politically, the union of West European countries was seen as a threat to be repulsed; ideologically, it seemed inappropriate that capitalists should overcome some of their contradictions. The Soviet Union therefore developed its policy of refusal to accord the Community juridical recognition, and got the East European members of Comecon to follow its example. Negotiations with the Community's member countries were permissible; negotiations with the Community itself were not.

Since the Community continued to exist and, indeed, moved towards the point of assuming full responsibility for trade negotiations, the policy of non-recognition became embarrassing for the Soviet Union and inconvenient for the other East Europeans. The Soviet Union began to moderate its attitude of uncompromising hostility to the Community; and the political obstacles to trade negotiations became less forbidding and, at the same time, more complicated.

Soviet and East European views of Community and Comecon

It was in the early 1970s that Soviet leaders apparently decided

---

5. For an analysis of this and subsequent developments of Soviet policy towards the Community, see Eberhard Schulz, *Moskau und die europäische Integration*, Oldenbourg Verlag, München 1975 (for the Deutsche Gesellschaft für Auswärtige Politik), p. 72 et seq.

to move towards a normal business relationship with the Community. But they seem also to have decided to link this policy with a strengthening of integration within Comecon, and in particular with moves towards a common commercial policy for the member countries.

Until 1968, with the exception of a brief period under Khrushchev's leadership, the Soviet Union showed little interest in the idea of integration within Comecon. The interest then came from other East European countries, which felt the need for specialization and large-scale production that would otherwise be beyond the reach of their small or medium-sized economies. In 1969, however, proposals for a Comprehensive Programme for further cooperation and the development of integration were launched in Comecon with the powerful backing of the Soviet Union, and in 1973 the Comprehensive Programme was agreed. The motive for the change of Soviet policy was evidently political: economic integration might help to maintain stability in Eastern Europe without the need for further military interventions.

Comecon had never concerned itself much about its members' trade with countries outside the group, and the Comprehensive Programme contained little on the subject. But a common external policy would, from the Soviet viewpoint, be a logical corollary to the Comprehensive Programme's design for the group's internal development. Some of the Soviet Union's East European partners have strong economic motives to negotiate with the Community on trade; and it may well have seemed convenient to the Soviet Union to secure their acceptance of a common external policy for Comecon in return for Soviet agreement on negotiations with the Community.

The East European governments, for their part, are faced by a dilemma. Most of them want to negotiate with the Community; and given the unequal bargaining power between the Community, as an economic superpower, and these small and medium-sized countries, a combination on the East European side for bargaining purposes could have intrinsic merit. But it seems that the idea of an East European grouping, working alongside the Soviet Union in Comecon as the Community works alongside the United States in OECD, is *mal vu* in the Soviet Union;[6] and the idea of a common

---

6. Explanations of the Soviet Union's negative attitude towards unions among other European countries are given in Eberhard Schulz, op. cit., p. 28 et seq.; and in P.S. Wandycz, "Recent Traditions in the Quest for Unity", in J. Lukaszewski (ed.), *The People's Democracies after Prague*, De Tempel, Bruges, 1970.

commercial policy for Comecon as a whole raises the issue of disproportion between the size of the Soviet Union and that of its East European partners, which together have only about one half of the Soviet Union's economic weight, quite apart from the disproportion of political and strategic strength. The Romanians in particular resisted the extension of Comecon's competence into trade with third countries; and it is likely that other East European countries also wished to preserve their autonomy in this field. Hence the long wait, of over a year, before Comecon arrived at the formula for its collective response to the Community's initiative on trade negotiations.

Hence, also, the ambiguousness of Comecon's formulation on the central political issue of the respective competences of Comecon and of its member governments. It was clearly agreed in principle that the responsibility would be divided in some way between them, because reference was made to agreements both between the member countries of each group and the "bodies" of the other, and between the two organizations. But there was no indication of what the division on the Comecon side would be, to reflect the Community's fairly clear definition of the scope of its common commercial policy (tariffs, quotas, import levies and export credit terms). The Community was left to guess about this; and the members of Comecon presumably expected to define Comecon competence later, in the course of preparing a detailed negotiating position or of the actual negotiations themselves.

Those East Europeans who wish to retain a maximum of autonomy in commercial policy doubtless hope that the group-to-group negotiations would concern only an umbrella agreement on general principles, and that the member governments of Comecon would themselves undertake with the Community the detailed negotiations on products, as well as continuing to make cooperation agreements with the Community's member governments on all economic matters not covered by the Community's common commercial policy. They must calculate that a division of competence arrived at in this way will be more favourable to them than one defined in advance of agreement with the Community that negotiations will take place. The Community's reply to Comecon indicated that its view may be different.

Community attitudes towards Comecon

The Community's attitude towards integration in Comecon is not much more favourable than the Soviet attitude towards the Community. The two attitudes are not exactly reciprocal, as there is no reason to suppose that the Community would view with disfavour integration among the Soviet Union's East European partners, symmetrical with the Community's own integration alongside, but not with the United States. Nor is there reason to presume that the Community would refuse to recognize the Comecon members' right to delegate certain competences to their group, should they decide how to define them and inform their trading partners of the decision. But proposals for integration concern not just the East Europeans but the whole group, including the Soviet Union; and Comecon competences in trade with third countries have not been defined. The Community's intention, in these circumstances, seems to be to avoid any action that would facilitate Comecon integration at the expense of the East Europeans' autonomy. In rebuffing the Comecon proposal for open-ended negotiations without prior definition of Comecon competences, the Community probably took the view that this would help to minimize the role of Comecon in trade negotiations.

This was not the only reason for the Community's stiff response to the Comecon proposals. There was also resistance to the apparent implication that the Community should be required to pay a price for the recognition of its member countries' right, which had been accepted by all its other trading partners, to conduct their commercial policy as a group; and there was a legacy of resentment at the Soviet Union's refusal to deal with the Commission, to which the Community's members had bound themselves by treaty to delegate certain negotiating functions, and at the attempts to place it on a par with the Comecon Secretariat which does not have these functions.

There are those on the western side who take a different view about Comecon integration from that implicit in the Community's policies, arguing that opposition to such integration would destabilize the European system. Given the Community's premise, however, it is still possible to form a different judgment about the desirability of open-ended negotiations with Comecon, on the grounds that the umbrella agreement which would emerge from them would impinge less upon the East Europeans' autonomy than would the consequences of the Community's failure to negotiate, which might be to increase their reliance on the major partner that does negotiate with them, that is to say the Soviet Union.

The Community and the Soviet policies towards integration on the other side both reflect attitudes with profound political significance. But it seems doubtful whether the failure to start trade negotiations should be attributed to these attitudes alone. The

Soviet Union has, as we have seen, evolved its policy to the point where it can be embodied in a formula, even if a somewhat vague one, for negotiations. On the Community's side, the decision to reject the Comecon proposal depended on a balance of judgment which seems fine enough to be open to revision if one or two new factors of significant weight were introduced on the other side of the scale.

Nor is the explanation that trade negotiations have been prevented by misunderstandings a sufficient one, although there have been enough of these. But the comedy of errors would surely not have stood in the way for so long if the real interests favouring negotiations had been strong enough.

This brings us to the economic interests that lie behind the policies towards trade negotiations. For there are good grounds to believe that the lack of economic interest in such negotiations on the side of either of the leading actors—the Soviet Union or the European Community—has counted for more than the major political differences, let alone the comedy of errors, in the failure to reach agreement to negotiate.

Differing Economic Interests

The European Community: substantial exports to the East, but what is reciprocity?

Its trade with Comecon is important to the Community. Exports to the eastern group comprise about one tenth of the Community's total exports to third countries, not far short of Community exports to the United States.[7] But it is not at all clear what the Community has to gain from trade negotiations with Comecon or its member countries.

For the last few years the Community has had a big surplus on its trade with Comecon, so that it could not expect to negotiate for higher levels of exports to the East until Comecon has begun to reduce this imbalance of trade. The eastern trading partners have, indeed, argued that they reciprocate any western trade concessions by spending all their export earnings on imports from the western countries. But this does not reciprocate the sort of concessions made by the West, for these affect not just the level but the pattern of

---

7. The trade between the Community and Comecon is analysed in John and Pauline Pinder, *The European Community's Policy towards Eastern Europe*, Chatham House and PEP, 1975.

trade. Cuts in tariffs or relaxations of quotas reduce the protection of particular industrial sectors, imposing a need for adjustment on those who work in them. After allowing for capital movements, western countries too spend on imports the money they earn for exports; and although the directness with which an eastern partner spends its earnings may be an advantage for western countries that are hard pressed by trade deficits, the spending of earnings cannot by itself be generally regarded as reciprocating the liberalization of specific tariffs or quotas.

Western countries have, in various international negotiations, sought for formulae that would constitute a real reciprocation; but despite the efforts on the part of some eastern countries to cooperate, it cannot be said that these attempts have met with much success. The Poles, when they acceded to the GATT in 1967, undertook, as reciprocation for any benefits that this might bring them, to increase their total imports from GATT members by 7 per cent. a year. But this was hardly a meaningful concession. For if the Poles earn or borrow enough to do so, they will anyway increase their imports by that amount; and if they do not get enough money, their commitment cannot be met.

A rather more sophisticated formula was found for the Romanians, the next to join the GATT in 1971, who agreed to raise their exports annually by a given percentage from each individual member of the GATT, thus committing themselves on not only the total value but also the direction of trade. This commitment was overtaken, as was that of the Poles, by inflation which raised the value of most flows of trade much more sharply; and the formula is also criticized on the grounds that rigidities in the direction of trade negate the principle of multilateralism which the western countries generally support.

The Hungarians, who acceded to the GATT in 1973, after they had introduced their New Economic Mechanism, argued that they had a market economy so their new tariff was a genuine instrument of economic policy, changes in which could affect the composition of trade and thus reciprocate concessions by other members of the GATT; and this was accepted as the basis for Hungarian accession. But this argument could not be used by the other Comecon members which do not claim to have market economies, even if it is fully applicable to Hungary, which western countries tend in any case to doubt.

In the Conference on Security and Cooperation in Europe, the Community pressed for better information and easier contacts for firms doing business with the East. This was a significant demand, which has been partly met by eastern countries;[8] but this again can hardly be seen as reciprocation for trade liberalization, and was not seen by either side in that way.

Although four of the five subjects listed in the Community's letters proposing trade negotiations were of interest mainly to the state-trading countries, one—that of mechanisms to deal with trade disruption—was of more interest to the Community. Some industries in member countries are much troubled by imports from the East: and this problem has recently irrupted into the field of services, with extensive Soviet undercutting of shipping rates. But negotiation about such mechanisms is hard to take seriously as an opportunity for reciprocation by the East. In the case of western exports to the East the issue of disruption does not arise, because the eastern countries do not import anything that could be expected to disrupt their planned economies, or allow the prices of imported goods to upset their domestic price levels; and there has been no question of the western countries being invited to negotiate about the ways in which this is done. The western countries would be acting no more restrictively than the eastern countries generally do, if they applied measures unilaterally to prevent disruption of their markets by imports from the East; and it is a concession to, not by, the eastern countries if there is negotiation about the procedures for applying them. It is only in relation to undercutting by Comecon countries in third markets that the western countries could not defend themselves in this way; and Soviet shipping is, perhaps, the first important example of this. Thus the Community in fact listed five subjects on which concessions would be made to the East, and not a single subject on which it might expect substantial reciprocity.

This is evidence not of any chance oversight, but of the fact that the Community does not know what to ask for in return for the concessions it would offer in trade negotiations. Nor does this reflect any special inadequacy on the part of the Community. Its member governments seem in general to have been as much at a loss in finding grounds for meaningful trade negotiations with their eastern partners, as distinct from a unilateral offering of concessions; and the same can be said of other western countries as a whole. Eastern governments know quite well what they want from western governments: the removal of quotas, reductions of tariffs or import levies, and other measures of trade liberalization. There has

8. See *Conference on Security and Cooperation in Europe, Final Act*, Cmnd 6198, HMSO, August 1975, p. 13 et seq.

been no such clarity on the western side.

This may at first sight appear to be an advantage for the East, who have been getting something for nothing; and we should not be surprised if we find on the eastern side a tendency to want to leave what is well for them, or at least may appear to be well, alone. In the CSCE, for example, the Soviet Union resisted the Community's pressure for recognition of the need for reciprocity for the guarantee of mfn treatment. But the appearance of an advantage for the East is deceptive, or at best temporary. For if the western partners do not expect to get any specific benefits out of negotiations, they will lack incentive to make any really significant concessions. There are exceptions to this, such as the major movement of liberalization that started with détente in the 1960s as western governments, one after another, took these trade decisions on political grounds. But in the mid-1970s, recession has rendered trade concessions hard to make and, with détente no longer politically glamorous, the political motive to make them is weaker. In these circumstances the eastern countries are not likely to gain much from negotiations with their western partners unless they offer convincing reciprocity. For the Community in particular, there is little inducement even to start negotiating, so long as the method of approach by Comecon presents political problems, on top of the uncomfortable trading concessions that the Community would inevitably feel constrained to make, and without the counterweight of expected economic advantage.

Substantial Soviet exports to the Community, but they encounter few trade barriers

The immediate economic interest of the Soviet Union in these trade negotiations is, for different reasons, surprisingly similar to that of the Community: that is to say, almost negligible. Like the Community, the Soviet Union has a major stake in the mutual trade; but also like the Community, the Soviet Union cannot expect to derive much advantage from trade negotiations with it of the type that have been usual in East–West relations up to now. This is because Soviet exports to the Community are mainly raw materials, which are not subjected to tariffs or to restrictive quotas. Since barriers to the Soviet Union's trade are not important, negotiations that would aim to reduce barriers are not important either.

Not that the Soviet Union has no economic claims to make to western countries. But it does not seem to have any really substantial claims to make in general trade negotiations with the

Community. Its most prominent and persistent demand, in the CSCE and elsewhere, has been for mfn treatment as of right. But although the United States does not accord mfn tariff treatment to the Soviet Union, the European Community does. Perhaps the Soviet Union fears that this treatment might be withdrawn, or that new tariff cuts resulting from trade negotiations might not be extended to it. But this possibility seems remote, and in a commercial bargain the Soviet Union would be unlikely to give much for the sort of guarantee against its occurrence that East European countries have secured by acceding to the GATT. The demand for mfn treatment with respect to quotas would be nearer the mark. But quotas affect the Community's imports from Eastern Europe much more than from the Soviet Union. The formulae agreed when they joined the GATT have made little or no difference to their rate of removal, which clearly depends not on a general legal formula but on hard and detailed negotiations over a period of time. In all, it is hard to escape the conclusion that the Soviet Union's mfn demand is legalistic or political rather than economic in motivation; and, more fundamentally, that this may reflect a view of general trade negotiations with western countries as fora in which legal rights are demanded and political points made, rather than bargains struck, in which each side gains something and each gives something. In so far as this is so, it is a serious obstacle to significant general trade negotiations, which western countries regard as vehicles for commercial bargains rather than legal demands or political points.

The securing of government-backed or subsidized credits has been a substantive interest of the Soviet Union, as of the East Europeans, but this relates to the cooperation agreements that are still negotiated with the Community's member governments, not to the trade negotiations for which the Community itself is competent. It is possible that the Community will come to assume some functions now classed under cooperation rather than commercial policy. It already has responsibility for export credit terms; an Export Bank, to provide as well as guarantee credits, has been proposed by the Commission though not supported by the Council; and it appears that the smaller member countries favour giving the Community more powers in the field of cooperation with state-trading countries.[9] But the larger member countries do not agree, and the provision of credits is not likely to enter into the proposed Community trade negotiations.

9. See *Agence Europe*, November 15/16, 1976.

The Soviet Union's exports of manufactures are continually increasing, and this will cause the liberalization of Community trade barriers to loom larger in Soviet thinking about trade policy in future. Until now, there has been little cause for the Soviet Union to worry about them so that the absence of negotiations with the Community has caused the Soviet Union virtually no inconvenience.

The adoption of the 200-mile fishing limit has, however, occasioned a striking exception to this rule.[10] Although only a tiny part of the Soviet Union's total economic activity, fishing in the North Sea is a tangible Soviet interest. As soon as the 200-mile limit was introduced on January 1, 1977, therefore, the Soviet Union sought negotiations with the Community on the amount of fishing to be allowed to Soviet vessels within that limit. The Soviet delegation explained, when the negotiations started, that this did not imply juridical recognition of the Community or open the way to general trade negotiations. But it did surely raise the question whether there can be formal negotiations about a product in which the Soviet Union has a tangible, though minor, interest without opening the way for formal negotiations on other products, such as beef, in which some East European countries have very much larger interests.[11]

The East Europeans' interest in negotiations

It is most unfortunate for the East Europeans that neither the Community nor the Soviet Union has a really significant economic interest in trade negotiations in any form that has been proposed so far. For the East Europeans do have big problems in exporting to the Community. A quarter of their exports are agricultural products, which come up against the protection demanded by the Community's farmers; and up to one half are manufactures, largely of "sensitive" products which compete with old industries in the Community, such as clothing, footwear or china, where the hard pressed firms and workers also demand protection. The GDR is an exception, because it enjoys, under a Protocol to the Treaty of Rome, free access to the market of the Federal Republic and even

10. See Angelika Volle and William Wallace, "How Common a Fisheries Policy?", *The World Today*, RIIA, February 1977.
11. For an analysis of the significance of Hungarian agricultural exports to the Community, for example, see Gabriella Izik-Hedri, "Die Auswirkungen der gemeinsamen Agrarpolitik der Europäischen Gemeinschaft auf Ungarns Westhandel", *Konjunkturpolitik*, Zweites Heft 1976, Berlin.

203

benefits under the common agricultural policy. Without any negotiations between East Europeans and the Community, this leaves it in a most privileged position. Bulgaria is less dependent on exports to the Community than are the remaining four East European members of Comecon. For Czechoslovakia, Hungary, Poland and Romania, however, their exports to the Community are vital, having reached, for Hungary, as much as some 8 per cent of gross national product. With their dependence on this trade, and the resistance to it from the Community's domestic interests, these countries face a constant predicament in their trade relations with the Community; and this has been sharply exacerbated by their need to export more in order to reduce their big trade deficits that resulted from the world inflation of commodity prices. Although the onus is on the East Europeans to produce competitive goods that the West Europeans will want to buy, the import restrictions that remain and the anti-dumping cases that have been proliferating in the Community during the current recession are evidence that this is far from being the whole truth. It is important to them that their exports to the Community should be less impeded by restrictions; and in so far as trade negotiations help to reduce the restrictions, they have a real need to negotiate.

Forms of Negotiations

Can existing channels suffice?

The meaning of juridical recognition is for jurists to explain. Evidently, the lack of such recognition does not prevent two parties from doing business with each other. The commercial representatives of East European countries have for years been visiting the Commission's offices in order to discuss specific problems, and recording agreements by the exchange of letters with the Commission. Now the Soviet Union, Poland and the GDR have undertaken formal bilateral negotiations with the Community about fish. Could there be enough recognition for any necessary business to be done without Soviet jurists having to admit that there was juridical recognition? If, for the Soviet Union, general bilateral trade negotiations with the Community are a sticking point, do we really need trade negotiations of that sort or could everything necessary be done in other ways? The question is far from academic, in view of doubts whether bilateral East–West trade negotiations have constituted a bargaining process in any meaningful sense, and of the amount of negotiating that is already done between the Community and the East European sides by means other than periodical set-piece bilateral trade negotiations.

Czechoslovakia, Hungary, Poland and Romania, as members of the GATT, are taking part in the multilateral trade negotiations. They will benefit from resulting mfn tariff cuts, and have the opportunity to articulate their particular interests. There is no reason to suppose that they would gain by introducing the subject of the Community's tariffs on manufactures into bilateral negotiations. Romania has the additional benefit of preferential entry for many products under the Community's Generalized Preference Scheme. For Bulgaria and the Soviet Union, which are not members of the GATT (although Bulgaria has observer status), the Community's tariff is not as yet of much importance.

The quotas that restrict imports of manufactures from Eastern Europe and the Soviet Union into Community markets have been liberalized until, with the exception of Italy, they affect only a hard core of sensitive products. Among these, textiles and clothing are the most important. Romania has already negotiated a Multi-Fibre Agreement with the Community, of the kind that has been devised within the framework of the Gatt to determine the size and rate of expansion of quotas on these products. Hungary and Poland have both gone far on the way to negotiate such agreements. There appears to be no reason of principle why similar agreements should not be negotiated with respect to other items that are subject to quotas. But in practice it seems difficult to secure any further improvements with respect to quotas from the Community at present. The Hungarians have found it hard to secure liberalization despite the Community's undertaking, along with other GATT members at the time of the Hungarian accession, to remove the quotas on its imports from Hungary "as soon as possible"; and the rising tide of protective reactions to imports from Eastern Europe during this recession has not yet been reversed. The Community does, however, in practice put together an offer to its trading partners whenever it starts new negotiations, so the East Europeans could expect to get more quota relaxations from formal trade negotiations with the Community than they do from present processes.

In agricultural products, the lot of countries that wish to export to the Community is not in general a happy one. East Europeans are not discriminated against in comparison with other suppliers; but this does not relieve them of their problems. The Community's beef ban in 1973 brought to a halt overnight about a sixth of

Hungary's exports to the Community,[12] accounting for over 1 per cent. of Hungarian GNP. East Europeans have, however, secured by informal negotiation a number of technical arrangements, such as the avoidance of supplementary levies on certain products, which have been of some help to their agricultural exports; and if they were to enter into formal bilateral negotiations with the Community, they would probably secure further improvements in the terms of access, as the Yugoslavs did in getting slightly preferential treatment for their exports of baby beef. The multilateral trade negotiations in the GATT concern agricultural as well as industrial products, and this may result in some improvements for the East European participants. The Soviet Union too could be among those that would benefit from a wheat buffer stock, about which the Community and other participants in the mtn are negotiating, in order to prevent shortages and wild fluctuations of price. But in general, the Community's partners are not likely to get much satisfaction out of the multilateral negotiations as far as agriculture is concerned.

Beyond the scope of commercial policy strictly defined, the Soviet Union and the East European countries still conduct bilateral negotiations with the several member countries of the Community, under the heading of economic cooperation. Given the Soviet Union's lack of real problems arising from trade barriers in the Community, these cooperation negotiations have probably served any economic functions that bilateral negotiations could in fact perform for the Soviet Union, at least until the appearance of the 200-mile fishing limits. For the East Europeans the cooperation agreements with western governments, and associated arrangements for credits, are important too. But the Community's commercial policy still presents them with many unresolved problems; and although tariffs and textile quotas can be dealt with in the framework of the GATT and multilateral negotiations or informal bilateral contacts can ameliorate their difficulties with other quotas and with the Community's agricultural protection, it seems likely that they would find formal bilateral trade negotiations with the Community a significant additional help.

What more would bilateral trade negotiations achieve?

There is reason to suppose that neither the Community nor the Soviet Union would expect to secure tangible economic concessions

---

12. See Gabriella Izik-Hedri, op. cit.

as a result of trade negotiations between the Community and the Comecon countries, but that the East Europeans have major interests which such negotiations might help to satisfy. Why is it thought that the Community should make concessions to them on the occasion of a negotiation in which they seem to have nothing to offer?

The answer lies in the Community's political processes. Decisions, which usually require the agreement of all nine member governments, are always hard to take; and they are particularly hard when domestic interests in one or more member countries are threatened. One of the things that concentrates ministers' minds on the need to decide today is the prospect that negotiations with a trading partner will begin tomorrow. In these circumstances they feel politically obliged to reach compromises on their national interests in order to arrive at a Community negotiating position.

Perhaps, moreover, the prospect of a general trade negotiation with the East Europeans would cause the member governments to bring their political interests to bear more than they do when issues relating only to particular products, such as textiles or beef, are involved. Even if negotiations offer little prospect of economic gain for the Community, a growth of trade and a stable economic relationship with the East Europeans is of major political importance. By the criteria of commercial policy, imports of clothing from South Korea, which is a member of the GATT without the complications that state-trading countries bring, may seem on balance to have priority; for a sound foreign policy, designed to look after the Community member countries' political and security interests, the balance is overwhelmingly the reverse. A general trade negotiation, which seems more important than a single product negotiation, might help the member governments to articulate this kind of political interest through the Community's decision-making process.

It is indeed an indictment of the weakness of the Community institutions if imminent negotiations with third countries are really required as a spur to taking decisions of so much political significance. The British, French, Germans and a number of other countries all liberalized their quota systems in the 1960s in order to promote détente. The Community itself managed to decide upon its Generalized Scheme of Preferences autonomously, without the necessity of negotiating about it with the less-developed countries; and if the member governments could bring themselves to take a similar decision about quotas on manufactures and access for agricultural imports from Eastern Europe, the set-piece bilateral trade negotiations would hardly be necessary. This is, perhaps, too much to expect when a recession is at its worst and pressures for protection consequently at their highest point. But there has been no indication that the problem might be solved in this way, even after the recession has begun to abate. Should the Community show itself capable of taking such a decision unilaterally, however, the need for bilateral negotiations to deal with immediate problems of commercial policy would almost disappear.

It is hard to escape a sense of absurdity in considering whether the Community needs the prospect of negotiations with third countries in order to take decisions that are, in effect, unilateral in any case because they are not made with the expectation of bargaining for something in return. We seem to be dealing not with economic fact but with political fantasy. But over the longer term, western and eastern trading partners surely will find how to negotiate in ways that involve a genuine reciprocation of benefits, and enable both sides to contribute to the expansion of trade and economic relations to optimum levels. These ways are not so likely to be found in the general context of the GATT as now constituted, which is concerned primarily with the problems of the western trading system, as in institutions and negotiations that deal specifically with the relations between market and state-trading economies. It is in opening up these possibilities for the future that direct negotiations between the Community and its eastern trading partners may be really indispensable.

The Future Development of Economic Relations

One view of the future of economic relations between East and West is that, with the growing use of market mechanisms by the eastern countries, multilateral negotiations, such as the GATT tariff rounds, will come to replace bilateral negotiations. Another view, which is held by this writer, is that the modern economy, with its complex and imperfect market system, increasingly requires bilateral negotiation between governments in West as well as East. This is reflected in the discussion in the GATT on safeguards, which would allow restrictions to be imposed on the import of a product from one particular country that was causing market disruption, implying negotiations between the importing and the exporting country about the size of the quota, the rate at which it is to be relaxed, and accompanying measures of adaptation. The same is shown by the Community's negotiations with Japan about ships and steel, by its negotiation of cooperation agreements with countries as diverse as India, Iran and Canada, and in many other ways.

It would be surprising indeed if the need for bilateral negotiations between eastern and western countries were to fade away at the same time as it is growing in the relations among the western countries themselves, and when the problem of devising more satisfactory ways of relating the two types of economy to each other is more important than ever and still as far from being solved.

The content of East–West negotiations

It has been argued that the key to successful negotiations is a form of reciprocity that makes sense to both sides, and that no form of reciprocity by the East has been found that makes sense to the western partners. Such reciprocity would have to concern the origin, composition or terms of imports into eastern from western countries.

The origin of imports, or more generally the direction of trade, could become an issue if the Community felt that the eastern countries' trading partners, such as the US and Japan, were being unfairly favoured at its expense. This is not happening now, but it is always a possibility.

The composition of eastern imports is a subject of real importance, on which there has been little attempt to negotiate up to now. The composition and terms of imports are what western trade negotiations, with their focus on levels of protection for particular products, are all about; and that is what the eastern countries seek to influence in their negotiations with partners in the West. One form of concession on imports by the eastern side would be commitments to import agreed levels of particular product-groups of interest to the western partners, such as computers or other high-technology products, ships or products from other industries suffering low conjunctural demand, or categories such as consumer goods which are important for some western countries and relatively little imported by the East. Such commitments could be on both quantity and price, and for the longer term as well as for periods of a year.

East Europeans may argue that this would be over-compensation for western liberalization, because the western government offers merely access to its market, while the eastern government would be committing itself to buy. One answer to this is that the eastern concessions, if qualitatively more powerful, could be quantitatively less. A better answer would emerge from a deeper examination of what either side is trying to achieve.

The aim of demands for trade liberalization is usually to secure a permanent place in the trade partner's market. This implies, if the liberalization is on an mfn basis and not just designed to replace imports from one source by imports from another, that the country liberalizing is in fact agreeing to produce less of that product in the future than it would without liberalization. In a market economy this follows from freer access to the market. In a directively planned economy, a change in the production pattern follows not from a change in access to the market, but from the decisions in the investment plan. A commitment to import a given product, therefore, if it is not just a diversion of trade from one source to another, is identical with a decision to invest less in the production of that product (or, if the product would not otherwise be available, of whatever would have been bought with the money now to be spent on it).

An import commitment that represented only a diversion of trade from a source where the order would otherwise be placed on grounds of price, quality, etc., would infringe the mfn principle that eastern as well as western countries consider it desirable to uphold. The only legitimate commitment, therefore, would be the trade-creating type that is equivalent to a commitment by the eastern partner on his investment plans. Seen in this way, concessions by market economies on market access would be reciprocated with concessions by planned economies on their investment plans. If the eastern country can claim that a concession on market access is worth less than a firm sale, because the benefit could be reaped by another supplier, precisely the same could be said of a particular western country's chance of benefiting from an eastern country's decision not to invest in producing a particular product.

This form of reciprocity would require a removal of the distinction, anyway artificial, between negotiations on trade and cooperation. In some ways the distinction between market access and investment decisions is itself artificial. In modern industries with capital-intensive and large-scale or specialized production, the western firms' investment decisions will be determined by the terms of access to the market; and the consequent pattern of investment will itself determine flows of trade that are stable for a long time. With respect to such industries, negotiations that appeared to concern market access on one side and investment decisions on the other would in fact concern investment decisions and long-term flows of trade on both. They would be akin to the specialization agreements that are made formally between governments on the eastern side and, often less formally, between firms in the West.

Such an evolution of the concepts of trade and cooperation would carry with it the need to negotiate, not just on commercial policy but at the same time on investment decisions and on the credits that help to finance them. It is hard to envisage such arrangements being made without a strengthening of bilateral negotiations, instead of their withering away. If relationships do develop in such a vigorous way, it is likely that the resolution of other issues such as commodity agreements and stocks, monetary arrangements and eventual convertibility, and the difficulties that inevitably arise in the external relations of integrating groups, would be facilitated by the system of bilateral negotiations as well as through common membership of multilateral institutions.

The present prospects for negotiations

Trade negotiations between the Community and its eastern partners might, then, lead on to major developments in the relationship between them over the long term, as well as being useful in alleviating some of the East Europeans' economic difficulties in the nearer future. The obstacles that stand in the way are political, but are reinforced by the lack of immediate material interest in such negotiations on the part of the Community and the Soviet Union.

The diplomatic and tactical decisions whereby the political obstacles can be overcome are not a suitable subject for a chapter such as this. But one suggestion may not be out of place. Negotiations are likely to begin once agreement is reached about the role of Comecon in relation to trade. The Comecon proposal indicates that the group as such is to have a role in trade negotiations, but fails to define it; the Community proposes to negotiate with Comecon itself on non-trade subjects only, and with the group's member governments on trade. The solution seems likely to be found in a definition of general principles for trade relations that would be agreed between the two groups as a whole, as a framework within which the governments of Comecon member countries could negotiate bilaterally with the Community about concrete problems relating to particular products. The economic section of the Helsinki Final Act contains many points on which agreement has already been reached; and it should be possible to take this work further. It might then be possible for the two groups, in addition to negotiating about the non-trade subjects, to agree formally that their trade relations would be conducted within the framework of the principles accepted by both sides at Helsinki and Belgrade, so that the East European countries that have a real need for detailed trade negotiations with the Community could begin them without delay. This would at the same time open out the prospect of going on from this starting point to a more far-reaching development of trade as well as cooperation relations over the longer run.

Part Four

COOPERATION IN HUMANITARIAN AND OTHER FIELDS

INTRODUCTION

In the third "basket" of the Final Act of the CSCE, the participating States declare that it is their aim: "*to facilitate* freer movement and contacts ... among persons, institutions ... and to contribute to the solution of the humanitarian problems that arise in that connection"; and "*to facilitate* the freer and wider dissemination of information of all kinds ..." In two further sections of this basket they agree on objectives, intentions and a series of measures with a view to promoting cooperation and exchanges in the fields of culture and education.

Together with the seventh principle of the Final Act, the inclusion of this basket was the result of Western insistence on extending détente to the freer movement of persons, ideas and information; thus countering the Soviet desire to restrict détente to relations between States and a recognition of the post-war political and territorial division of Europe.

The first two contributions clearly manifest the sharp disagreement existing on the implementation of this basket. There appears to be no meeting of minds concerning the "ideological struggle" between opposing systems as presented by Sheidina, and "the competition between societies" ruled by democratic or authoritarian régimes as advocated by Byrnes.

The sensitivity of the issues raised by the provisions of the third basket also reflects itself in the presentation and evaluation of the facts. The evaluation of Eastern and Western performances implied in Zeman's discussion of a number of cases which he reviews, diverges significantly from the conclusions and the careful and comprehensive analysis made in *the second semi-annual report by the US President to the Commission on Security and Cooperation in Europe.*

Chapter 11

CULTURAL EXCHANGE AND IDEOLOGICAL STRUGGLE: A SOVIET VIEW

by *Inna L. Sheidina*

It is no exaggeration to say that the issue of détente, of constructive interaction between States belonging to different socio-economic systems, is at the focal point of world public interest. And this certainly comes as no surprise since in the long run this issue is inseparable from that of ensuring stable peace—which is today synonymous with ensuring the very existence of mankind, the continuation of creative life on our planet.

Among the prerequisites of stable peace, the top priority undoubtedly goes to political and military problems; everyday life reminds us that quite often these are joined by the problems of economic and technological relations between States. But there exists yet another sphere of contacts between the peoples of the world which, without being the ground foundation of international relations, still plays a very special and significant international role. The sphere I mean is that of cultural exchange.

One can hardly name a different type of international links that is more conducive to mutual understanding and mutual knowledge, to the generation of sympathies and deep respect for the talents and capabilities of those who share with us the joys and vicissitudes of our journey in the Spaceship Earth. There is hardly any other kind of international contacts that might rival cultural exchange in its powerful and all-penetrating emotional and ethical charge.

In the absence of constant exchange of spiritual values between people there would be no progress of world culture. One would feel an irreparable gap, for instance, if one tried to think of European literature without Erasmus Roterodamus, or of world painting without Harmens van Rijn Rembrandt or Jerom Bosch, Pieter Breughel or Jan Van Eyck.

Actually, cultural exchange has gone on throughout the whole of world history, and it has developed both in space and in time; unseen ties bind each of us culturally not only with our compatriots, but with foreigners; not only with our contemporaries, but also with our predecessors. Hence, when we speak today about the necessity of developing systematic and varied cultural contacts, we mean that the spontaneous process of cultural exchange is in need of conscious and earnest guidance, because cultural interaction is truly vital not only for development of national cultures and world culture as such, but also for the generation around the globe of that atmosphere of mutual respect, trust and goodwill which is absolutely essential for genuine peaceful and good neighbourly relations between States.

Cultural Exchanges: Problems and Points of View

When taking a closer look at the problems of cultural exchange and also the exchange of information, publications, films and the like, it becomes evident that the problem goes beyond those self-evident considerations pertaining to the community of world culture and spiritual values of mankind that ring true for every ear. A closer look reveals a much more complicated picture as far as basic approaches and organizational patterns are concerned.

On the one hand, this sphere of international relations is not so rich in universally recognized, well agreed upon, long established norms of activity, as, say, diplomacy. This circumstance is still further enhanced by the momentous qualitative leap in the development of means of communication that occurred quite recently and opened truly unprecedented opportunities for influencing human minds irrespective of national borders.

On the other hand, it is particularly in this sphere that one strongly feels the remnants of the cold war in the shape of prejudice, of psychological inertia characteristic for both public figures and average people, in the shape of special infrastructure, of vested interests of some professional groups that made their careers during the cold war and now are either unwilling or outright incapable of thinking in different terms.

The notion of culture, of spiritual values, is closely bound with the ideals accepted by society, with its moral norms, its chosen priorities of goals and values—that is, with the social, or class, fibre of the society. An attempt to disregard the social aspect of culture can only breed misunderstanding. Let us not brush aside this crucial fact: by force of public ideals, moral and ethical standards shared in our country, we do differ from traditional Western interpretation of certain cultural phenomena and values. The cult of violence, cruelty, racial superiority, cynical amorality, propaganda of war or nationalism, are in our view incompatible with true culture. Our society, with its active collectivist approach, also finds unacceptable such themes as glorifying militant selfishness, or advertising the lures of a consumer's paradise ...

Our traditions and world outlook obviously make us disagree with some of the entries grouped under the term "culture" in a society that calls itself "self-indulgent" or "pleasure-orientated". Incidentally, I see that some of our doubts are shared by many Westerners. While reading sociological literature one frequently comes across descriptions of the so-called post-industrial culture in such words as cynical, disappointed, nihilistic, chaotic, superficial, weary, meaningless, alienated, fraught with collapse of traditional values, with increase in egotism, decline of interest towards society as a whole, bordering on outright antisocial behaviour, characterized by such symptoms of social pathology, as increase in mental illness, neurosis, divorce, suicide and the like. In the words of one American author, the evolution is towards an attractive, though slightly decadent society of idle consumers ...[1] I do not think it is too difficult to see the point in my society wishing to educate the younger generation in the spirit of rather different social values.

A hazy notion that the peoples of the socialist countries are denied access to those aspects of foreign life and culture that arouse their interest is quite erroneous. It can be verified by a very simple test, well within the reach of any foreign visitor to, for instance, the Soviet Union—by a chat with an ordinary Soviet man or woman. A chat will easily prove that on the average Soviet people are quite familiar with this or that Western country, with its history and geography, with its literature and fine arts. I dare say that no visitor to my country has ever encountered such total lack of knowledge about his native land and such absolutely bizarre questions as I happened to deal with while travelling with a Soviet exhibition across the United States of America several years ago under the programme of a Soviet–American cultural exchange.

The incoming information in its sum total is ample, comprehensive and diverse, but it is admittedly the product of conscious selection, it is devoid of sensational garish aspects, it does not stress some of the features habitual in the West—such as, for instance, the private lives of prominent figures in the arts, in political life, and the like. I assume that the word "selection" used by me will at once attract censorious attention—there now, the critics will say, she has

---

1. Herman Kahn and B. Bruce-Briggs, *Things To Come. Thinking About the 70's and 80's*. New York, 1972, esp. pp. 220–231.

admitted it herself! In the Soviet Union they "select" the information—and our demand is that of its all-out freedom!

I am convinced that the word "selection" is far from being so derogatory as some people are inclined to think at first glance. Everybody knows the famous motto of The *New York Times*—"all the news that's fit to print"; that is what the newspaper promises to give its readers. But surely there must be a way of judging what is "fit" and what is not. The very wording of the motto implies that there may be news unfit to print ... Thus it must be the editor who passes judgment on what merits the newspaper's space, and the editor's line of reasoning is aligned with the viewpoint of his employers, of the publishers, who might see things in a very different light than the wide reading public. Any information—its choice, its delivery—already implies a certain Weltanschauung, a certain ideological angle. And it is no wonder, it could not be otherwise, the inherent personal system of values, the world outlook of the one who "makes" information come into play automatically. But if the right to determine the angle is freely accorded to an individual editor or publisher, who more often than not is guided by narrow group interests, how, then, can one disregard in this respect the right of a State that clearly has the mandate of the overwhelming majority of the population?

Incidentally, the Intergovernmental Conference on Cultural Policy convened by the UNESCO in Helsinki in June 1972, when making recommendations as to furthering dissemination of ideas and cultural values that would facilitate peace, security and cooperation in Europe, pointed out that governments may feel it necessary to undertake protective measures to shield their respective national cultures from phenomena that are fraught with a negative corrupting influence on the younger generation.

Culture is a matter of momentous consequences. It can elevate and ennoble, but there exist also things which may be more appropriately called pseudocultural and which really contribute to degradation of personality. And here every society has the right to determine what answers its needs and what does not.

Does this kind of approach raise obstacles in the way of cultural contacts, does it unduly limit the stream of cultural exchange? I do not think so. The problem just boils down to foregoing attempts at forcing something down the partner's throat, at heaping upon him ideas or cultural standards that go contrary to his fondest belief, to his customs and traditions. Cultural exchange ought by all means to be free, but free is not synonymous to compulsory. An American scholar wrote recently that the gunboat diplomacy in our day belongs in the antique shop, and its place has been taken by the flourishing business of mass media and mass culture diplomacy.[2] If cultural exchange is going to be used purposedly as the equivalent to gunboat diplomacy, then it can be easily foreseen that instead of having a beneficial impact on the general international climate, it will exacerbate distrust, prejudice, bias, and prove to be another hindrance to notions of peace and friendliness.

Progress in Promoting Cultural Exchanges

Speaking of cultural exchange one is reminded that both in Russian and in English the very word "culture" denotes the sum total of the achievements of a society—in its material and in its spiritual development taken together, while the initial meaning of the Latin word was bound still closer with the material aspects of human life, with land cultivation. Hence, strictly speaking, a cultural exchange is not limited to theatrical tours or art exhibits. In the broad sense of the word, the exchange of achievements in basic sciences or in technological know-how also belongs to the category of cultural exchange. However, regardless of how you use the term, it is absolutely evident that within recent years we have witnessed a spectacular increase in the volume of international contacts under this category.

I shall quote just a few figures to illustrate the extent of Soviet participation in international cultural contacts. My country now has links in this field with 120 countries of the world; 83 official governmental cultural agreements are, at the moment, operational. After the Helsinki conference ended the Soviet Union, in keeping with the provisions of the Final Act, concluded quite a number of agreements pertaining to cultural and humanitarian spheres with various countries. These include the Soviet–Portuguese agreement on cooperation in the spheres of culture and science, the Franco–Soviet agreement on tourism, the Soviet–Turkish programme of cultural exchange for 1976–1978; there is also an agreement on furthering information exchanges between the Soviet news agency TASS and France Presse; a Soviet–Italian declaration was signed pledging both Governments to encourage a deeper mutual understanding and a mutual knowledge of each other's cultural heritage, to facilitate the learning of the Italian language in the USSR and

---

2. I owe the metaphor to Herbert I. Schiller, Professor of Communications of the University of California at San Diego.

of the Russian language in Italy, to promote contacts between young people of both countries, etc.

Let us turn to a different aspect—to literature. Here my country has excellent traditions in the field of translation from foreign languages. More than 300 American books and 150 (of each) English and French books are translated annually into the numerous national languages of the Soviet republics. In 1976 alone the Soviet Union published 1.5 thousand new foreign titles, the total reaching 60 million copies. According to the UNESCO figures the USSR publishes four times more books translated from foreign languages than the USA does, and nine times more than Britain.

The same is true of films and theatrical productions. During the last two years Soviet spectators saw 10 new American films, 14 French, 7 Italian ones, etc.; Soviet theatres present 130 contemporary plays by foreign authors (this does not include classical pieces).

We are sometimes reproached for the slow development of tourism. It is quite true that here we have not achieved the level we should like to; there is a large number of reasons for the way things are today: these include the non-convertibility of Soviet currency, the previous absence of infrastructure needed for tourism (hotels, services, etc.) because our country had first to satisfy much more urgent needs. Now the situation is undergoing some change. Within the last five years we have had a twofold increase in the number of foreign visitors to our country. About 15 million people came to the Soviet Union from abroad and about 11 million Soviet citizens went as tourists to other countries. We plan another half as much increase in these figures in the coming five years. The scope of our links also widens—we are now having guests from 155 countries, and Soviet tourists are visiting 130 foreign lands. The relative share of tourist exchange between socialist and capitalist countries is also growing—in 1956 only 25 per cent. of foreign visitors came from countries of a different social system, now the proportion has reached 40 per cent. The same is true of Soviet tourists going abroad—in 1956 only 19 per cent. went to capitalist countries and 20 years later the figure is 40 per cent.

Learning foreign languages is also closely connected with the notion of cultural exchange. The level of language learning in any country proves a reliable reflection of the general attitude towards foreign culture, of traditions of spiritual growth. Young people in the Soviet Union learn many languages spoken in every part of the globe, but if we take only the most popular foreign languages then

Soviet students in the system of secondary and higher education learning French number 2.5 million (compare this with 25 thousand French students learning Russian), those learning German number 11 million, and those learning English—12 million. In keeping with the Helsinki Final Act the Soviet Union is ready to aid any country in establishing Russian language courses; in 1973 we founded a special research centre to develop further the methodology of teaching Russian to foreigners—the Pushkin Institute of Russian Language, named after our great national poet.

Are we fully satisfied with the situation in the field of cultural exchange? Do we find it close to perfection?

Most obviously not. Far from being so, though I would like to stress that the situation today as such is a great step forward compared with what we had ten, not to speak of fifteen years ago. The level of contacts that seems no more than normal today might have been called chimerical in the recent past, after a quarter of a century of the Cold War and a virtual absence of cultural links. In bringing this fact to light my aim is not to encourage complacency, but to stress the need for a sober and careful attitude towards the progress in international relations that has been achieved by concerted efforts of many people, the need for sustaining and continuing these efforts in depth.

As Secretary-General of the Central Committee of the Communist Party of the Soviet Union Leonid Brezhnev stressed in his recent speech[3] that transmitting all the Helsinki agreements into reality depends in a large measure "on the general quality of interstate political relations, on what could be called the level of détente. The opponents of détente who seek to poison the international atmosphere hinder this activity". The reorganization and normalization of international relations together with the increase of mutual trust cannot come about simply as a result of an emotional explosion, of an enthusiastic wave; these call for routine everyday work without frequent dramatic breakthroughs. It is the kind of work that demands patience, perseverance, goodwill, continuity and single-mindedness. A different attitude, the one based on the expectation of the miraculous overnight appearance of glorious palaces of mutual love and general well-being, the way things happen in fairy-tales, is bound to be an illusion. Let us avoid this attitude. Nothing comes by itself. There is no magic available. We shall have to build those palaces with our own hands, on a day-

3. As quoted from *Pravda*, January 19, 1977.

to-day basis, all the time taking stock of the things already done and the things still in front of us. The years of the Cold War gave birth to the powerful infrastructure perpetuating it. Now we have to counter it with an infrastructure of peace.

Cultural Exchanges and the Ideological Struggle

By definition, the concept of culture features, among other constituents, ideology, that is the aggregate of notions about the world and the regularities of its development, of man's role and destiny and the like. There is a tendency to substitute ideology for the whole of culture, which certainly calls for objection, since culture is broader than ideology, though within the framework of culture ideology obviously takes up an important place.

Now, what is the meaning of the expression "the struggle of ideas", or "ideological struggle" and does this type of struggle hamper or inhibit cultural exchange and normal international relations as such?

In addition to its theory, the struggle of ideas on the international arena has already a history of its own. Ideology per se and ideological struggle emerged simultaneously with social classes, social struggle, and statehood. It was not "invented" by the Soviet Union and started long before the first socialist State in the world came into being. Naturally for quite a long time it was only within the State borders that the ideological struggle manifested itself as an important element of socio-political relations. Its use in the international arena was restrained due to the difficulties of practical ideological penetration across national frontiers, because the technological base for, so to say, massive long-distance communication of ideas was absent. Still, even in the past there were individual cases when ideological struggle managed to cross national thresholds centuries ago. The Austrian historian Alfred Sturminger, for instance, considers organized political propaganda to have been part of international life for millennia (the proponents of this view cite for confirmation the preaching of Pan-Hellenistic ideas and the use that has been made of this practice by Philip the Second and Alexander the Great). Other experts give a much later date, the Napoleonic wars, or still more frequently connect it with the emergence of "open diplomacy" at the end of World War I. The exact date is really unimportant for us now.

But what is of paramount importance is that the collision of viewpoints, of world outlook, the struggle of ideas, have long been, are now, and will continue to be an inescapable fact of life. There is no alternative. To be exact there certainly *is* an alternative, but it consists in total and absolute uniformity of modes of thinking of all those inhabiting the earth ...

We are today advocating peaceful coexistence under the conditions of continued ideological struggle. Now, if this concept be replaced by the one calling for peaceful coexistence on the basis of "ideological unity", what would that mean in terms of real life? I presume that in real life it would be tantamount to demand that the whole world adopt one of the two opposing ideologies—bourgeois or socialist. And in so far as neither side expresses a willingness to capitulate ideologically, this plan would turn out to be not a programme of peace, but a programme of embittered struggle and aggravation of tensions in the truest spirit of the new Crusades.

Not a whit more realistic is the plan for peaceful coexistence on the basis of an "ideological truce" under which each side would be supposed to stick to its own ideology, but renounce efforts at contention. This project could only be considered feasible by those who entertain the illusion that the wheel of history can be halted by mutual agreement. The interest that people take in what is happening in the world cannot be stifled. Human beings cannot but strive to comprehend the world—for the sake of estimating the future, but also in order to satisfy today's needs because it is impossible to find one's bearings in a contemporary constant torrent of change without at least hypothesizing its main channel. Wherever man lives, his day-to-day life poses scores and hundreds of poignant questions involving ideology. Man cannot be denied answers to these questions, for nowadays the wide masses have become an immense power which has to be reckoned with by any social system or any government. Thus no public policy is feasible today without some dialogue with the masses—which is pure ideology, and there is no doubt about it.

Most observers stress today an increased attraction towards problems of general social and spiritual environment, towards history and sociology; numerous schools of thinking calling themselves "microsociology", or "social engineering", or "social technology" and the like came into being; unprecedented enthusiasm for social forecasting loomed so large that it merited the name of a "futurology" explosion; the world was made familiar with newborn ambitious concepts aimed at a universal explanation of human history in its totality in response to the "Marxist challenge" (it will suffice to just enumerate a few names—Walt W. Rostow, Pitirim Sorokin, J.K. Galbraith, Zbiegniew Brzezinski in the

United States of America, Raymond Aron in France, Arnold Toynbee in Britain, Marshall McLuhan in Canada and many, many others). All of the above testifies to the fact that Raymond Aron was justly describing contemporary society as striving to satisfy its hunger, the hunger being probably more on the spiritual than the material side.[4] Given this acute interest toward things spiritual, toward the world of ideas, it becomes obvious that we are facing the issue of a collision of differing systems of spiritual values, of conflicting Weltanschauungen that give divergent interpretations of the world and the direction of its development.

Is that kind of collision fraught with danger for humanity? Does it jeopardize world peace? Does it block the way towards complete elimination of the bitter heritage of the cold war in international relations?

I am aware that many would answer the question in the affirmative. But widespread opinions are not necessarily true; it is well known that erroneous impressions may be extremely popular, still more so if there happen to be powerful vested interests dedicated to their perpetuation.

One of the lessons of history is that the largest wars of our century broke out not due to ideological divergence, or a different estimation of advantages and disadvantages of this or that social system, but to absolutely unrelated factors which embraced a search for profits, spheres of influence, sources of raw materials, new markets and the like. Hardly anybody is going to dispute the fact that long before the appearance of the first socialist State, when as yet there was nothing in the world to disturb its "ideological unity" in inter-state relations, the bourgeois world had been continuously rent by conflicts and wars. On the other hand history gives many instances of quite normal, good-neighbourly relations between countries with different political systems and ideologies.

Thus a wide schism in ideology between the United States, as a young bourgeois-democratic republic, and Russia, as an absolutist monarchy, did not prevent them from developing rather staunch loyalties for over a century. Neither did differences in ideology prevent an alliance between the Soviet Union, the United States and Britain during World War II. Today we also witness friendly relations between some countries divided by fairly insurmountable ideological dissimilarities. Thus past experience and present-day

---

4. R. Aron. *Les désillusions du progrès. Essai sur la dialectique de la modernité.* Paris, 1969, p. VIII.

reality tend to teach that if one does not deliberately exploit ideological differences as a pretext for aggravating relations, these differences will not hinder normal relations between countries belonging to different social systems. Under the conditions of a competition of two systems and the corresponding contest of ideas there is every possibility for doing away with the cold war and achieving not a diluted substitute for peace, but genuinely normal relations that will include good-neighbourly cooperation in many spheres of life. Our country has long adhered to this viewpoint. In the very first years of the existence of the Soviet Union the founder of our State V.I. Lenin stressed that we shall have to live together with capitalist countries on our planet, unless we planned "flying to the moon". It is true that today, from the purely technical point of view, "flying to the moon" has been made much more feasible, still all of us persist in intending to go on living on our old planet, hence we again express our readiness not to just coexist, but to collaborate in various fields.

Ideological Struggle and Psychological Warfare

The fact that an ideological contest is found inevitable and unremitting does not in any way imply that peaceful coexistence is compatible with any kind of activity aimed at influencing the minds of the people. It is one thing to engage in the ideological struggle, to argue about the understanding and assessment of reality, about the paths that lead toward ideals shared by the majority of mankind, about the merits or deficiencies of a social system. This kind of struggle, however acute the conflict of opinions may get, can be conducted within a proper framework of debate and need not incur danger to world peace and the improvement of international relations. It is quite another thing if one attempts to preach war and hatred between nations, to make slanderous allegations, to incite sabotage or to spread rumours aimed at sowing confusion and discord in a society. This can hardly be called an ideological contest, but would rather deserve the name of psychological warfare, of subversive activity. The latter is obviously damaging to the cause of peace since it breeds suspicion and distrust in international relations.

Ideological struggle being an objective process intrinsically inherent in international life—and in human life in general—the choice of its methods, modes, means and ends is certainly quite subjective and comes as a result of conscious decision-making by governments, ruling classes, political parties.

And in this respect the positive shifts that occurred recently in international relations are bound to introduce certain changes in those modes and methods of ideological struggle that were typical of the cold war period. The nature of the newly come shifts may certainly be interpreted in a narrow way, just as realization of the suicidal character of a nuclear war against the Soviet Union and hence switching over to non-military planes of rivalry between the opposing social systems. The importance of this transformation in approach is beyond a shadow of doubt. The point is whether it is going to remain the sole transformation.

As far as the Soviet Union is concerned we interpret peaceful coexistence as being much more than a mere absence of war. Peaceful coexistence potentially implies a genuine normalization of relations, a wide expansion of mutually beneficial cooperation. The whole problem of a relationship between opposing social systems does not boil down to the single consideration of the ratio between military and non-military modes of struggle. A lot of importance must be attached to the very means of contention within non-military spheres of relationship—in economy, politics, ideology, science and technology.

We ought to keep in mind that, after all, even during the cold war years these were the main spheres of rivalry—only the rivalry took certain specific forms typical of the cold war. On the plane of economic relations the forms employed included blockades, various trade restrictions, discriminatory rules and suchlike.

On the ideological plane the United States of America for instance openly opted for such forms as psychological warfare which was effected through specially established centres such as Radio Free Europe and Radio Liberty.

Now, if the turn for the better in international affairs leaves the above practices intact and only restrains the military aspect of confrontation, then there will be no reason to speak of the end of the cold war. After all, it was also conducted mainly in the non-military spheres and hence got the byname "cold". To really do away with it and consolidate détente we must renounce the forms and means of struggle that became ingrained during the cold war.

On the plane of ideology this means renouncing propaganda of belligerence and hatred for other countries, abandoning slander and various subversive techniques. Then the contest for people's minds will develop truly as a contest of varying outlooks that need not harm peaceful and friendly relations. Certainly, when we are reminded that, for instance, broadcasting guidelines openly direct Radio Liberty to press for change in the existing political system in the Soviet Union, we cannot but rate this radio station as a cold war vehicle steeped in psychological warfare and in no way compatible with the spirit of détente and with the basic principles of the Final Act adopted at Helsinki.

It is truly a pity that Western listeners do not in their majority speak Russian and do not hear what is being daily broadcast in Russian by Radio Liberty or Radio Free Europe; otherwise they would have a much better understanding of our singularly negative attitude towards their activity.

Recent months have also been marked by a new wave of a definitely malignant propaganda campaign related to the so-called "Soviet threat". Fomenting this kind of fictitious anxieties is really a well-worn trick. Every time, when new military budgets are being debated in the United States and in other NATO countries, a noisy campaign breaks out with the aim of exerting pressure on public opinion and coaxing more billions of dollars for military expenditure from the legislative bodies of the countries concerned (this is the kind of explanation we often hear from our colleagues in the Western academic community when we express our bewilderment with regular propaganda outbursts concerning the "Soviet threat"); as a "fringe benefit", political drives of this sort pose roadblocks in the path of new initiatives directed towards curbing the arms race. In the meantime the majority of knowledgeable specialists are very well aware that all the fuss about the "Soviet threat" is a deliberate tactical ruse and a deftly employed psychological operation. What makes the design still more obvious is the well-known fact that today there exist enough international communication channels and special mechanisms that allow to be aired, if need be, any doubts and anxieties as to the military measures taken by the other side and to seek all the desired information on the official governmental level, instead of fanning the excitement in the mass media.

In what way can we in the Soviet Union categorize the pressure tactics of that kind? We can only put it down as another routine in the ideological struggle—and the one that surely ought to have been discarded because of its potential for increasing misgivings and uncertainties between States.

As far as the true Soviet position is concerned, it has recently been firmly stated by L.I. Brezhnev, Secretary-General of the Central Committee of the Communist Party of the Soviet Union: "Not the policy aimed at achieving superiority in armaments, but the policy of their reduction, of lessening the military confrontation—that is the line we choose. In the name of the party, of the whole of our people, I proclaim that our country will never embark on the path of aggression, will never raise the sword against other peoples" ...[5]

My colleagues and I cannot but agree with those Western peace researchers who are convinced that alongside with normalized political and military relations between countries the international agenda today also includes psychological normalization or psychological disarmament. Elucidating this concept, a well-known American philosopher and psychologist Erich Fromm writes that it does not mean a renunciation of the ideological struggle, but that this struggle should "not be used to foster a spirit of war".[6]

We are aware that some scholars in the West see the main thrust of psychological normalization in the direction of legal restriction of certain forms of propaganda. True, to a certain extent, their approach looks a bit too formal. Safeguards against hostile propaganda can hardly be reduced to the signing of international treaties; likewise the struggle for world peace is waged chiefly by social and political means, not just by legal measures. But surely it would be wrong to underestimate the importance of the international legal mechanism that could play a prominent role in regulating government-to-government relations and various aspects of interstate activities, including the activity linked with an ideological contest, with the dissemination of ideas.

The problem of international law restricting propaganda and other types of ideological activity is relatively new and efforts in this direction could prove conducive to further improvements in the international political climate.

Incidentally, as regards official propaganda hostile to governments of other countries and calling for the overthrow of the status quo, Soviet Russia declared very early its willingness to refrain from such propaganda on a reciprocal basis, in response to similar commitments by the governments of capitalist countries. This was recorded in the very first treaties signed by the Soviet Government—the Brest Treaty (1918), treaties with Britain (1921), Poland (1921), Norway (1921), Italy (1921), and other countries right up until the 1933 exchange of letters between

---

5. *Pravda*, January 19, 1977.
6. Erich Fromm, *May Man Prevail? An Inquiry into the Facts and Fictions of Foreign Policy*, New York 1961, p. 16.

Franklin D. Roosevelt and Maxim M. Livinov establishing diplomatic relations between the USSR and the USA.[7]

Ending these remarks on the role of the ideological struggle in international relations I should like to stress once again that the competition of ideas, the contest of outlooks, cannot be abolished by decree or cancelled by mutual agreement. Cherishing expectations of the sort means closing one's eyes and ears to today's realities. And in our opinion it is most important to keep track of realities, however enticing illusions might be. Once you give in to illusions, disappointment is always close at hand, and it also breeds despair, cynicism, frustration, distrust towards any positive developments. Presumably such was the sequence of attitudes taken by many of those who now talk of their disappointed hopes in connection with the outcome of the Helsinki conference.

Prospects

If we stick to the firm ground of reality, if we do not underestimate the difficulties and disagreements, but press forward in every aspect of international activity included in the Final Act, then our progress will in time accelerate, international goodwill and trust will grow. And as suspicions, wariness, expectation of hostile attitude and attempts at subversion will be more and more relegated to the past, détente will be taking deeper roots in all spheres of international life, including wider cooperation in humanitarian fields and expanded cultural exchange, and all this activity will be becoming increasingly "normal", habitual, intertwined with the very fabric of State-to-State interaction.

---

7. *Dokumenty vneshney politiki SSSR* (*Documents of Foreign Policy of the USSR*), namely:

"Brest treaty", March 3, 1918, Article II—*Dokumenty* ..., Vol. I, Moscow, 1957, p. 121.

"Trade Agreement with Great Britain", March 16, 1921, Section A—*Dokumenty* ..., Vol. 3, Moscow, 1959, p. 608.

"Peace Treaty with Poland", March 18, 1921, Article Y—*Dokumenty* ..., Vol. 3, Moscow, 1959, p. 623.

"Provisional Agreement with Norway", September 2, 1921, Article YIII—*Dokumenty* ..., Vol. 4, Moscow, 1960, p. 301.

"Russian–Italian Agreement", December 26, 1921, Preamble—*Dokumenty* ..., Vol. 4, Moscow, 1960, p. 596.

"Exchange of letters between F.D. Roosevelt and Maxim Litvinov on the issue of propaganda", November 16, 1933—*Dokumenty* ..., Vol. 16, Moscow, 1970, pp. 642–644.

Chapter 12

CULTURAL EXCHANGE AND COMPETITION BETWEEN SOCIETIES: AN AMERICAN VIEW

by *Robert F. Byrnes**

The peoples and governments of all signatories of the Final Act, and indeed of the world, enjoy common benefits from the movement toward increased cultural exchange and other forms of peaceful relationships between East and West. At the same time, however, the individual States seek different national interests in these exchanges. Moreover, the concerns of the scholars, intellectuals, and artists who participate often differ in some degree from the interests of their governments. Consequently, increasing cultural exchange and competition raises complicated issues for the governments and societies involved.

The nature of thermo-nuclear war would be such that everyone in the world profits from efforts to reduce the likelihood of conflict. In fact, the prospect of nuclear war is so terrifying that most governments are interested in reducing strains and eliminating crises which might lead to annihilation. Moreover, the nature of the world in the fourth quarter of the twentieth century is such that all free governments, and those of many authoritarian States as well, recognize the advantages of cultural ties, particularly in reducing age-old cultural barriers, increasing knowledge and understanding of other peoples, and beginning the long, vital process toward cooperation in resolving common, indeed universal problems. The most effective expressions of such universal cooperation are those toward developing new strains of rice, grain and maize and spreading knowledge of these discoveries into every interested country. In relations between the West, the States of Eastern Europe, and the Soviet Union, such cooperative enterprises are not yet possible. However, the bilateral research cooperation agreements signed by the United States and the Soviet Union between 1972 and 1974 for eleven different fields of study (such as

---

* In preparing this paper, I have benefited from the opportunity for research and writing which the Netherlands Institute for Advanced Study in the Humanities and Social Sciences has provided.

agriculture, atomic energy, environmental protection, and medical sciences and public health), and similar agreements other Western States have with the Soviet Union, are at least a beginning toward peaceful cooperation between hostile States and may constitute a step toward a universal approach, which would benefit all.

Advantages of Exchange and Competition

American benefits

The initial steps which led to the cultural exchange agreement between the United States and the Soviet Union in March 1958 were taken by American scholars particularly interested in Soviet studies who wished to visit the country about which they were teaching and to carry on research in Soviet libraries. At that time, and still today, these scholars, and the intellectuals and artists who have participated in the exchange programmes, have sought principally to increase their knowledge and understanding of a different culture and political system, to learn from others who have the same scholarly and intellectual interests, and to obtain the advantages any educated person derives from widened horizons and access to new points of view. These aims are not unique to those interested in the Soviet Union and Eastern Europe, for they are only a part of the vast American effort since the Second World War to increase knowledge and understanding of the so-called non-Western countries and cultures, which American education had virtually ignored.

The American people support and assist these efforts to improve research and instruction throughout the educational system because they appreciate the importance of knowledge and understanding of others in this ever-shrinking world. Indeed, almost all Americans now understand, as almost none did in the 1940s, that they live in a small world in which all must cooperate to survive. In addition, Americans support closer cultural relations because they consider peaceful competition in intellectual fields more "safe and sane" than rivalry in arms or constant confrontations. Americans, and of course other Western peoples, are accustomed to cooperation and peaceful competition in ideas, as well as in trade. Expanding cultural relations with a rival, hostile State such as the Soviet Union therefore seems both natural and sensible. Above all, most Americans recognize the extraordinary advantages the United States and the West acquire in diverting competition from political warfare, an arms race, and endless crises to one in which the West is invincibly strong. Americans not only prefer transferring the competition to the safer cultural field, but were, are, and will remain confident that the United States and the West will emerge stronger and the world safer from such a test. The freedom and the intellectual vitality, effervescence, and openness of the United States and its allies and friends are the principal weapons of the West in peaceful intellectual competition. Indeed, Americans are delighted to participate in this test at every level, from jazz to computers, against what Sir Isaiah Berlin has called "the silence of Soviet culture".[1]

The American government from the beginning has endorsed this position of the scholars and the public because it shares the same values and views. Indeed, as time has passed, the government has come to appreciate the growing importance of this once "neglected aspect" of American foreign policy. Moreover, from the point of view of American national interest, increased cultural exchange and competition have brought at least a few Soviet and American citizens into contact and enabled those in an elite group on each side to demonstrate the interests of their governments and to learn about the other system, a process in which Americans believe both sides gain. These relations also provide the American government an opportunity to influence the Soviet political elite, a critical group, because in the last third of the twentieth century, as in the age of Louis XIV, "nations touch most at the top". In short, expanding cultural relations has not only brought the Soviet Union into the world from the isolation and ignorance which Stalin had imposed on it, but has also given the United States and other Western countries increased knowledge of Soviet policy and some slight leverage to use in the total Soviet–American relationship.

Over the years, some changes have occurred in popular and national American positions with regard to cultural exchange, and the relationships are somewhat larger and more significant than twenty years ago. However, the fundamental positions remain the same, just more deeply appreciated, understood, and supported.

Soviet benefits

The Soviet Union also obtains concrete advantages from cultural exchanges, which Soviet leaders declare an essential part of their doctrine of "peaceful coexistence". Americans cannot be certain of the meaning of this phrase, which remains "the general guideline of Soviet foreign policy", and which Soviet leaders have defined as

1. Isaiah Berlin, "The Silence in Russian Culture", *Foreign Affairs*, XXXVI Number 1 (October, 1957), 1–24.

"class war on the international level" and "the highest form of class struggle".[2] Cultural exchanges support the Soviet effort to persuade other governments and peoples that the Soviet Union has no aggressive designs or ambitions, that placid normalcy has returned, and that the Western States need not rearm or unite in defence. They also provide the Soviet Union respectability, still greatly needed after Stalin's twenty-five years of rule and its continuation by other leaders, and the opportunity to reward loyal Soviet scholars and cultural leaders. Finally, such relationships provide a fine opportunity to acquire access to the science and technology of Western societies. In the exchanges with the United States, more than eighty per cent. of the Soviet participants in the first fifteen years were scientists or engineers. In recent years, that percentage has risen to more than ninety per cent. of the total, thus demonstrating a powerful Soviet interest and advantage.

East European benefits

The peoples of Eastern Europe and their governments share many of the same interests as the American and Western peoples and their governments. In addition, they seek access to the wealth of the Western economies and to their scientific and technical achievements. They also seek to end the isolation long imposed on them during and after the Second World War and to return to their traditional relationships with Western Europe and its culture, which they share. This applies in particular to the peoples of Poland, Czechoslovakia, and Hungary, who have for centuries had powerful ties with the West. The peoples of Eastern Europe, in short, have an interest in overcoming the division of Europe at least as strong as that of the peoples of Western Europe.

Perspectives Since Stalin's Death

During the time when Stalin ruled, and today as well, the basic elements in international politics remain economic and military power, vitality and stability, resolution, and skill in diplomacy. In 1977, even more than twenty-five years ago, reaching agreements on disarmament and on crisis management remain more important than expanding cultural relationships. In short, SALT and MBFR are far more vital in the short run than is any mustard seed.

2. Georgii Zhukov, "Cultural Contacts: Two Approaches", *International Affairs* (Moscow), V, Number 11 (November, 1959), 19–27; *Communist*, September, 1973, editorial; *Pravda*, January 5, January 6, 1973.

However, in the long run, the role played by economic and intellectual relationships will acquire ever greater significance, not only in the reality of international politics but also in public understanding of those relations. In the long run, the competition of ideas may prove the decisive factor in the contest between two powerful systems.

During the last years of Stalin's life, no Western scholars were allowed to study in the Soviet Union, Soviet intellectuals (and other citizens as well) were prohibited from visiting even neighbouring states ruled by communists, and control over access to information within the Soviet Union, and from outside, was as tight as any government has ever managed. Not even a socialist State was allowed to send a commercial aeroplane into the air space of the Soviet Union so long as Stalin lived.

1977 is somewhat different, although many commentators have compared the gradual, slow opening of the Soviet Union and increased contact with the West to moving "the massive groaning gate of a medieval castle" and have described it as "the beginning of a beginning".[3]

In spite of the progress made in the past two decades, the patterns remain substantially the same. The divisions within Europe are much greater than they were a hundred years ago or even forty years ago, when Nazi Germany was ready to launch attacks upon its neighbours. Even the Final Act in Helsinki was signed only after more than two years of negotiations by 492 diplomats from thirty-five countries.

Progress since the mid-fifties

An American can best obtain perspective concerning these changes by reviewing the discussions which led to the March 1958 Soviet–American cultural exchange agreement. Ambassador William S.B. Lacy defined American goals as "removing barriers currently obstructing the free flow of information and debate on the vital issues of the day".[4] In his opening talk, he urged the Soviet Union as a great step toward peace to end censorship, to cease jamming Western radio broadcasts, and to abolish all controls over access to information and to travel. We have made perilously little progress toward those aims.

3. Senator Lyndon B. Johnson in the *New York Times*, January 28, January 29, 1958.
4. Joseph Quinn, *The Anatomy of East–West Cooperation: U.S.–U.S.S.R., Public Health Exchange Program 1958–1967* (Washington, 1969).

The Soviet Ambassador, Georgii Zarubin, on the other hand, described Soviet goals as "normalization of Soviet–American relations and the relaxation of international tensions". No one has agreed yet on the meaning of "normalization". Ambassador Zarubin also suggested the immediate exchange of fifty-six delegations in important fields of science and technology, a position which underlines one of the main purposes of cultural exchange for the Soviet Union.

The Soviet Union allowed twelve foreign correspondents to work in Moscow in 1953, compared with about 250 in 1977, twenty-five of whom are American (the Soviet Union has thirty-six correspondents in the United States.) The direct flights between New York and Moscow approved in the March 1958 agreement began eight years later. The exchange of classroom teachers accepted in 1958 began in 1974, with fewer than ten teachers each way. The Soviet Union signed the International Copyright Convention in February 1973. Forty-three Americans visited the Soviet Union as tourists the year in which Stalin died, and about 100,000 a quarter-century later. In this period, the largest number of Soviet tourists who visited the United States in any one year has never exceeded 600. The total number of participants in the cultural exchange agreement between 1958 and 1973 included 13,178 Soviet and 17,071 American citizens. In other words, some improvement has occurred.

For the Americans who launched these programmes, the academic exchanges remain the most significant symbol or touchstone. Between 1958 and 1975, about a thousand American senior graduate students and scholars spent from two months to two years in the Soviet Union, and approximately the same number of Soviet scholars and graduate students spent the same periods of time in the United States. During that period, 3,000 scholars and students from all the Western States studied in the Soviet Union. However, one must put these figures into perspective. For example, in 1976, 150,000 foreign students continued their studies in the United States and 25,000 in the Soviet Union. In each year since 1963, more scholars from Iceland have studied in the United States than have scholars from the Soviet Union.

Eastern Europe, in contrast, has been far more free, and exchanges have expanded far more rapidly than they have with the Soviet Union, although they usually began later. For example, a total of 1,000 Polish scholars studied in the United States between 1956 and 1960. Four hundred and twenty-two Czechoslovak scholars studied in the United States in 1967 and 1,000 in 1969 alone. One hundred and fifty-four Romanian scholars were in the United States in 1970. The University of Warsaw in 1976 launched an American Studies Center, with American faculty members in important instructional roles and a fine, open American library.[5]

Progress in recent years

Cultural exchanges have continued in a slightly different spirit and tempo since 1969 or 1970, although the pattern remains basically as established twenty years ago. It is difficult to determine the reasons for this Soviet relaxation: perhaps Soviet appreciation of the achievements of the previous years, the strain in Soviet–Chinese relations and the need to reduce pressures in the West, the "spring" in Czechoslovakia in 1968 and Soviet realization that Eastern Europe remains in disarray, and the Soviet discovery at about the same time of a growing gap in science, technology, and agriculture between the Soviet Union and the West. In any case, during the years in which the Western States and the Soviet Union were preparing for the Helsinki discussions, during the talks themselves, and since the signing of the Final Act on August 1, 1975, some improvements have occurred. These limited and uneven changes give some hope that other modifications will occur and that the Soviet system may mellow and adopt different foreign policies.

Thus, during these years, especially after the signing of the agreement, the Soviet Union has adopted a somewhat less rigorous attitude toward allowing emigration, particularly of members of divided families. It has at the same time forced some of its most distinguished dissidents to leave the Soviet Union, a barbarous practice but one which most Westerners consider an advance upon labour camps or psychiatric treatment. Travel by foreigners within the Soviet Union is under somewhat less constraint, but the right of Soviet citizens to travel abroad has remained unaffected.

With regard to access to information, progress has occurred. Thus, the Soviet Union ceased jamming such national government stations as BBC and the Voice of America in 1974. Since the signing of the Final Act, it has allowed some Western journalists multiple entry visas and has given them the same travel opportunities as it provides diplomats. The Soviet government at Helsinki agreed "gradually to increase the quantities and number of titles

5. Robert F. Byrnes, *Soviet–American Academic Exchanges, 1958–1975* (Bloomington, 1976), (276 pages) provides detailed information concerning academic exchanges, and other cultural exchanges as well.

of newspapers and publications imported", and has made some slight improvement in the number of Western newspapers available in hotels to which Western tourists are assigned. In academic exchanges, some slight improvement has occurred in admitting a higher percentage of Americans nominated who are interested in contemporary issues, in access to libraries and archives, and in travel for study-related purposes. In areas such as medical research and public health, less political than most, satisfaction is greater on both sides than it is, for example, in the exchange of publications.

The Eastern European States were far more free and less restrictive than the Soviet Union, but, even so, the changes there have been more visible and significant. In academic exchanges, for example, neither the United States nor its Western allies suffer the problems in admission or placement which they have in the Soviet Union. Western scholars travel freely within the East European countries, libraries and archives are open, and establishment of direct exchanges between institutions and even individuals has been easy. As one British observer described, cultural relationships with the Soviet Union involve climbing a wall and crossing a moat, while those with Eastern Europe involve going through a complicated turnstile.[6]

At the same time, the Soviet Union maintains a massive capacity for jamming foreign radio broadcasts and continues vigorously to jam Radio Liberty, Kol Israel, Radio Peking and Radio Tirana. Soviet hours of broadcasting to Western Europe and North America remain approximately fifty per cent. higher than those from Western Europe and North America directed to the Soviet Union. Yet, illogically but in accordance with the doctrine of peaceful coexistence and the simultaneous denial of ideological coexistence, the Soviet government continues both its intensive jamming and its vigorous campaign to close down Radio Free Europe and Radio Liberty. In addition, it has made a sustained effort since 1972 in UNESCO, in the General Assembly of the United Nations, and in the International Telecommunications Union to prevent radio and television broadcasts from artificial earth satellites into a country without that country's permission, activities not yet technically possible but which will one day raise critical problems for all governments which seek to control the flow of information.

Some of the conditions under which Western journalists work in the Soviet Union have improved, but they continue to live in

6. Sir George Weidenfeld, *The Publisher as Internationalist* (Denver, 1971), 2.

ghettos. Soviet agents follow them. The Soviet press has launched vicious and utterly unwarranted attacks upon some as spies. In February 1977, the Soviet government expelled a responsible American journalist, George Krimsky, apparently because Krimsky was maintaining contact with Soviet dissidents. This first expulsion since 1970 was followed by American retaliation against a TASS reporter in Washington. The Soviet Union continues to deny Western States the right to open reading rooms. It even censors Western publications which it imports under the International Copyright Convention for its research institutions. For example, the editors of *Science* discovered that Soviet officials are violating the contract under which they purchase and reproduce a number of copies of *Science*, by blotting out some articles, news items, editorials and letters to the editor before they distribute the issues.

Travel remains tightly controlled. For instance, American soil scientists in 1976 were not allowed to travel to areas which the Soviet government had previously agreed would be opened to them, and Western scholars encounter difficulties in obtaining research travel. Indeed, the scholars responsible for administering the academic exchange programmes note that the fundamental problems which appeared in 1958 still exist. Many Soviet citizens who have relatives abroad are denied the opportunity to leave the Soviet Union, even to visit. The Western press is full of information concerning Soviet citizens, especially Jews, who are not only not allowed to emigrate but are severely penalized for seeking exit visas. The Soviet government, and the East European States subsequently, even denied visas to the Commission on Security and Cooperation in Europe of the American Congress, which visited Europe in November 1976 as part of a fact-finding and review process of developments since Helsinki.

Above all, Soviet, Czechoslovak, East German, and to some degree Polish and Romanian treatment of dissidents in the past two years has raised a great threat to cultural exchange and competition. The arrest of a number of prominent Soviet dissidents, such as Andrei Tvordokhlebov of Amnesty International, Yuri Orlov of the Public Group to promote the Observance of the Helsinki Agreement in the USSR, and Alexander Ginsburg, a leading advocate of human rights, all darken the scene because of the dramatic character of these assaults on human rights, which are fundamental to any honourable intellectual exchange.

Similarly, the East German government's banning of Wolf Biermann, an utterly loyal Communist, for his songs in Hamburg, the house arrest of Robert Havemann, and the modulated pressures against West Berlin because about 100,000 East Germans have requested exit visas all remind Americans that the Berlin Wall and the death strips survive as denials of the qualities on which cultural exchange, indeed any kind of peaceful relations, rest. The ferocious attacks upon those who signed Charter 77 in Czechoslovakia and the arrest of some of those most prominent in the request that the Czechoslovak government honour its own constitution, a number of other agreements, and the Final Act, also indicate that failure to honour the promises of Helsinki is not confined to the Soviet Union and East Germany.

The Paradoxical Reversals of Position on Helsinki

The long negotiations about security and cooperation in Europe and the Final Act itself have proved far more significant than most Western observers thought likely. In fact, by the spring of 1977, both the Soviet Union and the United States had reversed the positions they had adopted eighteen months earlier, in one of the most striking paradoxes of recent international politics. At the time of the signing and for several months afterwards, the Soviet Union in particular praised the Helsinki Pact as a great achievement, one which marked the end of the Second World War and ensured stability in Eastern Europe through exchanged pledges of the inviolability of frontiers. In short, the Soviet view of the pact emphasized the past, and the Final Act is an important element in a Soviet defensive position.

On the other hand, most Western leaders signed the Final Act with reluctance. Most Western peoples, as well as dissidents in the Soviet Union and Eastern Europe, were deeply critical of the West for "sanctifying" the Soviet position in Eastern Europe and the Soviet Union's acquisition of 114,000 square miles of territory, in return for more Soviet promises for greater freedoms in the future. However, most Westerners now see some progress toward accepted Western standards and toward Helsinki commitments. Above all, they now believe that the Final Act offers dynamic possibilities for peaceful change within the conservative Soviet system.

Helsinki offers some promise for widening cultural exchange and competition, in part because the issue of human rights in the States which communists rule has emerged as a dramatic symbol, recognized as central for every person and every society, by those who restrict these rights and by those who struggle that they be honoured. These rights, which are an essential part of Basket

Three, are also included as Principle Seven of Basket One, which provides for "respect for human rights and fundamental freedoms, including the freedom of thought, conscience, religion, or belief". Discussion of their significance during the negotiations, the long and successful struggle to include them, and then, ironically, the Soviet acclaim of the Final Act all combined to raise this issue to an important position in international politics.

Moreover, the Final Act has provided a constitution or foundation which has legitimated and greatly encouraged the hopes of thousands of men and women in the Soviet Union and Eastern Europe that they will be able to enjoy a better and freer life. This reaction to the Final Act shows that hope springs eternal, that the desire for liberty never dies, even among privileged generations who had never known it. Those who have witnessed several times the "death" of the dissident movement have seen the civic courage and thrust for greater freedom rise again, this time based on an international agreement which the Soviet government has lauded. The personal character and courage, the good sense and restraint, and the civilized way in which the dissidents have responded to their governments' often vicious reactions have contributed greatly to Western comprehension of the human rights issue within each State, of the differences which exist among societies, and of both the necessity for and the difficulties in cultural relations and competition.

Indeed, this issue has dramatized the central difference which divides East and West, one on which scholars and workers, Frenchmen and Swedes, radicals and conservatives, are united. While most people cannot understand the complicated equations which enter the SALT for both sides, everyone can understand human rights, their central importance, and the hazards raised when governments deny them. This knowledge and understanding is especially great because developments in Greece, Portugal and Spain during the Helsinki negotiations and since August 1975 have underlined the contrast between East and West and encouraged the hope that other States will follow the path which the Spain once ruled by Franco has taken.

Fortunately for the West, the changes in the Mediterranean authoritarian States have occurred at the same time as the leadership of the Spanish and Italian Communist Parties have apparently revised some central ideological positions. These men and their organizations, which have considerable influence in parts of Eastern Europe and occupy an important position in the international grouping of communist parties, for reasons of principle or political expediency also support the Western position on human rights and on relaxations of controls in general. This helps strengthen the Western position, sustain the East European dissidents in particular, and exert a restraining influence upon regimes sorely tempted to throttle those who seek their constitutional rights, to repress all who question such actions, and to restrict the free movement essential for cultural exchange and competition.

The inclusion of the profound statement concerning human rights in a document thirty-five governments signed has also made this issue as legitimate a part of the agenda concerning relations between East and West as trade relations and threats to security. The Final Act provides diplomats of all countries an opportunity for making enquiries and for pressing other governments to meet approved standards of behaviour. It therefore acts as a deterrent to the Soviet and East European governments. At the same time, and perhaps more important because treaties have not always deterred governments, it reminds the Soviet government that it will pay a heavy price, including within many communist parties, if it violates agreements it sought so desperately and signed so enthusiastically.

Helsinki has excited profound scholarly, popular, and official support in the United States for these reasons and others. First, it represents both the culmination and the consequence of two decades of American experience in cultural exchange with the Soviet Union. As I indicated earlier, American scholars, the public, and the government support cultural exchange with the Soviet Union and Eastern Europe. Both sides have benefited; if they had not, the exchanges would not have survived. At the same time, American dissatisfaction has always been great and has increased over the years, in part because hopes were so high that conditions would improve. Moreover, continuation of the same pattern of problems and limitations has strained the attitudes of a people who consider change and improvement natural laws and who do not have the same sense of time and patience as some others, especially Russians. The period of exotic interest in the Soviet Union long ago ended. After twenty years, most scholars and artists want "to end scholarly tourism" and establish the kind of free movement with which all within Western society are familiar.

Developments which have occurred under détente have profoundly influenced these developments. Rightly or wrongly, most Americans believe that the Soviet Union has benefited significantly more than the United States from détente. The failure to make progress on MBFR, which was originally tied to Helsinki; "the great grain robbery"; disappointment concerning the absence of improvement in East German policies after Ostpolitik; the presence of thousands of Cuban troops in an Angola which had just liberated itself from Portuguese rule—factors such as these deeply influence the American view of Helsinki and American determination that its terms be honoured.[7]

Helsinki has drawn increasing attention from Americans for other reasons as well. The principles Basket Two and Three emphasize are central in American history and tradition. The return of American interest to Europe after a decade of involvement in Southeast Asia has contributed. Moreover, a period marked by the effort to end discrimination and to increase opportunity for blacks, womens' liberation, the movement against the war in Vietnam, Watergate, and the exposure of improper CIA and FBI activities, would almost inevitably produce concentrated interest upon the free movement of men and ideas and upon human rights in world politics.

In addition, the growing interest of scientists in international politics has become an important factor. Scientists have acquired a new concern in politics because of their appreciation of the role science and scientists play in modern technology, in national and international environment issues, in the exchange programmes with the Soviet Union, in Pugwash and other international conferences, and, above all, in war itself. This interest has been a most important element stimulating their work for peaceful relations with the Soviet Union and increasing their understanding of the Soviet system and policy. The prestigious National Academy of

---

7. Soviet participants in this conference will naturally speak concerning the Soviet view of the benefits both sides have obtained from Helsinki. The Soviet Union legitimately complains that the United States continues to delay and deny visas, a policy many Americans hope new legislation will revise, even though most trade union leaders will find it difficult to accept men like Shelepin as genuine union officials. However, legislation cannot remove the considerable difference between the number of Soviet books which Americans translate and publish and the number of American novels published in the Soviet Union because Soviet literature, and even the finest Soviet films, simply do not interest Americans (or other Westerners, for that matter). Other Soviet complaints are beyond remedy and derive from the simple fact that the United States and the West exist: Soviet ballet dancers will therefore continue to defect, emigrants will leave and be welcomed, dissidents excited and honoured, gallant underdogs and rebels supported. Neither the American government nor the Americans could or would adopt policies to help resolve these issues for the Soviet government.

Sciences and the large Federation of American Scientists have both become active in shaping American positions toward Helsinki. The National Academy of Sciences' cable to the Soviet Academy of Sciences in the fall of 1973 that any action depriving Sakharov of his rights would end scientific exchanges not only helped to preserve Sakharov's freedom, but illustrated dramatically the issue Sakharov raised and the power scientists wield. Indeed, the participation of American scientists over the past two decades in the Soviet–American cultural exchange has helped educate them concerning the ethics of science itself, the right of scientists to travel, and the need to protect freedom of inquiry and expression everywhere.

The threat to Sakharov in 1973 and to Solzhenitsyn in February 1974 and Soviet refusal to permit Sakharov to visit Oslo to accept the Nobel Prize in December 1975 helped to stimulate still another significant American response, the decision of the Congress early in the summer of 1976 to establish a joint Commission on Security and Cooperation in Europe to monitor observance of Helsinki and to advocate new steps towards security and peace. The election of Carter in November 1976 in a sense culminated the process of this approach towards Helsinki, especially human rights. In short, the Carter letter to Sakharov in February 1977 is part of a pattern which was developing throughout the 1970s, and will continue throughout the foreseeable future.

This escalation coincides with, and has been enlivened and strengthened by the dissident movements in the Soviet Union, Poland, Czechoslovakia, and East Germany. Pasternak, Sakharov, Solzhenitsyn, Amalrik, Bukovsky, and their courageous friends have helped educate millions. At the same time, Western knowledge of and interest in dissatisfactions and the dissident movements have helped both to stimulate and protect critics within the Soviet systems.

The Significance of Helsinki

On the American side, the reversal of position constitutes one of the most important consequences of Helsinki. This American view of Helsinki, particularly of the civil rights factor, makes the Final Act and its fulfilment burning symbols at a time when no other understandable issue dominates relations between the Soviet Union and the United States. It unites opinion in the United States, and it also brings the United States, its European allies, and even its most bitter critics among the neutral States together, not only with regard to the Soviet Union but also with regard to justice, human dignity, and the precedence of human rights in South Africa and Chile. At the same time, it has revived discussion concerning the nature of communism in a world-wide debate involving socialists and communists outside the Soviet Union. The remarkable evolution of Spain towards democracy and of Portugal to free its empire and to begin its own transformation, at a time when the Soviet Union remains frozen, dramatizes the issue and deeply affects views and policies of communists everywhere, notably in Italy and Spain. The new attitudes toward pluralism and peaceful change by these parties, the criticisms of the Soviet Union by even the most staunch defenders of Stalinism, and the discussions which led to the East Berlin conference of communist parties in the summer of 1976 all demonstrate that the impact of Helsinki has spread far beyond its anticipated limits.

The Dilemmas

The basic difficulty between the Soviet Union and the United States reflects the eternal contest between authority and freedom, between the State established on Lenin's ideas and that on those of Jefferson. The concentration camp and the Berlin Wall, the open library and the travelling scholar, are its appropriate symbols.

In addition, unrelated to any philosophical or ideological difference, the Soviet Union and the United States are suspicous rival powers, sparring against each other, consciously measuring advantages and disadvantanges in every relationship. Their national interests differ. Moreover, the two States and societies differ greatly from each other, with some in each society convinced that that society is morally superior, stronger, and sure to triumph. One State is an open, pluralistic political and social democracy with an advanced industrial economy, and the other is a closed, unitarian, proudly authoritarian State which has been trying to catch up with, or overtake and surpass, the West since the time of Peter the Great. Cooperation between States is always difficult, but it is especially complicated when the States are sensitive, are not entirely equal, and view the world through different sets of glasses.

The Soviet dilemma

The Soviet leaders clearly believe that the Final Act achieved great advantages for the Soviet Union. However, it has also led to an ever-increasing price, not only in stimulating and to some degree legalizing dissidence but also in exposing the system's major flaws and opening the character of the system to question. Soviet diplomats have sought to restrict these impacts by emphasizing "strict observance of the laws, customs, and traditions of each other" and "respect for the principles of sovereignty and non-interference". Insistence that coexistence does not apply to ideology or that the two systems can compete in every way except ideas is much like Nicholas I's search for a fire that would not burn. Cultural exchanges, trade, construction of factories in remote Soviet areas by Italian workers, importation of Western computers, the signature of agreements assuring human rights—all these introduce outside ideas into a previously closed system. The Soviet Union cannot be in the world, but not of it. It cannot join the world in every aspect but one, that of ideas, which inevitably enter along with the scientists, artists, and machinery it welcomes in order to strengthen the system and its economy. Moreover, the relaxation of controls within Eastern Europe, which is far more vulnerable than the Soviet Union to Western ideas, helps introduce these same virulent concepts into the Soviet Union. Intellectually, or ideologically, Eastern Europe is a barrier, not a carrier. How long can the Soviet Union tolerate the infections, the defectors, the dissidents, the clamour? What price must it pay to put the pandora loosed by détente and the Final Act back into the box? Will it in fact return to the box?

The American dilemma

The American dilemma is as acute. At the moment, the West has an apparent advantage in the eternal struggle with authoritarianism, aided in good part by the cultural exchange agreements, increased trade, and the Final Act, all of which serve to loosen the Soviet system somewhat. However, the exchange agreements themselves are a violation of the Western view that information and men should move freely among societies, without restraints of any kind. The agreements are like reciprocal tariff treaties. They provide for barter and horse-trading of artists, basketball players, language teachers, and scholars, just as though these men and women were bales of cotton. They also make cultural exchange and scholarly cooperation an essential element of foreign policy, subject therefore to restrictions imposed by two governments and dependent on diplomatic priorities unrelated to intellectual life. In fact, this kind of arrangement, which puts governments and their bureaucracies in control of cultural exchange, is an extension of Soviet practice into the glades of Western intellectual freedom.

Moreover, many Americans, particularly those who reflect upon the progress of the last twenty years, are convinced that the United States should not have cultural agreements with countries which are repressive, which censor information, harass and imprison critical scholars and other citizens, license and reward subservient intellectuals, and in general violate the precepts which are vital for civilized life. Indeed, they criticize agreements or other formal arrangements with such governments, because they are morally demobilizing and intellectually corrupting. They give respectability, dignity, and legitimacy to systems which openly flout their constitutions and charters which they sign.

In short, Americans face the dilemma which dealing with authoritarian regimes creates for democratic societies. They have begun to learn to live with totalitarian States, but their appreciation of the dilemma divides them on one hand, unites them on the other, and persuades the great majority that the way out of the dilemma is to press ever more resolutely and skilfully for the end of restraints, wherever they may be.

The Future

No one can predict with any confidence the future of this competition, which is part of a larger struggle and which will remain a long, gruelling contest. President Carter's vivid interest in cultural relations and human rights may assist toward joint progress in relaxing controls and expanding cooperation, as well toward concluding SALT II, ending all nuclear tests, and proceeding toward disarmament. On the other hand, American and Western determination to stand by their ancient values may lead the Soviet rulers to retreat to old fortresses and to be ever less cooperative in negotiations on disarmament and crisis management. In any case, progress will, at best, be grudging and slow.

Many observers believe that some Soviet leaders are beginning to appreciate that the old repressions will no longer work. They view the revival of the human spirit in Eastern Europe and the Soviet Union as part of an irreversible, irresistible force, as elemental as the growth of grass in the spring, which affects the advantaged third-generation communist as it does the Lithuanian Catholic or the Armenian nationalist. They see this continual "spring" as another illustration of the invincible power of ideas, flowing this time from the West to East. They ask: can authoritarianism survive in an ever-smaller, interdependent world in which revolutions in transportation and communication are bringing about the unbinding of all customs and controls?

Other observers see cultural exchange and competition as an unimportant element in international politics, in which technology, raw power, political organization, and determined leadership will move the entire world toward a universal authoritarian system or at least a series of powerful despotic States. They suggest that plural, open free societies cannot survive in this struggle, particularly because the West has lost its cohesion, spiritual base, and nerve. They ask: Can or will the Soviet system change? Are communism and liberty irreconcilable? Can democracy survive?

Both views are no doubt too cataclysmic. Today's conflict more resembles the Eastern Question or the Reformation than the fall of the Roman Empire or 1812.

Some proposals

The process of multilateral negotiations begun with the CSCE has far more importance than anyone thought possible in August, 1975. The thought and care with which the United States and the other Western States conduct negotiations will be especially important, because their position must represent Western values and strategies, reflect and sustain public support, and help move both sides into ever more constructive and cooperative policies. The United States must assist those who share Western values and who seek to move their States towards establishing open, free, and peaceful societies. It must encourage private citizens and organizations everywhere, because reliance upon the individual is a cardinal quality of Western society and because this issue is too critical to be left solely to governments.

The United States should continue to provide a helpful, constructive critique of the achievements and failures of the Soviet Union, the East European States, and of the United States itself in honouring the Final Act. It should seek to avoid a slanging match, but should press toward its basic goals—the elimination of restraints, such as jamming and censorship, and the expansion of freedoms. Jamming and censorship are in fact the true obscenities of this era. Progress in expanding trade should be related to progress in eliminating these controls.

The United States should welcome and encourage suggestions from other participants which seek to move beyond Helsinki toward greater security and cooperation. It should also try to move the discussion to a new, cooperative level by advancing proposals, with a specific agreed target date, which will promote American interests and those of the world so far as Americans can understand them.

These might include:

(1) Re-establishing the Informational Media Guarantee Programme for the East European States, assisting them to overcome hard currency shortages in the purchase of American publications and films. The West European and North American States might together sponsor such a programme for all Western publications and films. By January 1, 1979.

(2) Establishing common passport and visa requirements for all signatory States. By January 1, 1980.

(3) Agreement that travel be as free among all signatory States as it is now within the West European States. By January 1, 1981.

(4) Establishment of a large international programme, a combination of Rhodes Scholarship and Fulbright Fellowship, under an international selection committee, enabling a number of outstanding young men and women (the number proportionate to the size of each nation's population and the funding by contributions from each State, based on relative GNP) to travel and study freely in the other part of Europe, for two or three year periods. By January 1, 1982.

(5) Establishment of a bookstore in university territory in Moscow in which any Soviet institution or citizen may buy any Western book with Soviet currency, as Westerners can purchase Soviet and East European publications in Soviet stores in many Western cities. This store might also serve as a central purchasing centre for Soviet books, magazines, newspapers and films for Western educational institutions and individuals, using the rubles obtained from sales to purchase Soviet publications and the hard currencies from Western institutions and individuals to purchase the Western volumes for the bookstore. A Swiss or Swedish university should assume administrative responsibility. By January 1, 1983.

(6) Ending all cultural agreements, enabling individuals and publications to move freely from country to country, and encouraging institutions to make their own arrangements with each other, as they did in the Middle Ages and as they do today in the West. By January 1, *1984*.

Chapter 13

THE FINAL ACT, ITS IMPLEMENTATION AND "HUMAN CONTACTS"

by *Prof. Z.A.B. Zeman*

The Final Act may not be legally binding; it may be contradictory in places; it may be flawed in drafting because of compromises during the negotiations or because of difficulties in translation.[1]

Nevertheless, the Final Act helped to concentrate attention, of the public and of the governments, on East–West relations; it established a framework for their conduct; it put new items on the agenda; it may even have increased room for manoeuvre, for the smaller East European countries, in their foreign policy. Equally important, the Final Act and the negotiations preceding it have helped to indicate those areas in East–West relations on which agreement may be obtained; the areas of controversy were also better staked out.

The case of military matters for instance is quite straightforward. Developments in the implementation of the Final Act were simple to establish and report on. At the Belgrade review meeting all the participating States had consolidated lists of their complaints, and perhaps of their achievements, in the field of confidence-building measures. Such lists can be checked, double-checked, and agreed upon.

The Flow of Information

"Flow of information", on the other hand, is an entirely different matter. It cuts across the various sections of the Final Act: though it is dealt with mainly under section-Basket-3 of the Final Act, it concerns many aspects of Basket 2 as well, in the form of the availability of scientific, economic or commercial information.

We often hear the complaint, in the West, that information on economic developments in the East is very hard to come by. In my experience, this often is not the case. On the contrary; the wealth

1. Cf. for instance *Implementation Conference on Security and Cooperation in Europe*, East–West Institute, The Hague, p. 1.

of specialized literature and periodicals in East Europe is considerable, and so is the variety of information they contain. This is the view, for instance, of most of the research workers at UNECE, who specialize in East European economies.[2] At different levels, there appears to be lack of interest and understanding in the West in political, social and economic structures and developments in East Europe. In the Western media East European countries are sometimes presented in primitive ways—a monolithic Communist Party, pursuing repressive policies in an almost static society; more often, they are not presented at all, and East European societies therefore become visible to the West only at a time of one of the great crises, say in Budapest in 1956 or Prague in 1968. Of course faulty reporting is not a Western monopoly; complaints have been made both ways, with justification.

Nevertheless, the East Europeans, and especially the Poles, the Hungarians and the Czechs are keenly interested in all aspects of life in the West; and the East Germans share a cultural background as well as a political past with a major State of the West European community. Viewed from this standpoint, the East Europeans' claim that they know the West and its languages and cultures better than people in the West know East European civilizations does not sound all that far-fetched.

This is precisely the point from which the East Europeans launched their Third Basket offensive. Soon after the signing of the Final Act, the East Europeans started establishing their position. Namely, that they are translating more Western literature than the other way round; that they buy more Western books and periodicals than the West buys from them; that they show many more Western films. These statistics have been used again and again to prove that the East European governments observe the spirit and the letter of Helsinki better than do the West Europeans.

This cultural assymetry has a number of political consequences. To the Russians in, say, Moscow, the East Europeans of the smaller socialist States live in countries situated far to the West. In many cases, their standards are also closer to the West than are those of the Russians. It may therefore appear to the Soviet authorities that they have to protect their citizens against too much exposure to both Western and Eastern Europe: and tightening of "Socialist discipline" throughout the socialist camp is the way in which this cultural assymetry is coped with by Moscow. It would not be

---

2. Oral information, UN Economic Commission for Europe, Geneva.

surprising if too much public insistence on the continuation of ideological struggle was not a part of the same reaction.

We have noted that the Final Act and the negotiations preceding it contributed to a more precise differentiation between the neutral and controversial subjects on the East–West agenda. In the future therefore success of East–West negotiations should be more easily predictable, according to the subjects under negotiation.

Political controversy is underscored by the complexity of the matter under discussion, and by the different conceptual frameworks employed. We have briefly noted above the differences between, say, military matters and the flow of information.

In political terms, the clearest distinction has emerged between the subjects under Baskets 2 and 3. Scientists in the East and in the West have a certain set of problems in common, and an interest in solving them; political systems both in the West and in the East have an interest in promoting their work.

Tolerance of political opposition, on the other hand, varies from country to country, and from society to society. In Russia, for instance, public controversy on political issues has never been regarded as a sign of the government's strength; on the contrary. Any issues concerned with human rights, or political imprisonment, will therefore provide highly explosive material for any future East–West negotiations.

Similar distinctions have also emerged in much more specialized fields: take for instance broadcasting. Cooperation between, say, Eurovision and the East European Intervision often functions smoothly and to the satisfaction of all parties concerned; it is a neutral, technical subject, though it is not without far-reaching political implications. More openly political across-the-border broadcasts, say, London to Poland, or Moscow to France, are controversial, though not as highly controversial as the RFE or RL broadcasts.[3]

Human Contacts

In order to achieve "human contacts" some "movement of peoples" has to take place: both concepts are frequently employed by the Final Act. It is generally accepted in the West that most

---

3. "Broadcasting East–West", *Report No. 6, European Cooperation Research Group (EUCORG)*, April 1974.

Western countries do not place any barriers on emigration, whereas the Soviets do. This point was made for instance in the *First Semiannual Report by the President to the Commission on Security and Cooperation in Europe (Washington 1976)*. Nevertheless, one country's emigrant is another country's immigrant, and Western countries have tight laws on immigration; it is also doubtful whether really large movements of people, say, package tours from Germany to Bulgaria, constitute "human contacts".

The Final Act divides this broad category of movement of people into several more manageable subsections. Family visits and reunification was a topic with which the West German delegation had been closely concerned during the CSCE negotiations. Indeed, the first incidents after August 1, 1975 concerning family reunification occurred in the two Germanies. They concerned the expulsion of a newspaper correspondent from the GDR, and the practice of forced adoptions, on which he reported.

More recently, on March 14, 1977, Bonn protested in East Berlin over its refusal to allow West Germans to visit relatives in the GDR who applied to be reunited with them. At the same time, hundreds of people with relatives in the GDR were refused permission at the border to travel to Leipzig, where the Spring Trade Fair was then in progress. The bi-annual fair had for years been an opportunity for West Germans to meet their relatives in the East, at the price of an admission card to the Fair.

The recent difficulties arose as a growing number of East Germans—estimated at over 100,000—applied to be reunited with their relatives and fiancées in West Germany. Most of these applications were rejected by the GDR authorities, and the receipt of new ones was reported (*Financial Times*, March 16, 1977) not to have been acknowledged. Some 4,000 East Germans however have rejoined their families every year under the Basic Treaty of 1971 provisions. (According to several sources, the *total* number of East Germans who were allowed to emigrate was 10,200 in 1975, and 8,000 in 1974.) Though the vast majority of West Germans and West Berliners are still able to visit their families in the East, the GDR authorities regard these visitors as a source of inspiration for East Germans who want to leave the country.

Nevertheless, in view of the unfavourable age structure of the GDR population, of the growing labour shortage in the GDR and the CMEA area as a whole, an improvement on the past levels of permitted emigration is unlikely to take place. Though the decline in the GDR population had been much stronger in the 1950s and 1960s, the trend has continued ever since the construction of the

Berlin wall: 16.9 million inhabitants for instance in 1973 declined to 16.85 million in 1975.[4]

Of the different types of "human contacts" family reunions between the two Germanies will remain the subject which will attract most attention, especially in West Germany. It involves a large number of people and two States comprising the same nation. The Basic Treaty between the two Germanies is a more important instrument than the Final Act for the conduct of their relations; the Final Act provides a general background for the more specific East–West German agreements.

The practice of forced adoptions in the GDR—the first issue which made the headlines in Western Europe after the signing of the Final Act—appears to have been abandoned. The children who were to be kept back in the GDR soon started rejoining their parents who had fled the country: the total number of children who rejoined their parents in the Federal Republic between 1972 and early 1976 was put at 1,393.

Some advances in the area of family reunions have been made in the Soviet Union. For instance, the Swiss Embassy to Moscow reported that the requests from Soviet citizens to join their relatives in Switzerland have been dealt with by the local authorities with more speed and goodwill than before. The same was true of marriages between Soviet and Swiss citizens. The Embassy added that its administrative relations with the Soviet authorities have been easier and smoother since the conclusion of the CSCE (NZZ, February 5, 1976). Nevertheless, in a House of Commons debate on East–West relations on February 24, 1976, Mr. Roy Hattersley, then the UK Minister of State for Foreign Affairs, said that family reunions, as outlined in the Final Act, were not going well from the UK point of view. Emigration for family reasons has also become an issue in US–Polish relations, because of the strict laws which obtain in such matters in Poland.

The number of Soviet citizens receiving exit visas to join their families in the United States increased significantly in the first half of 1976. The following table reflects a general upward trend since 1970, with the sharpest rate of increase occurring in 1975:[5]

1970	230	1974	1,029
1971	287	1975	1,162
1972	494	1976	1,303
1973	758		

4. *Facts and Figures 1975*, Dresden.
5. *First Semiannual Report by the President*, p. 41.

It should be noted that this increase is largely due to Armenian emigration.

On the whole the process and number of instances of family reunification has been stimulated by the Final Act; apart from certain inconsistencies in administrative decisions (such inconsistencies have been reported especially from the Soviet Union with regard to bi-national marriages) the post-Helsinki developments appear to be encouraging.

In most cases, the diplomatic representations of the participating countries have dealt with family unifications, and with other human contact issues. But family reunifications are a humanitarian matter, and at least on one occasion (West German Red Cross, in the case of Czechoslovak children of parents resident in the Federal Republic) a Red Cross organization raised the matter with the authorities. The Red Cross was the only NGO specifically referred to in the Final Act; the Intergovernmental Committee for European Migration (ICEM) also expressed an interest in contributing to this work, though its contribution may be limited by its membership, which is quite different from CSCE participants.[6]

Emigration

Though emigration was not specifically referred to in the Final Act, it comes under several headings in its third part. Historical developments in Europe have resulted in a complex situation. Bulgaria, for instance, has a large minority of some 800,000 Turks; the Turkish Government has so far shown little interest in their emigration. Nor have some 200,000 Germans shown any desire to leave Hungary. Of the 286,000 Germans in Poland, on the other hand, 120,000 to 125,000 are to be allowed to leave over four years; the Poles made this concession in an agreement reached by Mr. Gierek and Mr. Schmidt in Helsinki, and ratified in the Bundestag in March 1976. The West German Chancellor had promised DM 1,300 million compensation for the Poles who had paid social security contributions in Germany during the Second World War, as well as a low interest credit of DM 1,000 million.

In Czechoslovakia, 80,000 Germans still remain; a delegation of the German Red Cross was to visit Prague in April 1976 to discuss the matter of their emigration with the Czechoslovak authorities. At the same time, the future of more than 600 children, whose parents reside in Germany and are of Czech or Slovak origin, was

6. *First Semiannual Report by the President*, p. 41 et seq.; and various press reports.

raised. Some 20,000 Germans, it has been estimated by the Red Cross, want to leave: in the past, 15,700 Germans left Czechoslovakia in 1968, 2,395 in 1971, 527 in 1973, 387 in 1974, and 182 in the first half of 1975. During the Helsinki conference, Mr. Husak was reported to have assured Chancellor Schmidt that he wanted to ease administrative measures with regard to emigration of Germans from Czechoslovakia.

In connection with some 400,000 Germans in Romania, Mr. Ceauşescu said that individual cases would be viewed with compassion; the future of the Romanian Jews became an issue in US–Romanian trade relations last year. Since the war, 250,000 Jews have left Romania for Israel, and 80,000 for other countries; some 80,000 still remain. After scrutiny by the US Congress of Romanian emigration practices, and President Ceauşescu's visit to Washington in June 1975, President Ford, during his visit to Bucharest in August, signed an agreement granting Most Favoured Nation treatment to Romania. It appears that since then, Jewish emigration from Romania has increased.

Measures have been taken in the Soviet Union to facilitate family reunifications and other forms of travel: reduction in the fee for an exit permit; application fee for travel documents is now payable only on the receipt of the document; the travellers do not have to receive as many "character references" as they used to do; the review period for failed applications has been reduced; children are now entered on passports without additional charges.

Other Areas of Human Contacts

Finally, some progress has also been reported in the remaining areas of "human contacts": travel for personal or professional reasons, tourism, religious contacts, sport and meetings among young people. It should be added here that a major complaint, often made in the West, concerns discrimination, in the Soviet Union and other socialist countries, in their policies of issuing passports and travel permits to their own nationals. It is argued that those East Europeans who receive permission to travel to the West are a narrow and privileged group: the purpose of the new dispensation under the Final Act is to broaden this group and make it therefore less privileged. However much they may desire to influence the decision-making of the East European authorities—this would involve influencing their cadre policy—there is little that governments in the West can do about this, apart from refusing the East Europeans visas: this is a frequent East European complaint. The length of time it takes to get Western visas for personal travel, and refusals to issue visas for professional travel, are often referred to.

This aspect of human contacts of the Final Act covers purely humanitarian concerns, such as the reunification of families, as well as travel for professional reasons: a broad spectrum of mobility. The policies of governments are however incoherent even within each section: one East European trade unionist is granted a visa to, say, Britain, while another is refused it; one bride is given a Soviet exit permit and passport while another is refused it. Administrative procedures have no doubt something to do with such lack of coherence, and they could perhaps be usefully examined in the case of each country, and reciprocal bi- or multi-lateral procedures could be agreed.

Conflicts and Limitations

On a different level, a specific incident stands out. While Jewish emigration in 1976 was slightly higher than in 1975 (11,700 Jews left the Soviet Union according to Soviet sources and 13,209 according to Israeli sources) it is still well below the years before the passing of the Jackson Amendment, in 1972 and 1973, when it was running at over 30,000 people a year.[7]

The Jackson Amendment tried to link a humanitarian concern— in this case Jewish emigration from the USSR—with US trade policy towards the Soviet Union. Neither the Soviet Jews nor American–Soviet trade benefited by the Amendment.

The incident showed the level of tolerance by the Soviets to outside pressure. There is a certain point beyond which their leadership cannot go, especially when pressure is seen to be exerted, in public. It is also likely, and has been argued in the West, that the room for manoeuvre at the disposal of those Soviet leaders who advocate the policy of détente is not very large. They have their opponents, the critics of détente, constantly at their elbows.

On the other hand, there exist certain political limitations in the West as well. Quite apart from the obvious limitations arising from political differences, there are other limits on Western readiness to cooperate more closely with the East. They may be described as

7. Cf. for instance *Implementation of the Final Act of the Conference on Security and Cooperation in Europe*, p. 117, Parliamentary Assembly, Council of Europe, Strasbourg, 1977.

procedural. Added therefore to suspicions of, say, Soviet policies in Africa, of the purposes of ideological struggle, or of the extent of the Soviet armaments drive, there is the sentence "we are not going to play the game by *Soviet* rules" which is being heard in the West.

It may mean anything from not giving visas to visitors from the Socialist countries selected by their own governments, to pressing the Soviets hard on the human rights issue. This attitude is no more than an expression of pique. Some of the ground rules for the game have been established by the Final Act; let it be played according to them.

This will have to involve much flexibility and goodwill on both sides, because its principles often cut across the specific provisions of the Final Act. In the case of human contacts, there are several specific issues which could be usefully reviewed in Belgrade. For instance administrative procedures with regard to issuing visas. They could be simplified and made more uniform, and classified according to the purposes for which the visas are being issued. Some progress, for instance in the case of issuing multiple visas to journalists, has already been made.

The question of emigration stands in a class of its own. It involves large groups of people; it has been vastly complicated by the exigencies of European history: it arouses emotion as well as publicity. Again, the conflict is not insoluble. The East, however, is currently suffering from a shortage of manpower; Western negotiators will have to bear this in mind, as well as the temporary surplus of labour in their own countries. Large and permanent movements of population have implications reaching far beyond humanitarian concern, or scoring propaganda points.

Chapter 14

IMPLEMENTATION OF BASKET THREE

INTRODUCTION

In the more than two years that have elapsed since the conclusion of the Final Act of Helsinki, citizens, scholars and governmental institutions in many countries have set themselves the task to observe, monitor and report on the Final Act's implementation by their own governments or those of other participating States. Several groups for promoting the observance of the Final Act have been set up in the USSR and East-European countries—they have faced a variety of repressive measures by their own governments.

The most authoritative scholarly analysis on the implementation of the Final Act to date can be found in: Jost Delbrück, Norbert Ropers, Gerda Zellentin, *Grünbuch zu den Folgewirkungen der KSZE*. Verlag Wissenschaft und Politik. Köln 1977.

In the US Congress a Commission on Security and Cooperation was created in June 1976 which was authorized and directed "to monitor the acts of the signatories which reflect compliance with or violation of the articles of the Final Act of the Conference on Security and Cooperation, with particular regard to the provisions relating to Cooperation in Humanitarian Fields". (Public Law 94-304 of June 3, 1976.) On February 24 and June 3, 1977 the Commission published two volumes of *Documents of the Public Groups to Promote Observance of the Helsinki Agreements in the USSR*. On August 1, 1977 the Commission published its "Report to the Congress of the United States on Implementation of the Final Act of the Conference on Security and Cooperation in Europe: Findings and Recommendations Two Years after Helsinki".

The President of the United States submitted two semi-annual reports to the Commission: December 1976 and June 1977. From these remarkably comprehensive and unique documents, we reprint in this chapter, Chapter 4 from the *Second Semiannual Report by the President to the Commission on Security and Cooperation in Europe*.

(Printed for the use of the Committee on International Relations. US Government Printing Office. Washington: 1977).

Cooperation in Humanitarian and Other Fields

Basket three of the Final Act contains a variety of provisions all sharing a common objective—the freer flow of people, ideas and information among the signatory States. During the CSCE negotiations, the United States and most other Western countries took the position that genuine security and cooperation in Europe require a dismantling of the barriers which stifle contact and communication between the peoples of East and West. While accepting the third basket at the Helsinki Summit, the Soviet Union and its allies have since tried to diminish the full extent of its obligation upon them. They have advanced arguments and interpretations which seek to blunt the purpose of basket three through token and selective implementation of its provisions.

This pattern, with some modification, persisted during the reporting period. Wary of the scheduled review of implementation at Belgrade, a number of Warsaw Pact Governments have in recent months tried to counter Western criticism of their implementation records through a carrot and stick tactic. On the one hand, they have offered concessions in areas least incompatible with the closed nature of Eastern societies but known to be of interest to the West. Thus, for example, certain countries have recently made efforts to resolve some long-standing family reunification cases and increase the number of Western periodicals available at selected newsstands. On the other hand, these same governments have often reacted harshly toward public criticism of their implementation records while retaining their fundamentally restrictive policies intact. Working conditions for Western journalists in Eastern countries deteriorated during the reporting period, and basic policies which assure rigid State control over the movement of people and information remained generally unaltered. The overall basket three implementation by the Warsaw Pact countries, though varying among individual States, remained well below the objectives of the Final Act.

Eastern countries responded to Western criticism of their implementation with charges that Western Governments, and particularly the United States, are "interfering" in their domestic affairs and seeking to mask their own implementation failures. While we categorically reject charges of interference and believe our implementation record to be generally excellent, we are reviewing aspects of our own implementation with a view toward a fuller compliance with CSCE provisions. For example, our visa-issuing practices are now under review to determine whether administrative and possibly legislative charges are required.

Similarly, the United States in March allowed expiration of restrictions on use of US passports for travel to Cuba, North Korea, Vietnam, and Cambodia. In April we removed restrictions on the travel of permanent resident aliens to all Communist and Communist-dominated countries. These actions demonstrate our desire to contribute to the CSCE objective of progressively reducing obstacles to the freer movement of all peoples.

Human contacts[1]

Despite some apparent efforts to improve their implementation records for the Belgrade review meeting, the Warsaw Pact countries have not fundamentally altered their policies on human contacts during the reporting period. Most Soviet and Eastern European officials continued to view travel or emigration to the West as a privilege to be granted or refused by the State rather than as a matter of personal choice.

Though the right of emigration is covered only indirectly in the Final Act (through endorsement of the Universal Declaration of Human Rights, which recognizes the right of individuals to leave and return to their own countries), family reunification and marriage between nationals of different States are specific CSCE concerns. These tend to intermingle in the Soviet Union, where family reunification is considered by the State to be the sole legitimate reason for emigration. Though Soviet officials claim possession of State secrets or hardship of other family members to be the only grounds for refusal of emigration applications, these criteria are in practice often arbitrarily invoked. Procedures in Eastern Europe follow a similar though sometimes less restrictive pattern. Applying for either permanent or temporary reunification with relatives abroad thus remains an unpredictable endeavour in Eastern countries, particularly when such relatives are considered to have left Eastern countries "illegally."

---

1. The material contained in this chapter, except where otherwise indicated, reflects the US experience with the member States of the Warsaw Pact. Our consultations indicate that the experience of other Western States follows a generally similar pattern.

Family visits and reunification

During the reporting period, the United States continued to make representations to all of the Warsaw Pact countries to request fulfillment of CSCE obligations in resolving the longstanding divided family cases of which the US Government is aware. The following numbers of such problem cases involving at least one previous refusal remained pending between the United States and Warsaw Pact countries as of May 1, 1977:

	Immediate families[1]		Nonimmediate families	
	Total cases	Individuals	Total cases	Individuals
Bulgaria	10	15	8	21
Czechoslovakia	30	74	13	19
German Democratic Republic	5	9	24	42
Hungary	7	12	0	0
Poland	136	247	810	2,467
Romania	218	327[2]	578	1,560[2]
USSR	124	359	—	—

[1] An immediate family is comprised of spouses plus their minor children. A nonimmediate family includes brothers, sisters, adult children, parents of adult children, etc. It was not possible to make this distinction in the case of the Soviet Union, the figures for which include both immediate and nonimmediate families.

[2] Approximate.

Despite US efforts, resolution of divided family cases continued to be a slow and often frustrating endeavour. Individual successes were often accompanied by the appearance of new cases, leaving the final tally worsened or unchanged. We have, however, continued our representations on this issue and monitored emigration trends on a country-by-country basis.

USSR

Our Embassy in Moscow processed a total of 2,574 Soviet emigrants to the United States in 1976, more than double the 1975 figure. The following table reflects the upward trend since 1972, with the sharpest rate of increase occurring last year:

1972	494	1975	1,162
1973	758	1976	2,574
1974	1,029		

While the high percentile increase for 1976 is a significant development, it should be noted that the absolute numbers are still relatively small. Also, much of the increase resulted from emigration of ethnic Armenians (69 per cent. of the total), many of whom immigrated to the Soviet Union after World War II, remained somewhat apart from the mainstream of Soviet society, and had, in the past, been immigrating to Lebanon rather than the United States. Soviet issuance of exit visas for the United States to Jews and other ethnic groups has increased only slightly since the CSCE.

In addition to tolerating Armenian emigration, Soviet authorities also increased the number of ethnic Germans allowed to resettle in the FRG. The 1976 total of 9,600 significantly reversed the slight downturn in 1975 and more than tripled the 1972 level, as seen in this table:

1972	3,100	1975	5,800
1973	4,400	1976	9,600
1974	6,300		

Nonetheless, a group of ethnic Germans refused exit visas protested their plight in an attempted demonstration in the West German Embassy in Moscow in May.

Issuance of exit visas to Soviet Jews destined for Israel increased in the last quarter of 1976 to produce a yearly total of over 14,000. Although this rise over 1975 halted the decline of the previous 2 years, Jewish emigration remained far below levels reached in 1972–73:

1972	31,500	1975	13,000
1973	35,000	1976	14,000
1974	20,000		

These figures indicate that the reforms in Soviet emigration policy announced in early 1976, such as the right to request reviews of refusals after six months instead of one year, apparently did not result in a greatly increased rate of Soviet Jewish emigration. At various times during 1976 there were also reports that some Soviet officials administered emigration laws more strictly by more narrowly defining family connections required to support an emigration application. Early 1977 figures have thus far shown approximately the same Jewish emigration rate as in 1976.

In a January 1977 press interview, the Director of the Visa and Registration Department of the Soviet Ministry of the Interior restated the Soviet claim that 98.4 per cent. of those who wish to emigrate from the USSR have their applications granted, and added that the number of Jews applying for emigration had declined by two-thirds since 1973. Though difficult to confirm or refute, the low refusal percentage may be technically accurate since the USSR discourages emigration primarily by penalizing applicants with loss of employment and sometimes shelter, thereby creating an atmosphere which inhibits submission of applications. A refusal percentage thus cannot be a reliable measure of Soviet tolerance on emigration matters.

While the Soviet Union has allowed some increase in overall emigration rates, it has not shown itself more forthcoming in resolution of "difficult" divided family cases. Since January 20, we have emphasized the administration's commitment to family reunification and gave the Soviets lists of 10 divided family cases resulting in particular hardship as well as a list of Soviet citizens refused exit visas to join relatives in the United States. This second list, the 19th in a series which the United States has presented over a period of 20 years, contained the names of 366 individuals in 128 family units. In talks with high Soviet officials we have expressed US interest in the resolution of a large number of cases of Soviet Jews refused exit visas for Israel.

Bulgaria

Following Bulgarian assurances in April 1976 that the divided families issue would soon be resolved, the Bulgarian Government made some effort to diminish the number of outstanding cases. In February Bulgarian officials informed our Embassy that they had reviewed all divided family cases with the United States of which they had knowledge. They stated that all the persons had been granted permission to travel to the United States except for two cases which had been refused and eight cases which were still pending. We have since noticed a tendency to resolve family reunfication cases more quickly.

Czechoslovakia

Czechoslovak authorities appear to have adopted a more flexible attitude in recent months, at least in cases involving separation of minor children from parents. In early November, Prague officials gave our Embassy a list of 20 children belonging to 15 couples in the United States and said that there was a likelihood the children would soon receive exit visas. Thirteen children have since obtained emigration permits. Although there was little progress on many other longstanding cases of reunification, the reversal of

Czechoslovakia's hard line on cases involving children was a welcome development, particularly since Prague released children to other Western countries as well. In April, we received indications that the Czechoslovak Government is considering a programme which might help resolve other divided family cases on which progress thus far has been extremely slow.

In April, the Czechoslovak press published a Czechoslovak woman's appeal to President Carter for assistance in return of her two children to Czechoslovakia. The children, living in California with foster parents, had been brought to the United States in 1968 by the father who subsequently died. The California State Supreme Court reversed an earlier San Bernardino Court decision and turned down the mother's request for the children in 1972.

German Democratic Republic

Emigration continued to be an especially vexing problem for the GDR, where an estimated 100,000 people are believed to have applied for permanent exit visas since the signing of the Final Act. Apparently dismayed by this trend, the GDR Government unexpectedly revived a 1963 regulation and for several hours on January 11 denied East Germans access to the FRG mission in East Berlin. Police officers informed prospective visitors that the mission could not be entered without prior written approval from the GDR Ministry of Foreign Affairs. In the exchanges which followed, the East Germans claimed that the FRG mission had been violating the Helsinki Final Act and interfering in internal GDR affairs, implicitly by assisting GDR citizens in emigration procedures. The FRG vigorously denied charges of wrongdoing and made clear its intent to continue advising individuals who visit the mission for assistance.

Most GDR divided family cases concern emigrations to West Germany, and the number of cases involving the United States is by comparison small. Nonetheless, we place high priority on resolution of these cases, and several times during the reporting period our Embassy in Berlin presented GDR officials with updated representation lists of both permanent and temporary reunifications still pending. In April, GDR officials indicated that they would resolve these cases shortly. This was repeated in an aide memoire presented to our Embassy on May 12.

Hungary

While strict on paper, Hungarian emigration policy has tended in practice to be relatively tolerant. In January, we passed to the

Hungarian Government a list of 7 unresolved family reunification cases involving 12 individuals in Hungary. We recognized the relatively positive efforts of the Hungarian Government in past reunifications of divided families, but emphasized that more could be done to resolve remaining cases. While the seven cases were still pending as of May 1, we remain hopeful of future progress.

Poland

Polish policy toward emigration has been relatively strict in recent years, leading to a large accumulation of divided family cases. On January 5, we passed to Polish officials copies of all the lists of divided family cases handed to Polish authorities since January 1, 1974—few of which have been answered directly—and a chronology showing 58 US representations on this issue in the same time frame. We emphasized that a continuing impediment to resolution of many cases appeared to be the narrow Polish definition of family, which excludes siblings and adult children, and expressed hope that the definition would be broadened. While there is still no evidence of a permanent change of policy, the Polish Government recently took favourable action on a few urgent, humanitarian cases.

Romania

Romanian performance on family reunification has generally improved since the signing of the Final Act, though the motivation likely rests more with the receipt by Romania of most-favoured-nation tariff status and access to Export-Import Bank credits from the United States than with its CSCE obligations. In recent months, however, Romania's processing rate has not kept up with the increase of new cases, leading to a considerable backlog. In our exchanges with Romanian officials, we expressed the hope that efforts to improve the situation would be made.

Emigration from Romania to the United States totalled 1,021 in 1976, somewhat above the 890 figure for 1975. Early 1977 figures indicate a decline in Romanian emigration to the United States and Israel as compared to 1976 levels. Emigration of ethnic Germans to West Germany rose sharply during the first quarter of 1977 but declined in the spring.

Family visits

Soviet and Eastern European policy on family visits continued to be restrictive and far below the objectives set by the Helsinki Final Act. Temporary exit visas for family visits to the West were generally issued only on invitation from abroad and to those individuals whose family and professional circumstances or age gave some assurance of return to the home country. Even under these conditions, however, exit visas could by no means be guaranteed. In cases where relatives were considered to have gone abroad "illegally," the prospects of family visits generally grew poorer still. In February, for example, the ballet star Rudolf Nureyev stated publicly that he had been trying for 14 years without success to get a temporary exit visa for his 72-year-old mother in the USSR.

Of the Warsaw Pact countries Hungary was the most flexible in this area and Bulgaria, Czechoslovakia, Romania, and the Soviet Union maintained the strictest policies. The USSR permitted 1,654 private citizens to visit relatives in the United States in 1976. While this is a very low absolute figure, it does represent an increase of 40 per cent. over the 1975 figures.

The United States continued to raise family visit cases on an individual basis with Eastern governments. Following our intercession, some countries have on occasion reversed unfavourable decisions on granting entry visas for family visits.

The Romanian Government indicated early in 1977 that persons of "Romanian origin" visiting Romania would be exempted from the lodging and currency exchange requirements for tourists. The definition of "Romanian origin" remained unclear, however.

Binational marriages

As of May 1, the following numbers of problem binational marriage cases were pending involving American citizens and citizens of the Warsaw Pact countries:

Bulgaria	0
Czechoslovakia	9
German Democratic Republic	11
Hungary	0
Poland	0
Romania	71
USSR	4

Policy toward East–West marriages continued to vary among Warsaw Pact countries. The Soviets remained uncooperative toward individual cases, while Czechoslovakia generally allowed exit after marriage but almost always prohibited departure of single persons for purposes of marriage. Some marriages were effectively obstructed by refusal of the Eastern country to grant an entry visa to the US fiance. In a January 20 demarche to

Romanian officials, the United States emphasized that the large backlog in marriage cases was a very negative aspect of our bilateral relations. The Romanians expressed the desire to make resolution of marriage cases more flexible in the future, although the backlog has for the most part continued to grow.

Travel for personal or professional reasons

During the reporting period, the most serious contravention of CSCE provisions on personal and professional travel occurred on December 30 when the GDR announced that as of January 1 all non-German visitors to East Berlin from West Berlin would be required to have visas, even for one-day visits. Previously such visas had not been required of visitors staying less than 24 hours. This move was contrary to CSCE commitments "to simplify and to administer flexibly the procedures for exit and entry."

The GDR also continued its practice of periodically obstructing travellers to East Berlin. Since early 1977, for example, a large number of former GDR residents who had left the country legally have been prevented from visiting East Berlin and the GDR despite possession of proper documents. Hundreds of formal complaints have been filed with the Travel and Visits Commission in Berlin. A new 10 mark fee on passenger cars entering East Berlin imposed by the GDR at the end of February has also served to complicate procedures for entry.

As noted in the section of this report on Basket Two implementation, Soviet authorities have recently imposed new visa procedures on some representatives of US commercial firms stationed in the USSR. These procedures serve to abbreviate the validity of Soviet exit/reentry visas, make travel on short notice difficult, and require businessmen to declare their itinerary outside the USSR. The United States raised these procedures with Soviet officials and pointed out their discrepancy with CSCE commitments. We also reminded the Soviets of our longstanding proposal, which has not been responded to by the Soviet Government, to issue multiple-entry visas on a reciprocal basis to commercial personnel.

An article in the Soviet weekly Literaturnaya Gazeta during the reporting period charged that the State Department had violated the Final Act by refusing a visa to the journal's editor (who is also a member of the Supreme Soviet) in retaliation for the Soviet denial of a visa to Chairman Dante Fascell of the joint Legislative-Executive CSCE Commission. The article claimed that there was no similarity between the two situations because the CSCE Commission had been created "unilaterally" and interfered in the internal affairs of the Socialist countries. In February, Senator Richard Stone, a member of the Commission, failed to obtain a visa to the USSR in a repetition of the Soviets' refusal of a visa to Chairman Fascell.

The United States continued its efforts during the reporting period to reach bilateral agreements for facilitating travel in the CSCE context. Following the generally small implementation of our April 1976 agreement with Hungary to issue diplomatic and official visas within seven working days, we proposed to Hungarian officials on January 19 the reciprocal issuance of one-year multiple-entry visas to diplomats and officials coming on temporary visits for official business.

During the reporting period, the United States proposed to Eastern European governments the reciprocal issuance to diplomats and government officials of multiple-entry visas valid for the specific period of official assignment in the other country, up to a period of 48 months. Presently, such visas are issued for a maximum 12-month period, thus necessitating annual revalidations. We specifically characterized the proposal as a step forward in the context of CSCE implementation.

In January, we reminded the Romanian Government that no response has yet been received to our earlier proposal to facilitate issuance of tourist, business, and transit visas by lengthening validities and making the visas multiple-entry.

Religious contacts and information

Soviet policy on religious contacts not officially approved by the Government remained strict during the reporting period, particularly in cases of contact between Soviet and Western Jews.

In December, Soviet authorities refused visas to seven American scholars invited to a Jewish Cultural Symposium in Moscow. When we took the matter up with Soviet officials, they maintained that the symposium was only a "political demonstration" and told us that six of the Americans were temporarily barred from the USSR and one permanently. Soviet authorities subsequently detained 13 of the symposium's organizers. Those remaining free condemned the action but were able to proceed only with the meeting.

A similar scientific symposium organized in Moscow by Soviet Jewish scientists four months later proceeded successfully with ten American and Canadian participants. Some of the foreign participants, who arrived on tourist visas, were warned against participating, however, and two were turned back at Leningrad.

In December, we raised with Soviet officials two incidents in which a total of seven Americans were detained at Moscow airport and not allowed entry into the USSR, apparently in some cases for carrying religious artifacts. The incidents were also disturbing because one group had been denied the right to call the US Embassy for consular assistance, a violationg of the United States–Soviet Consular Convention.

In a show of tolerance for officially approved religious contacts, on the other hand, the Soviet Government announced in April that it was granting permission to a New York interfaith organization to print and ship 10,000 copies of the Pentateuch (the Five Books of Moses) to the USSR as a gift to the Soviet Jewish community. The agreement came after two years of negotiation with Soviet officials.

The situation in Eastern Europe concerning religious contacts and availability of information continued to vary considerably. In Poland, Hungary, and Romania, for example, Westerners could generally have access to ecclesiastic organizations and individuals with relative ease, while in other countries obstacles were often raised. For the first time in 15 years, however, Romania, Hungary, and Czechoslovakia recently permitted delegates to attend the annual meeting of the European Council of Jewish Communities.

Tourism; meetings among young people; sports

East–West contacts continued during the reporting period through tourist travel, youth meetings, and sport competitions with no major changes. While the Warsaw Pact countries showed a preference for developing ties in these areas through state-organized and controlled exchanges, the United States hoped to see greater spontaneity through increased use of direct people-to-people initiatives.

In some recent examples of exchanges, delegations of young political leaders from the USSR and Poland visited the United States in May at the invitation of the American Council of Young Political Leaders. The Soviet delegation of 12 also participated in a five-day seminar with young political leaders.

The YMCA continued its exchange with the Soviets. It hosted a delegation of Soviet youth officials for ten days in February to evaluate its exchanges with the Soviet Union in 1976 and to make plans for 1977. In October it sent a delegation of 13 American women to the USSR to study the role of women in Soviet society, and in March it hosted 30 young Soviet professionals in the United States. Plans for a camp counsellor and physical education exchange sponsored by the YMCA are proceeding.

Tourist exchanges between Eastern and Western countries do

not appear to have increased substantially during the reporting period. Soviet authorities have in fact been discouraging tourism to the United States, as reported in the section of this report on Basket Two implementation.

Expansion of contacts

This section of Basket Three calls for further development of contacts between governmental institutions and nongovernmental organizations of the signatory States. Included in the Final Act by sponsorship of the Eastern side, this provision has been used by the Soviets to criticize exclusion of Communist labour representatives from visits to the United States.

In April, the United States refused visitors' visas to three Soviet labour representatives who had been invited to a longshoremen's union gathering in Seattle. In press articles and in a note to our Embassy, the Soviet Union again called this a violation of the human contacts provisions of the Final Act. We pointed out that it is a longstanding US policy not to recommend waivers of ineligibility for Communist labour representatives because labour exchanges with Communist unions would equate our free and voluntary trade unions with the Communist labour organizations. There is no specific Final Act reference to travel and contacts among labour representatives, and, when signing the Final Act, all CSCE participants were aware of our longstanding policy on this matter.

Information

The Warsaw Pact States continued during the reporting period to criticize Western implementation of CSCE information provisions. Such criticisms generally claimed that the Eastern countries publish more Western books and show more Western films than Western countries import from the East. The charges were facilitated by Communist access to statistics from state-controlled cultural outlets that do not exist in the West, thus making statistical comparisons difficult. There is, of course, nothing in the Final Act to suggest that there should be government-assured, statistical reciprocity in the numbers of books and films shown in East and West. Such a stipulation would imply a measure of State control over culture which Western countries, as well as the Final Act, reject. On the contrary, the Final Act supports the Western view that individuals should be free to choose what they read or see. In this respect, dissemination of information remains the Basket Three area in which the Soviet Union and its allies have made the latest progress in implementation since the Helsinki summit.

Dissemination of information

The number and range of Western books and films available in Eastern countries remain very limited. The choice of titles published and films screened is politically selective, and books which are published are often censored. The Soviet Union's own statistics show that over 50 per cent. of the books translated from American authors consist of scientific and technical literature while only 5.3 per cent. in 1973 and 11.8 per cent. in 1974 dealt with historical and socioeconomic topics.

Availability of Western newspapers and periodicals in Warsaw Pact countries remained poor during the reporting period. Only token numbers were imported and sold in select locations, if at all. At one point in early March, reports indicated that Czechoslovakia had curbed the importation of even Western European Communist newspapers, which had become increasingly critical of the Czechoslovak Government's policies toward human rights advocates. Subsequently, Bulgaria and Czechoslovakia, apparently with an eye to the Belgrade review meeting, initiated public sale of a few Western journals and newspapers. As in other Warsaw Pact countries, however, these were available in very small numbers and in select locations likely to be frequented by tourists and Western visitors. Also most issues were several days old, and expensive by Eastern European standards. There was little indication that Eastern governments allowed free access to Western newspapers through institutions such as major public and university libraries, which in Western countries often subscribe to Eastern periodicals and newspapers. Nor did most Eastern countries allow free and unhindered mail entry of newspapers paid for by Western relatives or friends.

In December, the Czechoslovak Government allowed an increase in the mail distribution of the USIS quarterly Czech-language publication "Spektrum" from 2,000 to 6,000 copies per issue.

Broadcasting

In October, the Soviet State Committee for Television and Radio Broadcasting signed a cooperative agreement with CBS to exchange TV and radio programmes as well as expertise and technology. NBC and ABC already had such agreements with the USSR. NBC has also contracted to televise the Moscow Olympics worldwide. In early January, Czechoslovak and Portuguese radios signed a cooperation and exchanges agreement. In February, France and the Soviet Union signed a cooperative agreement with reference to the CSCE. Despite such isolated ventures, however, the area of broadcasting remained contentious.

In January, for example, a Soviet press article denounced as "reactionary" the Russian-language broadcasting of Deutsche Welle, the British Broadcasting Corporation (BBC) and the Voice of America (VOA) because programming allegedly rests in the hands of political emigres from the USSR. A particularly strident propaganda campaign against the VOA was initiated in the Soviet and Czechoslovak media in early 1977. One Czechoslovak attack characterized the VOA as an "espionage radio station," and the Soviets broadened their attacks to criticize not only the VOA but the US Information Agency as a whole. While attacks on Radio Liberty and Radio Free Europe have been common for years, such a concerted campaign of criticism had not been heard since well before Helsinki.

Most Eastern attacks against Western broadcasting continued to aim at Radio Free Europe (RFE) and Radio Liberty (RL). A Czechoslovak press article in January defended the jamming of RFE as being fully in accord with the "letter and spirit" of the Helsinki Conference. The article claimed that RFE had been "secretly" instructed to work against the Belgrade review meeting and CSCE objectives. In a representation to our Embassy, the Soviet Government accused the stations of seeking to promote "national discord and enmity."

Other Warsaw Pact governments as well protested the radio stations as interference in their internal affairs. We continued to point out that the CSCE Final Act commits signatories "to facilitate the freer and wider dissemination of information of all kinds." We thus maintained that jamming, rather than broadcasting, violates the letter and spirit of Helsinki.

In a report to Congress in late March, President Carter reaffirmed American support for the VOA, RFE, and RL and requested funding to expand their transmitting facilities. He pointed out that the stations have been for many years "a vital part of the lives of the peoples of Eastern Europe and the Soviet Union."

In an Eastern example of positive implementation in the CSCE spirit, Hungarian television in late February showed the fourth in a series of East–West discussions on international affairs. As with the previous three broadcasts, Hungarian officials exercised no censorship and allowed Western panelists, who included prominent journalists, to speak openly on a broad range of East–West issues.

Cooperation in the field of information
This topic will be discussed in the following section of this chapter.

Working conditions for journalists
Working conditions for journalists in the USSR and Eastern Europe generally deteriorated during the reporting period, primarily because of the sensitivity of Communist governments to Western reporting of their human rights violations. The Soviet Union and several Eastern European countries mounted propaganda campaigns accusing the Western press of obstructing CSCE objectives by impeding East–West understanding. The Czechoslovak press, for example, accused Western newsmen of "slinking" around the apartments of dissidents and ignoring the true accomplishments of Czechoslovak workers. Also, American journalists continued to be attacked falsely in the Soviet press for alleged intelligence connections with the clear purpose of trying to restrict their contacts among Soviet citizens.

In early February, the Soviet Union expelled an Associated Press correspondent after charging him with illegal currency transactions. Earlier, the Soviet press had accused him of being an intelligence agent. This was the first expulsion of an American correspondent from the USSR since 1970. The United States protested the action and expelled a Tass correspondent in Washington in retaliation. The US Senate passed a resolution calling the Soviet action a contradiction of the spirit of the Helsinki Final Act.

In December, an American Washington Post correspondent was called to the Soviet Ministry of Foreign Affairs and accused of distorting Soviet politics to worsen Soviet–American relations. He was warned that continuation of such behaviour would have "consequences." Our Embassy in Moscow protested this incident to Soviet officials.

The Soviet Union subsequently called the arrest in Virginia of a Tass correspondent a violation of the Helsinki Final Act. In fact, the correspondent was arrested for repeatedly ignoring a traffic summons on the incorrect claim that he possessed diplomatic immunity.

In Eastern Europe, the GDR expelled a West German television correspondent in December after accusing him of defaming the

GDR. This followed the expulsion of a Der Spiegel correspondent in December 1975.

In two separate incidents in February, Czechoslovak authorities detained American correspondents from NBC and the New York Times. Each was removed from a train while departing the country and searched. Each also had papers confiscated. The New York Times correspondent was not permitted to contact the US Embassy. One of the incidents occurred on GDR, rather than Czechoslovak, territory, although it involved Czechoslovak officials. Our Embassies subsequently lodged vigorous protests with Czechoslovak and GDR authorities and termed such treatment of journalists unacceptable. A West German correspondent was similarly detained in Czechoslovakia at a later date. In early March, Czechoslovak police reportedly used tear gas on two Western journalists attempting to interview a dissident.

Although there is no permanently accredited US correspondent in Prague, Czechoslovakia has on several occasions in 1976 turned down temporary visits of US journalists. In late March, Czechoslovak officials informed our Embassy that American as well as other Western journalists would no longer receive visas to Czechoslovakia unless they agreed beforehand not to interview Czechoslovak dissidents. We were also told that correspondents whose work Prague considers "objectionable" would not be granted visas. We expressed our concern to the Czechoslovak Government regarding the application of such a policy and emphasized that the policy would work in exactly the opposite direction from the Helsinki CSCE commitment of promoting a freer flow of information and of improving working conditions for journalists.

In April, Romanian authorities denied a New York Times correspondent a visa but reversed themselves within 48 hours after representations by the US Embassy.

In December, the GDR proposed to us the reciprocal issuance of 1-year multiple-entry visas to permanently accredited correspondents. We reaffirmed our willingness to issue such visas as soon as the GDR lifted its longstanding refusal to accredit US correspondents resident in Bonn and West Berlin.

In other developments, a United Press International correspondent, the first from either East or West to reside in Leningrad, has opened an office in that city in reciprocity for the opening of a Tass office in San Francisco. Also, Yugoslav authorities sponsored a conference of some 100 journalists from the CSCE signatory States in Belgrade April 25–30 to discuss the role of the press in implementing the Final Act and the specific provisions on working conditions for journalists.

Cooperation and Exchanges in the Fields of Culture and Education

General considerations

Though still falling short of fulfilling the resolve expressed in the Final Act to "increase substantially" cooperation and exchanges, implementation of provisions relating to culture and education continued to be characterized by notable progress. Interest on the part of the Soviet Union and its Eastern European allies in maintaining and expanding formal exchange arrangements remained evident and in many respects appeared to grow. At the same time, however, some Eastern countries indicated what they perceived to be certain limits to cooperation and voiced their concern about "unregulated activities."

Recent measures taken by CSCE participants reveal some nuances in both the pattern and pace of implementation. From the US perspective, the most significant achievements centre on the Basket Three provisions relating to "extension of relations." Formal negotiations on the first intergovernment exchanges agreements with Bulgaria, Czechoslovakia, and Hungary have been concluded and the agreement with Hungary was signed in April. Agreement has been reached with the Governments of Romania and the Soviet Union on programmes for future activities under the existing bilateral exchanges agreements; discussions on implementing programmes with Bulgaria and Hungary are in progress. We have proposed that a United States–German Democratic Republic cultural programme of reciprocal exchanges be developed, outlining specific types of activities that might be undertaken in the near future. The initial GDR response to this proposal has been positive. If accepted, it would significantly enhance the presently limited exposure of American artists in East Germany. In mid-May, the GDR proposed to us for discussion several other areas of cultural cooperation. The United States has responded positively to this initiative and discussions on expanded cultural exchanges are underway.

New direct exchange agreements, primarily involving educational institutions, also contributed to the recent increase in formal, cooperative arrangements. At the same time, progress in extending relations on the level of direct contracts and communications among persons working in the fields of culture and education continued to be hindered in some Eastern countries by fear of ideological contamination.

Another factor affecting implementation was the continued importance of political considerations in the implementation activities of the USSR and the Eastern European States. It has become increasingly evident in recent months that as the date for the Belgrade follow-up meeting draws nearer, the Eastern governments are becoming more sensitive to the need for demonstrating a credible implementation record. The increased weight of this factor was illustrated during the reporting period by the more frequent references in Eastern media to cultural and educational affairs in an explicit CSCE context, as well as by the somewhat more forthcoming Eastern attitude to new forms of cooperation. While the effort to document and defend their own records appears to have encouraged the Soviet Union and the countries of Eastern Europe to take further small but positive steps, it has also led to an increasing number of polemical attacks on Western performance.

Politicization of cultural and educational relations was also heightened by the reactions of Eastern governments to recent human rights activities in their countries. Linking dissident activity with exposure to Western "bourgeois" influences, Soviet and some Eastern Europe press articles presented increasingly strident warnings of the ideological limits to cooperation, particularly in cultural fields, and hints of a curtailment of further progress in East–West exchanges. This media campaign has shown that the Soviet Union and, to varying degrees, its allies, still adhere to the position advanced by Soviet Deputy Minister for Culture Popov, that cooperation and exchanges "without boundaries or barriers" are unacceptable.

The remainder of this section notes specific activities which relate to the Final Act's provisions on cooperation and exchanges in the fields of culture and education. The listing is by no means all inclusive but rather a representative sampling of recent activities.

Cooperation and exchanges in the field of culture

Books and publishing

There was considerable activity during the reporting period in the area of publishing and book and library exchanges. Representatives from the US private and public sectors met on February 17, under the joint auspices of the US Advisory Commission on International Educational and Cultural Affairs and the Government Advisory Commission on International Book and Library programmes. The group—which included officials from the Departments of State and Commerce, USIA and the CSCE Commission, as well as representatives from publishing, film, and library associations—discussed Basket Three implementation with particular regard to the role of the private sector in book and library programmes. A prime topic of discussion was consideration of developing a currency convertibility programme similar to the defunct information media guarantee programme.

During the last weeks of November, a delegation sponsored by the American Library Association (ALA) visited the Soviet Union to develop a plan for library exchanges between the two countries. Although the Soviet Ministry of Culture appeared eager to exchange personnel, the ALA deferred consideration of a formal exchanges agreement until it could assess the results of two bilateral seminars on the subjects which may be held in 1978. The US National Archives and the USSR Main Archival Administration also began discussions on an agreement which, inter alia, would provide for exchanges of archivists and joint publication of a collection of historical documents. Details of the programme remained to be worked out.

In the area of publishing, one significant development was the February visit to the United States by a delegation from the USSR's All-Union Copyright Agency. The group signed an agreement with the National Technical Information Service on the translation and publication in the United States of six Soviet journals, including the publications "Kommunist," "USA: Economy, Politics, Ideology," and "Space Biology and Aerospace Medicine." The agreement also provides for publication of seven collections of articles from Soviet journals on questions of politics, economics, philosophy, and agriculture. The Soviet delegation met with representatives from the Association of American Publishers, as well as with officials of major American publishing houses specializing in fictional works. In the course of these meetings, the representatives of Doubleday, Harper & Row, Simon & Schuster, Time-Life & Little, Brown indicated that they are considering publication of works by Soviet authors. McMillan noted that it will publish this year the first of ten works of Soviet science fiction, and the Times Mirror publishing group signed an agreement to issue English language editions and coproductions of Soviet works on art and medicine.

The Soviet delegation also inquired about possible representation by American companies at an upcoming Moscow international book fair. Among others, the publishing houses McGraw Hill International, John Wiley & Sons, Times Mirror,

Harper & Row, Ballantine Books, Plenum, Addison-Wesley, and Prentice-Hall International expressed a willingness to participate.

One major Soviet work currently being published in the United States is an English translation of the "Bol'shaya Sovetskaya Entsiklopedia" (The Great Soviet Encyclopedia). The Franklin Book Programs, a nonprofit organization established 25 years ago under the auspices of the American Book Publishers Council and the ALA, has also begun translating European and Soviet scientific works under a contract with the National Science Foundation. New areas of activity relevant to the Final Act which this organization is considering include the translation of foreign books for publication in the United States and the promotion of international book exchanges by means of conferences, exhibits, and newsletters.

Citing the December visit to the United States by a Soviet delegation of translators and literary experts and the residency of a prominent Soviet writer at the Universities of Kansas and California during the fall semester of 1976, the official organ of the USSR Union of Writers in January characterized recent exchanges with the United States as "very fruitful." The one Soviet complaint was that "anti-Soviet propaganda" allegedly hampered acceptance of Soviet literature in the United States.

Examples of recent activities with Eastern European countries include a visit to Romania by Prof. Richard Ellman, who lectured on James Joyce and American poetry at the Universities of Bucharest and Galati; a 1-month lecture tour of several US universities by a Romanian professor of comparative literature, and the participation by prize-winning Hungarian poet Otto Urban in a 4-month international writers programme at the University of Iowa.

Films and broadcasting

Specialists from Hungary, Poland, and the USSR were among the broadcasters from 16 countries participating in a 2-month study tour of US radio and television facilities organized by Syracuse University and sponsored by the Department of State this spring. Following an orientation programme in Washington, the radio specialists participated in an international broadcasting seminar at Syracuse University and attended the annual National Association of Broadcasters convention. While in the United States, project participants also had on-the-job assignments at American broadcasting stations. Eva Starodomskaya, a Soviet television journalist, visited the United States in April and attended the international programme for foreign women journalists sponsored by the American Women in Radio and Television. Ms. Starodomskaya is the first Soviet participant in this annual programme.

On November 23, CBS presented a 1-hour, primetime television programme filmed in Romania and featuring Gymnast Nadia Comaneci. This programme was subsequently broadcast on December 5 by Romanian television. Hungarian television presented on April 24 a report on United States–Hungarian relations. The programme, the first Hungarian one specifically on this topic, included interviews with Senator Sparkman, Congressmen Bingham and Vanik, and Department of State Counsellor Nimetz. Earlier in April, Hungarian television presented a programme analyzing the status of the SALT talks. It included comments by New York Times correspondent David Binder on the US media's reaction to Secretary Vance's trip to Moscow. In February, NBC signed an $85 million contract with the Soviet Olympic Committee for coverage of the 1980 Olympics, and in mid-March Polish television began broadcasting the first of 16 half-hour programmes produced in collaboration with the Kosciuszko Foundation, a private American organization.

Other contracts with Eastern Europeans in this area included a visit to Hungary by American film expert Henry Bietrose. While in Budapest, Professor Bietrose gave lectures on "Documentary Film-Making in the US" at the College of Dramatic and Cinemagraphic Arts and participated in a film workshop. The Polish film "Nights and Days" and the East German film "Jacob the Liar" were nominated for Best Foreign Film in this year's Oscar competition, a prize won in 1976 by the Soviet–Japanese coproduction "Dersu Uzala." The East German film archives presented a week-long retrospective of films by the American film pioneer D.W. Griffith in East Berlin in April.

Performing arts

Highlighted by the Los Angeles Philharmonic Orchestra's tour of Bulgaria, Czechoslovakia, Hungary, Poland, and Yugoslavia in November and December, live performances by American musicians continued to play a major part in our cultural programmes in the Soviet Union and Eastern European countries. During the reporting period, the following US performing art groups and individual performers travelled to Eastern European countries under State Department sponsorship: Nitty Gritty Dirt Band to the USSR (April 28 to May 24); the Blackearth Percussion Ensemble to Romania (April 4 and 5); the Mississippi Delta Blues Band to Romania (May 2 to 11); and dancer Judith Jamison to Romania (February 24). In May a group of US theatre directors visited the Soviet Union at the invitation of the Soviet copyright agency to view a selection of Soviet plays. The Arena Theatre of Washington produced "Catsplay," a play by the contemporary Hungarian playwright Istvan Orkeny.

A number of Soviet performing art groups visited the United States during the reporting period, including some which changed the previous emphasis upon classical performances. In December, for example, the folk group "Pesnyari" performed in 11 US cities during a 2-week tour that included a recording session in Nashville. In the same month, an Armenian group performed before audiences during a 3-week tour of the west coast. In March, Soviet playwright Roshchin and theatre director Yefremov spent 2 weeks in San Francisco assisting in the production of Roshchin's "Valentin and Valentina" by the American Conservatory Theatre. They then spent a week visiting other US theatres. Examples of the more traditional types of Soviet performances in the United States included the 2-month tour of the eastern United States by the Leningrad Symphony Orchestra and a series of performances by Daniel Shafran, a leading Soviet cellist. In addition, a number of Eastern European performers toured the United States.

Exhibits

As in the case of live performances by individuals or groups, exhibit exchanges continued to be a successful form of cultural cooperation. In the Soviet Union, the bicentennial exhibit "USA—200 Years" drew crowds which exceeded during the 1-month showing all records set during 17 years of USIA exhibits in the USSR. Other US exhibits in the USSR included the USIA exhibit "Photography USA," which was displayed during the reporting period for 1-month showings in Tbilisi, Ufa, and Novosibirsk.

Soviet exhibits in the United States included a display devoted to the history of Russian costumes at the Metropolitan Museum of Art in New York, and an exhibition of Russian and Soviet paintings from Moscow and Leningrad at the same museum. The latter exhibit is the largest Soviet art show ever displayed in the United States. In December, the Soviet exhibit "Scientific Siberia" completed its tour of the United States with a final showing in New Orleans.

In Eastern Europe, the most activity pertaining to exhibits was in Poland. An exhibition entitled "200 Years of American Painting" ended its four-city tour in December. A USIA-sponsored "Shakers" exhibit was displayed for 1-month showings at Wroclaw's Architectural Museum and Krakow's Ethnographic Museum, and the Polish Government agreed to the showing of another USIA exhibit entitled "Reflections: Images of America" during the first half of 1977 in Katowice, Szczecin, Bydgoszczand, and Gdansk. The Hungarian Cultural Institute also agreed to accept this USIA exhibit, which will open in June. With the exception of a display of graphic arts from the New York Metropolitan Art Museum in 1973, this will be the first individual US exhibit in Hungary outside the framework of the annual Budapest Trade Fair.

The "Reflections" exhibit also appeared in Sofia, Bulgaria, from December 10 to January 10 and was the first US cultural exhibition in Bulgaria since World War II. In Romania, the exhibit was shown in Bucharest (October 1976) and Craiova (January 1977) and opened in Oradea in March of this year. Another USIA exhibit in Romania focused on American agriculture. Romania and Polish exhibits recently in the United States included displays of rugs and tapestries at the Chicago Museum of Science and Industry. The Bulgarian Government has agreed to provide a display of "Thracian Art" this summer at the Metropolitan Museum in New York. Arrangements are also proceeding for a major exhibit of works from East Germany's Dresden Museum. The exhibit is scheduled to open in Washington, D.C., in early 1978.

Exchange visits among specialists

While not falling within a particular category, there were a number of visits and meetings of experts during the reporting period which served to implement the mutual understanding provisions of the Final Act. Included among these was a visit to the United States by a delegation of Soviet youth leaders under a project sponsored by the YMCA. Representatives from Hungary, Poland, and the USSR were among economists from 20 countries participating in March in 4 weeks of State Department-sponsored meetings in the United States with their American counterparts.

On April 28, 94 Polish agricultural specialists completed a 13-month stay in the United States during which they lived and worked on American family farms under a new 4-H Council exchange. A smaller number of Americans from the 4-H Council went to Poland under the same programme. A second group of Poles arrived in May for a 1-year stay, and the 4-H Council is discussing a similar programme with Hungary.

Recent travel of this nature by Americans to the Soviet Union included a visit by political scientist Harold Isaacs to research and educational institutions in Moscow, Leningrad, and Kiev, where he spoke on ethnicity and politics in American society; a trip by a delegation of US mayors to Moscow, Sochi, Minsk, and Leningrad to strengthen links between American and Soviet cities; and the participation by a delegation sponsored by the American Council of Young Political Leaders (ACYPL) in a seminar with Soviet counterparts in Odessa. The latter trip was reciprocated in May with a visit to the United States by a delegation from the Soviet Committee of Youth Organizations.

Similar exchanges of visits occurred with Eastern European countries. For example, the second-ranking member of the Bulgarian Committee on Art and Culture visited the United States from January 24 to February 3, meeting with American poets and writers and touring American cultural institutions in Washington and New York. A similar event was the visit by a delegation of California mayors to Romania, where they were received by President Ceaușescu. American futurologists Dennis and Donella Meadows also visited Bucharest and lectured at various Romanian institutions on energy and population questions.

Multilateral activities

As a result of actions taken at its 19th General Conference in November 1976, UNESCO during the 1977–78 biennium plans to continue programmes to further European cooperation. It plans also to initiate a number of new activities recommended by the Helsinki Final Act.

As its contribution to the setting up of a cultural data bank recommended by the Final Act, UNESCO will make a systematic inventory of existing cultural documentation facilities to facilitate optimum use of existing resources. Studies of European cultures at the national and regional levels will be continued, and UNESCO will also publish a detailed annual calendar of cultural events in Europe, as recommended by the CSCE. In addition, the UNESCO European Centre for Higher Education, located in Bucharest, has begun to implement a full programme of activities which promise to increase understanding and cooperation among educational institutions on the postsecondary level in Europe, Canada, and the

United States. The problem of the education of migrant workers and their families will also be the subject of a number of UNESCO activities.

Cooperation and exchanges in the field of education

Extension of relations: access and exchanges

Probably the most encouraging aspect of cooperation in this area was the increased number of direct institutional exchanges. An indication of Soviet willingness to proceed toward the expansion of such arrangements was an article in the journal of the "Institute of United States and Canadian Studies." It praised the October 4, 1976, agreement between the State University of New York and Moscow State University—the first agreement for direct exchanges between American and Soviet universities—and spoke in glowing terms of the prospects for future direct exchange agreements. Several US universities have made proposals for direct exchanges with Soviet universities, and in March a Soviet delegation of officials from Kiev State University visited various US universities and discussed possibilities for such exchange agreements.

Direct exchanges agreements continued to increase in Eastern European countries. The University of Kansas recently established a new programme with Warsaw University for undergraduate and graduate students as well as teaching assistants in various academic fields. Warsaw University also signed a direct exchanges agreement in March with Kent State University, bringing to over 20 the number of United States–Polish agreements of this type.

Together with the University of Nebraska, Iowa State University in December concluded a direct exchanges agreement with the Romanian Academy of Agriculture and Forestry Sciences. A recent encouraging development was the prompt implementation of a new agreement in urban planning between Johns Hopkins University and Bucharest University. Another new institution-to-institution arrangement discussed with Romania recently is a proposal for exchanges between the University of Kentucky Business School and the Romanian Academy of Economic Studies.

Other educational programmes and visits

Interaction between professional organizations and visits by educational specialists and teachers also continued during the reporting period. In April, a Soviet delegation headed by the USSR First Deputy Minister of Education participated in a US–

USSR seminar on teacher education organized by the Council for International Exchange of Scholars. Following the seminars, the group visited teacher training institutes at three American universities. The following month a Soviet delegation on vocational and technical education travelled to the United States to return a Soviet visit by a US group in January 1976.

Following discussion started over two years ago, the American Bar Association and the Soviet Lawyers' Association reached agreement on legal exchanges between the United States and the Soviet Union. The agreement called for a series of bilateral seminars on legal topics, individual placement of lawyers in legal or business firms of the two countries, and exchanges of lecturers in law. Because of difficulties on the Soviet side, implementation of the agreement was delayed and a planned seminar and other legal exchanges may not take place this year. In a related development, Moscow State University in January accepted the first American law professor under the Fulbright lecturer programme. In April, the GDR doubled its academic exchange programme through the International Research and Exchanges Board, which arranges exchanges between American and Eastern academic institutions.

History, a traditional field of academic cooperation, continues to evoke interest and interaction. In March, two prominent Bulgarian historians participated in a 2-day conference at the University of Vermont on the centennial of Bulgarian independence. Talks were also held on strengthening ties between the newly established international documentation centre on Bulgarian history and interested institutions in the United States. These talks resulted in the signing of a cooperative agreement. In April, seven Romanian scholars attended a meeting at Ohio State University on the centennial of Romanian independence. The group subsequently visited other universities and academic centres in the United States and attended a symposium in Detroit on Romanian history. Americans also exchanged views with Eastern European colleagues from Bulgaria, Hungary, Romania, the USSR, and Yugoslavia during the second international colloquium of the Commission of the Balkan Countries Today, which was held in Bucharest in November.

Examples of related activities during the last months of 1976 included a lecture by Prof. Rudolf Tokes of the University of Connecticut on "East–West Relations" at the Institute for Historical Research of the Hungarian Academy of Sciences and participation by Librarian of Congress Daniel Boorstin in a roundtable seminar at the same institute. Dr. Boorstin also visited

Bulgaria and Romania. US electoral specialist Richard Scammon travelled to the Soviet Union in April and lectured on US national politics and elections and met with Soviet political leaders and journalists. That same month poet John Balaban and Prof. Christopher Given, American Fulbright lecturers in Romania, travelled to the University of Sofia to give lectures to students of literature; the trip marked the first time Fulbright lecturers have been invited to Bulgaria since the Bulgarian Government terminated the programme in the 1960s. In May Alton Fry of the Council on Foreign Relations visited the USSR and Poland to lecture on international affairs and disarmament. In May a three-person delegation from the Council for International Exchange of Scholars also travelled to the Soviet Union to discuss an expansion of the Fulbright lecturer programme with the Soviets. In February two professors from Moscow's Higher Trade Union College travelled to Chicago to lecture at Roosevelt University, and in March the director of the USSR Institute for Scientific Information on the Social Services visited US libraries, research institutes, and universities at the invitation of the Department of State.

Science

Provisions for cooperation in the field of science primarily fall under Basket Two of the Final Act. Scientific contacts in an educational, as opposed to a research, context, however, are also specifically encouraged in Basket Three. Many ongoing activities of this type are encompassed within the direct exchanges agreements noted above.

Other examples of activities in this field included talks by Dr. Rene Dubos with environmental and biological specialists at the Soviet Academy of Sciences, lectures by Prof. Kenneth Frey on plant genetics during a six-day visit to the Romanian Academy of Agricultural and Forestry Sciences, and a roundtable discussion at the Romanian Space Council and National Council for Science and Technology, at which American specialist Karl Heize discussed aspects of the space shuttle and other US space projects. A major US programme was a 35-day tour of American science and technology museums, organized by the Association of Science-Technology Centres and sponsored by the Department of State. Representatives from Czechoslovakia and the USSR were among the 14 participants who, in addition to visiting science museums throughout the United States, also attended the first International Conference of Science and Technology Museums held in Philadelphia.

Language

Although statistics compiled by the Modern Language Association through 1974 indicate a downward trend in study of established foreign languages in American schools, the United States has continued to encourage the study of foreign languages and cultures through domestic and international programmes. As in other fields, many of the international projects undertaken by the United States in the area of language study are encompassed and developed within programmes of direct exchanges or other university-to-university arrangements. Agreements have been signed between Ohio State University and Middlebury College and the USSR's Pushkin Institute of the Russian Language which will enable American students to study Russian in Moscow. In addition to an exchange of Russian language students and teaching specialists, Ohio State and Pushkin Institute will sponsor in 1978 a conference on teaching Russian. Together with existing exchanges between the State University of New York and the Thorez Institute of Moscow, and similar exchanges scheduled for summer 1977 between Bryn Mawr College and the Pushkin Institute, the new arrangement significantly expands the language-teaching ties between the two countries.

On the elementary and secondary school levels, the United States also expanded efforts in bilingual education. Wide-ranging programmes offering part of the curriculum in a second language for the millions of American students whose native language is not English are now an established aspect of US educational policy, with State and Federal funding of over $200 million annually. Today some form of bilingual teaching is mandatory in 11 States, whereas six years ago no State had such requirements. This year the Department of Health, Education, and Welfare will sponsor 627 bilingual projects in 68 languages. Moreover, it continues to encourage the development and maintenance of foreign language and area specialists with particular emphasis given to less widely studied languages and, through the promotion of ethnic studies, has attempted to underscore the contribution that various ethnic and cultural minorities have made to the life of the Nation. Of interesting potential for the future is the new section 603 of title VI of the National Defense Education Act which was passed by the Congress in 1976. It authorizes support for the stimulation of "locally designed educational programmes to increase the understanding of students in the United States about the cultures and activities of other nations in order to better evaluate the international and domestic impact of major national policies."

EPILOGUE:

A DEEPENING SENSE OF UNCERTAINTY

by *Frans A.M. Alting von Geusau*

On Thursday, March 9, 1978, the Belgrade Follow-up Conference ended its work with the adoption of a brief Concluding Document. For almost five months, representatives of the thirty five participating States—according to the Document:[1]

> "held a thorough exchange of views both on the implementation of the provisions of the Final Act and of the tasks defined by the Conference, as well as, in the context of the questions dealt with by the latter, on the deepening of their mutual relations, the improvement of security and the development of the process of détente in the future".

As the previous chapters had been completed shortly before the opening of the Belgrade Conference, we intend in this Epilogue to examine some of the more important conclusions reached in the light of the Conference's outcome.

The Belgrade Follow-Up Conference

Several months before the Belgrade Conference opened on October 4, 1977, indications were already manifold that its chances to be a vehicle for improving the process of détente were most unpromising indeed.

Soviet/Cuban intervention in Africa and the human rights issue in Eastern Europe, had exacerbated East–West relations and manifested the divergent goals pursued by participating States under the common label of détente.

The United States continued to emphasize that détente should be used as an opportunity to promote mutual restraints— also in policies outside Europe—and further agreements, bilaterally as well as in Belgrade. The new American Administration, moreover, came out in support of the human rights movements in the Soviet Union and Eastern Europe. It announced its intention to employ

---

1. The Text of the Concluding Document appeared in *Atlantic News*. Bruxelles, March 15, 1978. 12th year. No. 1009.

the Belgrade Conference as an occasion to *review* implementation of the Final Act, in particular as regards its seventh principle and the third basket.

The Soviet Union began to emphasize its view of détente as an irreversible process towards the victory of "Socialism", which was not to restrain its policies in any way. It showed little or no interest in using Belgrade as an opportunity to reach further agreements, and resisted the idea of reviewing the implementation of the Final Act. A review of the implementation of the seventh principle and the third basket in particular was seen by the Soviet leaders as interference in the domestic affairs of socialist States.

The review part of the Belgrade Conference was dominated, as a consequence, by sharp exchanges of view on human rights issues between the American and Soviet representatives.

The other Western, non-aligned and neutral States prepared for an overall review of the implementation of the Final Act, but emphasized that they would prefer to avoid reciprocal recriminations and accusations. They also prepared proposals on a number of additional steps aimed at furthering détente and cooperation.

As the negotiations dragged on, it became increasingly clear that the Conference would formally end in failure unless the participating States agreed to bow to the Soviet demand to conclude it with an empty document. During the first part of the Conference, the Soviet delegation refused to engage in a meaningful debate on the implementation of the Final Act. When the Conference resumed in January 1978, the Soviet Union rejected any effort to produce a document reflecting at least the substance of negotiations.

The Concluding Document, therefore, only refers to "a thorough exchange of views", adding:

> "It was recognized that the exchange of views constitutes in itself a valuable contribution towards the achievement of the aims set by the CSCE, although different views were expressed as to the degree of implementation of the Final Act reached so far".

In fact, the exchange of views had been neither thorough nor valuable; the phrase: "different views were expressed" is diplomatic Volapük for complete disagreement and deadlock.

The Concluding Document also states that such a "thorough exchange of views" was held "on the *deepening* of their mutual relations, the *improvement* of security and the *development* of the process of détente in the future" (emphasis added). Indeed, about ninety proposals had been tabled to these ends. But: "before much serious negotiations could be done on these proposals the meeting had to move on to draft a Concluding Document".[2] And the Document says on them: "Consensus was not reached on a number of proposals submitted to the meeting".

The number of proposals on which consensus was not reached was ... about ninety.

The outcome of the Belgrade Conference thus supports *Ghebali's* final conclusion[3] that the Ten Principles' sole merit has been to reveal the fundamentally unsatisfactory nature of the concept of détente itself. Still, as befits a multilateral diplomatic conference, it can always find an escape from formal failure in continuing itself. The participating States therefore decided: "in conformity ... with their resolve to continue the multilateral process initiated by the CSCE ... (to) hold further meetings among their representatives". Five further meetings, each to begin on a given date and at a given place, have been agreed upon: a second "of these meetings" in Madrid (November 11, 1980), to be preceded by a preparatory meeting in Madrid (September 9, 1980); a meeting of experts (Montreux, October 31, 1978) "charged with pursuing the examination and elaboration of a generally acceptable method for peaceful settlement of disputes aimed at complementing existing methods"; another meeting of experts (Bonn, June 20, 1978) "to prepare a scientific forum"; and a third meeting of experts (La Valetta, February 13, 1979) to "consider cooperation in non-security fields within the framework of the Mediterranean chapter of the Final Act".

It is difficult to escape the conclusion, that the Concluding Document of the Belgrade Conference is a particularly disappointing one, even by the modest standards of achievement one has learned to apply to East–West and "all-European" multilateral negotiations.

Despite agreement to continue the process initiated by CSCE, détente remains uncertain at best. Or, should one now conclude that uncertainty has deepened?

In the following sections, we shall review some of the arguments in the preceding chapters in the light of the Belgrade Conference.

---

2. Richard Davy, "No progress at Belgrade". *The World Today.* April 1978, p. 132.

3. In chapter 4, *supra*, p. (57).

Détente and Disarmament

The linkage between détente and disarmament prior to and during CSCE resulted from two different approaches to the desired process of détente in Europe.

By proposing negotiations on MBFR as a condition for participating in CSCE,[4] member States of NATO hoped *both* to induce the Soviet Union to make concessions in the area of its greatest military strength, *and* to limit the danger of impending unilateral reductions in NATO countries.

The non-aligned and neutral countries proposed both a discussion on disarmament at CSCE,[5] and the inclusion of so-called Confidence Building Measures in the Final Act as a means to facilitate disarmament by diminishing distrust.

Whereas the Soviet Union accepted MBFR talks primarily in order to gain Western acceptance of CSCE, few incentives for agreement on force reductions in central Europe remained after Helsinki, according to *Griffith*.[6] Détente, we are told moreover by the Soviet Union, is the outcome of a shift in power relations in favour of the Soviet Union, resulting from the continuous strengthening of the Soviet and Warsaw Pact military forces. The Soviet arms build-up and the growth of Soviet naval power has become apparent especially since Helsinki. The substantially increased Soviet offensive capability in central Europe and the deployment of naval units in the Mediterranean and Norwegian seas may not as yet reflect the intention to strike. They obviously have gone well beyond the needs for defence and deterrence and cannot but raise suspicion in the West that they are to serve purposes incompatible with Western security and European détente.

It has reversed the trend towards unilateral reductions in NATO and accelerated the efforts to keep abreast of the Soviet Union in the development of new technologically advanced weapon systems.

The new approach *Teunissen* advocated[7] has not been tried and MBFR negotiations continue to be a process without end.

According to *Acimovic*,[8] confidence building measures have indeed been implemented. At the Belgrade Conference, the non-aligned, neutral and West-European countries tabled several proposals to

4. Compare Teunissen, chapter 6, *supra*, p. (93).
5. A similar proposal was made at Belgrade.
6. Chapter 1, *supra*, p. (5).
7. Chapter 6, *supra*, p. (93).
8. Chapter 7, *supra*, p. (132).

improve and expand CBM's such as: notifying manoeuvres below the 25,000 man threshold, notifying large scale military movements, and according better treatment to observers. The Soviet Union rejected all such proposals and no consensus could be reached as a consequence.

Since the conclusion of the Final Act, renewed attention has been given to the problem of nuclear weapons in Europe.

First of all, NATO offered in December 1975 to reduce the number of tactical nuclear warheads in Europe as part of a first stage in MBFR.[9] The Warsaw Pact States proposed, in the Autumn of 1976, to conclude a treaty on the no-first use of nuclear weapons between the States participating in CSCE.[10] Neither proposal has so far received serious attention by the other side. A second reason for this renewed attention since 1977 may be that nuclear arms-control has been given "priority-treatment" in the Special Session of the UN General Assembly on Disarmament.

A far more disturbing reason for this renewed attention, however, lies in the development of nuclear weapons itself, as has been described by *Griffith*.[11] The increasingly asymmetric character of this new phase in the nuclear arms-race is eroding the balance of deterrence between the two alliances and has so far precluded any meaningful progress in SALT II.

SALT II appears to have joined the CSCE and MBFR talks in the sense that they are no longer referred to as negotiations to reach agreement, but as "continuous processes" ... the current euphemism for persistent deadlock.

In the Summer of 1977 the nuclear debate took an ominous turn, when it became known that the US Administration considered to replace part of their tactical nuclear warheads by the Enhanced Radiation Reduced Blast Warhead (ERRB) better known as the neutron bomb. This is not the place to review the highly emotional debate on the neutron bomb, nor to explain its technical features. What does concern us in this Epilogue is the highly negative impact the neutron-bomb issue has had so far on the process of détente. From a military point of view, the ERRB warhead is considered to be most effective to offset the vast Warsaw Pact superiority in tanks and armour. As the latest example of the ongoing qualitative nuclear arms race, its deployment can be

9. Chapter 6, *supra*, p. (93).
10. Chapter 5, *supra*, p. (79).
11. Chapter 1, *supra*, p. (5).

prevented only by a conscious political decision to exercise self-restraint. Such a decision may contribute to arms-control, provided that the other side—i.e. the Soviet Union—reacts in kind by measures of self-restraint in the areas of its greatest strength. Unfortunately, the Soviet leaders have taken the opposite course. They have mounted and organized a vicious propaganda campaign—around the world and inside Western Europe—against the neutron bomb, with the specific purpose of dividing NATO and exploiting Western weaknesses. The apparent success of the Soviet "stop the neutron bomb" campaign—especially in The Netherlands—has induced the CPSU to further organize and broaden resistance in Western Europe against (NATO's) nuclear weapons in general. At the same time the Soviet Union continues to substantially improve its (strategic and tactical) nuclear capabilities. In the absence of any Soviet willingness to restrain the build up of its own nuclear and conventional forces—or to revise its offensive strategic doctrine—arms control talks cease to be meaningful and détente becomes irreversibly meaningless.

Cooperation in the Field of Economics

The classic functionalist adage that limited economic cooperation fosters more economic cooperation and contributes to the reinforcement of peace and security found expression—as we saw—in the Final Act. It also induced *Bognar* and *Pinder*[12] to be cautiously hopeful about taking matters somewhat further at the Belgrade Conference. Pinder in particular suggested that Belgrade might assist in a *rapprochement* between the European Communities and COMECON. As we know, Community proposals to improve cooperation suffered the same fate as the other proposals made at Belgrade. The pace of negotiations between the European Communities and COMECON has been too slow so far to expect any meaningful progress in the foreseeable future.

For the near future the potential destabilizing impact of excessive allocation of resources for military purposes—already hinted at by *Bognar*[13]—is likely to become more serious a problem for East–West economic cooperation. Recent Western estimates on Soviet defence spending indicate "that the Soviet leadership has placed a much higher value on military power than many Western

12. Chapters 9 and 10, *supra*.
13. Chapter 9, *supra*, p. (172).

observers had previously thought".[14] If so, it helps neither the Eastern capacity to expand trade nor Western willingness to provide even larger long-term credits to do so.

Cooperation in Humanitarian and Other Fields

According to the Concluding Document of the Belgrade Conference:

> "The representatives of the participating States ... reaffirmed the resolve of their governments to implement fully, unilaterally, bilaterally and multilaterally, all the provisions of the Final Act".

Two months later—in May 1978—*Prof. Yuri Orlov* was sentenced to 12 years of jail and banishment; a new wave of arrests among signatories of the Charter 77 Manifesto was reported from Czechoslovakia. Their offences? Prof. Yuri Orlov, until his arrest in February 1977, had been the leader of "The Public Group to Promote Observance of the Helsinki Agreements in the USSR".[15] The aim of the group, formed in Moscow on May 12, 1976, is to promote observance in particular of the seventh principle and the third basket of the Final Act. And the signatories of the Charter 77 Manifesto?

> "Charter 77 is a free and informal and open association of people of various convictions, religions and professions, linked by the desire to work individually and collectively for respect for human and civil rights in Czechoslovakia and the world—the rights provided for in the enacted international pacts, in the Final Act of the Helsinki Conference, and in numerous other international documents against wars, violence and social and mental oppression".[16]

The "offence" for which these men and women are persecuted, harassed, dismissed from their jobs, beaten up, interrogated, and sentenced or exiled, is that they have asked their government to apply to its own citizens what it has pledged to do in the Final Act and other international agreements.

---

14. Hannes Adomeit and Mikhail Agursky, *The Soviet Military-Industrial Complex and Its Internal Mechanism*. National Security Series, No. 1/78. Centre for International Relations, Queen's University, Kingston, Ontario, p. 3.

15. The Documents of the Group have been compiled by the Staff of the Commission on Security and Cooperation in Europe. Congress of the United States, February 24, 1977.

16. From the English translation of the Text. *International Herald Tribune*, February 1, 1977.

According to the judge, who tried Prof. Orlov, his activities—to promote observance of human rights—constituted "anti-Soviet agitation and propaganda". If governments of the other States participating in CSCE or the Belgrade Conference express concern about such violations of human rights, it constitutes interference in the internal affairs of the Soviet Union or—as we have read[17]—psychological warfare and subversive activity.

The grave situation, reflected by these events and arguments should not be underestimated. The Final Act of Helsinki has been negotiated for the purpose of agreeing on a "code of conduct" for détente, and as such ought to be subject to review of its implementation in all parts and by all participating States. The third basket forms an integral part of the Final Act and as such expresses a common objective to cooperate towards a freer flow of people, ideas and information.[18] No participating State can deny any other participating State the right to review and discuss compliance, and to propose improvements.

As the Belgrade Conference approached, there were many good reasons to seek discussion on these matters. Following the emergence of human rights groups in the Soviet Union and Eastern Europe, demands to observe the seventh principle had been met by repression, thus focusing attention on its violation. The third basket, moreover, was a unique one in the sense that governments had pledged to take specific steps, rather than merely to refrain from or continue with certain activities. Progress in implementing the third basket had been made but was minimal.[19] Soviet efforts to avoid discussions on these problems,[20] had the opposite effect of focusing attention on them. The Belgrade Conference, as we saw, failed to reach agreement on any of the modest proposals to improve cooperation, introduced by West European representatives. At best, it may have helped to continue the interest in and the monitoring of progress and violations in this respect.

It is in the light of these cautious efforts, that the Orlov trial is likely to further endanger détente. Because "the sentencing of Mr. Orlov ... serves sharp notice that Mr. Brezhnev sees no present reason even to feign a minimal compliance with his 1975 promises".[21] A regime which so practices oppression at home and

17. Sheidina. Chapter 11, *supra*, p. (216).
18. Chapter 14, *supra*, p. (259).
19. See chapters 11–14, *supra*.
20. A variety of tactics have been used. See e.g. Davy, *loc. cit.* p. 129.
21. *The Economist*, May 20, 1978, p. 19.

contempt for commitments abroad can be no reliable partner in the further development of détente.

The Growing Malaise

By the end of the sixties—and despite the Soviet invasion of Czechoslovakia—one could nurture some hopes that the emerging era of multilateral European negotiations might improve security by progress towards arms-control and crisis-management.

The Final Act of Helsinki did not create a new structure for peace and cooperation, but its solemn conclusion on August 1, 1975, could justify expectations that it might contribute towards more cooperation in Europe. The atmosphere, Helsinki had created according to *Mates*,[22] was much less burdened by total confrontation and showed encouraging signs towards gradually dismantling the cold war and blurring the ideological lines of division between East and West.

By mid-1978 and in the wake of the disappointing Belgrade Conference most of these modest hopes and expectations have turned out to be unfounded illusions.

The *negotiating relationship* between the Soviet Union and the United States has eroded to a point where even the SALT II process is in danger. Hopes for progress in arms control have turned into fear that the arms-race is no longer under control.

The rapidly increasing military involvement of the Soviet Union and Cuba in *Africa* has made this continent *a new object of East–West confrontation*. Confrontation in Africa has become a heavy burden on East–West relations in general.

At the same time, the *ideological lines of division between East and West* are becoming sharper again by the relentless repression of human rights groups in the East, the stepping up of subversive activities conducted by the CPSU in Western Europe, and the vitriolic propaganda campaign against the United States (nicknamed "the ideological struggle").

The most disturbing aspect of these trends is not the break-down of the code of détente—an agreed "code" never existed—but *the break-down of the capacity for negotiated crisis-management*.

For this latter break-down, three causes may be given: the "paralysing lack of consensus on foreign policy in the United States"; the "immobilizing uncertainty over the problem of suc-

---

22. Chapter 3, *supra*, p. (42).

cession in the Soviet Union";[23] and the internal political weakness of Western Europe in the face of American indecision and growing Soviet military power.

As *Loewenthal* writes further:[24]

> "the dangerous fact is that this period of probable pre-decision line-up in the Soviet leadership coincides with the lack of consensus in the United States ... For this means that *possible major Soviet decisions are being prepared in a situation in which the Soviets have the impression that they have nothing to hope and nothing to fear from the United States, and indeed from the West in general* ... Just as the Soviets may come to the conclusion that it is not worth while to meet American negotiators halfway in the hope of economic advantages, because those will be blocked in Congress by the opponents of negotiation, so they may also conclude that there is no need for restraint in crisis areas from fear of American counteraction, because that would equally be blocked by the opponents of foreign commitments".

Given the totalitarian character of the Soviet system and its "procedures" for succession of leadership, the chances for more restraint in crises, for exorcising the demon of ideology, and for willingness to accommodate with the West are not very great.

Consensus in the United States and the West in general may return, as a consequence, but the danger that it will return too late and at the wrong moment, cannot be dismissed.

Totalitarian regimes and pluralist democracies are no natural partners for peace in the long run. In final analysis, there is no synthesis between détente as an irreversible process towards the victory of totalitarian lawlessness; and détente as a policy to promote human rights, arms-control and a freer flow of persons, ideas and information.

Détente, as a consequence, is bound to be uncertain. When the totalitarian side, emphasizes its irreversibility and appears to act accordingly—as it does since 1975—the sense of *uncertainty cannot but deepen.*

---

23. From Richard Loewenthal, "Dealing with Soviet-Global Power". *Encounter*, June 1978, p. 89.
24. *loc. cit.* p. 90.

INDEX OF AUTHORS AND SUBJECTS

n (note) = footnote

ABC, 272
Academic exchanges, 236
ACDA, 167
Aćimović, Ljubivoje, 11, 67n, 77, 132–149, 291
Acte final, cf. final act
Adenauer, Konrad, 153n
Adomeit, Hannes, 294n
Adoptions, forced, 253, 254
AFLCIO, 165
Africa, 52, 73, 79, 181, 296
Aggression, 86
Airforces, 118–120, 122
ALA, 278
Albania, 49, 60
Allemagne, 59, 70
Allison, T., 21n
Alting von Geusau, Frans A.M., XVII–XIX, 67n, 288–297
Amalrik, Andrei, XVIII
Amalrik, Jacques, 129n, 244
America, 79, 81, 221, cf. USA; Etats Unis
American:
   armaments politics, 158
   economic interests, 160, 161, 168
   foreign policy, 150, 161
   Government, 159
   indecision, 297
   –Polish Trade Commission, 166
   –Romanian Economic Commission, 166
   Security Council, 156
   society, 157, 161
   –Soviet accord, 166
Andras, Charles, 9n

Andren, Nils, 5n, 8n, 13n, 22n
Angola, 73, 243
Antagonism, 49, 54, 56
Antarctic Treaty, 81, 93
Antinomie des conceptions, 72–73
Apunen, Osmo, XVIIn
Arab States, 113
Argursky, Mikhail, 294n
Arkwright, Francis, 181n
Armée rouge, 37, 38
Armenians, 255, 263
Arms:
   control, XVIII, 12, 25, 77, 93–96, 123–126, 129–132, 293, 296
   race, 80, 83, 130–133, 145, 168, 228, 296
   reduction, 79
Aron, R., 225n
Arts, 280–281
Asiles psychiatriques, 39
Aspin, Les, 125n, 160
Assemblée nationale, 28
Atlantic:
   Alliance, 26, 106, cf. OTAN, NATO
   Charter, 105
   Declaration, 128
   gap, 19
Australia, 178
Austria, 135, cf. Autriche
Auto détermination, 63
Autriche, 65, 69, cf. Austria

Backfire bomber, 129, 165, 167
Balance of forces, 87, 99, 102, 109, 126
Balkans, 23, 82, 92
Bangla Desh, 17

299

Bank of America, 40
Barnet, Richard J., 155n
"Baskets" 1, 2 and/or 3, 11, 12, 26, 37, 48, 51–59, 64, 152, 162–166, 215, 243, 250–252, 259ff, 276ff
BBC, 237, 273
Beam, ambassador –, 97
Beecher, William, 22n
Belgium, 89, 91
Belgrade-1977, XVIIn, 11, 12, 43, 46, 51, 58, 66n, 68, 87, 145–149, 162–167, 192, 194, 212, 250, 258, 260, 272, 275, 288, 291–295
Bender, Peter, 9n
Benelux, 100, 109
Berlin, 10, 29, 36, 47, 49, 97, 153, 265, 268, 275
Berlin, Sir Isaiah, 233
Berlin Wall, 240, 245, 254
Bertram, Christoph, 13n
Bettati, Mario, 62n
Bietrose, Prof. Henri, 280
Binder, David, 280
Bingham, 280
Birnbaum, Karl E., 5n, 7n, 8n, 13n, 22n
Blech, Klaus, 8n
Bloc-free constellation, 56, 149
Bognár, József, 171, 172–189, 186n, 293
Boltin, Ye. A., 9n
Bonn, 7, 10, 22, 36, 253, 275, 290
Book exchanges, 271–272, 277
Boorstin, Daniel, 285
Borders, 57
Borklund, C. W., 157n
Bosch, Jeroen, 216
Brandt, Willy, 7, 8, 10, 33, 95, 97, 98, 154
Brazilia, 25
Brejnev, 30, 32, 33, 34, 35, 38, 41, 64, cf. Brezhnev
Breughel, Pieter, 216
Brezhnev, 3, 6, 80, 95–97, 100, 105, 124, 222, 228, 295, cf. Brejnev
Brezhnev doctrine, 33, 57, 58, 62, 64, 71

British nuclear force, 106, 124
Broadcasting, 227, 237, 238, 252, 272, 273, 279
Bromke, Adam, 9n
Brookings Institution, 118
Brosio, 98
Brown, George S., 126n
Bruce-Briggs, B., 218n
Brunner, Guido, 8n
Brzezinski, Zbigniew, 17n, 128, 129n, 224
Bucharest, *Bucarest*, 31, 88, 256
Budapest, 251
Bukovsky, 244
Bulgaria, 10, 101, 106, 162, 204, 255, 262, 264, 276
Bundestag, 255
Bundeswehr, 14, 97, 114, 122, 255
Burgos, 69
Burt, Richard, 19n, 21n, 127n, 130n
Byrnes, Robert F., 215, 231–249, 237n

Calcutta, 28
California State Supreme Court, 265
Campbell, John C., 9n
Camps, M., 175n
Canada, 60, 100, 209
Canby, Steven L., 13n, 127n
Capétiens, 29
Capitalist countries, 179, 180
Carter, President, 12, 24–26, 36, 39, 45, 46, 69, 125n, 129, 150, 151, 156, 158–161, 167, 168, 244, 247, 265, 273
CBM's, 11, 15, 291
CBS, 270, 280
Ceausescu, President, 31, 256, 283
CEE, 33, 69, 70, cf. EEC; European Communities
Ceilings (forces), 90
Censorship, 239, 247, 272
Central Europe, 79, 81, 82, 88–92, 94–97, 99–102, 142, 154, 155
CEP-accuracy, 20
Chaban-Delmas, Jacques, 26, 34
Charter, 77, 240, 294
Charvin, Robert, 63n

300

Chernenko, Konstantin, 63n
Chicago Council on Foreign Relations, 161
Chile, 245
China, 10, 49, 110, 124, 125, 129, 150
Chine populaire, 30, 38
Chinese border, 14
Christian Democrats, 17
Chypre, 59, 65, 68, 69, cf. Cyprus
CIA, 243
CIES, 127
Civil rights, 150
Class struggle, 3
CMEA, 177, 180, 181, 185, 253, cf. Comecon
CM's, 15, 19–22
Code of conduct, XVIII
Coexistence, 41, 93, 125, 226, 233, 238
Coffey, J.I., 13n
Colonial wars, 55
Cold War, 6, 26, 42, 50–53, 85, 132, 144, 150, 157, 160, 177, 178, 216, 222, 226, 296
Comanesi, Nadia, 280
Comecon, 40, 171, 192–201, 204, 211, 293, cf. CMEA
Committee on International Relations, US –, 260
Communist:
  construction, 3
  parties, 18, 47
Comprehensive Programme, 195
Concluding document, 289, 290
Condominium, 33, 34
Confidence building, 139, 140, 143, 148, 291
Congress, 77, 125, 156–159, 163, 167, 168
Congress Commission S.C.E., cf. Security and Cooperation
Conventional forces, 85
Cooperation, 26, 27, 42, 54, 56, 147, 153, 179–182, 185, 202, 211, 260, 276, 293
Copenhagen, 102, 104
Copyright Convention, 236, 239
Corbeilles, cf. "Baskets"

Coudenhove-Kalergi, 29
CPSU, 3, 95, 124, 293, 296
Crimée, 34
Crisis-management, 296
Croatian crisis, 22
Cruise missiles, 165, 167
CSCE, XVII, XVIII, 3, 8–12, 26, 57–59, 61n, 64–72, 77, 82, 87, 89–100, 104, 129, 132–135, 138, 141–145, 164, 171, 199–202, 262, 268–271, 273–278, 290ff, 295
Cuba, 296
Cuban crisis, 26, 27, 38, 93
Cultural:
  agreements, 246ff, 249
  exchange, 216, 217ff, 220ff, 231, 236, 242, 276ff
  relations, 232ff, 277
Cyprus, 135, cf. *Chypre*
Czechoslovakia, 10, 22, 26, 27, 88, 100, 162, 204, 205, 234, 240, 255–256, 262, 264, 265, 270, 274, 275, 276, 294, 296, cf. Tchécoslovaquie
Czempiel, Ernst-Otto, 77, 150–167, 154n

Dabrowa, Ambassador Dr. Slawomir, 118, 119n, 130
Davy, Richard, 290n
DDR, 7, 10, cf. RDA
Deadlock, 289, 292
Dean, Robert L., 9n
Debré, gouvernement, 27, 32
Décalogue, 58, 61, 62, 62–68, 70–73
Delbrück, Jost, 259
Democratic Study Group, 159, 160
Denmark, 135
Détente: XVII, XVIII, 3, 5, 16, 18–26, 32, 39, 46, 50, 58, 64, 72, 73, 77, 83, 88, 95, 99, 146, 149–156, 159–163, 168, 177, 191, 201, 207, 215, 227, 230, 242, 257, 288, 293, 295, 297
  concepts of –, 3
  opponents of –, XVII, 78, 156–158, 161
  Soviet-American –, 3, 78
Deterrence, 153, 173, 174, 291, 292

301

Devillers, Philippe, 9n
Deutsch, John, 19n
Deutsche Welle, 273
Digby, James, F., 19n
Disagreement, 289
Disarmament, 77, 80, 93, 94, 130, 132, 133, 136, 153, 291, 292
Dissidents, 12, 37, 237, 239–241, 244, 275
Distribution system, 190
Dobrosielski, Marian, 77, 79–92
Droits de l'homme, 36, 38, 39, 64, 65, 69, 72, cf. Human rights
Dutch foreign policy, 117
Dzirkals, Lilita, 9n

Earth satellites, 238
East-Berlin, 7
Eastern Europe, 7, 10, 12, 17, 22, 26, 44, 47, 162, 163, 164, 168, 171, 194, 195, 204–207, 212, 234, 238, 240, 246, 251, 270, 295
East-Germany, 7, 8, 12, 22, 240
East–West:
 balance, 23, 97
 confrontation, 12, 49, 54, 151, 157, 296
 cooperation, 5n, 50, 178, 180, 189
 dialogue, 43, 193, 273–274
 exchanges, 271ff, 277
 negotiations, 113ff, 203ff, 209ff, 290
 relations, XVII, XVIII, 5, 26, 50, 51, 56, 86, 100, 122, 133, 171, 176, 177, 178, 179, 182, 183, 185, 231, 250, 254, 296
 trade, 9, 11, 12, 160, 161, 163, 167, 177, 181, 192, 204ff
ECM, 19
Economic:
 cooperation, XVIII, 171, 172, 189, 193, 293
 management, 187, 188
 order, 55
 relations, 177, 178
Education, 276, 284ff
EEC, 10, 11, 171, 185, 193, cf. CEE; European Communities

Egalité souveraine, 62
Eisenhower, 29
ELINT, 19
Ellman, Prof. Richard, 279
Elysée, 27, 32
Emigration, 255, 256, 257
Emigration from USSR, 164, 253, 262–264
England, 221
Environment, Conferences on, 12
Erasmus, 216
Erickson, Hohn, 13n
ERRB, 292
Escalation, 85
Espagne, 59, 69
l'Est, 59, 6^1, 64, 65, 70, 72
Estaing, Giscard d' –, 24, 26, 27, 34, 35
ETA, 69
Etats-Unis, 30, 32, 33, 35, 38, 39, 41, 59n, 60, cf. America; USA, United States
Eurocommunism, 6n, 22, 45, 49, 52, 53
Europe, 20, 21, 24, 26, 28, 31, 42, 43, 46, 50, 52–54, 56, 59, 65, 70, 72, 74–85, 92, 97, 99, 100, 126, 142, 143, 146, 163, 171
European:
 Communities, 43, 44, 52, 105, 171, 185, 192ff, 211ff, 293, cf. EEC, CEE
 Left, 44
 Parliament, 43
 relations, 48
 security, 132, 135, 139, 145, 149
Eurostrategic balance, 128, 129, 131
Eurovision, 252
Evans, Rowland, 156n
Exchange, free –, 246ff, 249, 276
Exhibits, 281–282
External economic activity, 178, 182, 188, 189
Eyck, Jan van, 216

Family reunions, 253–255, 261, 264
Fascell, Dante, 268,
FBI, 243

FBS, 117, 124, 127, 128
Federal Republic, 7, 24, 25, 86, 93, 94, 100, 111, 114, 183, 203, cf. GFR
FGR, cf. GFR
Final Act, XVII, XVIII, 51, 57–60, 65, 67, 83, 86, 136, 138n, 144–148, 171, 211, 215, 220, 228, 230, 235, 240–242, 250ff, 259ff, 271, 274, 289–296
Financial relations, 183, 184
Finland, 65, 135
First use, no –, 87, 110, 292
Fischer, Robert Lucas, 13n
Flynn, Gregory A., 8n
Fontaine, André, 3, 26–41
Force reductions, XVIII, 14, 77, 79, 95–98, 104, 115, 148, 291
Ford administration, 35–38, 45, 150, 156, 161–165, 256
Foreign Relations, Council on –, 6n
Fouchet, 31
France, 3, 17, 18, 26, 29, 31, 38, 41, 44, 87, 99, 100, 110, 114, 127, 128, 140, 143, 220, 221
Franco-allemand, traité –, 29
Frank, Paul, 8n
Free, Lloyd A., 25n
French:
 forces, 86
 nuclear force, 106, 124
 participation, 14, 101
 Presidents, 3
 revolution, 173
Fromm, Erich, 229n
Frontières, 59, 60
Fulbright:
 Fellowship, 249
 lecturing, 285, 286

Gasteyger, Curt, 12n
GATT, 199, 202, 205–209
Gaulle, Général de, 24, 26, 27, 30–32
Gaullism, 17
GDR, 57, 89, 100, 162, 203, 204, 253, 262, 265, 268, 274–276

General Assembly, U.N. –, 81, 82, 238, 292
Geneva, 10, 42, 43, 47, 48, 50, 62n, 100, 136, 149
German:
 reunification, 10
 settlement, 7
 treaties, 10, 11
Germany, 93, 265
Gérontocrats, 26, 38
Getler, Michael, 22n
GFR, 81, 86, 87, 89, 90, 91, 93, 127, 183, 263, 265, cf. Federal Republic
Ghébali, Victor-Yves, 3, 57–73, 67n, 68n, 290
Gibraltar, 59
Gierek, 255
Ginsburg, Alexander, 239
GNP, 79, 160, 249
Golan, Galin, 18n
Goldman, Marshall, 9n
Goodpastor, Gen. Andrew, 13n
Gomulka, 31
Grande-Bretagne, 30, 32, 33, 38, 41
Gray, Collin S., 13n, 22n
Great-Britain, 15, 17, 87, 91, 95, 100, 114, 127, 128
Greece, 241
Griffith, D.W., 280
Griffith, William, E., 3, 4, 5–25, 180, 291, 292
Groll, Götz von, 8n
Gromyko, 41, 88, 129n
Gotman, Patrick, 181n

Haftendorn, Helga, 7n, 93n, 94n, 95n, 97n
Hanoï, 32
Hassner, Pierre, 16, 22n
Hattersley, Roy, 254
Havemann, Robert, 240
Heisenberg, Wolfgang, 124n
Helsinki, XVII, 22, 26, 36, 42–44, 46–48, 50–53, 57–60, 63, 68–70, 79, 110, 136, 145–149, 162–168, 219, 237, 240, 244ff, 291, 294
Heneghan, Thomas, E., 17n

303

Henze, Gerhard, 8n
Hiroshima, 84
Hitler, 8
Holland, 89, 91
Holst, Johan Jørgen, 13n, 17n, 19n, 21n, 22n
Hotpeace, 16
Human:
  contacts, 252ff, 260, 261
  history, 224–225
  rights, XVIII, 12, 26, 38, 58, 150, 151, 156, 164, 165, 239ff, 252, 261, 274, 289, 294, 295, 296, cf. *Droits de l'homme*
Hungary, 10, 38, 100–102, 113, 162, 182, 183, 188, 199, 204, 205, 234, 262, 265, 269, 270, 273, 276
Huntzinger, Jacques, 13n
Husak, 256

ICBM's, 128
ICEM, 255
Ideological:
  contamination, 277
  disarmament, 13
  struggle, 13, 224, 226ff, 296
IISS estimate, 108
Illyitch, Wladimir, 35
Ilyichew, 19n
Immigration, 253
Implementation records, 260ff, 276ff, 288ff, 295
Indépendance nationale, 29, 30, 33
India, 17, 124, 181, 208
Integration:
  in Comecon, 196ff
  in the Communities, 197
Indochina, 30, 154
Intégrité territoriale, 60
Interdependence, 174, 175, 189, 191
Interprétation de l'Est, 63
Intervision, East European, 252
Invasion russe, 38, 296
Iran, 209
IRBM's, 20
Irlande, 59
Isaacs, Harold, 283

Israel, 30, 34, 124, 256, 264
Italy, 17, 18, 38, 44, 47, 69, 101, 139n, 205, 220, 241
Izik-Hedri, Gabriella, 203n, 206n

Jackson, 39, 128, 156, 160, 164, 166, 167, 257
Jamison, Judith, 28
Jamming of radiostations, 237, 238, 273
Japan, 5, 6, 24, 124, 155, 167, 178, 180, 208
Jefferson, 245
Jobert, Michel, 26, 33, 34
Johnson:
  President, 154
  Senator Lyndon B., 235n
Journalists, 274
Juridical recognition, 194, 195, 203, 204

Kahn, Hermann, 218n
Kaiser, Karl, 6n
Kaufmann, W.W., 19n
Kekkonen, 82
Kendall, Donald, 160
Kennedy, 25, 30, 151, 154
King, Robert, R., 9n
Kippour la guerre du, 34
Kirilline, 32
Kissinger, Henri, XVIII, 5, 10, 23, 24, 25, 32, 34, 39, 45
Kol Isreal, 100, 104, 105, 125, 150–157, 163, 165, 238
Korea:
  North –, 261
  South –, 207
Kossyguine, 41
Kostko, Yuri, 13n, 94n, 99, 103, 109n
Krell, Gert, 158n
Kremlin, 26, 28, 31, 33, 38, 41, 78
Krimsky, George, 239
Krushchev, 6, 195

Lacy, Ambassador William S.B., 235
Laird, US Secretary of Defence, 97

Lambeth, Benjamin S., 17n
Lance missiles, 91
Landes, David S., 5n
Languages, study of, 287
Larrabee, F. Stephen, 9n, 16n
Latin America, 159
Lawrance, R.O., 127n
Lebanon, 263
Legvold, Robert, 8n
Leipzig, 253
Lenin, V.I., 35, 226, 245
Leningrad, 275
Libertés fondamentales, 69
Libre-échange, 64
Lieber, Robert J., 17n
Livinov, Maxim M., 229
Loewenthal, Richard, 296
Lomonossov, 29
London, 22
Londres, 32
LSI, 20
Lukaszewski, J., 195n
Luxembourg, 89

Macmillan, 29
Madrid, 290
Mahgreb, 181
Maizière, General Ulrich de, 109n
Malta, 65, 135
Mansfield, Senator, 10, 14, 97
Marché commun, 30
Mark 12-A, 129
MaRV, 19, 20
Marxist:
  goals, 6
  –Leninist ideology, 5
Mates, Leo, 3, 8n 42–56, 296
MBFR, 11, 13, 14, 15, 21, 22, 95, 101, 103, 105, 166, 234, 243, 291, 292, cf. MFR
Meadows, Dennis and Donella, 283
Mediterranean, 15, 20, 23, 82, 99, 142, 241, 290, 291
Meissner, Boris, 8n
MFN-treatment, 156, 157, 164, 166, 193, 202, 205, 210, 256, 266

MFR, 100, 101, 103, 104, 106, 107, 117, 121, 123, 124, 129–131, 134, 135, 144, cf. MBFR
  NATO proposals, 111ff
  Warsaw-Pact draft treaty, 106ff, 119ff
Michael, Louis, 126n
Middle East, 18, 19, 24, 35, 38, 55, 124, 181
Military:
action, surprise –, 122, 131
  impact, 158, 159
  involvement, 296
  manoeuvres, 11, 37, 134, 136–140, 144, 148, 292
  observers, 139, 144, 148, 292
  power, 293
  resources, 176, 184, 293
  stability, 130
Minsk, 100
MIRV, 19, 20, 128
Mitterrand, François, 34, 35
MLF, 153
Monnet, Jean, 27, 34
Montreal, 30
Montreux, 290
Morris, Federic A., 21n
Moscou, 27, 30, 32, 33, 35, 38
Moscow, 6, 7, 9–12, 14–25, 45, 49, 80, 88, 98–100, 151, 155, 160, 165, 167, 236, 251, 262, 263, 269, 270, 272, 274, 294
MPLA, 73
MRCA, 118
MRP, 28
MURFAAMCE, 77
Mutual:
  benefits, 179, 180
  Force Reductions, 79, 88, 89, 91, 94, cf. MFR and MBFR
  Security, 189
  understanding, 216
MX, 129
Myrdal, Alva, 130n

Namara, Mc., 125
Napoléon, 29

Nations Unies, 36, 58, 60n, 67, 69, cf. United Nations
NATO: 14, 15, 17, 26, 44, 49, 77, 79, 82–91, 94, 95, 98–106, 108–131, 134, 135, 163, 228, 291, 292, 293, cf. OTAN, Atlantic Alliance
collective ceiling plan, 112, 113, 116
Naval forces, 138, 148, 291
Nazi Germany, 235
NBC, 272, 275, 280
Neal, Fred Warner, 161
Negotiations, rounds of, 113ff
Nerlich, Uwe, 8n, 13n, 17n, 19n, 21n, 22n
Netherlands, The, 135, 136, 293
Neutralité, 66
Neutron bomb, 129, 292, 293
New Economic Mechanism, 199
Newhouse, John, 13n
Nike-Hercules, 119
Nimetz, State Counsellor, 280
Ninčič, Djura, XVIIn
Nitze, Paul H., 97n, 125n
Nixon administration, 10, 150
Nixon, President, 32, 33, 99, 103, 125, 154, 155, 157
Nobel Prize, 244
Non-aligned countries, 43, 48, 50, 54–57, 65–67, 138, 149, 289
Non-alignment, 42, 45, 54, 55, 56
Non-intervention, 26, 57, 58, 64, 69, 73
Non-proliferation, 24, 82, 85, 93, 154
Non-recognition, 194
North–South antagonism, 17
Norway, 135
Norwegian seas, 20, 291
Novosibirsk, 28
Nowak, Robert, 156n
Nuclear:
  arms control, 93, 292, 293
  attack, 86
  defence, 117, 292
  states, 131
  war, 5, 6, 80, 105, 231
  weapons, 14, 15, 77, 79, 81, 83, 88–91, 95, 105, 119, 125, 128, 292, 293

l'Occident, 33, 36, 39, 62
OCDE, 40, cf. OECD
Occupation militaire, 62
Oder-Neisse, 36
OECD, 17, 25, 177, 195, cf. OCDE
Offensive strategic doctrine, 293
Olympics, 272, 280
OPEC, 127
Oppression, 295
Oreanda, 97
Orkeny, Tstvan, 281
Orlov, Prof. Yuri, 37, 239, 294–295
Osimo, 71
Ostpolitik, 6n, 7, 22, 23, 59, 154, 243
OTAN, 29, 68, 69, cf. NATO, Atlantic Alliance
l'Ouest, 59, 61, 62, 64, 65, 72
l'Oural, 28
Outer Space Treaty, 81

Paix mondiale, 29
Paris, 32, 35
Parsky, 160n, 166
Participants to MFR talks, 101
Passports, 261
Pasternak, 244
Patolichev, 166
Pawelczyk, Alfons, 13n, 114n, 121n
Pays Baltes, 59n
PCF, 35
PCUS, 34, 35
Peace, 56
Pékin, 34
Peking, 19
Pentagon, 85, 125, 157
Pentateuch, 270
Pershing missiles, 85, 90, 91, 117, 119, 122
Persons, movement of, 215
Peter the Great, 245
PGM's, 15, 19, 20, 21
Phantoms, 90, 117, 122
Phnom-Penh, 30
Pinder:
  John, 171, 192–212, 198n, 293
  Pauline, 198n
Pitsounda, 34

306

Planck, Charles, R., 93n
Pliouchtch, 39
Pluralité des textes, 68
Podhoretz, Norman, 18n
Poland, 7, 10, 22, 37–40, 47, 81, 85, 89, 91, 100, 130, 198, 204, 215, 234, 254, 255, 262, 266, 270, cf. Pologne
Political sensitivity, 177, 194
Pologne, 69, cf. Poland
Pompidou, Georges, 24, 26, 33, 34, 100, 105
Popov, 277
Portugal, 17, 18, 36, 44, 69, 220, 241
Povolny, Mojmir, 9n
Prague, 31, 32, 38, 95, 251, 255, 264, 265, 275
Principes du Décalogue, 64–67, 71
Proliferation, 153, cf. Non-Proliferation
Psychological warfare, 226ff, 295
Publishing exchange, 278–279
Pugwash, 82, 243
Pushkin Institute, 222

Quarles van Ufford, Ambassador Jhr. Mr. B.E., 102, 109, 111n, 118n
Quinn, Joseph, 235n
Quotas, 193, 199, 207

Radio:
  Liberty, 227, 238, 273
  Free Europe, 227, 238, 273
  Peking, 238
  Tirana, 238
Rakmaninov, Y., 61n
Rapallo, 33
RDA, 36, 37, 69, 70, 71, cf. DDR
Reagan, Ronald, 150, 156
Record, Jeffrey, 116n, 118n, 127n
Red Cross, 255, 256
Relations Franco–Soviétiques, 27
Relations, US–West European –, 25
Religious contacts, 269
Rembrandt, 216
Remington, Robin Alison, 9n
Republican administrations, 160, 161
République Fédérale, 31, 32, cf. GFR

Resor, Stanley, R., 111n
RFA, 36, 70, cf. GFR
Rhodes Scholarship, 249
Richardson, Secretary of Commerce, 164
Robinson Jr., Clarence A., 125n
Romania, 7, 10, 43, 46, 101, 113, 135, 162, 166, 196, 199, 204, 205, 256, 262, 266, 270, 275, cf. Roumanie
Rome:
  declaration of, 95, 112
  Treaty of, 192, 203
Roosevelt, Franklin D., 230
Ropers, Norbert, 259
Roshchin, 281
Ross Johnson, A., 9n
Rostow, Eugen V., 18n
Roumanie, 31, 62, 65, 67, cf. Romania
RPV's, 20
Rubinstein, Alvin Z., 17n, 18n
Ruehl, Lothar, 13n, 95, 105, 112n, 114n, 120n, 127n
Rumsfield, US Secretary of Defence, 127n, 156
Russell, Harold, 63n, 64n
Russia, 15, 21, cf. USSR, Soviet Union

Sakharov, Andrei, XVIII, 37, 244
SALT-I or II, 15, 20–22, 25, 35, 40, 41, 53, 92, 96, 98, 105, 117, 124, 127–130, 150, 158, 165–167, 234, 247, 292, 296
SAM-2 air defence system, 119
San Francisco, 275
Satelite broadcasts, 238
Sattler, James F., 111n
Scandinavian countries, 99
Schiller, Herbert I., 220n
Schlesinger, US Secretary of Defence, 127n, 155n, 156
Schmidt, 7, 69, 255, 256
Schmückle, Gerd, 94n
Schulz, Eberhard, 194n, 195n
Schumpeter, Joseph, 158
Schwartz, Hans-Peter, 6n, 8n
Schwerin, Otto Graf –, 8n
Science, 286

307

Scientists, 243, 244
Scoville Jr., Herbert, 129n
Sea-Bed Treaty, 81
Seattle, 271
Secretary of Defence, 157
Sécurité, 73, cf. Security
Security, 9, 132–135, 140–147, 171–176, 189, 291
Security and Cooperation in Europe, US Congress Commission on –, XVIII, 163, 239, 244, 253, 259, 268, 278
SED, 70
Selection of information, State –, 218, 219
Senate, US –, 126, 128
Shafran, Daniel, 281
Sheidina, Inna, L., 215, 216–230, 295n
Shelepin, 243n
Shipping rates, 200
Shulman, Marshall D., 8n
Sibérie, 28, 40
Sidorenko, A.A., 126n
Siegler, Heinrich, 93n
Simon, Secretary of the Treasury, 166
Sino-American rapprochement, 23
Sino-Soviet:
   détente, 19
   Split, 6
SIPRI, 83, 84, 87
SLBM's, 128
Sloss, Leon, 127n
Smith, US Ambassador G., 124n
Soames, 32
Sobakine, Vadim K., 72n
Social:
   aspects of culture, 217, 218
   systems, 227, 245
Socialism, victory of –, XVII, 73
Socialist:
   construction, 3
   countries, 26, 85, 178, 183, 186
   economies, 179, 182
   reform process, 186
   struggle, 223
Solzhenitsyn, Alexander, XVIII, 244

Sonnenfeldt, la doctrine, 31, 163
South-East Asia, 124
Southern:
   Africa, 18, 24, 245
   Europe, 17
Soviet–American:
   condominium, 3, 24, 26, 33, 34
   relations, 52, 97, 160, 166, 230, 233, 236, 274, 276
Soviet:
   aims, 9, 10, 11, 13, 125
   army, 90, 108, 111, 112, 164
   authors, XVIII
   détente policy, 6, 23
   dissidents, 12, 237, 239, 240, 244
   hegemony, 9
   Jews, 18, 156, 164, 239, 263, 264, 269, 270
   leaders, 5, 26
   model, 44, 49
   peace policy, 124
   power, 20
   pressure, 7
   Society, 17, 218
   tourism, 221
   treaties, 229
Soviets, 11–15, 18, 23, 25, 41
Soviet Union, XVII, 3, 5–7, 10, 12, 16, 22, 25, 41–46, 50, 77, 78, 96–100, 126–129, 136, 150, 156, 162, 164, 171, 192, 194ff, 204, 206, 240, 291, 295, 296, cf. USSR, Russia
Soviet–US trade, 18, 23
Spain, 17, 18, 44, 134, 140, 241
Sparkman, Senator, 280
Specialization agreements, 210
SS-20, 20, 41, 129
Stalin, 6, 28, 37, 233–236
Staradomskaya, Eva, 279
State secrets, 261
Stanley, Timothy W., 8n
Steenwijk, Ambassador de Vos van, 115n, 118, 120
Stevens, Arthur G., 159n
Stevenson, 156, 160, 164, 166
Stoel, Max van der, 72n
Stone, Senator Richard, 269

Strategic, cf. SALT
 parity, 125
 weapons, 85, 129
Stroganov, Oleg, 68n, 69n
Sturminger, Alfred, 223
Strohm, Carl Gustaf, 22n
Suède, 65, cf. Swedish
Suisse, 65, 66n, cf. Switzerland
Swedish:
 Institute of International Affairs, 8n
 proposal, 134, 140
 University, 249
Switzerland, 135, 249, 254
Szenfeld, Ignacy, 9n

Tactical weapons, 85
Tanks, 292
TASS, 220, 275
Tatu, Michel, 124n
Tchécoslovaquie, 26, 27, 31, 32, 37, 39, 62, 69, cf. Czechoslovakia
Tchervonenko, 35
TERCOM, 20
Teunissen, Paul J.M., 77, 93–131, 291
Third World, 42, 56, 176, 181, 183, 184, 190
Threshold, 83, 87, 131
Tiflis, 96
Tinbergen, Jan, 184n
Tindemans, 69
Tito, 23
Tlatelolco, treaty of –, 81
TNW, 81–88, 92, 117, 118, 124
Tokés, Rudolf, 6n, 285
Totalitarian nations, XVIII
Tourism, 270
Trade: 23, 190, 198ff, 211
 barriers, 201–203, 210
 credits, 202
 disruption, 200
 negotiations, 198ff, 202ff, 207, 208, 209ff
 Reform Act, 166
Transportation, conferences on –, 12
Trieste, 71
Troop reductions, 14, 15, 106, 111, 115, 122, 123, cf. MBFR, MFR

Tsipis, Kostov, 19n
Turkey, 137, 220, 255
Tvordokhlebov, Andrei, 239

U-2, 153
UDR, 34
Ulbricht, 7
Ulster, 59, 69
Unaligned countries, 43, 48, 50, 54, 55, 57
Uncertainty, 297
UNCTAD, 127
Undiminished security, 102, 103, cf. Security
UNECE, 251
UNESCO, 219, 221, 238, 283
UNITED:
 Kingdom, 15
 Nations, 81, 82, 88, 127, 238, cf. Nations Unies
 States, 7, 9, 10, 12, 14, 18, 19, 23, 24, 44–46, 77, 78, 81, 93, 97–101, 140, 142, 154, 157, 158, 254, cf. America, Etats Unis, USA
Urals, 26, 28
Urban, Otto, 279
URSS, 28, 29, 30, 31, 32, 33, 35–40, 59–61, 63, 64n, 69, 70–73, cf. USSR, Soviet Union, Russia
USA, 3, 5, 6, 25, 26, 82, 84–87, 100, 150, 164, 165, 178, 180, 195, 221, 228, 260ff, cf. America, Etats-Unis, United States
US–Soviet bilateralism, 100, 152, 161
US–USSR:
 Consular Convention, 270
 negotiation, 296
 trade, 166, 268
USSR, 26, 28, 57, 89, 134, 136, 137, 140, 142, 150, 157, 164, 220, 262, 294, cf. Soviet Union, URSS, Russia

Valetta, La –, 290
Vance, Cyrus, 155n, 158, 280
Vanik, 156, 160, 164, 166, 280
Varsovie, 31, 32, 33, 37, 38, 59, 68, 70, cf. Warsaw

309

Vienna, 14, 53, 77, 79, 82, 89–92, 93, 100, 101, 130, 135, 144, 148
Vietnam War, 10, 24, 32, 35, 154–158, 160, 165
Visas, 263ff, 268ff, 275
Vladivostock, cf. Wladiwostok
VOA, 273
Volle, Angelika, 203n
Vugdelic, Vladimir, 72n

Wagner, Wolfgang, 8n
Wallace, William, 203n
Wandycz, P.S., 195n
Warnke, 25, 41, 167
Warsaw, 47, 237, cf. Varsovie
Warsaw-Pact:
  countries, XVII, 15, 43, 45, 49, 79, 84–89, 93, 94, 100, 103, 111, 115, 129, 131, 134, 260, 262, 270–273, 291, 292
  draft treaty, 106ff, 119ff
Washington, 7, 9, 10, 22, 25, 41, 151, 154, 157, 162, 165, 256
Watergate, 24, 158
Watts, William, 25n
Weapon:
  systems, 19, 291
  technology, 20, 291
Weidenfeld, Sir George, 238n
Weizsäcker, von, 84
Well, Günther von, XVIIn
West-Berlin, 7, 22
Western:
  Alliance, 3, 9, 22, 44, 46, 103, 104, cf. NATO

Communist parties, 45, 47–49, 56
Europe, 5, 6, 10, 12, 19–21, 24, 25, 43–46, 85, 100, 104, 105, 126–128, 155, 160, 180, 204, 234, 293, 296
initiative, 13
Society, 17
World, 43, 77
West European integration, 14
West-Germany, 6, 7, 9, 10, 12, 14, 15, 21, 22, 25, 93, 95, 97, 100, 117, 154, 253
Wettig, Gerhard, 8n, 9n, 13n
Whetten, Lawrence, 7n
White House, 52
Whitt, Darnell M., 8n
Wieck, Hans-Georg, 8n
Wilson, President, 151
Wilson, Prime-Minister, 95
Wladiwostok, 117, 128, 129, 165, 167
World War I, 5, 225
  II, XIX, 225, 232, 234, 240, 255, 263

Yefremov, 28
YMCA, 270
Yochelson, John, 13n
Yugoslavia, 7, 10, 12, 22, 23, 43, 47, 49, 57, 62, 65, 67, 69, 113, 135, 139n, 206, 275

Zarubin, Ambassador Georgii, 236
Zellentin, Gerda, 259
Zeman, Z.A.B., 215, 250–258
Zhukov, Georgii, 234n